SCHOLAR-SPY
The Worlds of Professor Sir Peter Russell

Professor Sir Peter Russell (1913–2006) was one of the great British scholars of the twentieth century. Russell, who held the King Alfonso XIII chair of Spanish Studies at Oxford from 1953 to 1981, belongs to those who not only moved with equal facility between history and literature, but made lasting contributions to each as scholar, teacher and mentor, not least to Javier Marías who wrote him into a succession of novels including his *magnum opus*, *Your Face Tomorrow*. Russell was also a key figure in the development of Hispanic Studies in Britain and, as shown in this volume, the last to have a conspectus on its evolution both cultural and administrative from the 1930s to the 21st century. To all these endeavours he brought an intensely human and logical approach, the product not only of a massive intellect but of a wealth of personal experience which made him more than a scholar and a man of letters.

Russell's service to his country both before and during the Second World War stands comparison with his academic career. Recruited into secret intelligence in the late 1930s, Russell was sent to Spain during the Civil War where he was unmasked as a spy and barely escaped with his life. Drawing on an array of sources private and public, this biography goes on to uncover his service in wartime intelligence which involved him in the effort to usher the Duke and Duchess of Windsor out of Lisbon in 1940 and as an MI5 counter-espionage officer in the Caribbean, West Africa and Southeast Asia.

At the epicentre of this volume, as of Russell's being, is his swirling mental world, one reconstructed from the detailed and often harrowing revelations found among his papers after his death. This material, of indisputable richness, itself represents an absorbing case study in mental illness and its evolution and treatment on Freudian principles in mid-century. The result is a fully documented, deeply researched and compelling picture of a fascinating figure, his relationships, his writings and his years as professor and servant of the state, one that aims to reach beyond academic biography while asking pertinent questions as to the motivations and impulses that attend every scholarly enterprise and the mind and experiences underpinning it.

Bruce Taylor was born in Chile in 1967 and educated at the University of Manchester and at Oxford where he received a D.Phil. in Modern History in 1996. He has published in the fields of early modern Spanish history and particularly naval history, in which he is a leading author. He lives in Southern California and is a freelance translator.

SCHOLAR-SPY
The Worlds of Professor Sir Peter Russell

BRUCE TAYLOR

LONDON

SPANISH, PORTUGUESE AND LATIN AMERICAN STUDIES IN THE HUMANITIES

Scholar-Spy: The Worlds of Professor Sir Peter Russell
by Bruce Taylor

The rights of Bruce Taylor to be identified as author of this work have been asserted by him in accordance with the Copyright, Designs and Patents Act, 1988.

© Bruce Taylor, 2024

All unauthorized reproduction is hereby prohibited. This work is protected by law. It should not be duplicated or distributed, in whole or in part, in soft or hard copy, by any means whatsoever, without the prior and conditional permission of the Publisher, SPLASH Editions.

Published by SPLASH Editions, 2024.

All rights reserved.

The cover photograph shows Peter Russell in Oxford, *c.* 1946.

ISBN 9781912399406

SPLASH Editorial Board
Tomás Albaladejo
Alejandro Coroleu
Catherine Davies
Jeremy Lawrance
Ana Lessa-Schmidt
Ana Gabriela Macedo
Bernard McGuirk
Rui Gonçalves Miranda
Francesca Pasciolla
Rebeca Sanmartín Bastida
Gareth Stockey
Barry Taylor

Contents

Preface	9
Author's Note	12
Abbreviations	13
Chapter One A Colonial Childhood	15
Chapter Two Cheltenham and Oxford (1927–1939)	64
Chapter Three *S'en va-t-en guerre* (1939–1946)	121
Chapter Four Dark Tower	169
Chapter Five Master of Studies (1946–1987)	222
Chapter Six Iconoclast: Academic Writings (1934–2006)	286
Chapter Seven Awaiting the Reaper	326
Appendices	
I Stephen Gilman and the Valle Lersundi Archive	354
II Oxford University Spanish Syllabus (1931–1932)	366
III Graduate Students Supervised (1951–1984)	368
IV University Lectures and Classes Imparted (1938–1981)	376
V Publications	381
Sources	399
Index	412

Peter Russell as he reached Oxford in 1931.

In grateful memory of
Professor Kenneth Stockdale Reid
(1913–1992)

This woven raiment of nights and days,
    Were it once cast off and unwound from me,
Naked and glad would I walk in thy ways,
    Alive and aware of thy ways and thee;
Clear of the whole world, hidden at home,
Clothed with the green and crowned with the foam,
A pulse of the life of thy straits and bays,
    A vein in the heart of the streams of the sea.

                    SWINBURNE, 'The Triumph of Time', ll. 281–8

Preface

For all that Peter Russell held a prominent academic position, published many books and articles, lectured widely, was an occasional broadcaster and received numerous accolades culminating in a knighthood, he can in no respect be regarded as a public man, nor did he have any interest in popular acclaim or personal enhancement after being elected to his chair. Only for a brief period in the mid-1960s did he sit on the highest councils of his chosen profession, and for all his distinction as a scholar scarcely any of his books can have sold more than a few thousand copies and none are in print at the time of writing. Great as was his contribution to Spanish and Portuguese studies both academically and intellectually, his interest lay in fields having comparatively little resonance in the Anglosphere much before or after the *annus mirabilis* of 1992, the gifted though sceptical visitor to a series of ancient pools issuing few ripples visible to any beyond the student or expert. Although forty or so graduates were supervised by him over half a century at Oxford and elsewhere, his influence was largely confined to the academic circle of which he formed the centre, his gifts dispensed in the immediate sense among a relatively small community of people. His accomplishments like those of any modern scholar are on record, his publications stored and tabulated, his legacy secure to the extent his achievements have outlived him and will I suppose outlive the last of those who knew him before fading with the effluxion of time, a reminder of when the *studia humanitatis* could still call the most brilliant into its ranks.

So why this biography, a poor substitute for the autobiography he never thought to write? The answer lies in the life-enhancing effect he had on those on whom he shone the beam of his attention or who came within its range, born not only of his power of mind, gift of communication, roving curiosity and breadth of experience, but also of his encompassing humanity, one not free of equally human flaws. Guarding this outward persona was a reserve that in turn derived from the extraordinary and indeed frightening degree of emotional depth and inner turmoil it was his life's endeavour to master. It was, too, the combination of these facets of personality and the vaguely perceptible hinterland they enclosed that invited such fascination in those who gained access to him, influential for most, imitated by some and elevated into creative inspiration by others, notably the novelist Javier Marías. He seemed to know us intimately but not we him to any great degree, no matter where or how long we looked to find purchase. There lay much of the allure, and there also some of the explanation for his near-complete absence from the published memoirs and biographies of the many luminaries with whom he rubbed shoulders over the course of his life and career. My aim is therefore to capture this personality by exploring the many contexts from which it developed and to present it as a coherent whole or sequence of wholes with the benefit of his intimate writings. If it also serves as a record of an imposing product of British civilisation and experience in the twentieth century then its purpose shall have been doubly served.

I came to know Peter Russell by introduction in 1992. What began as the patient and sympathetic mentoring of a young scholar staring into the deepening abyss of his ignorance progressed by degrees into a friendship in which one party could hardly help having his mind broadened and the other found a place to repose some of the things of his life through a gradual lifting of his reserve. That privilege which I enjoyed until his death in 2006 has since been given dimension by the active contribution to this biography of two dozen of his students, colleagues and fellow scholars whose memories, records, insight and criticism it has been my good fortune to receive while gathering the many strands of his life. They are, in approximate order of association with him, Alan Forey, Ronald Truman, John Rutherford, David Gallagher, Maria da Graça de Almeida Rodrigues, Tom Earle, Nigel Griffin, John Wainwright, Anthony Pagden, Colin Thompson, Daniel Waissbein, David Hook, the late Sir John Elliott, Alastair Saunders, Eric Southworth, Felipe Fernández-Armesto, Colin Wight, Clive Griffin, Jeremy Lawrance, Julian Weiss, the late Ian Michael, the late Javier Marías, Richard Kagan, Lee Fontanella, Madeline Sutherland, Ted Parks, Xon de Ros, João Gouveia Monteiro and Kirstin Kennedy. From several of these the assistance has extended beyond practical kindnesses to sharing what can only be described as a sentimental journey, and I am indebted to them for helping me unfold and reconstruct the canvas of Peter Russell's life and mind. In doing so they have heightened my awareness of how much richness he brought into our lives, and reminded me too of how much friendship and *savoir vivre* so many of them have brought into mine, in some cases over the whole of my adult life. A separate word of acknowledgment is due to Anthony Pagden for having given me unrestricted access to Russell's archive, of which he is the literary executor. Likewise to Nigel Griffin and Jeremy Lawrance, once and always my teachers, who have not only unstintingly shared and contributed much of the material appended to this volume but also commented extensively on it. To Eric Southworth, generous with his time, vivid in his memories, unerring in his judgements. To Alastair Saunders and Daniel Waissbein who many times have opened my eyes to unsuspected dimensions of Russell's life and personality. And finally to my godson Frederick Morgan who has reached those places in the Oxford library system I could not from California. Other assistance and acts of generosity are recorded in the footnotes but none beyond myself could be held accountable for the contents of this work. My gratitude also to Barbara and Sarah Russell for their generous support in the earlier stages of this project, and always to my wife Bettina whose loving spirit has provided the backdrop to the writing of this book. To them all I would fain offer, what some are no longer living to receive, my heartfelt thanks.

'E[s]t tu, Brute?' Peter would ask with characteristic ambiguity whenever I appeared in his company, and often in the composition of this biography have I wondered whether I was engaged in the reputational assassination of a man I loved and who silently placed the highest value on his privacy and our confidentiality, an impression sharpened by my realisation of how often he felt his trust in others to have been misplaced. As frequently I have found myself aghast at the mental torment in which much of his life was spent, or yet shaking with mirth at the quips strewn through his journals and correspondence, memory calling forth intimations of the former and iterations of the latter at Belsyre Court. Peter would I suppose have appreciated the spectrum of responses elicited by his variegated life and personality as they are revealed in these pages, though a concern remains for when next we meet. Equally I'm aware that the pungent richness of his journals, particularly in the late 1940s, draws much of this narrative vortex-like in their direction. The dangers of both biographer and reader placing too much reliance on such material are, as he knew so well, a feature of the genre as of all archivally-based writing, and I've endeavoured to place them in their context of time, mood and place without recourse to suppression. Readers will draw their own conclusions but should in any case advance with caution.

Bruce Taylor
Los Angeles, Calif.
September 2024

Author's Note

Readers may need to be familiarised with the names given by the University of Oxford to the terms of the academic year: Michaelmas (winter), Hilary (spring) and Trinity (summer). More than fifty years after it was abolished it may also be helpful to remind them of the traditional currency of the United Kingdom: there were twelve pence to a shilling (known as a 'bob') and twenty shillings to a pound (also known as a sovereign or a 'quid'). Among the many coins engendered by this system was that known as 'half a crown', worth two shillings and sixpence. Finally, all photos are from Russell's archive except where indicated.

Abbreviations

ALRTP 'À la recherche du temps perdu', Peter Russell's memoir of his boyhood in Christchurch, New Zealand and Southsea, England, 1913–1926, manuscript, August–December 1935, 40 pp.
ANZ Archives New Zealand, Wellington
BNAE British National Antarctic Expedition (1901–1904)
DMI Directorate of Military Intelligence
DSO Defence Security Officer (MI5)
GKCK George Kolkhorst's correspondence to Charles Kennedy from 1949–57, Taylor Institution Library, Oxford, MS.Fol.E.20; available in an unpublished edition by I. D. L. Michael (2006), 99 pp.
JMA Javier Marías Archive, Madrid
OCTU Officer Cadet Training Unit
OUA Oxford University Archive, Oxford
OUSC Oxford University Spanish Club
PELR 'Peter Edward Lionel Russell', word-processed account of his life up to 1953 deposited 'for possible necrological use' with the British Academy in November 1992, 4 pp.
RMR Rita Muriel Russell, *Life Story*, 1964, word-processed copy ed. Hugh Russell, 67 pp.
RSSR 'Recollections of the Second Spanish Republic', Peter Russell recorded on 26 May 1998, Taylor Institution Library, TAPES.137
SIFE Security Intelligence Far East (MI5)
SOE Special Operations Executive
TNA The National Archives, Kew
    KV Security Service
    WO War Office

CHAPTER ONE
A Colonial Childhood

In the summer of 1935 Peter Russell, then twenty-one, began writing the memoir of his childhood in New Zealand he titled *À la recherche du temps perdu*. When in early December of that year news reached Oxford that his grandfather was near death in faraway Christchurch, Russell returned to his manuscript with heightened emotion. The result not only captures the nostalgia of a young man responding to the force of events in the context of his own geographical and cultural displacement, but also the immense presence in his life of someone who 'always [...] gave even me as a child the idea that he had everything perfectly under his control and knew exactly everything that was happening and would happen.' [1] Those who knew Peter Russell in later years might readily have applied the same description to him, just as surviving photos show how strongly he resembled his grandfather at the end of his own life seventy years later. Though few were aware of it, the intervening decades in fact served to confirm to Russell how little he shared of the ineffable certainty he identified both in his grandfather and in the other key figure in his life, his mother Rita. In the context of 1935 Russell's Proustian memoir of a vanishing world offers an early insight into the formation of an intellect destined to shape so many lives and minds in the coming decades, but that dimension is in every sense for later. For the present it is necessary to look back further still to the nineteenth century and there trace the life and career of the personality upon whom the fortunes of the family rested then and still: Peter Russell's grandfather Thomas Gregory Russell.

*

The gravestone Thomas Russell erected for his family at Linwood Cemetery in Christchurch in around 1916 records his birth at Colchester in Essex on 24 October 1850. [2] He was born into a Baptist family, the eldest son of Gregory Ruffell Russell, a bricklayer and subsequently a builder of Elmsett, Suffolk, and his

---

[1] 'À la recherche du temps perdu' (MS.) (hereinafter ALRTP), 9.
[2] <billiongraves.com/grave/Thomas-Gregory-Russell/9112245>.

wife Miriam Warren of Colchester. The family, then five-strong and residing in London, emigrated to Tasmania in the clipper *Whirlwind* which sailed from the Thames on 4 January and reached Launceston on 3 April 1855 after a voyage of eighty-six days. Although hardly untypical, the passage can without exaggeration be described as a nightmare during which forty-four passengers succumbed including twenty-three to scarlet fever together with a crewman who plummeted to the deck from aloft, the voyage marked also by severe weather, structural damage to the ship requiring docking, and a restive crew.[3] Like the other 391 souls in steerage who survived the journey, the Russells were bounty immigrants whose passage was funded by the colonial government under a scheme by which recruiting agents were paid to find suitable tradespeople and skilled labour in Britain and ship them and their families out to the young colony. The *Launceston Examiner* for 3 April carried this report of the new arrival and her human cargo together with what was reckoned to await them:

IMMIGRANTS.

The long expected 'Whirlwind' has arrived, and several hundred souls will be added to the population. The emigrants have passed through a fearful ordeal. An accident to the rudder compelled the commander to put into Portsmouth, where the necessary repair could have been effected in a few hours, had not the use of the empty government dock been denied by the official personage in charge who eats the salt of that nation whose funds furnished the accommodation. Scarletina broke out: its victims were removed to an inhospitable hulk, for which the British government charged a high price, forgetful of the first duties of humanity; inclement weather aggravated the disease, which assumed a serious type, and carried off a number of victims. Twenty-three died on the passage, and although the survivors are healthy and robust, the loss of relatives and friends casts a shade of sorrow on the enterprise. We deeply sympathise with the bereaved, and the painful circumstances in which Mr. Drake has been placed must evoke the kindest feelings of his friends. His was no mercenary mission, and though he may not calculate on the gratitude of those he has sought to benefit by a removal from comparative penury to immediate plenty and ultimate affluence, he has earned their respect, and will secure the esteem of the colonists. His

---

[3] <belindacohen.tripod.com/woolnoughfamily/id9.html>.

position has been one of great responsibility, much risk, incessant anxiety, and no profit. When years have elapsed, he may expect adequate acknowledgment from those he has served, and not till then. The captain, too, has had his trials: his crew have been in a state of insubordination in consequence of the proper and rigidly enforced rules that excluded the seamen from intercourse with the emigrants, and the sailors have, at the conclusion of the voyage, struck. The misguided men will soon learn that here their misconduct will not be countenanced—that punishment will visit the refractory—that extravagant pay no longer prevails, and that the gold-diggers, on the average, do not make ordinary wages. We trust the hopes of the emigrants have not been unduly elated, and that they will be prepared to accommodate themselves, as thousands more affluent have done before them, to the exigencies of a new country. The farm labourer and mechanic will not be carried off by force at any wage they may demand: the unmarried females will not be surrounded by sighing lovers, solicitous to make then brides. Australia is a land where privations must be endured, and hard work encountered. At the end of the vista, which is not long, there is settlement and independence to the industrious, the economical, and sober. Every young woman will find a husband in process of time, but before she obtain a good one she must show by her behaviour she deserves him. Everything will be new to the emigrants; they must be surprised at nothing, and become quickly reconciled to the condition of the colony. If they display those qualifications of temper and aptitude which make people useful they will be appreciated, and experience consideration and kindness from their employers, who will in general promote their welfare to the utmost. We repeat, hard work, frugality, and sobriety for a time will inevitably lead to independence; but those who seek the latter by the shortest line must be prepared to 'rough it' for a season.

If we are to believe the letter sent by one of these agents, the immigrants had all found a safe berth within a fortnight of *Whirlwind* being brought up to the Tamar below Launceston:

LAUNCESTON EMIGRATION AID SOCIETY. We have been politely favoured with the following extract of a private letter to a friend, from the gentleman who selected the emigrants by the *Whirlwind*: 'Launceston, 17 April. Perhaps you may have heard of our arrival here. If not, I must tell you that, about a fortnight since, we put our emigrants ashore, and such a shipload never reached the colonies before: serious, clean, healthy, hard-working, God-fearing people. They were soon all engaged, and at good wages, and I am pleased and even proud at the results of my mission. I am happy to say that all who saw the people speak in strong terms of approbation, and their employers are more than satisfied.' [4]

For the Russells this consisted of settlement at Quamby Brook, twenty-five miles west of Launceston, from where young Thomas was at length sent to Horton College, a now-defunct Methodist establishment near Ross halfway between Launceston and Hobart. [5] Aside from Thomas the other two children who reached Tasmania with Gregory and Miriam Russell were Susan Helen (b. 1852) and George Warren Russell, the latter born in Haggerston, London in 1854 and destined for a notable career as a newspaper owner and politician. [6] Another son John Ruffell (subsequently editor of the *Dannevirke Advocate* and founder with George of the *Manawatu Herald*, both in New Zealand) appeared in 1856 followed by Miriam (1858), Joseph (1859), Jabez (1863) and finally William Henry (birthdate unknown; still alive in 1950). [7] In later years Peter Russell was able to familiarise himself with life at Quamby Brook in the early days from a Miss Williams, a family governess with whom he had tea among copies of the *Morning Post* in Shepherds Bush one afternoon in 1934. [8]

The next major recorded development in the history of the family comes in 1871 when Gregory and Miriam Russell moved again, this time to New Zealand. The vessel in which they did so, the iron-hulled full-rigger *Euterpe*, has by some

---

[4] *The Sydney Morning Herald*, 25 April 1855, cited in <belindacohen.tripod.com/woolnoughfamily/id9.html>.
[5] Julian Evans, 'Lt. "Teddy" Evans and Hilda Russell, 1902–1913: Biographical Research' (2011), 4, at <pdfs.semanticscholar.org/ee0e/d769fc03fbf19562da14446e908de46411b2.pdf>.
[6] <teara.govt.nz/en/biographies/2r31/russell-george-warren>.
[7] <www.geni.com/people/Gregory-Russell/6000000024310452858>; Hugh Bernard Langford Russell, *One Man's Journey through Life* (Edinburgh: privately published, 2008), 130; Miriam and Jabez succumbed in their early twenties.
[8] Diary, 23 Dec. 1934; 'a real character'.

miracle survived to be preserved in San Diego, California as the *Star of India*, and it was one of Peter Russell's unrealised ambitions to visit her, ever conscious of the oceanic travel that had shaped the fortunes of his family as much as it had his life and imagination. Whereas the elder Russells settled in Wellington on the North Island, Thomas established himself in Canterbury on the South Island where he pursued training in accountancy, the first step in a remarkable business career. His first decades in New Zealand are summarised in the biographical notes taken during the painstaking research carried out into the early settlers of the Canterbury region by George Macdonald, information complemented by the memoirs of his daughter Rita, Peter Russell's mother. [9]

Among Thomas Russell's first business ventures in New Zealand was the purchase of a farm at Walmate in South Canterbury, but it was as an accountant that he started his married life with Helen (Nellie) Stringer of Christchurch in 1874. [10] Another early venture was the acquisition of the book debts of a local firm, Hutchinson & Co. and, less successfully, the purchase of the licence of the Jollies Pass Hotel sixty miles north of Christchurch in 1876. The latter enterprise left him bankrupt after a claim declaring the establishment to be 'an injury to the neighbourhood' was upheld in court and the business apparently shut down. Nonetheless, Russell recovered and built up a successful accountancy practice in Christchurch where he stood for election to the position of city auditor, albeit coming bottom in the poll. In 1883 he matriculated at Canterbury College to read law, which he accomplished by the breathtaking feat of passing all three years of exams in as many terms and being admitted to the New Zealand Bar in October 1884. He first entered practice at Kaiapoi ten miles north of Christchurch before opening law offices at 55 Cathedral Square in the regional capital from which he would drive to courts in the outlying communities by pony and trap. Not content with practicing as a barrister and solicitor in many prominent criminal and civil cases, Russell's mastery of commercial law is set forth in the weighty tome he published on the subject in 1908. [11] Already in 1898 he had established the *New*

---

[9] <collection.canterburymuseum.com/persons/10767>. The research was carried out between 1952 and 1964 and is housed in the Canterbury Museum in Christchurch; Rita Muriel Russell, *Life Story*, 1964, word-processed copy edited by Hugh Russell (hereinafter RMR), 1.

[10] <collection.canterburymuseum.com/persons/88923>. One of Nellie's brothers was Sir Thomas Walter Stringer KC (1855–1944), a New Zealand High Court judge who took silk in 1893, was appointed to the Supreme Court in 1914 and knighted in 1928.

[11] T. G. Russell, *Commercial Law as Applicable to New Zealand: A Practical Statement of the*

Zealand Magistrates' Court Reports (closed in 1952) and in 1905 took over the *Mercantile Gazette of New Zealand* (founded in 1875) which together with its affiliated journals remained under family ownership until 1980, the business having to be bought out after becoming overleveraged following expansion to new premises. He apparently also took ownership of the *Gazette Law Reports* (founded in 1876) which closed in 1951; an obituary in the national press recalled his high standing in the New Zealand legal profession. [12]

Peter Russell's maternal grandfather, Thomas Gregory Russell (1850–1935), seen c. 1930. Moustache apart, the two bore the closest resemblance in the closing years of their lives.

Peter Russell's maternal grandmother, Helen (Nellie) Russell (née Stringer) (1856–1915), c. 1910.

Thomas and Helen Russell had in the meantime begun a family, initially at Chester Street in Christchurch where three daughters were born of whom only the first, Ethel Nellie (1875–1964), survived infancy. However, these were

Law Governing Those Matters which Are Dealt with Every Day by Business People, and Intended for the Use of the Legal Profession, Law and Commercial Students, and Business Men Generally (Christchurch: Whitcombe & Tombs, [1908]).

[12] 'Obituary. Mr. T. G. Russell.', *Auckland Star*, 12 Dec. 1935, 10, at <paperspast.natlib.govt.nz/newspapers/AS19351212.2.119>.

followed by Gerald Warren (1879), Hilda Beatrice (1883), Rita Muriel (1887) and finally Cecil Ruffell (1892–1961). The house in which Peter Russell's mother Rita was born on 22 November 1887 was an imposing property (since demolished) built on land acquired by Thomas Russell in the suburb of Fendalton in the 1870s and which he named Quamby, a nod to his youth in Tasmania. *The Star* of Christchurch printed this description of it at the time of its sale to the McLean Institute (a retirement home) on 3 March 1909:

> The house itself is built of black pine, totara, and kauri [...] It is lavishly fitted inside, the papering and general decoration being of a most artistic nature. The rooms are spacious and airy and are all fitted with gas. The bedrooms open onto a wide sunny balcony [...] The drawing room is probably one of the largest of its kind in Christchurch and will seat 40 persons with ease. [13]

Rita's memory of Quamby over fifty years later is not only atmospheric in itself but provides a vivid portrait of the upper-middle-class life entered by the Russells in New Zealand as the nineteenth century drew to a close:

> Quamby was a large square house considerably altered in later years. It stood in 5 acres of land comprising about 2½ of garden and 2½ in paddock. Our house was approached by a fine avenue of red beech which gave good shelter in wet weather and there were fine trees for us children to climb. They must have been planted in the '70s. On the front lawn was a tall monkey puzzle tree and several other large spreading trees.
>
> We kept a cart horse and a pig besides a lot of poultry. We made our own butter and bread. We had two tennis courts, one grass the other asphalt, two greenhouses, one full of grapes and lovely smelling musk. Along the border of the property was a swift flowing little river full of trout. This river [the Waimairi] turned the waterwheel which pumped artesian water up to a tank 20–30 feet above ground. We had a swimming bath about 31 feet long fed with water from the water tank overflow. The bath was always flowing in, and out; this made the water always very cold. [...] I learnt to swim in our swimming bath. Father used to take us to the bath up the garden in frosty weather and we had

---

[13] Evans, 'Lt. "Teddy" Evans and Hilda Russell', 6.

to plunge in through thin ice. At other times we had to have a cold bath in the house, sometimes I had it and at other times I pretended to do so.

[...]

At Quamby was an old two-roomed cob cottage; it belonged to Mr Fendal, the first man to live in Fendalton which was called after him. The early settlers built these cob cottages made of mud, straw and I believe a certain amount of manure. The walls are about 15 inches thick, as hard as rock and very warm. They are trying to trace and to save these cottages but most of them have been destroyed. Ours at Quamby has gone, being pulled down by the McLean Institute who later bought our house for old indigent gentlefolk. One room we used for all the garden tools and the other, which was the bedroom, we used as a changing room for the swimming bath next door. The front of the cottage had a magnificent peach tree across it. The garden contained apple trees, pears, plums, Japanese plums, greengages, apricots, currants, gooseberries, raspberries, peaches, walnuts and hazelnuts, asparagus and medlars. [14]

Quamby, the house Thomas Russell built in the Christchurch suburb of Fendalton in the 1870s. This photo taken c. 1900 presumably shows one of the three daughters of the house on the balcony: Ethel, Hilda or Peter Russell's mother Rita.

[14] RMR, 2–7.

Nor is the wild beauty of the New Zealand landscape or the impression of the Colony as a pioneer society ever far from her narrative:

> Soon after father moved to Quamby he bought Rakaia Island. It had 800 acres of land and was in the middle of the Rakaia riverbed. There was a homestead where we stayed and also 'Whites' about 2½ miles away which was generally occupied by shearers and farmworkers. [...] We children had some good times at the island. I was about six or seven at the time. We used to bathe in the river without any fear. Sometimes the river was in flood and great big trees came hurtling past on their way to the sea. Crossing this river in flood to get to the island was a very hazardous business. One time when I went to the island with Cecil and father we were told at Southbridge that the river was in flood. When we arrived there we could see that it would be impossible to drive across in the buggy. So the horses were taken out and harnessed, father got on one horse with me sitting in front of him, Cecil in front of the man who came for us. We had about four or five separate rivers to cross. The horses swam and the water came well up over my knees. Fortunately, these horses Eva and Charlie were used to river crossing. We arrived safely at the homestead a day or two later. Our man was able to cross the river with the two horses and bring the buggy back with our luggage. The house was quite a nice one with a big sunny veranda in front. Our own family quarters had been added on at the side. There was no bath and the toilet was under a lot of pine trees. It was very drafty and full of big spiders. We used to go for lovely picnics on the island. There was some beautiful native bush at the top end. Very often we would ride there. I remember tying a pillow on a horse and using it as a saddle. Another time I got on the back of a cow. I only had time to think how hard her back was when I was shot off. [15]

So much for the backdrop. What of the major figures in her life? Rita Russell made no bones about her father's character:

> He was a very hard Victorian man. When we were children we were all very afraid of him and had not the least affection for him at that time.

---

[15] *Ibid.*, 10. Rakaia Island, about 20 miles west of Christchurch, is formed by the courses of the braided river of the same name.

> Owing to being so afraid of father, many a night I have sat for over half an hour trying to make up my mind to get up and kiss him goodnight. I would be longing to go to bed and would unbutton my boots while waiting. [16]

The relationship clearly warmed as the decades passed but Thomas Russell expected to be obeyed and was never a man to be crossed. Much as one would like to offer a similar pen portrait of Rita's mother Nellie Russell, scarcely any mention is made of her in her daughter's memoirs and the impression is of an unobtrusive personality entirely dominated by that of her husband. Where Rita herself is concerned the inescapable picture from her writings and the descriptions of those who knew her is of a somewhat austere, even flinty woman, undemonstrative without being cold, disillusioned without being cynical, intelligent without being curious, petty without spitefulness, perennially blunt and guileless, strangely devoid of passion and emotion though dutiful, generous, honest and fair-minded, gregarious in her way but scarcely ever a participant where participation was most needed: in the inner life and natural emotional needs of her sons, the elder in particular, much as they loved her and evidently she them. Rita's recollection of her schooldays provides an insight into the detached single-mindedness and strength of will Peter Russell came to recognise as among her enduring character traits. Here is her account of the events leading to her expulsion from St Hilda's Collegiate School in Dunedin four years after her arrival there at the age of twelve in June 1900:

> This school was run by Church of England sisters. The Head was a Sister Geraldine, a woman very plain to look at and utterly devoid of sympathy or understanding, as hard as nails and very unsuitable to be in charge of young girls. [...] One afternoon at 4.30 I was looking out of my cubicle window at a family named Hislop in the garden of the house opposite. Suddenly there came a terrific rap on a window to my right. It was Sister Geraldine. She was furious and looked it. She came to my cubicle and gave me a good talking to at bedtime. I used to do a lot of mischievous things and make the girls laugh at the wrong times. A little later on she came again to my cubicle at bedtime and told me she would give me a week in which to improve or else I have to leave school. In my heart of

---

[16] *Ibid.,* 4–5.

hearts I did try that week. However, at the end of that week she came again and said I'd not tried to improve. I was very bitter. She said she'd asked my parents to remove me at the end of the term. I showed no sorrow or regret and I don't think I ever forgave her for such unjust judgment or treatment. I genuinely tried to improve and she had not noticed or believed it. When Sister Geraldine heard that I was going to a Roman Catholic convent school she told me to write and ask my parents if I could stay at St Hilda's, but I did not do so. My pride would not let me, neither did I want to stay. [17]

Rita's report on exiting the Lower IV and St Hilda's in 1901 unsurprisingly describes her academic performance as 'not very satisfactory' but no one meeting her in later years could have any doubt as to her intellect. [18] By the time she left the unnamed convent school three happy years later in 1904 the Russells of Christchurch had been caught up in what has come to be known as 'the heroic age of Antarctic exploration'.

*

On 6 August 1901 the barque-rigged steamship *Discovery* sailed from Cowes on the Isle of Wight for the Antarctic. Built at Dundee as the last wooden three-masted vessel of her kind in the United Kingdom, she was the chief asset of the British National Antarctic Expedition, the brainchild of Sir Clements Markham of the Royal Geographical Society. Although formed under the joint sponsorship of the RGS and the Royal Society and constituted with both exploratory and scientific aims, the BNAE was effectively under Admiralty authority and manned largely by naval personnel with numbers made up by civilian experts and members of the Merchant Navy. The expedition was commanded by Capt. Robert Falcon Scott RN whose first polar voyage this was. Scott was informed that the objects of the expedition were twofold:

> *(a)* to determine, as far as possible, the nature, condition, and extent of that portion of the South Polar lands which is included in the scope of your expedition; and *(b)* to make a magnetic survey in the southern regions to the south of the 40th parallel, and to carry on

---

[17] *Ibid.*, 11–12. Possibly Saint Mary's Convent School, Christchurch. I am grateful to John Huggett of Dunedin for his assistance with the St Hilda's archives.
[18] Evans, 'Lt. "Teddy" Evans and Hilda Russell', 6.

meteorological, oceanographic, geological, biological, and physical investigations and researches. None of these objects is to be sacrificed to the other. [19]

The base station for the expedition was to be Christchurch, and particularly its port of Lyttelton lying eight miles to the southeast which *Discovery* reached on 29 November 1901. Scott and his men received an outpouring of public and private generosity in New Zealand and *Discovery* sailed restowed and heavily laden with supplies and gifts (including a herd of sheep) to a rousing sendoff on 21 December. Putting in at Port Chalmers to replenish her stocks of coal and bury a seaman who had fallen from aloft while returning the enthusiastic cheers of the thousands lining the shore, *Discovery* then turned her bows towards the Antarctic. She was not to return for another two and a half years of toil, exhaustion, sickness and danger in the name of science and exploration during which Scott, Ernest Shackleton and Edward Wilson marched to the then unmatched latitude of 82° 17' S, approximately 530 miles from the pole. It had originally been intended for *Discovery* to carry out further seaborne reconnaissance and survey work before the winter of 1903 set in but these plans were thwarted by the fact that the ship remained beset throughout the polar summer. Resupplied by the relief ship *Morning*, Scott instead planned further sledge journeys in late 1903 with a view to returning to Britain via New Zealand the following year.

It is not known what contact if any the members of the expedition had with the Russell family during the three weeks *Discovery* lay at Lyttelton in December 1901, but any absence was made good by Sub-Lieutenant E. R. G. Evans RN, Second Officer of the relief ship *Morning*, who sailed in her from London in July 1902, the vessel fetching Lyttelton on 16 November. Edward Evans, always known as 'Teddy', was a larger-than-life figure, a tornado of pluck, patriotism and manly vigour of a type not unfamiliar in late imperial Britain. Born into a legal family in London in 1881, Evans joined the Navy in 1896 after education at Merchant Taylors' School (from which he was expelled) and HMS *Worcester*, the Thames Nautical Training College at Greenhithe. Appointed as a sub-lieutenant to the battleship *Majestic* in 1900, he was among no less than seven of her officers and men (led by Scott himself) to join the BNAE, in Evans' case after importuning Markham for inclusion in the crew of the *Morning*. Evans, who became a national

---

[19] Cited in Ann Savours, *The Voyages of the* Discovery: *The Illustrated History of Scott's Ship* (London: Virgin Books, 1992), 22.

hero for his exploits as a destroyer commander during the Great War and eventually reached the rank of admiral, was as his obituary stated 'perhaps the naval officer whose name was more widely known to the public than any other of his generation. For this' the obituarist continued 'he was himself largely responsible, for he was never one to hide his light under a bushel, he revelled in publicity and enjoyed being in the public eye.' [20] He was, wrote fellow expedition member Apsley Cherry-Garrard in his diary, 'a shallow man with none of Scott's complexity or Wilson's thoughtful altruism'. [21] For all that these character traits occasionally could and did take on a somewhat absurd aspect, there can be no doubt that Evans was a man of great personal courage, conviction, endurance and resource, and one on the whole much liked and respected by his brother officers and the men serving under him — this in a Service which placed no great value on intellect and traditionally looked askance at self-advertisers. Vain and ebullient, Uncle Teddy was one of the characters of Peter Russell's youth, a link to the most exciting era in the history of his family and to the upper reaches of society; it was, after all, through Teddy Evans that Russell once danced to jazz with Queen Maud of Norway, Evans' second marriage being to one of her ladies-in-waiting.

It was this man who by the time *Morning* sailed from Lyttelton in fulfillment of her second relief mission to the Antarctic in November 1903 had become engaged to Thomas Russell's second surviving daughter Hilda, then aged nineteen. As his biographer wrote, 'There was notable hospitality at the Russell house. Evans was given a standing invitation to lunch. Soon he was calling it his second home. Hilda Russell, he told his parents, was "a beautiful and upright girl". His friend Gerald Doorly described her as "one of Christchurch's fairest".' [22] The marriage took place at St Barnabas' Church, Fendalton on 13 April 1904 on Evans' return from the polar regions and was attended by the entire BNAE including Scott with a guard of honour supplied by men of the cruiser HMS *Tauranga*. [23] The reception was held at Quamby where following naval tradition the cake was cut with a sword. Among the gifts received by the couple was a silver casket from the officers of *Discovery, Morning* and the second relief ship, *Terra*

---

[20] *The Times*, 22 Aug. 1947.
[21] Cited in Ranulph Fiennes, *Captain Scott* (London: Hodder & Stoughton, 2003), 189.
[22] Reginald Pound, *Evans of the Broke: A Biography of Admiral Lord Mountevans K.C.B., D.S.O., LL.D.* (London: Oxford University Press, 1963), 47. Lt Gerald Doorly was Third Officer of the *Morning* and one of Evans' contemporaries in HMS *Worcester*.
[23] Evans, 'Lt. "Teddy" Evans and Hilda Russell', 7.

Nova.²⁴ Lt and Mrs Evans spent their honeymoon walking through the spectacular landscape of the South Island before the expedition, including the newlyweds, began sailing for home in May. ²⁵

Nor was this all. Among the bridesmaids at St Barnabas was Mr Russell's youngest daughter Rita who within a month of the wedding had become engaged to another member of the expedition, Evans' best man Lt Michael Barne of the *Discovery*. Barne was born into the Suffolk county gentry at Sotterley Hall in 1877 and entered the Navy as a midshipman in 1893. Picked out by Scott from the wardroom of the *Majestic* as 'especially fitted for the voyage where there were elements of danger and difficulty', Barne served the expedition as assistant magnetic observer and carried out several sledging journeys including a sixty-eight-day foray onto the Ross Ice Shelf in late 1903 during which he suffered severe frostbite. ²⁶ Rita's memoirs yield little information on her engagement on 6 May 1904 which can only have been formalised with her father's consent, but Elspeth Huxley's biography of Scott notes that Barne

> enjoyed some tender exchanges with the bride's younger sister Rita, who worked a table cloth and cushion with his crest on it for his cabin, cleaned his bicycle, and gave him a potted fern. He hung an enlargement of her photograph in his cabin and painted her name on the trunk she was taking back to her convent school. Cycling to her home in the dark to say goodbye, he met her pedalling towards the ship on the same errand; they collided. Next day he watched her waving from a train till it was out of sight; no wonder he was 'beastly sick' at leaving Christchurch. ²⁷

Surviving examples of Rita's needlework leave no doubt as to the quality of those tokens of her affection.

The marriage having been announced in March 1905, Rita sailed for England unaccompanied, reaching London in July to be met by Barne and her

---

[24] <antarcticsociety.org.nz/wp-content/uploads/2018/05/Antarctic.V33.3.2015.pdf>.
[25] Admiral Lord Mountevans [E. R. G. R. Evans], *Adventurous Life* (London: Hutchinson & Co., 1946), 73–4.
[26] Cited in Savours, *The Voyages of the Discovery*, 30; see also 41–2, 54–5, 79–81 & 90–1.
[27] *Scott of the Antarctic* (London: Weidenfeld & Nicolson, 1977), 136. All told at least eight of Scott's men were married or became engaged to New Zealanders before the expedition weighed anchor.

elder brother Gerald, then a surgeon practising in Gower Street.[28] The party immediately entrained to the naval town of Gosport in Hampshire where Hilda and Teddy Evans were then living. Here Rita experienced a change of heart. Although as she recalled 'The marriage would have been a good one, there was money and position [...], [i]t was while here that I decided I simply could not go on with this marriage. I suffered from shyness all my life till I was about 36 and at this time I felt I simply could not face all that would have been expected of me, so I ended it.'[29] In his notes to her memoirs Rita's son Hugh made the following remarks based on conversations with her in later years:

Robert Falcon Scott poses with his wife Kathleen, the Lord Mayor of Cardiff Charles Hayward Bird and lady mayoress, and Lt Edward Evans and his wife Hilda (née Russell, extreme right) in June 1910, shortly before Terra Nova *sailed on her fateful expedition to the Antarctic.*

> I do not think that she ever visited Sotterley or met Michael's parents. She certainly never mentioned it. However, while at Gosport she learned what would be required of her as Michael's wife and with neither of her

---

[28] News of the announcement was reported in *The Press* (Christchurch), 27 April 1905, 5. Gerald Russell had been trained at the University of London.
[29] RMR, 13. Rita turned thirty-six in 1919.

parents there to advise, support and guide her she, normally rather shy, must have felt she could not cope, have taken fright and decided to terminate the engagement. [30]

Aside from the trials of being a naval officer's wife, the plausible suggestion has also been made that Barne's colonial fiancée was deemed unacceptable by his aristocratic family, his mother being the daughter of the 5th Marquess of Hertford. [31] Be this as it may, the episode was one on which Rita naturally looked back with some bitterness: 'It was simply absurd that I should have been allowed to become engaged, he was 13 years older than I was. I was 16 years 5 months old. I had never had anything to do with the male sex.' In the event, Mike Barne soon found another bride, went on to give distiguished service during the Great War and lived until 1961, the last survivor of the BNAE. Meanwhile, the response to this turn of events in New Zealand was all too predictable: 'The family were very angry and I was told I must go back to school.' This Rita did for a little over a year at a finishing establishment on the Rue de la Source in Brussels before returning to what was no doubt a frosty reception in Christchurch in December 1907; an attempt to postpone this by joining Teddy and Hilda when the former was assigned to the West Indies Station came to naught after the Admiralty rescinded the appointment.

Rita's sundering of her engagement in 1905 can in retrospect be seen as ushering in a long period of upheaval in the history of the Russell family. On 28 October 1910 the *Terra Nova*, the base vessel of Scott's second expedition to the Antarctic reached Lyttelton. With her came Hilda and Teddy Evans (second-in-command of the expedition), Scott's well-connected sculptor wife Kathleen and the bulk of his party, many of whom were to become household names over the course of the next few years. However, relations between Kathleen Scott and Hilda Evans had become strained since *Terra Nova* sailed from Cardiff on 15 June 1910 and broke down in New Zealand. 'On one occasion [Hilda]' whom Kathleen thought childish 'sulked and refused to go to a reception because the invitation had arrived a day later than the Scotts'.' [32] The mortal danger presented by the impending expedition no doubt lay at the root of the strained atmosphere, but the immediate cause of the rupture was Scott's reinstatement of Petty Officer

---

[30] *Ibid.*, 63–4.
[31] Evans, 'Lt. "Teddy" Evans and Hilda Russell', 9.
[32] Louisa Young, *A Great Task of Happiness: The Life of Kathleen Scott* (London: Macmillan, 1995), 116.

Edgar Evans after an incident of drunkenness ashore had prompted Teddy Evans to remove him from Lyttelton. Scott's decision upset both Teddy and his wife who, felt Kathleen Scott, was a bad influence on Evans, 'working him up to insurrection' with the result that he went to Scott 'excited by vague and wild grievances, the only reasonable one concerning [Petty Officer] Evans'. Scott smoothed down Teddy's ruffled feathers but the outcome was a blistering row between the two wives. Mike Pryce recounts the story:

> Capt. L. E. 'Titus' Oates reported that 'Mrs. Scott and Mrs. Evans had a magnificent battle; they tell me it was a draw after fifteen rounds. Mrs. Wilson flung herself into the fight after the tenth round and there was more blood and hair flying about the hotel than you see in a Chicago slaughter-house in a month, the husbands got a bit of the backwash and there is a certain amount of coolness which I hope they won't bring into the hut with them, however it won't hurt me even if they do'. It is interesting to speculate on the effect this disharmony amongst the wives had on the expedition as a whole, especially once the civilising effects of New Zealand had been replaced by the harsh reality of the southern continent. Once at sea all was well, but Kathleen decided that if her husband ever mounted another expedition, the selection of men and their wives deserved more consideration. 'If ever Con [the name by which Scott was known by his intimates] has another expedition, the wives must be chosen more carefully than the men — better still, have none'. [33]

Traditional gender roles aside, one may suppose that Hilda Evans was, among other things, unwilling to exhibit the deference traditionally shown among wives in British service circles to the spouse of the ranking officer, these contrasting with the rarefied society in which Kathleen Scott was accustomed to move in London and elsewhere. Be that as it may, to this unpleasantness an unwelcome reminder of the past was added before *Terra Nova* sailed from Lyttelton on 26 November 1910. As Rita recalled, 'Hilda gave a dance for members of the Expedition and their friends. I was there but no one asked me to dance, why I don't know.' The reason was not far to seek: disgust among Michael Barne's friends at her breaking off their engagement five years earlier. In another of his notes to her memoirs, Rita's son Hugh reported having seen an earlier draft of this record in which her

---

[33] Mike Pryce, 'Centenary of Scott of Antarctic' at <nzshipmarine.com/nodes/view/ 1077>.

feeling of humiliation and distress was made manifest. [34] In the wider context of the expedition, however, when the moment of parting came off Port Chalmers on 29 November all differences between the wives were eclipsed by the numberless hazards that awaited their men. Kathleen Scott:

> I didn't say goodbye to my man because I didn't want anyone to see him sad. On the bridge of the tug Mrs. Evans looked ghastly white and said she wanted to have hysterics, but instead we took photos of the departing ship. Mrs. Wilson was plucky and good ... I mustered them all for tea in the stern and we all chatted gaily except Mrs. Wilson who sat looking somewhat sphinx-like. [35]

The story of the *Terra Nova* Expedition and the disaster that befell Scott and his companions in their quest for the Pole in early 1912 need not be rehearsed in any detail here. Although he came within 160 miles of the Pole, Teddy Evans was not among those selected by Scott for the final push. This did not come as a surprise to Evans who was physically much depleted by his exertions and regarded by some as quite literally not pulling his weight, but the disappointment was real enough. One of those chosen to proceed with Scott and ultimately to his death was Lt Henry Bowers who committed these words to his diary on that occasion, a record both of his friend's sadness and of his great love for his New Zealand wife: 'Poor Teddy — I am sure it was for his wife's sake he wanted to go. He gave me a little silk flag she had given him to fly on the Pole.' [36] As it was, Scott and the rest of his party reached the Pole on 17 January 1912 only to find that Amundsen had beaten them to it, before themselves succumbing to exhaustion and malnutrition on the return journey. It was not until February 1913 that the world at large learnt of the tragedy but Teddy Evans, upon whom command of the expedition had devolved, had in the intervening period rejoined his wife in Christchurch in April 1912 crippled by advanced scurvy. He owed his survival on the journey off the Polar Plateau and back to McMurdo Sound to the devotion of his companions during one of the brutal sledge journeys which characterised the expedition. Rita left this memory both of his homecoming in Christchurch and the episode as a whole:

---

[34] RMR, 67.
[35] Young, *A Great Task of Happiness*, 117.
[36] Cited in Fiennes, *Captain Scott*, 304.

A Colonial Childhood

> Teddy looked very ill when he arrived. He was suffering from the aftereffects of scurvy. His legs were very swollen but he soon got better when he had fresh food. A few weeks later Amundsen came to lunch and told us all about his run to the South Pole. He asked Teddy why Scott did not make more use of his dogs. Amundsen said his dogs did all the work, and pulled all the stores, now and then he killed and ate one, and fed the dogs too. [37]

It is one of the questions that has exercised historians of the heroic age of polar exploration ever since.

However, further disaster lay in store. In March 1913 the Evanses sailed in the *Aorangi* from Wellington and then in the SS *Otranto* from Sydney, the ship bound for London via the Suez Canal. Bill Conroy takes up the story:

> On Monday 14 April, when the *Otranto* was cruising along the coast of Italy, Hilda was taken ill with what later proved to be peritonitis. She was attended by the ship's doctor and a medical specialist who was travelling as a passenger on the ship. On the 15th an emergency operation was carried out, which seemed to have been successful, and when the ship reached Naples on Thursday Hilda was conscious. However, in the early hours of Friday morning, when the ship was at sea, her condition began to deteriorate and Hilda died at about midnight on 18 April. [38]

Hilda Russell was buried at Toulon, her coffin borne by officers of the *Otranto*. Back in Christchurch the Russells had grim forewarning that all was not well: on the evening of the 18th Rita had read a notice in *The Evening Post* reporting her sister to be seriously ill at sea between Naples and Toulon. The following morning came a cable informing them she had died. The family received a detailed account of Hilda's last illness from her aunt Ada who happened to have joined the *Otranto* at Port Said:

---

[37] RMR, 17. See also Pound, *Evans*, 119, for a very similar account of the same occasion; as Pound acknowledges Rita Russell (ix) he no doubt met or corresponded with her.

[38] Bill Conroy, 'The Final Tragedy: Remembering Hilda Evans', *Antarctic* [New Zealand Antarctic Society] 33.3 (2015), no. 233, 26–8; 28, at <antarcticsociety.org.nz/wp-content/uploads/2018/05/Antarctic.V33.3.2015.pdf>. Note, however, that her nephew Dr Hugh Russell describes Hilda as having had an ectopic pregnancy rather than peritonitis before succumbing to the embolism; RMR, 65.

> She told me she saw Hilda sitting up on deck looking rather ill. It was apparently very painful for her to get up or sit down. Two or three days later an urgent operation was successfully performed by a Melbourne surgeon. The next day the ship called Naples, and Hilda was so well she sent the others on shore to do some shopping. One of the passengers had given up a de luxe cabin to Hilda. Early next morning Hilda became unconscious and died at midnight from embolism. Poor Teddy was nearly crazy with grief. [39]

As Evans had condoled with Kathleen Scott after the death of her husband, so Kathleen set aside earlier differences and hurried to his side at the first opportunity:

> Lady Scott, with true womanly sympathy, made a special journey to Charing Cross and waited for more than an hour in order to greet Commander Evans and to offer him in his time of sorrow a word of comfort and a welcome. The meeting between the widow and the widower was a touching scene. [40]

Much of the sentiment expressed by Evans in his two autobiographical works can be taken with a grain of salt but there is no disputing the sincerity of the lines he devotes to his late wife:

> This part of the book is the hardest for me to write, and so I shall just say that no words of mine could ever pay high enough tribute to the beautiful and upright girl who shared my fortunes and inspired me to help and work for my fellow creatures for the next nine years of my life, and who died in 1913, just before I reached England after Scott's last expedition. [41]

Within a year Evans had seen to the installation of an impressive stained-glass window at St Hilda's Collegiate School in Dunedin which his wife (and Rita after her) had attended. Indeed, Evans remained close to the family, to the extent of altering his name by deed poll to add 'Russell' as a fourth given name. As he

---

[39] RMR, 19. Ada Stringer was Hilda's and Rita's maternal aunt.
[40] Cited in Conroy, 'The Final Tragedy', 28.
[41] Mountevans, *Adventurous Life*, 74.

recalled, 'We made friendships in that lovely land of fine and generous Britons of the kind that are broken only by death.' So it proved.

These events belonged to the generation ahead of Peter Russell who could only live them vicariously, mainly through his mother. Shortly after his return from the war in 1946 he recorded this valedictory experience of her and of that era:

> Tonight a broadcast version of Scott's journey to the Pole which Mother listened to with intent sadness. It is curious that she should have been so closely linked with those strangely chivalrous conquistadores of the Edwardian age. [42]

'Thy Will Be Done' reads the tablet on Hilda's grave in Toulon.

*

In the intervening years Rita Russell continued her search for a husband, of which the boating party she gave on the Avon in Christchurch for the officers of a visiting warship may be an instance. It was, however, no easy matter being a suitor to one of Thomas Russell's daughters. Rita's elder sister Ethel (then aged twenty-five) had eloped with her future husband Will O'Callaghan after her father refused permission for them to marry as Will's assets consisted of no more than a bicycle. [43] Rita recalled her father's chaperoning style in the following terms:

> Father used to allow me to bring boys to the house, he sat in the room with us, pretty tame for the boys and for us. At 9.00 p.m. father used to get up, take out his gold watch, open it then shut it with a tremendous bang as a warning that it was time for the boys to leave. They did! [44]

Nonetheless, the pressure to find a match remained and the result was a marriage of convenience. Rita's account of how she met her husband could scarcely be more laconic: 'In September 1912 [her younger brother] Cecil brought Captain H. B. Wheeler to dinner. Actually he was asked for Saturday, he came on Friday. I saw him many times, then followed a very unromantic courtship and I became engaged, it was all fixed up while walking along the street in New Brighton.' [45]

---

[42] Journal, 11 Feb. 1946.
[43] RMR, 16. Ethel O'Callaghan died in 1964.
[44] *Ibid.*
[45] *Ibid.*, 18. New Brighton is a coastal suburb of Christchurch.

Wheeler may have introduced himself as a captain or else Rita's memory was defective but he was in fact still in the rank of lieutenant. At all events, the marriage was a low-key affair at St Barnabas' Church, Fendalton on 30 November, just two months after their first meeting. The service was followed by a reception for fifty guests at Warwick House, a local hotel. With the bride's parents away on a planned two-year voyage to Europe via Japan, China and the Trans-Siberian Express while the new family home, Knowlescourt, was under construction, no invitations were sent and the guest list confined to close relations.[46]

Peter Russell's paternal grandparents: Lieutenant-Colonel John Langford Wheeler, Army Ordnance Department., and Lydia Wheeler (née Porter).

Hugh Bernard Wheeler was born in Halifax, Nova Scotia on 5 January 1883, a fact which at length allowed his sons to claim Canadian nationality. He was the son of Major (eventually Lieutenant-Colonel) John Langford Wheeler of the Army Ordnance Department and Lydia (*née* Porter), the former of Lechlade in Gloucestershire and the latter apparently from the Isle of Wight. A member of what used conventionally to be referred to as 'a good family' complete with heraldic achievement, Wheeler's birth in Nova Scotia came as a result of his father's posting to Halifax with its impressive array of coastal batteries, a fact Peter

---

[46] The death of their daughter Hilda in April 1913 caused Thomas and Nellie Russell to curtail their planned two-year journey to England and return to Christchurch.

Russell was able to verify in the garrison baptismal records during a visit in 1988. [47] Bernard followed his father into the Army, first as a Lieutenant in the Hong Kong Volunteer Corps from 1901–02 and then gazetted a Second Lieutenant in The Queen's Own (Royal West Kent Regiment) on 24 March 1903. [48] Although he received the expected promotion to Lieutenant the following year, Army life clearly did not suit Wheeler who resigned his commission in April 1905. He then accompanied his parents and three surviving siblings to New Zealand where his connection with the Army was resumed, being appointed a Lieutenant in the Reserve in January 1909, followed on 17 March 1911 by appointment to the New Zealand Staff Corps in the same rank. [49] However, change of scene brought no enhancement of zeal and Wheeler was soon under the scrutiny of his superiors for lack of officer-like qualities. Indeed, steps were being taken by June 1912 to give him the option of resigning his commission before his services were officially dispensed with. Wheeler survived this episode but his performance continued to leave much to be desired. Here is his commanding officer's report following a stint at a training camp in Palmerston North in July 1913:

> I have to report that the work of [Temporary Acting] Captain H. B. Wheeler N.Z.S.C. during the first period of this Course was far from satisfactory. He does not know his drill, was incapable of imparting instruction in it, had a bad word of command, and took very little interest in his work; in fact he was so bad that I asked for permission to keep him here for the second period. [50]

Although competent at office work, Wheeler's desultory service record as it unfolds over 400 pages is one of deficient energy, slackness, self-indulgence and

---

[47] PER to Charles Kennedy, Oxford, 12 May 1988.

[48] *The London Gazette*, 19 May 1903, 3154; Wheeler's service record in the British Army is contained in The National Archives, Kew [TNA], WO [War Office] 339-43150. His service record in the New Zealand Staff Corps is held in 405 pages at Archives New Zealand [ANZ], Wellington, at <ndhadeliver.natlib.govt.nz/delivery/DeliveryManagerServlet?dps_pid= IE19153613>; summary of service on applying to the New Zealand Defence Forces on 21 June 1910, on 397.

[49] Russell, *One Man's Journey*, 2. The siblings were Ernest, Margery and Hildreth who was cashiered from the Coldstream Guards in 1907; an elder brother Lionel died in Amoy (Xiamen) in 1905.

[50] ANZ, service record, 29 July 1913, 17.

creative explanations. As one exasperated officer put it, 'Whether it is due to stupidity or not I am not prepared to say but I have constantly noted that when furnishing an excuse he will give one reason at one time and a totally different one a short time afterwards — a course of action, which, whatever the cause, does not reflect to his credit.'[51]

Lt Bernard Wheeler and Rita Russell on their wedding day, 30 November 1912. They are at Knowlescourt, the bride's newly completed family home in Christchurch.

[51] *Ibid.*, 6 June 1912, 26.

This then, was the man Rita married, who had in addition accumulated a number of debts by the time he met her. No mention is made of these in Rita's memoirs but the details were shared with her son Hugh:

> Father was looking for a wife who was well-off financially; he had no means beyond his Captain's pay and was in debt. Mother paid off his debts before the marriage and it appears to have been a not inconsiderable sum. Thus, after the marriage she was not best pleased to find that he still had a lot of debt to be paid off. [52]

The reaction of Thomas Russell who neither met Bernard Wheeler before he married his daughter nor presumably had much opportunity to enquire as to his assets and prospects is to be imagined. In the event, the Wheelers were supported by the bride's father throughout their marriage and their first marital home on Carlton Street in Christchurch was rented and furnished at his expense.

In appearance Bernard Wheeler was a stoutish dapper man of good height and good looks, albeit with a somewhat awkward bearing. Peter Russell remembered him thus:

> He was tall and square-faced, dark and rather plumpish, always well-dressed and with a terrific shine on his shoes. [*Marginalia:* thick eyebrows. I remember male smell of his handkerchiefs.] He walked in a slow upright manner and had rather a nasty habit of laughing and rubbing his hands together suddenly, sometimes. [53]

Of Bernard Wheeler more later, but this is the moment to introduce another of the salient features of Peter Russell's youth, one which remained vivid in his mind's eye all his life: the Russell family home at 274 Papanui Road in Christchurch, known as Knowlescourt. In 1909 Thomas Russell decided to sell Quamby and commission the design and construction of a mansion nearby in the affluent northern suburb of Merivale. [54] Knowlescourt was designed in the

---

[52] Russell, *One Man's Journey*, 2.
[53] ALRTP, 22–3. Wheeler's physical examination on joining the New Zealand Permanent Forces at Wellington on 3 Jan. 1911, described him as standing 5' 11" tall, weighing 12 stone and with grey eyes; ANZ, service record, 393.
[54] Information on the sale of Quamby in 'Holly Lea: 123 Fendalton Road' at <my.christchurchcitylibraries.com/holly-lea-123-fendalton-road/>.

English Arts and Crafts style by J. J. Collins of Armson, Collins and Harman, one of the oldest architectural firms in New Zealand. [55] Boasting twenty rooms the uppermost of which offered distant views of the Southern Alps, the house had half-timber detailing, was roofed with terra-cotta tiles shipped from Marseille and, girt by an impressive brick wall, took a year to complete at a cost of £3500. Fitted with every modern convenience including central heating, it was equipped with porcelain bathroom and kitchen fittings by Doultons and furnished entirely from the catalogue of a company on the Tottenham Court Road. Nor did Mr Russell stint on ornamentation, with carved interiors, Venetian glassware and an assortment of antiques and decorative art including the marble statue of Dante's Beatrice he left in his will to the McDougall Art Gallery in Christchurch. Peter Russell had this evocation of it:

Knowlescourt, the mansion built by Thomas Russell in the Merivale suburb of Christchurch. Completed in 1911 and demolished in 2011 following the Canterbury earthquakes of 2010–11. The photo dates from c. 1925.

I remember the drawing-room — a rarely-visited place with glass cupboards of china and glass of a valuable nature. Then there was the

---

[55] '1897_record_form', PDF downloaded by author from (defunct) New Zealand Historic Places Trust website. The plot on which the property was built was on the corner of Knowles Street. See Laura Dunham, 'The Domestic Architecture of Collins and Harman in Canterbury, 1883–1927', Ph.D. thesis, University of Canterbury, 2013, 115–16 & 386–7, at <core.ac.uk/download/pdf/35471212.pdf>. The firm had already designed a building for Russell on his Rakaia Island property in 1894; 226.

little room away up in the roof where I used to sleep and which had a rope ladder as a fire escape. It used to be very ghostly up there at night. Next to it was the large and luxurious bedroom where Aunt Winnie slept when she visited the place. Then there was the clock on a landing upstairs which had a low mellow chime and was most attractive. And the rather mysterious place of basket chairs known as the maids' sitting-room. And the bathroom with its electric heater with big bulbs which glowed attractively. [56]

It was not only the structure and amenity of the house but also the life carried on inside it that imbued Peter Russell with some of the assurance that, outwardly at least, was such a distinct part of his personality:

Sunday night dinner. Lights, silver, finger bowls, table napkins, all sorts of attractive food. Hugh eating till he began to gasp. Grandpa telling his giant stories in the study with the lights out. Grandpa playing the organ in the morning before breakfast. Bowls of porridge with real rich cream. The nice smell of boot polish and marble in the cloakroom. Collecting sycamore seeds and making propellers of them so that they revolved quickly when one ran. Uncle Gerald in the darkroom and the mysteries of red, yellow etc. shutters, hypo and the like. [57]

Another denizen of Knowlescourt was his Uncle Cecil, recently returned from the University of Wisconsin with a degree in Civil Engineering:

[…] Uncle Cecil had a room by the greenhouses filled with all kinds of mechanical contrivances, mostly wireless parts and there he would construct wireless sets amid a rich smell of shellac and soldering stuff. I used to go there and watch him for a long time very often, rather intrigued by the sight of an uncle who wore ugly American suits, said 'yep' and had a whole gamut of conversational grunts. […] Sometimes a set would be finished and then he would twiddle about with it a lot and eventually put earphones to my ears and tell me America was coming through. [58]

---

[56] ALRTP, 4. Winnie was the sister of Thomas Russell's third wife, Gertrude Brown.
[57] *Ibid.*, 1–2.
[58] *Ibid.*, 5.

Russell's early addiction to the radio and the keen interest in film and photography he cultivated later in life no doubt owed something to his uncles and memories of Knowlescourt. It was here too that he began a lifetime of voracious reading, later recalling having worked his way through much of Knowlescourt's library by the time he turned twelve. [59] However, the preeminent feature of Knowlescourt was Thomas Russell himself:

> I can see him in his white coat working in the greenhouses, potting flowers and proudly showing me his petunias and other creations. There was a warm earthy smell in there and the scents of all sorts of flowers. Other times I can see him at afternoon tea in the study, with his tallish wiry body, acute blue eyes, white moustache and white-haired head with a big shiny bald patch on top. His face was always alert and keen and one knew that, though slightly deaf, there was little he missed. He used often to smile at his jokes or add some tale he had heard but if something ruffled him the wrong way his anger was cold and short and he said little but made no doubt as to his feelings. In the study was a smell of cigar smoke which I always associated with him. There also was the big organ which he would play in the early morning or in the evening. When he played the organ he liked to have no one in the room as if he seemed to derive some special satisfaction from being alone with his music. He was always quietly but well dressed in well-tailored suits and gave even me as a child the idea that he had everything perfectly under his control and knew exactly everything that was happening and would happen. He enjoyed his wealth because it was all his own and because he could help and further all who needed and deserved his assistance. Action and energy of mind and body were essentials in his life. [60]

No one who heard Peter Russell describe Knowlescourt in later years could doubt that he spent the happiest years of his life under its aegis.

The Russells moved into Knowlescourt in the summer of 1911 and remained in the property until, much to the distress of the family, it was sold by Thomas Russell's widow in 1943. At some point after the Second World War Knowlescourt was subdivided into four flats and was in use as a bed-and-breakfast

---

[59] *Ibid.*, 8.
[60] *Ibid.*, 8–9.

at the time it was first heavily damaged and then ruined in the Canterbury earthquakes of September 2010 and February 2011. The house was demolished in November of that year, among the more prominent losses to the city's architectural heritage which largely erased Christchurch as the Russells had known it. Loving Knowlescourt as he did, it would have pained Peter Russell beyond measure to see the symbol of his family's wealth and the rock-like solidity of his grandfather to whom he owed so much shattered and destroyed. An eye surgery now occupies the site.

*

In early 1913 and within a few months of her marriage Rita Wheeler found that she was expecting her first child. Early in the pregnancy her husband was posted to Rangiora eighteen miles north of Christchurch to which she briefly decamped before returning on account of an undisclosed health issue, dismal lodgings and bad food, the last straw being the bluebottle she found in her soup. Here, bereaved by the death of her sister Hilda in April, she prepared for her confinement:

> I took a house in Hawthorne Road Papanui and a few months later Peter was born. I went to the house of the nurse, Mrs. Wright, three days before he arrived. Peter was born at 6.35 a.m. on Friday October 24th which was also father's birthday. He weighed 11½lb. The birth was not easy and the doctor stayed the night. At 7.30 p.m. the night before I saw the train passing on the way to Lyttelton; father and [her sister-in-law] May were on board. He was going to Wellington and she to London. Next morning while father was having his breakfast at the Royal Oak Hotel a telegram was handed to him wishing him a happy birthday and telling him he had a grandson. [61]

The infant was christened Peter Edward Lionel Russell Wheeler. His given name seems not to have had any precedent in the family but Edward was surely a nod to Teddy Evans while Lionel apparently commemorated an elder brother of his father who had succumbed in China in 1905, an assumption supported by Russell's determination to drop it from his initials in later life. More pertinently, beyond the bare details of parturition cited above Rita's memoirs convey

---

[61] RMR, 19. May Russell was the first wife of Rita's elder brother Gerald. Russell, *One Man's Journey*, 1, records the birth weight as 12½ lb.

absolutely nothing of the arrival of her son in her life or that of her husband with whom an already tenuous relationship was fraying.

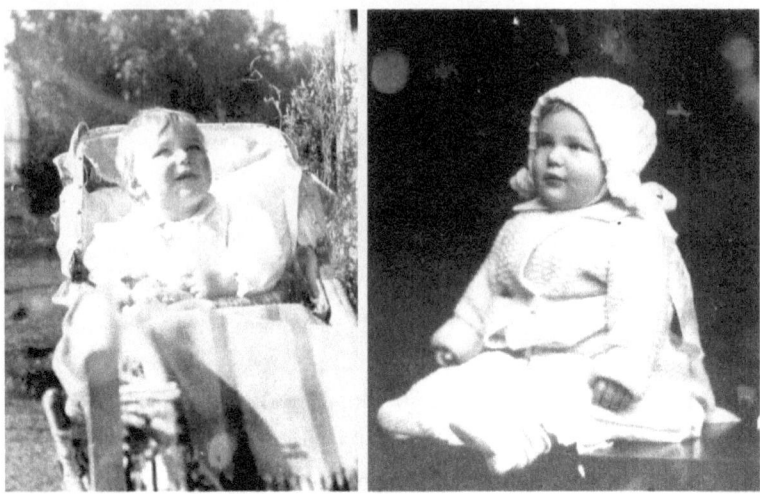

The earliest surviving photos of Peter Wheeler, seen shortly before he made his first visit to Britain in 1914.

As earlier the family found itself caught up in the wider conjuncture, in this case the Great War. Rita's first inkling of what lay ahead came with the sudden cancellation of her husband's leave in the spring of 1914 just as the family was preparing for an extended stay with her parents-in-law at Havelock North on the North Island. The following year Wheeler was recalled to his old regiment, the Royal West Kents, and on 18 May 1915 the family boarded the SS *Turakina* at Wellington for a forty-seven-day voyage to Plymouth via Cape Horn calling at Montevideo, Rio de Janeiro and Tenerife. At this point Rita's memoirs make one of their few mentions of her sons unrelated to health, in this case concerning Peter at about twenty months: 'At the last place [Tenerife] a lot of German ships were interned; the ships' officers used to have dinner at a hotel there. We dined in this hotel and Peter made a great nuisance of himself by continually joining these officers, why I don't know.' [62] Rita, it will be noted, tended to record surprise at situations she found untoward or chose not to analyse in any detail. Peter Russell would later maintain that his mother had only accompanied her husband to Britain to become pregnant, which she duly did at Aldershot or Oxford in late

[62] RMR, 20.

1915. It was while staying at the since demolished Clarendon Hotel in Oxford that she had one of the psychic experiences so characteristic of the age, recalled here in the clipped terms so characteristic of herself:

> It was here that one Sunday in 1915 I had a premonition that something was wrong in New Zealand and I felt I must sit down and write to mother, which I did. Next day I received a cable to say that she had died after an operation. She had actually died at the time I felt something was wrong. [63]

Helen Russell died on 20 December 1915 at the age of fifty-nine. Rita's memoirs make no further mention of her but Peter Russell later recalled how his grandfather would drive to Linwood Cemetery and lay flowers on her grave every Sunday morning. [64] Aside from her husband's imminent posting to France, this circumstance no doubt influenced Rita's decision to return to New Zealand to have her baby, which she did in the SS *Arawa* in late January 1916, being joined by her father for the last leg of the voyage between Hobart and Wellington. Returning to Knowlescourt, she gave birth to Hugh Bernard Langford Wheeler on 9 August, an event that again elicits only the briefest coverage in her memoirs.

Rita had apparently agreed with her husband that she would return to Britain with the children at the earliest opportunity, but by the end of the year she and the boys had contracted scarlet fever and not until they were out of quarantine in February 1917 could the journey be undertaken. Rita's earlier wartime voyages had been uneventful and completed at no great risk but this third journey was a very different proposition. On 1 February, sixteen days before the SS *Rotorua* sailed for Britain via the Panama Canal and the United States, Germany resumed unrestricted submarine warfare against Allied shipping. Here is Rita's record of the latter part of the voyage for which she engaged the services of a nurse to look after the boys:

> We went to Newport News in Virginia to coal, I went up to Richmond with the family and stayed there three days. We were to sail under sealed orders but the night we left I bought a paper and read that our ship was leaving for England that very night, there were seven women and children

[63] *Ibid.*
[64] ALRTP, 9.

on board. We had fire drill every day, really escape drill. The ship's boats were all lowered until even with the decks and fully provisioned. In mid-ocean a small Greek ship came to us to ask her position, I can see her now, she was regarded as highly suspicious and the Captain was called out of his bed, but all was well. Some of the women were neurotic and a number of squabbles took place. I made Hugh a kapok lifejacket, it fastened well round him, and had a big strong handle that he could be carried by; fortunately he did not need it. As we neared England I slept in half my clothes. Of course the ship was blacked out. As we passed Land's End early in the morning [of 22 March] a lamp signal came from the shore telling the Captain that a hospital ship [HMHS *Asturias*] had been sunk there the night before. The weather was fine but very cold. As soon as we passed the mole at Plymouth we all went down and had drinks. We arrived at noon [on the 22nd]. We left the ship at 1.00 p.m. and she left for London at 3.00 p.m. I had decided to leave the pram on board but at the last minute decided to take it with me. [65]

Later that afternoon the *Rotorua* was torpedoed and sunk twenty-four miles east of Start Point by the German minelaying submarine *UC-17* with the loss of a single crew member and over £400,000 worth of mutton, beef, cheese and butter, enough said Rita to supply London for a month. *Rotorua* had been shadowed into Plymouth by the ace U-boat commander Oblt.z.S. Ralph Wenninger who, so Peter Russell later held, refrained from attacking her on humanitarian grounds before despatching her once the passengers had landed. True or not, this was one of several deliverances and experiences in his life he would use to rebut casual criticism of this or that nationality or personage, in this case the Germans.

The Wheelers were reunited on the tug into which the passengers of the *Rotorua* disembarked at Plymouth, Bernard meeting his son Hugh for the first time. Rita eventually took a flat over a wine merchant's shop in Southsea and settled down to the austerities of life in wartime Britain with severe rationing punctuated by visits to nearby Stokes Bay where lived Elsa, the Norwegian who became Teddy Evans' second wife in January 1916. [66] Naturally enough, the war placed added strain on what was already a tenuous marriage:

---

[65] RMR, 22. *Asturias* had been torpedoed by *UC-66* on 20 March and was beached on the Devonshire coast with the loss of thirty-five lives.
[66] *Ibid.* Rita became godmother to their first son Richard, born in August 1918.

> I remember when Bernard came over from France on leave and went out to tea, I gave up our ration tickets and while I was pouring out the tea he had eaten the two tomato sandwiches and cake. Another time he had his own and my ration of bacon for breakfast, he looked at it and said 'What's this? I can get more in France.' I replied 'well you'd better go back to France.' [67]

Boorishness and defects of character were one thing, but Rita seems never to have appreciated the hellish reality experienced by her husband in Flanders where he served with the British Expeditionary Force from March 1916.[68] Although Wheeler was finally promoted captain in November 1915 after being restored to the Royal West Kents for war service in May, within eighteen months he had been relegated to staff duties as a Lieutenant 2nd Class though retaining his substantive rank as Captain. In June 1916 Wheeler wrote to the commanding officer of the New Zealand Expeditionary Force in France applying for promotion to the rank of major. 'My reason for making the application,' he wrote 'is that, owing to the rapid promotion obtaining amongst Officers of the New Army, I am under the unpleasant necessity of serving Junior to Officers here who received promotion to Captain after only a few months service.'[69] The request was denied. After a spell on secondment as Draft Conducting Officer to the Chinese Labour Corps, Wheeler returned to the West Kents with whose 8th Battalion he was wounded 'for the fourth time', suffering injuries to his legs and face on 26 September 1918. Then on 16 October he was gassed during operations east of Cambrai 'causing vomiting and laryngeal irritation, and at the same time, as the result of the shell explosion, he was hurled to the ground from a bridge on which he was standing, severely spraining his left ankle'. Wheeler was evacuated for convalescence in Devon two days later, reaching Exeter on the 19th. His wife's response needs no elaboration:

> I don't know what happened to him in France. After he was gassed he was sent to Miss (Major) Yarde Buller's convalescent home near Exeter. He was very angry because I did not go down and see him, but he was not very ill, it was a day's trip to get there and I had Peter and Hugh to look after. After a month at this place he came home on leave with orders to return [to France], he never did and although he had letters telling

[67] *Ibid.*, 22–3.
[68] TNA, WO 339-43150.
[69] ANZ, service record, Wellington, 15 June 1916, 288.

him to return he took no notice of them. His main idea was to get a ship back to New Zealand. [70]

Rita Wheeler (née Russell), c. 1915. Her dress is embellished with her own needlework.

Rita Wheeler with her sons Hugh and Peter at Southsea, 1917.

Probably she contrasted his fate with that of her cousin Neil Ruffell Russell, the barrister son of her uncle John who rose through the ranks to become 2nd Lieutenant in the Auckland Infantry Regiment before being killed at twenty-nine during the Ludendorff Offensive in March 1918. Whatever the case, Wheeler eventually secured a passage home for himself and his family but neither his bungling arrangements in connection with the journey (not assisted by his having resigned his commission in the Royal West Kents on 6 December) nor his selfish behaviour *en route* did other than inflict further damage on his marriage:

> He went to New Zealand House in London and saw the authorities. They told him they would do what they could to get him berths in the 'Oxfordshire' sailing for Auckland about December 15th 1918, and they told him they would let him know. As we heard nothing he went up again to see them and when he came back he told me they said they thought it would be all right and we could go ahead with our arrangements. We

[70] RMR, 23.

sent our luggage on to Liverpool and gave up the flat. We arrived at New Zealand House and the man when he saw us said 'what are you doing here? I never let you know you could have a passage.' I said I understood it was all settled and all our luggage has gone to Liverpool. The result was we were given a two-berth cabin for four. After a few days one of the officers offered Bernard a berth in his cabin. I had to get up early every morning to take the boys into breakfast at 7.30 a.m. Bernard would not get up on alternate days to do this, however I made him look after them while I went and had my breakfast at 8.00 a.m. I was hungry by then. [71]

They are the recollections of a woman who had lost all respect for her husband.

The voyage, the first for which Peter Russell retained vivid memories, took the family via Suez and Colombo:

I also remember seeing the Rock of Gibraltar and coming to Suez where Egyptian magicians came on deck and produced chickens from their mouths and sleeves and made half-crowns vanish in handkerchiefs. I can also remember seeing the mountains on both sides of the Red Sea and learning that 'Moses' had lived there and seeing a man in white robes on a camel and also the barren arid point of Cape Guardafui. About Colombo I remember a great deal. I can see the bay full of ships and the pier at which we landed and a ride in a rickshaw along hot yellow streets where nearly naked black men and quite naked children played and moved. Then there was the Galle Face Hotel where we stayed and Mother engaged a black ayah to look after Hugh and myself all the time we were there. He was terrified of her and screamed and howled. I was sorry for her that he should be so afraid because she was black and I remember that I was rather afraid myself but for this reason tried to hide it and be friendly and kind to her. One other thing I remember about the Galle Face was eating steamed haddock for breakfast in the company of the ayah and other white children and being taken to a bazaar full of trinkets, carpets, black ivory elephants, noise and queer smells. After that I recollect nothing of the trip except the Cocos Islands where we were to pass close by and see the remains of the *Emden*. There I have a most

---

[71] *Ibid.* The matter receives extensive coverage in Wheeler's service record. Rita had the indignity of being required to repay the New Zealand Government the cost of her and the boys' passages in eight £5 installments.

vivid memory which seems too fantastic to be true of a yellow sandy shore with palm trees and a man driving along the shore in a horse carriage which might have come off a Cheltenham street. [72]

On reaching Auckland in early 1919 the ship was ordered to anchor for twenty-four hours in the Quarantine Station as a precaution against the Spanish 'Flu. During this time a young widow committed suicide by pitching herself through a porthole into the harbour, her body found on the ebb tide next day in a tragedy that captured the desolation of the moment for all on board. It is interesting that neither Rita (nor Russell himself, for that matter) made mention of the person ultimately responsible for the quarantine of the *Oxfordshire* and other vessels arriving in New Zealand, G. Warren Russell, who held the portfolio of Minister of Internal Affairs and Minister of Public Health in the national government of William Massey between August 1915 and August 1919. [73] A younger brother of Thomas Russell and one of the outstanding New Zealand politicians of the early twentieth century, Warren Russell had in October 1918 taken the decision to allow the SS *Niagara* to dock in Auckland and was blamed for the ensuing (though in fact unrelated) outbreak of Spanish 'Flu that claimed over 8,000 lives and effectively ended his career as a Liberal politician. Incidentally, the arrival of the *Oxfordshire* at Auckland meant that Rita and the young Peter had completed four sea voyages between Britain and New Zealand in as many years, a total of approximately 50,000 nautical miles and 200 days afloat, typical of the restlessness he always associated with her and no doubt the bedrock of his formidable grasp of shipping and geography.

The family returned to the comforts of Knowlescourt where Thomas Russell had reached the age of sixty-eight. Widowed three years earlier and financially secure, he might reasonably have been expected to slip quietly into his dotage in the potting sheds and greenhouses of his Christchurch mansion but this was not

---

[72] ALRTP, 15–16. The German raider SMS *Emden* had been sunk by the cruiser HMAS *Sydney* on 9 Nov. 1914.

[73] <teara.govt.nz/mi/biographies/2r31/russell-george-warren>. See his *New Zealand Today: "A Priceless Gem in the Imperial Crown"* (Christchurch: G. W. Russell, 1919) and a utopian novel, *A New Heaven* (London: Methuen, 1919, but written c. 1902). As Minister Russell was, however, approached by the family to help settle a service claim for backpay brought by Bernard Wheeler in April 1916, a request that reached the office of Prime Minister William Massey the following month; ANZ, service record of Hugh Bernard Wheeler, 265 & 294.

Thomas Russell's way. An early enthusiast of motoring, in 1916 he made the first of two voyages to the United States during which he secured import rights for Buick cars, establishing New Zealand Automobiles Ltd. for the purpose. This energy also extended to his personal life and in 1917 he married twenty-nine-year-old Doris Baldwin, one of Rita's oldest friends and six months her junior. The following year he took Doris, by now pregnant with his child, to the United States where she contracted the Spanish 'Flu in New York City:

> She was six months pregnant and pregnant women had no chance of recovery. She ran a high temperature and father who never liked to think anyone was ill, treated her himself and got her temperature down to normal but next day it soared and she was taken to hospital where she died. As it was not possible to get her buried for some weeks he decided to take her body back to New Zealand. It must have been a terrible trip, the stations were piled up with coffins, and where they changed trains he had to identify Doris's coffin. Eventually he got on the boat for New Zealand. […] At Auckland the coffin was taken off by Lighter so as not to attract the attention of passengers and father had to go down a rope ladder, a shameful thing to expect an elderly distressed man to do. When they went to lower the coffin into the grave it was too short and they had to wait while it was enlarged. [74]

This return journey was not perhaps as terrible as it might have been because Mr Russell's eyes lighted on a fellow passenger, thirty-three-year old Gertrude Brown, daughter of the founding professor of chemistry at the University of Auckland. Several trips to Auckland during the course of 1919 resulted in his engagement to Gertie and the announcement that he would be bringing her to live at Knowlescourt following their marriage which took place in Auckland in February 1920. Gertie outlived Thomas Russell but it was subsequently alleged that his three wives were not the extent of his amorous life following his first marriage to Nellie Stringer in 1874. During the trip he and Nellie had made to Europe between 1909 and 1910 while Knowlescourt was under construction Mr Russell stayed in Tours with a retired officer in the French marines whose acquaintance he had made in the 1870s, Martial Gadrat. [75] While there he met

---

[74] RMR, 25; additional information in Russell, *One Man's Journey*, 5.
[75] <www.geni.com/people/Marcelle-Blair-Suzanne/6000000078280434966>. I am grateful to Mauro Herlitzka of Buenos Aires for his assistance with this section.

two of the daughters of the house, Madeleine and Suzanne, and during the visit Gadrat reportedly asked Mr Russell if he would look after his daughters should they ever go to New Zealand. As Rita recalled, this outwardly highly unlikely scenario eventuated in 1912 with the arrival of Suzanne:

> I often wonder if father paid her fare. It was not a very pleasant surprise when she arrived, and she stayed about 18 months. She was quite nice but her clothes smelt terribly of perspiration and nearly made us all sick. This caused a great argument on Sunday nights when Gerald and May and Uncle Harry Stringer came to supper, nobody wanted to sit next to Suzanne and when the meal was over mother used to open the big window wide; no matter what the weather was like, the room had to be aired. [76]

The one occasion on which Suzanne proved her worth at supper was when Amundsen dined at Knowlescourt in 1912, at which French was the lingua franca. Suzanne eventually moved out and at length married a decorated officer in the New Zealand Staff Corps in London in 1917. This, however, was by no means the last of the Gadrats since Russell's last will and testament of 1935 made provision for the payment to Madeleine of £500 on his death and a £100 annuity thereafter, which Peter Russell later declared to be in connection with a child fathered by Mr Russell though no evidence has been found to confirm this. In any case, not until Madeleine's death in 1977 were these charges on the estate curtailed by the family by which time two or three generations of a Touraine family had been in receipt of largesse from New Zealand.

*

Meanwhile, Rita Wheeler had domestic trouble of her own. Although her father bought the couple a bungalow on Weston Road in Christchurch the household could scarcely make ends meet, particularly after Wheeler resigned his remaining commission (that in the New Zealand Staff Corps) in August 1920 on being told it had been decided to terminate his employment. Unable to secure assignment to the New Zealand Army Ordnance Department or find civilian employment, Wheeler slumped into a shiftless existence:

---

[76] RMR, 17. Harry Stringer was Rita's maternal uncle.

I never worked so hard in my life. Bernard with no job and not trying to get one. Father made me an allowance and I could just manage on it. I had to do all the housework, washing, ironing and the garden. I well remember after 2½ hours ironing and I was still doing it at 2.00 p.m. when Bernard came in from town and said 'where's my dinner'. I said 'oh get out I feel something in my head is going to snap'. He left and I finished the ironing; he changed his shirt every day. I decided to go and see father and ask him to give Bernard a chance and a job, and he did. He gave him a job helping to unload and assemble Buick cars. He had to be at work at 7.30 a.m. which meant I had to give him breakfast before 7.00 a.m., he stuck this job for six weeks only then announced he would not be returning. I heard later that he avoided all the heavy work and walked around with a feather duster dusting assembled cars. He said the work was beneath him; it was the beginning of better jobs if he had only stuck it. He never got another job, he used to pick and choose over jobs advertised in the papers, the job he wanted never came and he would not consider the others. Things became worse and worse. I asked him to get a job and we'd start again. It was no use. The boys got on his nerves if they cried and several times he threatened them with his razor strap. Finally after some words with Peter, he struck me. My exact words to him were 'you've threatened to do that several times, and now you've done it and that's the end, you can get out'. He went up to his father, Ernest and Hildreth at Wairoa but his father sent him back and said his place was at home. When he first left I gave him all I had — £50. I went up to Hanmer for a rest, and he went back to Wairoa, he did this several times and did some very odd things about the house so that I became afraid of what he might do. [77]

Rita had evidently lost her 'shyness'. The demise of this marriage did not of course escape the boys' notice, even if their memories of their father were by no means all bad:

I remember my Father playing what were called 'fun jokes' which were all kinds of games in which he hurled us about. As far as I can

[77] *Ibid.*, 25–6.

remember he was always very kind and indulgent to us in spite of occasional fierce outbursts. Indeed it was Mother who was the disciplinarian with the handle of a feather duster but she was also the one to whom I turned when in trouble and needed assistance. I had a very acute perception of all things in those days and can remember the quarrels which used to take place in the poisoned atmosphere of my Father's inability to find congenial work and the consequent strain of housework etc. on my Mother. There was one terrible day when I hid under my bed and watched them strike each other. After that my Father's absences with his family in Wairoa became more frequent. Grandpa tried to assist him in a severe sort of way. I can remember once seeing him working in one of Grandpa's garages. He was generous and always stood for something different from the ordinary humdrum life of home and school. [78]

Whatever Wheeler's personal shortcomings, evident enough before the Great War, these can only have been magnified by what was then known as shell shock or neurasthenia and is now diagnosed as post-traumatic stress disorder. Between July and September 1920 he had a six-week confinement for neuritis at Rotorua Military Hospital, supposedly due to the effects of gas poisoning but possibly part of a failed effort to secure a war pension on the ground of invalidity. [79] Although his service record gives the impression of a serial malingerer, the fact that Wheeler was admitted to the Queen Mary Army Convalescent Hospital in the spa town Hanmer Springs eighty miles northwest of Christchurch after the separation leaves little doubt that his condition was officially recognised. [80] The boys visited him there at least once:

> People wandered around the grounds which had a number of places where one could drink the waters. The soldiers were all dressed in a blue sort of uniform. I was then a toddler. We wandered around with father and we chatted to a soldier who became very incensed with my cough. It must have been a very annoying cough, as it was to me, because I could

---

[78] ALRTP, 21–2.
[79] ANZ, Wheeler record, 29 July 1913, 106–10.
[80] The establishment of this hospital owed much to the efforts of Rita's uncle G. W. Russell as Minister of Public Health and was opened by him on 3 June 1916; <teara.govt.nz/en/biographies/2r31/russell-george-warren>.

not control it. He kept on telling me to stop and said that it was just a habit. [81]

Rita, however, exhibited as little sympathy for her husband's plight at Hanmer Springs as she had during his post-gassing convalescence in Exeter: 'In the meantime Bernard went to the Army Convalescent Hospital at Hanmer where he made himself very unpopular complaining all the time.' [82] After consulting her brother Gerald and her father she instead went to court and petitioned for divorce in December 1924, which became absolute on 2 April 1925:

> Just as the court began, the door opened and in came Bernard; there was no need for him to do so, the case was undefended. Father undertook to educate the boys, and to be responsible for their upbringing. It was soon over; I forgot to say that the divorce was on a three-year separation; several times Bernard broke the rule that we must not meet. The decree was made absolute, and on that day he came to Christchurch, met Peter and Hugh, the latter brought him home to our new house in Heaton Street and showed him all over the house. I was home late and missed him, just as well. [83]

This may have been the end for Rita but it could hardly have been so for her sons who like so many children of divorced parents longed for a reconciliation:

> When he finally went away his occasional visits were great joys, perhaps for this reason, and I remember how often I used to watch over the gate towards the end of the street to see if any of the people coming down the street were him. […] I must've been about seven when I asked Mother one sunny afternoon in the back garden if she was 'separated' from him in the presence of Miss Leuchars. I shall always remember the look on her face as she said 'yes'. I think that after that I always hoped somehow to bring them together again and would try to

---

[81] Russell, *One Man's Journey,* 4.
[82] RMR, 26.
[83] *Ibid.* The decree absolute is held in the Christchurch Archive, Supreme Court of New Zealand for the Canterbury District, D1246/1924, Wheeler, Rita Muriel v Wheeler, Hugh Bernard.

do so but Mother always had some unhappy tale of him to remind me of on those occasions. [84]

In fact neither Peter nor Hugh ever saw their father again. By 1925 several members of the Wheeler family had moved to Australia where Colonel Wheeler purchased his son Ernest a farm at Kojonup 160 miles southeast of Perth while Bernard settled on an army pension in the Sydney suburb of Mosman. Rita encouraged the boys to write to their father but the letters went unanswered and the effort sadly tapered off. In the event, the severance of contact was not total though by the early 1930s Peter Russell had come to regard his father with some disdain. In a diary entry for 30 June 1933 he records having 'Received letter from Father talking about job in Nauru with the phosphate company. It would be splendid if it came off but it won't.' [85] A letter sent to Russell from his grandfather in Kojonup in January 1935 mentions that 'Bernard has sent me some sheets of your literary productions which I have read with great interest', this being the period when his grandson was publishing short stories and had aspirations to a career as a novelist. [86] Three months later Colonel Wheeler cabled Rita with the news that her ex-husband had died in Mosman on 5 April at the age of fifty-two. As Peter Russell later put it, he walked into a pharmacy one day and 'dropped dead', the cause of death recorded as coronary thrombosis with wartime gassing as the secondary cause. [87] Rita remitted £15 towards the cost of erecting a memorial at the Northern Suburbs General Cemetery in North Ryde and Peter corresponded with his grandfather until at least 1938. [88] The Wheelers' farm in Kojonup was a tenuous affair in the unforgiving setting of Western Australia, of which Colonel Wheeler's letter of January 1935 gives a flavour: 'The last six months I must say have been very trying ones for us all with the pressure of the farm work, machinery and labour troubles etc., and the disappointments we have had through the low prices realized for our wool and surplus sheep etc.' The death of Colonel Wheeler and Ernest within a few months of each other in 1943

---

[84] ALRTP, 22–3. Miss Leuchars was the last of the boys' many governesses.
[85] It didn't. In January 1935 Wheeler, now aged fifty-two, wrote petitioning the New Zealand Staff Corps for employment; unsurprisingly he was turned down. ANZ, Wheeler record, 29 July 1913, 50.
[86] Col. J. L. Wheeler to PER, Kojonup, 2 Jan. 1935. Russell sent funds for the upkeep of the grave in 1967.
[87] Russell, *One Man's Journey*, 43–4.
[88] Col. J. L. Wheeler to PER, Kojonup, 16 Oct. 1935 and 19 Nov. 1938.

brought an end to the endeavour, the latter having run the business as a gentleman farmer who employed labour to do all the work. [89] It was a character trait the Russells will have recognised from Bernard Wheeler. Hugh no doubt spoke for both brothers when he wrote in his memoirs that 'I would dearly love to have had some sort of relationship with him, but I doubt if he missed me.' [90] Peter Russell's verdict in later life was altogether blunter: 'Bastard.' The use of an epithet, so rare in his lexicon, not only captures Wheeler's shortcomings as a man and as a father but the role he played in the mental torment Russell was fated to suffer in future decades, product of the greatest breach of trust a parent could possibly visit on a child, that of sexual abuse.

Peter Russell had lost all interest in his father's family by the end of the Second World War but Hugh and surprisingly enough his mother retained their curiosity, and the former assiduously sought and cultivated contact with his Wheeler relatives in Australia, New Zealand and London. Of these Hugh and Rita's meeting with Bernard's brother Hildreth in a working-class suburb of Auckland in December 1950 proved much the most memorable:

> Hillie met me at the door and I was suddenly amazed to see this huge old man who must have been well over 6 feet tall. He had closely cropped hair, mainly grey, but red hairs still apparent. He seemed to be rather poor and his house had a somewhat frowsty smell about it. A woman was in the background who he said was his wife; they met in a Salvation Army Hostel where she was a Lass. She was told to bring us some tea, which duly appeared on a sort of tray on which were laid three white earthen pottery cups. She then took her departure from the room and Hillie handed the cups round. [...] The room we were in was furnished with a long table, a bench and a few chairs. Hillie presided over the feast from the end of the table. He was wearing a long jacket about which there was a suggestion that in better times it might have been an army coat; this was worn unbuttoned as if the buttons had long since gone. He spoke in a good, educated, upper-class English accent which sounded extremely odd in the circumstances. He told mother that she should be heartily ashamed of herself for divorcing father; he said that she had tarnished the family's escutcheon! [91]

---

[89] Russell, *One Man's Journey*, 271.
[90] *Ibid.*, 6.
[91] Russell, *One Man's Journey*, 272–3.

Peter Russell would recount this episode with a characteristic guffaw. Years earlier he had noted the similarity in appearance between his two grandfathers but there the comparisons ended. [92] The fortunes of each family and the opportunities they took and missed in the context of Britain's long colonial enterprise in Australasia could scarcely have been more different.

Already in October 1929 Rita had taken the decision to change the family name from Wheeler to Russell by deed poll. The reason was twofold. Not only had Bernard Wheeler and his family largely exited their lives, but Thomas Russell had no male heirs in the direct line amongst his children, his elder son Gerald's second marriage having produced a daughter Suzanne before Gerald's death in 1925 while his younger son Cecil (d. 1961) was born with spina bifida and never married. In Peter's case this meant that he took his fourth given name as his last. Distressing as it was at the time, this development formalised the process by which Peter Russell's grandfather and to some extent his uncles Gerald and Cecil had replaced his father first in his life and increasingly in his affections, a step he in later life interpreted 'as an attempt to eliminate the existence of my father from my conscience'. [93] In fact, Bernard Wheeler was being declared dead by the family as early as 1927, eight years before the event.

*

Peter Russell's first formal education after kindergarten came in 1920 in the muscular environment of St Andrew's College, Christchurch, a Presbyterian establishment opened in 1917 in the grounds of a large private house off the dusty Papanui Road. [94] Outwardly St Andrew's presented an attractive prospect with its kilted pipe bands, rugger and *haka* against the backdrop of the grassy swards and woods through which the Waimairi meanders before draining into the Avon. Inwardly it was a temple to corporal punishment in the Scottish tradition, starting with liberal use of the tawse on the younger boys and moving on to the cane as they got older. As Russell recalled, neither his ability to spell far better than any of his peers nor being 'the best reader in the class and usually top of the forms for which I received prizes for "General Excellence"' kept him from being beaten in his turn:

---

[92] ALRTP, 17: 'Colonel Wheeler looked rather like Grandpa except that he was shorter and his face was less keen.'

[93] Javier Marías Archive, Madrid [hereinafter JMA], PER to Javier Marías, Oxford, 30 Jan. 2002.

[94] I am grateful to Lisa Clark and Pip Dinsenbacher of St Andrew's College, Christchurch for kindly furnishing records and photographs of Russell's school career.

> When I went to the school I was a little boy in a junior class and was taught by a woman teacher called Mrs Mayne. She was middle-aged, dark hair, dark eyes, capable-looking without being old-maidish. We learnt reading, arithmetic and writing. Discipline was kept by a strap. We learnt copperplate writing in copybooks for which a great deal of fearful work was required. Blots in the copybook were punished by cuts from the strap on the palm of the hand. I was terrified of this. My writing was always free from blots but one day I made one and was panic-stricken. We always had to sit with our arms folded when not writing so I tried to cover [the] blot with [the] corner of my folded arms but she found it out and I received some cuts from the strap and was terribly humiliated. [95]

By his own account a rather lonely and introverted child, Russell clearly elected to keep as low a profile as his academic distinction and imposing physical stature allowed:

> Though I was as big and strong as the rest I used to hate playing rough games or fight with the other boys as I was afraid of being beaten by them and the humiliation would have been unendurable. Nor did I break rules as I was too afraid of being punished. On one side of the classroom were double doors leading into a big room used as a museum and library. We always started with fear when this door opened as it meant often the entrance of the headmaster — a short, plump, dark, full-faced man whom we called Aka (from his initials A. K. Anderson) and his appearance I once heard my mother call sensual. He was a real figure of dread to us boys as he ruled by the cane and his appearance sometimes meant a summons to his study. When he talked and made jokes or smiled we all laughed uproariously or smiled broadly, waiting anxiously the moment of relief when he disappeared again. [96]

Then came graduation to the middle school. Russell continued to show distinction in English, Spelling and Geography in particular and garner many prizes, but there was more to school than that:

---

[95] ALRTP, 29–30.
[96] *Ibid.*, 30–1.

Life was much more complicated. The boys were of all classes. The boarders had a continual feud with the dayboys whom they despised. They wore grey open shirts and were a much tougher lot and often bullied the dayboys. [...] The urinal was smelly and covered with green moss; a boy called Wood — a crudish country lad — used to show me how he could piss right over the wall high into the neighbouring urinal. [97]

The rule of the tawse. Hugh and Peter Wheeler in the uniform of St Andrew's College, Christchurch, c. 1921.

Peter Wheeler seated extreme left at St Andrew's College, November 1923. Courtesy of St Andrew's College, Christchurch.

A particular torment was sports generally and gym especially:

[97] *Ibid.,* 33 & 38.

The horror of doing gymnasium exercises at a weekly drill hour when we were supposed to swing and turn somersaults on the parallel bars and the rings. I was very poor at this, not because I couldn't as of my self-conscious fear that I mightn't be able to. I once ran away from school and hid in a field nearby but was brought back by prefects sent out to search for me. [98]

In this, however, family help was at hand:

I didn't like school much and often malingered to try to escape it. Usually I failed but a good trick was to pretend to a pain in my chest. I went to see my uncle Gerald the doctor who lived in a house on a street corner in the same long road where Knowlescourt was. His waiting room smelt slightly of chloroform. He was in these later days a kindly man with a big nose, short, and kind eyes. To my surprise he didn't reject my purely imaginary claim to pains in chest but said I had a heart murmur and had better not play football. This suited me admirably. [99]

But it was the sadistic culture of corporal punishment that left the deepest mark in every sense:

Our lives in school were entirely ruled by fear. Menteath had a thick strap hardened in saltwater. If a boy talked or did bad work he had to go up in front of the class and bend over and receive three or four terrific whacks with the strap. This beating became the chief element in the school lives of many of the boys — owing to its frequency none could escape indefinitely. Cheating was especially strongly punished. One day one of the Myers boys was caught and beaten in front of the class until the blood began to come through his trousers. The science of beating became one of our major interests and we took a professional interest in it. It was always rather sickening to watch a boy getting it though. To cry under such treatment was the cardinal sin. The one hour a week on Wednesday afternoon was the worst period of all as then an English

---

[98] *Ibid.*, 38–9.
[99] *Ibid.*, 33. The heart murmur was later found to have been misdiagnosed.

master called Stewart took the class. He was probably the cleverest and most hard-working of the masters but to us he was a real terror as he carried in his pocket a terrible strap and if we could not parse the sentences correctly he would take it out and administer one or two terrific blows with it on the palm of our hands, numbing the whole hand with pain and making it swell. This man was the most dreaded of all. [100]

Leaving aside the trauma to which he was exposed, no wonder Russell always recoiled from unreasoning discipline, loutishness and traditional displays of masculinity. To Russell, indeed, '[t]he terms seemed to go on interminably and monotonously and my chief desire in life was to grow up and be free of them.' [101] The decision taken at Knowlescourt in late 1925 that the boys should complete their education in England therefore came as a distinct relief: 'I cannot remember feeling much regret even at leaving my friends to whom I promised to write regularly. England had always seemed too fascinating a place to be true and so it was as if one had suddenly been given the right of entry to a childish heaven.' [102] Where the decision itself was concerned, Russell later wrote that '[i]n those days families in New Zealand (and Australia) who could manage it often transplanted their sons and daughters to England to complete their secondary education so there was nothing specially unusual about this', though his mother may also have looked to remove herself and her sons from Christchurch society in light of the divorce. [103] The real wrench was leaving his wider family and Knowlescourt itself:

> The last thing I remember of Knowlescourt was just before our departure for England. That afternoon I remember going all around the house and garden taking a last look at everything but in the excitement I hadn't really understood until I reached the cloakroom and looked at myself in the mirror there and wondered how long it would be before the mirror saw me there again. It was a shattering moment. [104]

---

[100] *Ibid.*, 35–6.
[101] *Ibid.*, 40.
[102] *Ibid.*, 39.
[103] 'Peter Edward Lionel Russell' (hereinafter PELR), the four-page word-processed account of his life up to 1953 prepared by Russell 'for possible necrological use' which he deposited with the British Academy in November 1992.
[104] ALRTP, 6.

As it turned out they had seen each other for the last time.

Out of this rich tapestry of wealth, tragedy and experience, of intellect and pragmatism, sensitivity and deprivation, industry and fecklessness encompassing a world joined by lengthy sea voyages and shaped by catastrophic events came the Peter Russell who reached England in 1926.

CHAPTER TWO
Cheltenham and Oxford (1927–1939)

Among the lesser sadnesses in Peter Russell's life was the demise of the ocean liner as the chief means of long-distance travel. Aside from the evolved culture attaching to it, particularly in the first class to which he became accustomed, this sentiment was due in part to what in later years he looked back on as the happiest interlude in his life: the voyage he took with his mother and brother from Wellington to London in the cargo liner *Port Melbourne* in 1926. Not only did he have a twelve-year-old's unfettered excitement at all that lay ahead in England but the journey itself found his mother at her most contented. The ship sailed from Wellington on 20 February, his grandfather and aunt Ethel having accompanied the family from Lyttelton to see them off. As recorded in the diary the young Peter kept of the voyage, *Port Melbourne*'s course took her across the Pacific, through the Panama Canal and the Caribbean and at length to London which she reached after a voyage of forty-one days. Apart from the usual shipboard activities indulged in by the boys from deck games to dancing, they were also able to experience the functioning of the vessel at first hand, including coaling and painting. The highlight of the voyage was the friendship the family struck up with the ship's 2nd Engineer, an officer by the name of Anscombe. Russell later speculated that Anscombe and his mother had had a shipboard romance, and his diary mentions those days during which he joined them ashore after *Port Melbourne* docked in London. Whatever the case, relations were sufficiently close for Russell to sleep in his cabin, though not for many years did he understand why Anscombe had insisted on keeping the door propped open at all times. Of all the many lengthy sea voyages Russell took in a life punctuated by oceanic travel under different circumstances none ever matched this idyll, and the intimate knowledge of ships and shipping and the fascination with the sea and maritime geography that underlies so much of his work and psyche no doubt owes much to this journey.

The arrival in England on 2 April was otherwise somewhat inauspicious. Peter and Hugh found London grimy and oppressive, the country at large lurching towards the General Strike which was declared on 3 May. Rita settled in Cheltenham where it was intended to place Hugh in the Cheltenham College

Cheltenham and Oxford (1927–1939)

Junior School as a day pupil, while Peter was due to enter as a boarder for Sedbergh School in Westmoreland after a spell at Dane Court School at Parkstone in Dorsetshire and a summer of study with a tutor. The selection of Sedbergh, a particularly austere exercise in muscular Christianity operating under the premonitory motto of 'A Stern Nurse of Men', seems to have been made at the recommendation of Teddy Evans abetted by the famous London agency of Gabbitas and Thring but the choice was disastrous. There followed one of the defining episodes in Peter Russell's life, recorded here by his brother Hugh:

> Peter and his tutor seemed to get on very well. I cannot recall how long he stayed with the tutor, but don't think it was very long, and it was the autumn term when he was taken up to Sedbergh by train to Kendal and then on by taxi and I think he must have felt very lonely and abandoned. The College had an excellent record, and the boys were probably mainly from the north of England. He never complained, however, but his stay at Sedbergh was to be very limited. Early in his first term he developed a sort of paralysis of both legs; the doctor at Sedbergh was worried lest this should indicate a worsening of his cardiac condition and sent him back home by ambulance. He had had a heart murmur since birth and had not been allowed to take strenuous exercise. He was assessed on arrival and it was decided that he needed to be told to walk again. There seemed to be no change in his alleged cardiac condition. So a nurse came daily who was accustomed to teaching people to walk and this he managed fairly quickly. In retrospect this seems to have been a reaction in a highly strung boy to the situation in which he found himself and we were thankful indeed that he was all right. [1]

Nowhere in Russell's papers (or in his mother's) is any mention made of this episode of catatonia, nor is he known to have discussed it. The condition is associated not with any physical ailment but with depression and post-traumatic stress disorder of which the introspection, desire for solitude and extreme sensitiveness he recorded of his childhood and exhibited throughout his life would provide early evidence. In the event, it was another year before Russell had recovered sufficiently to enter the Cheltenham College Senior School as a boarder in September 1927 after further tutoring. Tellingly, Rita took the risk of

---

[1] Russell, *One Man's Journey*, 20.

recording Bernard Wheeler as deceased on her son's school application, an effort no doubt to avert searing questions on the divorce and excoriating judgement on Wheeler's dismal army career, one all too easily followed in the pages of the *Army List*.[2] The expedient can only have been partially successful. Two years later she completed the process by changing the family name from Wheeler to Russell by deed poll, an experience her son later described as being 'nullified'.[3]

As it was, Russell's past preceded him at Cheltenham and he was never able to live down the impression quickly formed by the school authorities of a temperamental hypochondriac with an overbearing mother. The confidential notes entered in his academic record reveal not only the prejudices of Russell's masters but also their difficulty grasping the sophisticated mind and highly sensitive personality that had come into their hands:[4] 'Passed for Sedbergh, but too delicate for it. Now quite fit, but no football [i.e. rugby]' begins the ledger in Autumn 1927; 'Bad health largely imaginary' (Summer 1928); 'Knowing that he has a "temperament", he must strive to control it, and then he will do well under F. H. P[hilpot, his housemaster]' (Autumn 1928); 'Some progress clearly, and signs that he is ceasing to fuss'; 'Would do better if his Mother went away. Temperamental' (Spring 1929); 'Now grows pleasant and gets on with others'; 'Most satisfactory as the fads and complications drop away' (Summer 1929); it should be added that Russell won the form prize in both of these years, and the next. The following term, Autumn 1929, coincided with his change of name from Wheeler to Russell; Cheltenham couldn't resist a dig on a subject on which Russell no doubt faced close scrutiny from every quarter: 'Very good in his work and a much improving fellow, his new name we will learn to adopt with his new character.' For Spring 1930, during which Russell had an appendectomy and first announced his intention of going up to Oxford, the verdict was 'Works, but disturbed by home influences and unsettled objective.' Cheltenham plainly expected Russell to complete a full course of study in the school before trying for

---

[2] Cheltenham College Archive, application form of Peter Edward Lionel Russell Wheeler, 18 May 1927. Bernard Wheeler had however revived sufficiently to be mentioned as living in Australia at the time an application for a Kitchener Scholarship was considered for his elder son in January 1931; NA, WO 339-43150.

[3] JMA, PER to Javier Marías, Oxford, 4 Sept. 2000: '[A]bout 1928 [actually 1929] my mother (no expert in the psychology of adolescents) changed her and our names by a legal 'deed poll' to "Russell". On another occasion, if you like, I could tell you all about what happens when a schoolboy's identity label is forcibly changed…'

[4] Cheltenham College Archive, confidential academic record of P. E. L. Russell.

the Laming, its closed scholarship in Modern Languages at The Queen's College on which he had set his sights: 'He goes ahead well and I'm sure will not mind if Queen's College do not decorate him this year'; a rationale for this prediction seems to have been that Russell was 'Able and works but no style yet. History insincere' (Autumn 1930); when Russell was duly awarded his scholarship the following term this grudging entry was made in his record: 'I'm very sorry that he is to leave earlier than is good for him. He has got a great deal out of College and should do well at the University, where his Laming Scholarship does him much credit'; among the last comments, redolent of the whole, were 'Thinks he is now infallible. Disposition still warped by Mother' (Spring 1931). So it was that Peter Russell left Cheltenham with a scholarship after just three years and two terms; his departure can hardly have come soon enough.

Peter and Hugh Wheeler at Cheltenham College. It was during their time here that the family surname was changed to Russell by deed poll in 1929, the approximate date of these photos.

So much for Cheltenham's experience of Russell; what of Russell's experience of Cheltenham? This passage he committed to his diary three years after his departure in September 1934:

Read a book called *Pyramid*; not so bad as a school-book goes. Set me thinking of my own school days; I did not enjoy them owing to rather great[er] sensibility and knowledge than most of my contemporaries, and to a foul inferiority complex which has now gone. I remember even now how I hated the repression and standardisation of it all, the aching for solitude and escape from the discipline. However there were good things too. I still remember joy of success at work, and the lucky air about me in those days which let me have much more of my own way than otherwise. I am still uncertain about my physical inability and my dislike to play team games. I play golf and swim badly but with great enjoyment but team games bore me beyond belief. Why? Then there were various romantic but innocent friendships. Now such things are over I look at them with a slight touch of sadness [...]. What else? Solitary cross-country runs in the dusk over black earthy fields and green parklands, walks in the rain, coming first in form-rooms and feeling the intellectual pall over one's fellows, Sp[ecial] house with Mango Meeyne whose careless freedom gave scope to one's individuality, the first time I took charge of sweatroom [i.e. preproom], Sunday evening in Chapel in winter with candles casting long shadows, moving full-throated hymns and the Chaplain's 'God bless you etc.', smiling at Mike or Seddon in Chapel, debating, peaceful evenings reading Stevenson and Kipling in Library, field-days cutting wood in the woods and snow with Scouts, eating sausages in Tucker with Brown or someone, taking skiff on river and rowing upstream, glory of that day when I won the Scholarship — so it wasn't so bad after all! Though there were also many things which I still remember with disgust and dislike, though some of them were due to my superior 'rebellious' attitude. [5]

Evidently Russell had come early to a realisation of his unusual intellect and emotional intelligence, one that extended well beyond his peer group. This was due not only to extreme acuity of mind but a decidedly logical and pragmatic approach to life in every arena except his own psyche. Deriving from this was an unerring ability to draw the attention of others to absurdity or manifest stupidity (often their own), first as a means of subsistence and eventually as a crushing

---

[5] Diary, 20 Sept. 1934. Lionel Birch, *Pyramid* (London: Philip Allan, 1931). Russell apparently lodged in a private boarding house in his final term at Cheltenham.

weapon in its own right. With it came powers of leadership. 'He certainly has personality and can always be relied upon to respond to any responsibility entrusted to him' Philpot said of him in his report for Summer 1930 as Russell approached his seventeenth birthday, and he was duly appointed a house prefect. [6] Naturally, the extreme sensitivity remained as it would always remain. Complimenting him on 'A most satisfactory term' that Spring, Philpot had the insight to add that 'it is a pity, however, that he allows himself to worry at times both about himself and his future'. [7] That future was stated both on entering and leaving Cheltenham to be the Consular Service, to which the Civil Service was added in 1931. It was not to be.

The Cheltenham interlude was not therefore one on which Russell could look back with much pleasure. His brother Hugh's experience of the Junior School no doubt compared with his own in the Senior:

> I had not enjoyed my time at school. There was a lot of what today would be called bullying and I had never confronted this before. I assumed that all English people experienced it. It involved much verbal unpleasantness and sometimes physical bullying as well. I, of course, was in a different situation from that of most English pupils. I was a stranger who could not easily be classified by class or social group. I had no father around and my accent was somewhat different from that of the others. I never, therefore, became a member of the school community as I would have liked. This, particularly, was a group very conscious of itself. [8]

Nonetheless, as in his relations with his father ten years earlier, Peter Russell's severance from Cheltenham was far from total, while the psychological effects of both those eruptions in his life were never erased. Meanwhile, his undergraduate diaries record one Old Cheltonian dinner ('rather pathetic') and several enjoyable visits to the school to watch sporting fixtures and see old friends including Philpot, acknowledging 'plenty of bonds of sympathy still'. [9] Three years after leaving he noted that 'I can't arouse much sympathy for the "Old School" as an institution. I hate it in fact but it has a deplorable sentimental interest

---

[6] P. E. L. R. Russell, Cheltenham College, report for Summer 1930.
[7] *Ibid.*, report for Spring 1930.
[8] Russell, *One Man's Journey*, 32.
[9] Diary, 11 Nov. & 10–11 Dec. 1932 respectively.

presumably because of the few good friends I had there.' [10] Lacking the benefit of experience, one suspects that Russell found himself drawn back to grasp and reconfigure what had afflicted him as well as to receive plaudits for his success. There the subject rested until a notice in the *London Gazette* concerning one of his Cheltenham peers in the summer of 1939 restored it to the forefront of his mind:

> It was a period in which fears of various kinds played a large part; fear of compulsory games, not as an idea but because, starting late at them, I feared I would be bad at them and my pride could not tolerate that. So I spent a lot of time trying to avoid them and at the same time desperately wanting to be good at them. The mental enjoyment and physical pleasure of many cross-country runs remain; the agony of will to keep going over ploughed fields, streaming sweat and warm baths afterwards with their glorious lassitude. I also remember enjoying rowing in fours and skiffs on the Severn at Tewkesbury; the trips in the lorries there and back, the showers in the boat-house with room full of naked boys; the doughnuts and cream pastries on sale there afterwards. I even learnt to box but had little success. I do not think this was funk as much as fear of not being good. One thing that can be said about a public school is that it impresses itself indelibly on the mind; perhaps this is its most serious fault. The tension of experience is such that many never experience anything so strong again and in consequence their lives constantly flow backwards to it, as it were, and one gets the professional OLD BOY. Memories are innumerable — [Headmaster H. H.] Hardy's address to the new boys in the Library, his fixed stare at the boys as they left Chapel, my horror when faced with a piece of equipment to blanco and buttons to polish, the smell of 'boy' always about one, a smell slightly stale deriving from dirty underwear, sweat and soap, days of fear when I expected to be beaten by the College Prefects for walking over the field when the Flag was up [...] Chapel, bellowing the hymns; period of religious fervour associated with Confirmation. This led for a term or two to getting up early on Sundays and going to Communion as long as the novelty of the ceremony lasted; it was followed by a period of atheism based on feelings as vague as those which had produced the

[10] Diary, 16 Sept. 1934.

Cheltenham and Oxford (1927–1939)

religious fervour! Days in Scout Troop. In some ways this was most agreeable thing of weeks [*sic*]. Wearing corduroy shorts, khaki shirt and scarf that gave one a feeling of freedom which could be savoured to the full on expeditions in the Cotswolds for mapping the country, or building fires, learning signalling and following tracks across the park and woods. I think all that helped to teach one an appreciation of Nature and the interest and spiritual delights of the countryside which I have always been most thankful for. How many moments of solitary ecstasy in the Cotswold valleys, or fir-covered hills of the Black Forest or in the Tyrolese Alps can be traced to that Scout Hut at Cheltenham where one learnt to look at Nature and savour its pleasures for the first time! Smells and scents of soil, grass and trees. Then there was work. I won prizes constantly and without trouble and was usually top of every form I entered. Looking back on it I cannot see any special mental aptitude or sensitivity I then had to account for this. I certainly worked hard both to please Grandpa and because my pride could not tolerate my not being top of my various forms. I suppose there was aptitude but it must have been entirely un-self-conscious. [...] It is interesting to recall all this but [it] probably only represents an attempt to see that posterity get its due from one!' [11]

The Laming Scholarship notwithstanding, not for some time did his impressions of Cheltenham crystallise into an enduring bitterness, a conviction enhanced no doubt by the distaste for the place shared by an earlier inmate, his friend Maurice Bowra. [12] The war had an anaesthetising effect, Russell writing on his return that 'I find that my schooldays are now so far away that I can enjoy the smug placidity of Georgian Cheltenham without remembering the resentments of adolescence', but a final rupture awaited. [13] In a letter to his solicitor and Cheltenham contemporary in 1961 Russell made reference to the fact that 'When I was a fellow of Queen's College here in the late 1940s I had a lot of tiresome difficulties on an official matter with the then Headmaster and I fear I have, since then, entirely lost touch with Cheltenham, which is, perhaps, a pity.' [14] The matter

---

[11] Journal, 15 July 1939.
[12] Leslie Mitchell, *Maurice Bowra: A Life* (Oxford: Oxford University Press, 2009), 16–21.
[13] Journal, 22 Feb. 1946.
[14] PER to A. R. A. Seacome, Oxford, 17 Aug. 1961. The headmaster in question was Alan Guy Elliott-Smith. Russell had in fact been in private correspondence with a former master, C. T.

in question related to an attempt by Cheltenham to have changes made to the terms of the Laming Scholarship of which he had himself been a recipient in 1931. Decades later Russell delivered his final verdict:

> In those days it was a school which specialized in training boys for the Indian Army or the British Army and for the Indian and Colonial Civil Services and the emphasis was all on producing conformist types preconditioned for such careers. Though I did quite well scholastically at Cheltenham I was never at home with the demand to conform to a new set of class-bound English social values whose rationale I never succeeded in understanding. [15]

These formative perceptions and the geographical and cultural displacements that marked his youth bring us to some of the defining characteristics of Russell the scholar, at once fascinated by the interplay of societies, determined to stand alone and ever ready to take up the cudgels against received ideas and conventional wisdom with devastating critiques made from the inside.

*

Much as he resented Cheltenham it was here that Russell first came into contact with Spanish and took the first steps on what became his professional career:

> I am often asked how I came to be interested in Spanish. The answer is wholly prosaic. I did not wish to repeat another year working at French and German for the Higher School certificate, which I had already obtained. Taking up Spanish, rather surprisingly then an optional subject at Cheltenham College, offered a way out and also gave me the satisfaction of doing something rather out of the ordinary. [16]

Aside from his juvenile reading at Knowlescourt and elsewhere and the contents of school libraries with their tales of Elizabethan derring-do and Tennyson's *Ballad of the Revenge*, Russell recalled his first exposure to Spain as coming

---

Priestley, in 1958.
[15] PELR, 1. Not, of course, that Russell was proof against some of these same values. 'We were all' he recalled in 1935 'anxious to convince each other of the vast wealth of our parents'; ALRTP, 20.
[16] PELR, 1.

through French literature in the work of Merimée and Gautier's *Voyage en Espagne* (1845). [17] In the months after leaving Cheltenham in the spring of 1931 Russell took the opportunity to visit the Peninsula for the first time, his recommended reading from Oxford being José María de Pereda's novel *Sotileza*, set among the fisherfolk of Santander and partially written in their argot. His arrival by slow train in Madrid on 15 April was inauspicious, it being the day after Spain was declared a Republic and King Alfonso XIII went into exile. A few weeks later on 11 May he witnessed the burning by Anarchists of the Jesuit residence on the calle Flor together with its priceless library, archive and artworks. Stopping to question one of the perpetrators as to his motive, Russell was informed 'Porque los jesuitas son dueños de los tranvías madrileños' ('Because the Jesuits own the trams of Madrid'). It was the beginning of a lifetime's observation of the passions and quirks of Hispanic society. Still only seventeen, Russell lodged with a widow at calle Serrano 36 who took in foreign students. After a month he made his way to Granada and completed a memorable first visit to the Peninsula by signing on as the cabin boy of a MacAndrews Line steamer at Barcelona. By the time it reached the Port of London three weeks and a dozen Iberian ports later in August he was fluent in Spanish.

The first forty years of the twentieth century have been described as 'the golden age for Oxford undergraduates' and in Britain at least have left a more lasting cultural impression on the present time than any university in any epoch. [18] During this period the University comprised approximately 5,000 mostly male students of whom three quarters were products of the public school system, the balance coming from the grammar schools. At Oxford, where the pursuit of science had been badly neglected in the late nineteenth century, a majority of undergraduates and staff studied the humanities, of which Classics enjoyed the greatest prestige followed by History and English. Of the colleges, few of which had more than 200 members, those with the highest academic reputation were Balliol, Merton, New College, Queen's, Corpus Christi and Somerville, with Christ Church and Magdalen occupying the top of the social pecking order. Researchers as they came to be understood after the Second World War were still comparatively few, nor was research the passport to academic appointment it later became:

---

[17] 'Recollections of the Second Spanish Republic', recorded on 26 May 1998, Taylor Institution Library, TAPES.137 [hereinafter RSSR].
[18] Noel Annan, *The Dons: Mentors, Eccentrics and Geniuses* (London: Harper Collins, 1999), 136.

Fellowships were sometimes awarded immediately on the result of performance in finals but were often obtained by hanging around for a year or two hoping to impress in meetings of academic societies and by picking up some teaching. No one boasted of 'breakthroughs' in research. [...] A don would be known to be engaged in a particular line of enquiry but his scholarship was a by-product of his main duty — which was to teach. The tutors, not the professors, were the gatekeepers to the academic pastures. [19]

What do Russell's copious diaries and memoirs reveal of the young man who came up to read French and Spanish at Queen's in October 1931? What did he find there? Established in 1341 but housed in one of the greatest Baroque ensembles in England, Queen's was among the larger Oxford colleges with a student body of around 200 and 22 fellows. The college Russell joined as a Laming Scholar was just emerging from the fifty-two-year tenure of Provost J. R. Magrath, the last ten of which he had spent immured in his lodgings as a virtual recluse. Russell's friend in later years Oliver (later Baron) Franks had come up to Queen's as a Classical scholar from Bristol Grammar School in 1923 and by the time of his arrival was a philosophy fellow at the college. Although the impression from Russell's diaries is that the stratification had eased somewhat by the time of his arrival eight years later, this description in one of Franks's letters home gives an idea of the status he will have enjoyed as a scholar:

> In Hall we have definite tables but not definite places. Our table consists of all of the freshers who are scholars or exhibitionists — about 15 or 20 in all. The senior scholar [...] has to sit at the end of the table and if he is not there I as second scholar have to take his place. Apparently any Classical scholar takes precedence over any other scholar or exhibitioner. [20]

Russell first appears in College records via the interview notes taken by Provost E. M. Walker at the time of his matriculation in October 1931: 'Has been four months in Spain. Rows. Not musical.' [21] His earliest surviving adult diaries

---

[19] *Ibid.*

[20] Alex Danchev, *Oliver Franks: Founding Father* (Oxford: Oxford University Press, 1993), 16.

[21] I am grateful to Amy Ebrey of Queen's College for sharing Provost Walker's notes; email to

date to January 1932 and there can be no doubt that Russell took to Oxford immediately, recalling his undergraduate years as 'totally happy ones' and college life 'like Liberty Hall' after the privations of an English boarding school. [22] Living in college throughout except for a year in digs in 1934–5, his undergraduate years began in a conventional mix of alcohol, amusement, sports and clubs, punctuated by a few close friendships and unconsummated infatuations. Russell's bibulous phase, if it can be called that, was largely over by his second term ('Giving up beer and entertainment for lack of money in favour of work'), although he was 'progged' (fined by the University Proctors) for the minor offence of being caught drinking in The Pheasant on St Giles during the interval of a review at the Oxford Playhouse, city pubs being off-limits for students ('Blast it! 10/- gone'). [23] 'Thank God I gave up being a hearty' wrote Russell in his diary for 11 November 1932, but those who knew the august professor in later decades will also have to fit another incident of high spirits into their picture of Russell the undergraduate, albeit as part of a group effort: 'Visited the Proctor this morning with James, Monty and others and came off with a quid a head for damage to Lincoln etc. on the night of Wednesday last!' [24] Then there was sport, including a not altogether successful spell rowing for Queen's, along with sailing, golf and tennis, none of which survived Russell's first year. Less formally he enjoyed 'messing about in boats' on the Isis and the Cherwell and was a keen sunbather, with the inevitable reddening and peeling of his pale complexion that ensued. As most of Russell's photos from the 1930s have been lost the best visual recreation of this dimension of his world may lie in the drawings of the Spanish artist Gregorio Prieto whose album of prints was published in Oxford by Joan Gili in 1938. [25]

Although pressure of work caused Russell to cut down on his social activities as time passed, he often gave tea in his rooms and began the tradition for which he became famous and through which his generosity, depth and power of engagement were fully displayed: taking friends to dinner, usually singly. A favourite spot was that fixture of the Oxford scene, the now vanished George Café on the corner of Cornmarket and George Streets. Russell was an observational

the author, 16 Jan. 2023.
[22] PELR, 2.
[23] Diary, 12 May & 11 Oct. 1932 respectively. Ten shillings in 1932 equates to approximately £30 in 2024.
[24] Diary, 3 March 1934.
[25] *Students: Oxford-Cambridge, 20 Drawings* (London: Dolphin Bookshop Editions, 1938).

writer and the stream of consciousness he set down in his commonplace book in around 1933 allows the atmosphere of the place to be re-created:

> Sizzling of grille[d] steaks. Luscious warmth of hot meat. Babble of confused conversation and voices in distance. Coughs. Smell of Worcester Sauce and beer. White tablecloths and misty mirrors showing the same people dining away into a distorted distance. Rattling of plates and dishes. Rare [?] tinkle of cash register. Tall thin waiter with large hooked nose moving rapidly about flicking table napkins. Various men sitting at tables. Outstanding cufflinks. Proud red hands on white table. Empty glasses and smoking cigarette. Grey check coat, red pull-over, neat hair. General atmosphere white and light and dark yellow. Little brown pages in brown buttons. Various floating succulent odours. Small box in corner, glass panels with pay-clerk, sour-faced with flaxen hair. [26]

Standing 6' 1", Russell was a dapper dresser to go with his devastating good looks and a diary entry for 7 November 1933 has this record of his daily attire: 'Today am wearing black pull-over, black and white check coat, grey flannels, black-grey fixed-collar shirt, green tie, grey socks and black shoes.' Nor are descriptions of the décor of his rooms in college omitted, with prints and woodcuts decorating the walls in a room otherwise dominated by books and the prized radio set on which he could pick up Lisbon and Barcelona, a birthday gift from his mother: 'Have finished my room quite nicely I think — pale green and marigold. An Utrillo, two Cézannes, a Gauguin and two Austrian Tyrolese woodcuts.' [27] In fact, modern art was one of his passions, the impetus of the *plein air* hobby he took up with some skill in the 1950s. A visit to Paris in the autumn of 1933 had provided the necessary inspiration:

> This morning I went to the Jeu de Paume Museum of modern foreign art and was really inspired to see what rigour and promise there is abroad in the art world — more so than in contemporary French art I think. Spain and Belgium seem to be doing the best work. England has of course begun now to arrive at the Cézanne stage with Sickert!

[26] Commonplace book, 25.
[27] Diary, 14 Oct. 1934.

Nothing in painting will ever equal the epoch of Cézanne, Manet, Monet, Sisley, Gauguin, Van Gogh and Picasso. I can spend hours gazing at their stuff. [28]

His diaries also show him to have been a keen filmgoer, farces starring Ralph Lynn and Mary Brough being particular favourites. Hollywood productions on the whole left him impressed only as to their vacuousness and helped persuade Russell, ever the analytical purist, that the coming of the 'talkie' presaged the end of the medium. A keen student of theatre, here are the conclusions he set down after an otherwise enjoyable screening of Georg Wilhelm Pabst's German classic *L'Atlantide* in 1933:

> It is obvious that these talkie films filled with talk are bastards because a film is most of all an art which touches always the fringe of reality. Too much talk and most of the modern subjects render it into a sort of bastard theatre, forgetting that in each case the mediums and aims <u>must</u> be different, hence decay of the cinema. [29]

Of much greater consequence were clubs, including the French Club but particularly the Oxford University Spanish Club of which he was Secretary in 1932 and President in 1933. The club had had an ephemeral existence before being refounded by Fernando de Arteaga and George Kolkhorst (on both of whom see below) in November 1927, telegrams being sent inviting King Alfonso XIII and the dictator Primo de Rivera to be its honorary president and vice-president respectively. [30] Neither was *en poste* by the time Russell was making his contributions to the OUSC programme, which included a play reading in June 1932, a talk on popular Spanish music (with records) in May 1933, and especially the club's annual banquet attended by the Argentine ambassador Manuel Malbrán at the Randolph Hotel on 3 March that year at which he delivered a ten-minute speech in Spanish. A splendid photo survives of the occasion together with the President's writeup in the *Oxford Times*, Russell characteristically giving full credit to a fellow OUSC committee member for his organisational efforts.

---

[28] Diary, 9 Sept. 1933.
[29] Diary, 27 May 1933.
[30] *El Imán: Revista del Oxford University Spanish Club*, ed. E. L. G. Powys, P. G. Smith & L. de Oriols (Oxford: Holywell, 1928), 4–12, at 5.

Spanish at Oxford: The annual banquet of the Spanish Club held at the Randolph Hotel on 3 March 1933. Russell is standing fourth from the right as President; two places to his right is Professor Entwistle. The most distant seated figure in the far corner of the room is Dámaso Alonso (wearing spectacles). Just discernible as the most distant seated figure on the near side of the room is George Kolkhorst, silhouetted against the double doors and craning for the camera. Sitting next to each other halfway along the near side of the far wing of the table are two of Russell's undergraduate contemporaries, Ronald Hilton (back largely to the camera) and Janie van den Bosch (in the light-coloured dress).

Among the distinguished speakers during Russell's presidency of the OUSC was Américo Castro, 'A fine but rather theatrically Spanish sort of man and much too condescending. Still his book on Cervantes is a work of genius.' [31] The latter opinion he would revise. In later years Russell recalled the Argentine embassy being unstinting in its supply of both funds and speakers to the OUSC, in stark contrast to what he remembered as a complete lack of interest in promoting Hispanic life and culture shown by its Spanish counterpart, this period coinciding with the tenure as ambassador of one of Russell's favourite writers, Ramón Pérez de Ayala (1931–6). [32] In this, however, Russell's memory fails him since Pérez de Ayala was the club's guest of honour on 24 February 1932 at which he gave a speech. [33] Closer to home, the essayist Joseph Addison had been up at Queen's in the 1680s and an intellectual society established there in his memory. Russell was elected to the Addison first as a member in February 1934 and then as its president for 1934–5, accepting the former as 'a compliment in its way but [it] puts me under an obligation to other people which I hate. Nevertheless it will perhaps help me in my climb to the heights of Abraham and Byron!' [34] Out of this came what he reported to have been a well-received paper on Ibsen in October 1934, an early mark of his scholarly range.

This narrative therefore brings us to Russell's main concern at Oxford, his academic studies. These initially encompassed Spanish and French, to which Portuguese was added when that language first became available in the University in January 1934. As Russell recalled nearly fifty years later, the establishment of Portuguese at Oxford was the work of the then King Alfonso XIII Professor of Spanish Studies, William Entwistle, with generous government funding from Lisbon and teaching imparted by a young Portuguese lecturer, António Gonçalves Rodrigues. [35] Where the teaching of Spanish at Oxford was concerned, the earliest surviving reference dates to the late sixteenth century, but not until 1858 was the

---

[31] Diary, 28 Feb. 1933. An anonymous summary of Castro's lecture at the Taylorian and informal talk at Rhodes House are given in 'Professor Castro in Oxford', *The Oxford Magazine*, 9 March 1933, 528–9. *El pensamiento de Cervantes* (Madrid: Editorial Hernando, 1925).
[32] RSSR.
[33] See the handwritten speech given in response by Kolkhorst enclosed with the Taylor Institution's copy of the 1928 number of *El Imán*; ALMA: 990209434290107026. Russell's diary makes no mention of the occasion.
[34] Diary, 5 Feb. 1934. The allusion is to the heroic but fatal assaults made by General Wolfe at Québec in 1759 and Byron at Missolonghi in 1824.
[35] *Prince Henry the Navigator: The Rise and Fall of a Culture Hero*, Taylorian Special Lecture, *10 November 1983* (Oxford: Clarendon Press, 1984), 3–4.

subject imparted on a consistent basis under the lapsed Catholic Lorenzo Lucena, an Andalusian. [36] Even then Spanish did not get onto a solid footing until the creation of the Faculty of Medieval and Modern Languages in 1903, the Oxford establishment requiring some persuasion that these were subjects deserving of serious study alongside Classics. The Honour School of Modern Languages graduated its first (male) students in 1905 (women had to wait until 1920), and nine years later the Faculty of Medieval and Modern Languages became institutionally separate having previously come under the Faculty of Arts. English and Modern Languages only parted company in 1926, and from 1927 it was possible to read for two languages instead of just one. [37] If that limitation had earlier prompted many of the brightest candidates to opt for Cambridge instead, other problems proved harder to overcome. Whereas Cambridge boasted twenty college scholarships in modern languages, Oxford in 1926 could offer only six or seven, reflecting what remained an overwhelmingly University-driven pursuit. Much of the intake in modern languages was of a low standard by comparison with that expected of Classical candidates ('disgracefully low' in the case of those reading for the two-year Pass degree), resulting in scholarship places going unfilled. This was compounded by the curriculum of the Honour School of Modern Languages which imposed a disproportionate emphasis on Philology on students many of whom were comparatively or completely new to their languages. It was a criticism made of the School by the Balliol history don and Curator of the Taylorian F. F. 'Sligger' Urquhart in 1926 and fully acknowledged by Cesare Foligno, Serena Professor of Italian, in 1930, describing it as '[a] dry subject for those students who are not particularly gifted in that way, and one that can only be usefully pursued distinct from literature; for it tends otherwise to degenerate into a painstaking memorising of obsolete forms and the parrot-like recording of etymologies of old and dialectical texts and to bring about a disproportionate prevalence of phonology and morphology'. [38] Other charges proffered against the Modern Languages School were of it being too literary and linguistic, the School itself acquiring a corresponding sensitivity to the preparation given its students in

---

[36] Ian Michael, 'Afterword: Spanish at Oxford, 1595–1998', *Bulletin of Hispanic Studies* (Glasgow) 76 (1999), 173–93. More generally, see Sir Charles Firth, *Modern Languages at Oxford, 1724–1929* (London: Oxford University Press, 1929).

[37] Anon., 'Modern Language Scholarships at Oxford', *The Oxford Magazine*, 4 Feb. 1926, 249–50, with reply by G. F. Fisher, *ibid*, 11 Feb. 1926, 290.

[38] Cesare Foligno, 'The School of Modern Languages', *The Oxford Magazine*, 15 May 1930, 705–8, at 706.

history, with a focus, influential in Russell's case, on 'thought'. A rather dismal picture is completed by a shortage of teachers and Faculty representation at University level fragmented by the claims of each language, together with a degree of misogyny visited on what was and remained the most co-educational branch of study in the University.[39] This state of affairs not only fed the reigning prejudice against Modern Languages, one that fell heavier on Spanish than French, Italian and German, but often restricted graduates to employment as teachers rather than the careers in commerce and diplomacy originally envisaged for them. The upshot was that the pre-war Faculty had something of the air of a teacher-training establishment, and it would be another twenty years before modern languages at Oxford took on the mantle of a 'humanistic school' as traditionally understood. Directly or otherwise, Russell was destined to share almost every aspect of this reality successively as scholar, graduate, teacher, lecturer and Fellow in the Faculty of Medieval and Modern Languages at Oxford from 1931.

'My climb to the heights of Abraham and Byron.' Russell front and centre as President of the Addison Society for 1934–5.

The first titular professor of Spanish at Oxford was the Catalan Fernando de Arteaga y Pereira who was appointed in 1919 having been taken on as a Spanish

---

[39] A somewhat rosier impression is, however, presented in William J. Entwistle, 'Modern Language Studies in Oxford', *The Oxford Magazine*, 16 Feb. 1933, 427–9.

teacher in 1894 and in whose name a prize fund was established in 1929 for the best work in Spanish in the Final Honour School. In the meantime the University had taken receipt of two significant benefactions. The first of these was the £10,000 given by Henry Laming to Queen's in 1916 for the establishment of an annual scholarship in either Spanish or Russian, additional funds becoming available on his death for Travelling Fellowships. This was followed in 1920 by the creation by Guillermo de Osma of the Studentship that bears his name and of which, like the Laming Scholarship, Russell was a recipient in 1934. To these were added the King Alfonso XIII Professorship of Spanish Literature funded by private benefactions from William Morris (later Lord Nuffield) and the Anglo-Chilean press magnate Agustín Edwards but established under the auspices of the Lord Mayor of London in 1927, the University having awarded Alfonso the degree of Doctor of Civil Law the previous year. [40] The King's contribution was confined to a signed photo, since lost. The first holder, appointed in 1928, was the celebrated writer, Liberal politician and statesman Salvador de Madariaga who soon found he had little vocation for the position or feeling for the University and was in Oxford only sporadically before being sent by the new Republic as its ambassador to the United States in 1931. [41] His impression that the electors were alive to what he later confessed to be his 'inherent shortcoming' for the appointment may not have been far off the mark. Nonetheless, these developments together with the splendid library and expanding research facilities offered by the Taylor Institution which had opened its doors 'for the teaching and improving of the European languages' in 1845 completed the institutional context of Hispanic studies as Russell encountered them in 1931, even if Spanish remained a minority activity at Oxford, with only eight students graduating in that language that year and thirteen in 1939, all of them in conjunction with French.

Turning now to the syllabus in Spanish, Appendix II contains the lecture and class list for the first year Russell was up at Oxford, 1931–2, which encompassed Entwistle's arrival as professor. Spanish followed the tripartite division of literature along historical or dynastic periodisations characteristic of most of the Faculty, the Middle Ages in its case yielding to the Golden Age in 1516 and to Modern Literature in 1700. [42] The latter course of study was notable for the

---

[40] See OUA/UR 6/SPC/1B, file 2 for a summary account of the foundation of the chair.
[41] Salvador de Madariaga, *Morning Without Noon: Memoirs* (Farnborough, Hants.: Saxon House, 1974), 124–6.
[42] For the syllabus, see *University of Oxford Examination Statutes* (Oxford: Clarendon Press), published annually.

inclusion of properly 'modern' (i.e. post-1900) authors both on the syllabus and in one of its standard texts, Fitzmaurice-Kelly's *Oxford Book of Spanish Verse*.[43] The expansion was almost certainly due to the newly appointed lecturer Dámaso Alonso (see below), but in later years Russell would recall how the rest of the Faculty took it as evidence of a lack of seriousness in Spanish studies (the French syllabus, for instance, closed in 1870), although German and Russian soon followed suit.[44] This was also the era of the Pass School, which in the case of Spanish was introduced in 1923 and phased out in 1947, its students being confined mainly to language classes and nineteenth-century and contemporary Spanish literature, whereas their counterparts in the Honour School were exposed to Romance philology, historical linguistics and Medieval and Golden Age literature; Spanish colonial and Spanish-American literature (1500–1919) and Catalan were added together with Portuguese early in Entwistle's tenure. Not the least innovation was the appointment of one María Victoria de Lara to lecture in Golden Age prose in place of the absent Madariaga in Hilary 1932, perhaps the first woman instructor in Spanish at a British university.

Russell's surviving undergraduate output is represented by two essays concerning Calderón probably written for Kolkhorst in 1934. The first, 'Taste versus thought in Calderón', begins with Hegel and shows the influence of Russell's exposure to aesthetic theory via Clive Bell's *Art* whose notion of 'significant form' he noted in his diary as having made 'a great difference to my outlook on all sorts of things'.[45] The second essay, 'Consider the four chief genres of Calderón and their relation to the work of Lope in the same field', opens with reference to the Post-Impressionists and proceeds by way of Terence, Aquinas, Racine, Shakespeare, Molière and Murillo. While not lacking in inspiration, neither offers any great penetration of Calderón's *oeuvre* or much insight into Russell's genesis as a literary scholar, the first inkling of which comes in the article on Pirandello he produced in 1934, his earliest known published academic work.[46] If this reduced sample provides evidence of a certain lack of depth in pre-war standards in Spanish at Oxford, one supported by some of the examination papers set, that impression is reinforced by Russell's memory of exercises in prose composition under Dámaso Alonso as recalled for this biography by a group of his students and colleagues, in this case Eric Southworth:

[43] Oxford: Clarendon Press, 1913, and subsequent editions.
[44] RSSR.
[45] Clive Bell, *Art* (London: Chatto & Windus, 1914); Diary, 6 Jan. 1934.
[46] 'Pirandello' in *Miscellany* (Oxford: The Queen's College, 1934), 10–14.

> [Y]ou'll remember Peter's accounts of how Prose was 'taught' pre-war: you brought your version along, it was glanced at perfunctorily (if as much), and you were then directed next door, to copy out the tutor's yellowed Ideal Form. Peter said that once one realised that next week's perfection was on the desk underneath this week's, the temptation was to scribble that one down as well, and then present it next time as one's own work. But it made no difference to the format. [47]

Nonetheless, Russell's diaries and subsequent writings and utterances leave no doubt that he was exceptionally fortunate in his teachers. [48] Although giving priority to Spanish, he drew much from the tuition and support of Wilfred House, the first Laming Resident Fellow and first Praelector in French at Queen's. A decorated veteran of the Great War but lacking formal qualifications in French, House was also the administrator of the Laming bequest and therefore responsible for awarding Russell his Scholarship. Writing House's obituary nearly sixty years later, Russell recalled how '[i]t was largely due to his presence that, by the mid-'30's, Queen's had become a major centre for modern languages among the men's colleges.' [49] Beyond anything House taught Russell on French language and literature or awarded him in furtherance of his career were the human qualities he imparted, forged in an environment far removed from Oxford:

> His success as a teacher and organizer of teaching was reflected in consistently good Finals results. He took immense trouble over his pupils and always treated them, even the unsatisfactory ones, as adults, employing towards them a patterned urbanity that some of us would later recognize as more typical of a regular officers' mess than that of a senior common room. House, though he would only speak of his experiences in the First World War to those who had shared them, was plainly much influenced by what they had taught him as a young officer

---

[47] Eric Southworth, 26 June 2020. See also *Oxford University Examination Papers. Second Public Examination. Honour School of Modern Languages* (Oxford: Clarendon Press, 1932–5).

[48] This appreciation is mirrored in the memoirs of one of Russell's contemporaries, Ronald Hilton, who read French and Spanish at Christ Church and Magdalen from 1929–37; *Spain, 1931–36, From Monarchy to Civil War, An Eyewitness Account* (2000), at <historicaltextarchive.org/books.php?action=nextpre&bid=11>.

[49] 'Harry Wilfred House (1895–1987)', *The Queen's College Record* 6 (1987), 4–6. Russell's diary records him having tea with House and Mr and Mrs Laming on 11 Nov. 1933.

about man management. He expected his pupils to call him by his Christian name but this was never allowed to become an excuse for matiness. In his reserved way House was a shrewd judge of character. The files of individuals he left behind him showed that he assessed with remarkable accuracy his pupils' merits and weaknesses and was good at divining what the future probably held for them.

These words would hardly be worth citing at such length did they not so accurately reflect Russell's own teaching style and approach as it emerged from the crucible of another war. They also explain the certain community of sentiment he came to enjoy with other soldier scholars including Maurice Bowra, survivor of Passchendaele and Cambrai, and Charles Boxer, twenty-five years a regular officer in the British Army and ultimately prisoner-of-war of the Japanese in Hong Kong.

Among the most accomplished scholars teaching Spanish at Oxford was the philologist, poet and literary critic Dámaso Alonso, a former pupil of Ramón Menéndez Pidal whose arrival coincided with Russell's own in 1931. Alonso not only lectured on and tutored Russell in Valera, Baroja, Clarín, Pardo Bazán, Azorín and Gabriel Miró (all in Spanish), but gave him his first instruction in literary criticism of which he is remembered as one of the finest Spanish practicants of the twentieth century. In many respects a strange man, a hypochondriac and jealously protective of his wife Eulalia, Alonso was nonetheless an excellent tutor and in later years Russell recalled his practice of taking a bad poem by some prominent poet and explaining exactly what its deficiencies were, 'a very useful exercise in forming some kind of critical sense'. [50] He also gave Russell an introduction to pursue his studies through the racket and fug of tobacco smoke characteristic of the library of the Ateneo de Madrid. Within two years Alonso had left to take up a chair at Valencia having been interviewed in Madrid by a selection board including the philosopher Miguel de Unamuno, a public event Russell was able to attend in person. [51]

---

[50] RSSR.

[51] Diary, 7 April 1933: 'This afternoon went to the Universidad Central with Janie [van den Bosch, a Dutch student of Spanish at Lady Margaret Hall] to attend the public exam of Alonso for his professorship at Valencia. Tiny room with old Unamuno, Salinas and Artigas. Very queer and amusing listening to Alonso's lengthy talk about himself.' The Generation of '27 poet and writer Pedro Salinas was at that time teaching at the Centro de Estudios Históricos in the Institución Libre de Enseñanza in Madrid; Miguel Artigas y Ferrando was then Director

Russell's next important teacher was Madariaga's successor as King Alfonso XIII Professor, William James Entwistle, appointed in 1932. A product of the University of Aberdeen, Entwistle came to Oxford having been Lecturer in Hispanic Studies at the University of Manchester (as part of the Faculty of Commerce), and then inaugural holder of the Stevenson chair of Spanish at Glasgow to which he was elected in 1925 at the age of twenty-nine. Russell would later, and among many other criticisms, privately describe Entwistle as having a tendency to 'assiduously go about missing the point' and more than one student remembered him as a difficult lecturer ('bewilderingly erudite') but, after his death in 1952, and particularly in his 1992 memoir and subsequent utterances, Russell recalled him as 'a brilliant polymath whose work in various fields has been unjustly forgotten' and indeed 'the last of the polymaths I have known in Oxford'. [52] On a personal level the debt was clear enough, since not only did the polyglot Entwistle introduce Russell first to Medieval and Golden Age Spanish literature and then to the history of the Peninsula, but took him as his protégé, endorsing his application to extend his degree by a year, a step Russell believed (rightly) would guarantee him the first on which he was resolved. This patronage extended to Entwistle sitting Russell down one day in the autumn of 1933 and telling him 'all I must do to get a fellowship in Spanish', to supporting him in pursuing a doctorate in history against administrative opposition, and to securing a University lectureship for him twelve years later, among many other favours. [53]

The other key figure in Russell's undergraduate formation was George Kolkhorst who was appointed Taylorian lecturer in Spanish in 1921, University lecturer in 1926 and Reader at Exeter College in 1931. It was Kolkhorst who as Russell recalled had run Spanish at Oxford during Madariaga's frequent absences. Universally known as 'the Colonel' owing to a purported commission in the Portuguese medical corps or more likely his decidedly unmilitary bearing,

---

of the Biblioteca Nacional in Madrid.

[52] Journal, 7 Feb. 1948, PELR, 2, and RSSR. See his 'William James Entwistle (1896–1952)', *The Oxford Magazine*, 16 Oct. 1952, 6–8, and 'Entwistle, William James (1895–1952)', *Oxford Dictionary of National Biography*, <doi.org/10.1093/ref:odnb/33024> (revised version, 25 May 2006). See also Alfred Ewert, 'William James Entwistle', *Proceedings of the British Academy* 38 (1952), 333–43, and R. D. F. Pring-Mill, 'William James Entwistle', *Romanistisches Jahrbuch* 5 (1952), 43–7.

[53] Diary, 7 Nov. 1933. Something of Entwistle's personality and teaching style can be traced in conjoined pieces by Sylvanus Griswold-Morley and Albert E. Sloman, 'William James Entwistle: Two Memoirs', *Bulletin of Hispanic Studies* 29 (1952), 183–92.

Kolkhorst was a wealthy aesthete of Irish extraction who spent his childhood in Chile before moving with his family to a luxurious *quinta* (country estate) at Dafundo outside Lisbon. [54] As with House, Russell left a record of him in words that *mutatis mutandis* might be autobiographical:

> His contacts with Spain began towards the end of the 1914–18 War, when he was employed there for a time on government work. Though he always found some aspects of Spanish life and culture unsympathetic, others deeply interested him, and he took the unusual step for man of his intellectual ability of specializing in Spanish when he went up to Exeter College, Oxford in 1919. [55]

And like House before him, albeit for very different reasons, the eccentric Kolkhorst was not the subject of universal approval among his peers, not least at Exeter which he pointedly excluded from his substantial will: 'I desire to leave nothing to my College Exeter College Oxford as my College has never done anything at all for me.' [56] Russell, who knew Kolkhorst as well as anyone by the time of his death in 1958, wrote these lines in his obituary of him:

> He turned out to be an exceptionally gifted, if unorthodox, teacher, and found fulfilment in pouring into his lectures and tutorials his penetrating gifts as a literary critic, his flow of verbal wit, and his amused but always sympathetic interest in human beings — especially young ones — and their behaviour. Until the 1930's the main burden of Spanish teaching at Oxford fell on his shoulders, and there is no doubt that the successful establishment of the subject there owed a very great deal to him. [...] His pupils also knew him as a delightful and stimulating tutor. Lectures and tutorials, even on what looked like the most routine subjects, turned in his hands into high drama into which even his most idle or most sophisticated pupils found themselves actively drawn. Many *almas*

---

[54] See John Betjeman's pen portrait of Kolkhorst in *Summoned by Bells* (London: John Murray, 1960), 96–8.
[55] 'Mr. G. A. Kolkhorst: Gifted Teacher of Spanish', *The Times*, 16 Sept. 1958.
[56] In later life Russell recalled Kolkhorst refusing to set foot in Exeter after one of the fellows, Dacre Balsdon, upbraided him for bringing in a guest who was wearing plus-fours; see I. D. L. Michael's unpublished edition of Kolkhorst's correspondence to Charles Kennedy (1949–57) [GKCK] (2006), 67.

durmientes [sleeping souls] owed their awakening to Kolkhorst's unorthodox methods, while the more wide-awake ones emerged enlightened, excited and sometimes properly chastened, by their weekly tussles with him. All had cause to remember the kindness, humanity, and sense of humour he was incapable of concealing behind the façade of formidableness he sometimes liked to assume. [...] Those who had the privilege of hearing him using these gifts are unlikely to forget him or them, or to remain unaware of the enduring influence which a natural teacher of Kolkhorst's calibre can have even on those whose background and interests may be very different from his own. [57]

Among the many lessons Russell surely learnt from House and Kolkhorst were the talents and potential offered by otherwise unorthodox figures in the institutional setting of Oxford, an appreciation he deployed to the full in future decades. It may also have been from Kolkhorst that Russell acquired his distinctive Spanish accent which he would describe as *castizo* (linguistically 'pure'), [58] the counterpart of the elegant Oxford drawl some phoneticians claimed was unique to Queen's in the '30s:

> On the way, the Spanish he had learnt in South America was dropped and replaced by the patrician Castilian which used to impress both Spanish visitors to Oxford, and his own pupils. It was modelled on the speech of the late Duke of Alba, who befriended him when he was staying at the Instituto de Valencia de Don Juan, and whose blending of scholarship with *grandeza* he much admired. [59]

---

[57] 'George Alfred Kolkhorst (1897–1958)', *Bulletin of Hispanic Studies* 36 (1959), 51–2.
[58] Xon de Ros, a native of Barcelona, remembers Russell speaking Spanish with 'unanglicized elegance'; notes to the author, 16 Sept. 2020. Others noted that Russell's Spanish accent was 'all his own'. Where written Spanish and Portuguese were concerned he relied on native speakers to check his work but was let down in this respect in the introduction to his edition of *Celestina* (1991), one marred by 'hundreds and hundreds of inaccuracies, incorrections, wrong turns of phrase, and plain mistakes'; Daniel Waissbein, email to the author, 27 Oct. 2020.
[59] 'George Alfred Kolkhorst (1897–1958)', 51. One occasion when these linguistic skills were drawn on was the visit to Oxford by Unamuno in February 1936 when Kolkhorst had to serve as interpreter, Don Miguel having no English; RSSR, and for a report of the visit, see Entwistle's 'Don Miguel de Unamuno', *The Oxford Magazine*, 10 Nov. 1938, 369–70.

Not only that but it was Kolkhorst who served as a link to the *jeunesse dorée* of the 1920s, the world of Harold Acton, Evelyn Waugh, Cyril Connolly, Robert Byron, Anthony Powell, Osbert Lancaster and John Betjeman, the world of the writers to which Russell aspired. [60] Nor was it lacking in refinement, of which the dinner party he attended at Kolkhorst's famous set of rooms at 38 Beaumont Street on 5 November 1934 was the first of many over the next two decades: 'In evening had a marvellous dinner-party with the "Colonel" at his lodgings on Beaumont Street. Dinner just right (warmed port etc.) conversation brilliant, drinks pleasant and then Kolkhorst read a typical paper on the Baroque.' [61] The friendships made in these salons also brought Russell into the orbit of the young Dean (later Provost) of Wadham, the classicist Maurice Bowra (who had a long-running feud of sorts with Kolkhorst) which included John Sparrow, fellow (later Warden) of All Souls, Rosamond Lehmann, Enid Starkie and Iris Murdoch, though he was never a Bowrista, however much he owed to his patronage. [62] In later years he would smile at the memory of lively parties at Yarnton Manor, the residence Kolkhorst bought outside Oxford in 1936 with its tapestries, Fabergé and collections of Oriental carpets, porcelain and jade for which Russell gained an abiding affection. [63] The eccentric staff, infestations of mice and assortment of vicious, slobbering and flatulent dogs were another matter. Here is his account of a visit he made between wartime postings in February 1945:

---

[60] Journal, 15 March 1948: 'Colonel in better form than for some time; possibly I was too. He reminisced about the Hypocrites Club with that delicate suggestiveness which reminds one of the president of a woman's club talking smut. Also about his aristocratic young friends of the twenties who seemed bores to me.'

[61] More raucous occasions in these rooms are captured in the writings of two of Kolkhorst's friends, John Betjeman in the long poem *Summoned by Bells* (London: John Murray, 1960), 96–8, and Osbert Lancaster in *With an Eye to the Future* (London: Century Hutchinson, 1986; first published 1967), 72–7. See also Bevis Hillier, *Young Betjeman* (London: John Murray, 2003), 140–6 & 176–7.

[62] 'I like Maurice Bowra, but he is hardly a colleague. Besides I think he permits himself to say very foolish things — without, of course, looking it. But the folly of his technique remains. There have — in the world's history — been greater than he. Though he is — in his own narrow, specialised microcosmos — great'; Kolkhorst to Charles Kennedy, Yarnton, 8 June 1951, in I. D. L. Michael's unpublished edition of that correspondence [GKCK], 76–7.

[63] A serialised article devoted to the house and its contents in the 21 and 28 Dec. 1951 numbers of *Country Life* prompted a burglary of the property while Kolkhorst was in residence in early February 1952, an episode from which he never recovered; Kolkhorst to Russell, Yarnton, 8 Feb. 1952.

I spent the weekend with my friend who has a manor nearby — a weekend in cloudcuckooland but amusing all the same though over a long period I should feel somewhat like an exhibit myself — my bedroom had among other things two Tournai tapestries (xv cent.), a pantryful of Ming and Tang pottery, a Samarkand carpet, a Louis Quinze settee, a full-sized piece of Japanese armour and a number of far from dumb mice. [64]

This relationship is recorded in the voluminous, brilliant though obsessive correspondence Kolkhorst sent Russell and the latter's friend Charles Kennedy in the post-war years, some of which prefigures the Colonel's slide into dementia which periodically had him admitted to the Warneford psychiatric hospital in Oxford prior to his death in September 1958. [65] Although his need for privacy and aversion to promiscuity would serve as a barrier to other than passing engagement, Russell was also on the periphery of another circle with an interest in Spain, that of W. H. Auden, Stephen Spender and Christopher Isherwood whose novels would in time make him nostalgic for pre-war Berlin. Two distinguished undergraduate friends were Walter Eytan, later a codebreaker at Bletchley Park and noted Israeli diplomat, and John Oakes, Rhodes Scholar, iconoclastic journalist and member of the Ochs family, the publisher entity of *The New York Times*. These and other social contacts honed an already powerful mind into a formidable tool of perception, intuition and expression which was never blunted.

*

This privileged immersion does not however entirely encompass Russell's formation as a scholar which was driven by a burning ambition to succeed in the eyes of his grandfather and benefactor Thomas Russell and also his mother Rita. 'God grant I may be worthy of Grandpa' he wrote in his diary on the eve of his nineteenth birthday, 23 October 1932. Exactly two years later he committed this to paper:

---

[64] PER to Maj. J. B. Heigham, Oxford, 26 Feb. 1945.
[65] Kolkhorst's correspondence to Kennedy from 1949–57 is currently held on revocable loan at the Taylor Institution Library, Oxford, MS.Fol.E.20; it is available in an unpublished edition by I. D. L. Michael [GKCK]; that to Russell, denser, more private and not shared with others in his lifetime, remains unpublished. The tone of the correspondence is well captured in Russell's journal entry for 28 Sept. 1948: 'The trouble with the Colonel as a correspondent is that all his writings are *belles-lettres*; more than a little French, in fact.'

If I could have my years again expect I should change many things but if I did I shouldn't be as I am which might be distressing as on the whole I would not like to be anyone else. For the future my first hope is to please Grandpa and myself by being a) a fellow b) a writer. If I can write as I think I can all will be well and I think that writing of some kind is possible. At any rate I hope that I may receive a 'first'. Secondly and equally important I hope that always Mother may never have cause to regret me.

Russell had arrived in Oxford with every intention of making good the academic promise that had won him the Laming Scholarship, and he proceeded to do just that, taking a first in Spanish and French with Portuguese as a subsidiary subject in the summer of 1935 and remembered among the brightest students of his generation. Years later Kolkhorst told him that '[a]s an Undergraduate, you were full of sterling promise. You were a Child being true Father to the Man. And looked it ... No Peter Pan you.' [66] As it was, much of the four years he spent as an undergraduate constituted a tug-of-war between his bounden duty to excel in his studies and his keen desire to become a novelist. 'Am I going to be a don, an author, a schoolmaster or a publisher?' he wondered in his diary on 6 January 1933. There can be little doubt that it was the second of these outcomes he cherished most, in pursuit of which he continued the voracious and omnivorous course of reading that had begun at Knowlescourt but which now served to feed his literary aspirations. [67] As to his literary influences at this time, an early enthusiasm arising from his undergraduate study was French drama, particularly Racine, 'the noble poet of humanity' with his 'silvery delivery and force' and aesthetic fascination. [68] 'The French classical tragedy' he wrote after watching performances of *Britannicus* and Molière's *Les Précieuses ridicules* at the Comédie-Française 'is real literature and one can see it trying to escape from its medium and become purely an aesthetic literary creation all the time. The realities are entirely unimportant and only serve as links for a universal tragedy of all men and women. Hence the declamation rules etc. It's all marvellously beautiful when one realizes this.' [69] Among the poets he had a particular

---

[66] Kolkhorst to PER, Yarnton, 5 June 1947. Russell's first recorded social contact with Kolkhorst was his hosting the latter for tea in March 1934.
[67] Russell's diary for 1932 contains a list of seventy titles read over a nine-month period.
[68] Diary, 31 Dec. 1934 & 28 May 1933 respectively.
[69] Diary, 31 Aug. 1933.

attachment to Swinburne — 'the real practical Swinburne of *Atalanta* [*in Calydon*], "The Triumph of Time" and "A Last Farewell"' which 'threatens to become an obsession — I wonder why?' [70] Any understanding of Russell's psychosexual makeup and insecurities, his sense that human desire is by its nature self-destructive, would provide a ready answer to that question, as it would to his interest in Oscar Wilde and subsequently Vicente Aleixandre. Outside of English and Hispanic letters his favourite writers at this time included Stendhal and Chekhov though there is no elaboration on the preference. Where the direct influences on his own writing were concerned, Russell made this entry in his diary: 'How to reconcile Anatole France and Conrad is my worry. Perhaps by adding [Arnold] Bennett and Azorín?' [71] Again, no elaboration is provided on this assortment. He enjoyed the innovations in Hemingway's shorter works ('Interesting and valuable because they are entirely lacking in the conventional trappings of the short stories. They are just fragments which occur — an argument in the waiting room, a boat ride etc., with a cruel and bitter reality yet impressionistic') and was intrigued by his interest in things Spanish. [72] Elsewhere Russell's Romantic formalism served as a barrier. The expurgated *Lady Chatterley's Lover* with its examination of class and heterosexual narrative he 'did not like much'. [73] Dickens he found problematic, telling evidence of his literary priorities and intellectual conceit:

> Dickens' form is often thoroughly careless and bad, he never betrays any sign of being a man of any culture whatever, his reaction to moral and social problems have all the undesirable characteristics of a smug and egoistic age, he has, in most ways, as much subtlety as a bull and yet he continues somehow to be one of the very greatest of novelists. It is, I think (not alone) entirely due to his ability to depict a series of unforgettable characters which make one feel that life must be worth living in a world where so many people are so interesting. His method seems to be rather dubious if examined closely but it has no effect whatever on his success. [74]

---

[70] Diary, 25 Aug. 1933.
[71] Diary, 18 Sept. 1932.
[72] Diary, 6 Sept. 1934.
[73] Diary, 3 April 1932.
[74] Journal, 5 July 1936.

Later came Dostoyevsky and above all Gide whom Russell presumably met when he was awarded an honorary doctorate at Oxford in June 1947 and through his friendship with Gide's biographer and sponsor Enid Starkie.

Russell went to the length of retaining the services of the Cambridge Literary Agency in 1931 in pursuit of his aspirations in that direction and his diaries record his stringent efforts to allocate the time necessary to make them reality while fulfilling his academic requirements. He also wrote for the journal *Isis* which in March 1933 printed the first in a succession of short stories influenced by Conrad but told in the manner of Somerset Maugham: 'The Pool' ('no matter how bad it is') concerning death and redemption in rural Spain. [75] This was followed by another in May — 'Red Earth', set in coastal Cornwall — at which time Russell noted that 'There is a rumour of my taking up a share on the staff of the *Isis* but on the whole I'd prefer not to.' [76] Never much of a team player in the conventional sense, this response was consistent with his lifelong aversion to avoidable administrative commitments, but it no doubt also reflected his justified misgivings about the wisdom of pursuing the vocation of a writer by contrast with the solidity of academic endeavour: 'Perhaps my future path lies in that direction and perhaps it is just youthful ebullition.' All the same, he persisted with youthful confidence in his abilities ('As usual spent day working and thinking of all the brilliant things I am going to write'), describing another of his short stories — 'The Witch', a tale of the supernatural set in rural Ireland — as 'too good for the *Isis* but too short for anything else'. [77] Later he confessed in his diary that 'It is possible that I have become an intellectual snob but it is pleasing and genuine'. [78] Only rarely in his diaries, or in his life, did Russell entirely lose his power of detachment but these are among the earliest recorded signs of the operation of a massive but effectively suppressed ego which two decades later brought him to a state of mental collapse.

Intermittently the nineteen-year-old Russell laboured on a novel, or rather a succession of novels, which were planned, started, postponed, resumed, recast and abandoned before the Second World War. Work began on an *opus* set in a Cornish coastal village under the title *Lenten Lilies* (subsequently *The Woven Raiment: A Fantasy*) in early 1932. [79] A vehicle for his recently evolved theory of

---

[75] Diary, 1 March 1933.
[76] Diary, 10 May 1933.
[77] Diary, 27 July & 12 Oct. 1933 respectively. Published in *Isis* in October 1933.
[78] Diary, 21 May 1934.
[79] The revised title is from Swinburne's poem 'The Triumph of Time'; see the epigraph to this

beauty and the child in prose of Algernon Charles Swinburne, the surviving incomplete draft reveals it to be tastefully written but mannered and precious in the extreme. Here are the opening lines:

> Spring was come to Pirran on David's birthday. Already the noise of the wind as it swept inwards from the sea bore with it a faint promise of wild roses and here and there in the valleys the timid wenbrush lay in bright clusters of yellow bloom amongst the dark winter grass. The troubled sea itself had begun to take on the sapphire hue of summer and lay tossing gently as if still unwilling to rest after the fierce winter storms. The mournful crying of the gulls as they circled slowly around the black rocks was tempered by a new and more urgent note — the demand for life of the countless unborn.

Russell eventually despaired of acquiring the necessary grasp of Cornish life and language and shifted the narrative to 'a small half-industrial town which does not need such intimate country knowledge and will enable me to express my hate of the bourgeoisie successfully'. [80] Between whiles he planned an Andalusian travelogue and a novel on Boabdil, the last Emir of Granada. [81] By the end of 1934 the anti-bourgeoisie project had in turn been abandoned in favour of 'the "something different" Oxford novel' [that] is in my mind and must be produced now that I have decided to give the other up, at any rate for the time being'. [82] 'Surely I'm not going to be a humorous writer' he had recorded in January 1932, but if Russell's evolving sociopolitical views had earlier contributed to the change of setting from rural to urban, his decision to strike out on this new path may be tardy acknowledgement of the direction in which Waugh, Powell, Graham Greene and others were taking the genre. [83] Perhaps the die was cast in 1932 when he read James Joyce's *Ulysses* ('a revelation but not I think an instrument of conversion'; later he recanted of that view) and then *Dubliners* in 1934 ('a

---

biography.
[80] Diary, 20 June 1932.
[81] Diary, 30 June 1932.
[82] Diary, 31 Dec. 1934.
[83] Russell's papers do however contain a brief farce titled *Life's a Dream or All the World's a (Revolving) Stage* with a cast including Noah, the Brontë sisters, Lord Lloyd (a contemporary political figure of extremely conservative views), the President of the United States, Queen Elizabeth I and Éamon de Valera.

thrilling if sickening piece of work'). [84] As it was, these literary aspirations gradually yielded to his academic responsibilities, among other obstacles. He acknowledged as much in August 1936:

> The novel I have planned for so many years gets no further. I am unable to make the really (for me) severe effort required to write even a short story. The mental plan is so reluctant to commit itself into the clumsy hands of concrete vocabulary and expression. Yet one day I shall write a really worthwhile novel. [85]

No such day dawned. A couple of weeks later he explored the dimensions of the problem:

> I feel sure that if I was a Catholic or a communist or someone of that sort who has this world and the next all neatly arranged in a conveniently narrow and tightly closed cell I should produce something worthwhile but when one is drifting in a mental chaos somewhat like Greco's *Vista de Toledo* as to light and strain it is not easy to start trying to produce what one hopes would be a work of art out of the void as it were. [86]

A year passed without alteration:

> Since 1934 I have not had anything published in the line of pure literary effort but I do not see why scholarly erudition should not prevent literature on small scale as well. Alas, if only I were a poet! Imagine the thrill of expressing freely one's lyric emotions! [87]

In this Russell had come to the heart of the matter. As one reader has noted of his unpublished work, 'ultimately, PER was just too introspective and private to be able to communicate fully as a creative writer'. [88] Nonetheless, though his ambition in this realm had eventually to be set aside altogether, Russell brought a many-layered style to his scholarly prose which was not only as complex as the

---

[84] Diary, 6 April 1932 & 24 Sept. 1934 respectively.
[85] Diary, 3 Aug. 1936.
[86] Journal, 19 Aug. 1936.
[87] Journal, 25 Sept. 1937.
[88] Jeremy Lawrance, email to the author, 15 Aug. 2020.

man but also perfectly suited to the critical approach that became the hallmark of his work. If his surviving *oeuvre* in prose is any guide then this turn of events can neither be wondered at nor altogether regretted. Certainly, Russell scarcely ever mentioned it again.

*

By the time Russell reached Oxford in 1931 the lotus-eating generation of the previous decade had largely though by no means entirely departed. Moreover, with the onset of the Depression the mood changed perceptibly from the unbridled hedonism of the 1920s to the enhanced awareness of the 1930s. [89] From a political standpoint sympathies and attachments ranged across the spectrum with a growing taste for pacifism as the decade wore on, one made notorious by the Oxford Union debate in February 1933 at which the motion that 'This House will under no circumstances fight for its King and Country' was carried with a substantial majority. The incident went unmarked in Russell's diary and in the way of these things he later recalled it as having had rather more impact outside the University than in it.

No political animal in the conventional sense, Russell's private diaries and memoirs show him to have broadly sympathised with the Right into the late 1930s, a position informed no doubt by the chaos he had witnessed in Spain in the spring of 1931, and to a lesser extent by the shockwaves caused by the 'mutiny' of the Atlantic Fleet at Invergordon in September which forced Britain off the Gold Standard; on this his Uncle Teddy Evans, by then rear-admiral commanding the Australian Squadron, will have given him the official view. Also of concern was the episode of labour unrest known as the Depression Riots in New Zealand in 1932. 'Shall I join the New Party?' Russell asked himself, or was asked, on 7 January 1932, a reference to the organisation founded the previous year by Oswald Mosley and shortly to form the nucleus of the British Union of Fascists. That same day he watched the Atlantic Fleet put to sea from Portsmouth, wondering 'Is it [the] last time?' Essentially a pacifist and for a time at least a member of the OU Liberal Club, Russell's inclinations were plainly less ideological than a matter of politico-cultural expediency, and he was hardly alone in viewing the fascist movements that developed in Italy and Germany as the best hope for countering communism. A diary entry in June 1932 summarises Russell's political outlook in the early 1930s: 'I see Chile is going Socialist. The

---

[89] Dacre Balsdon, *Oxford Now and Then* (London: Macmillan, 1970), 172.

hope of Europe is Italy and Germany now, also Empire free trade without jingoism. The last chance of democracy is at hand.' [90] He took a similar position on the Church: 'Whatever we may think of the Roman Catholic religion, the Church Universal is the world's greatest bulwark against Communism' even if '[t]o the average modern man the Church exists as the cold repressing hand of a dead past'. [91] He prized democracy (as he interpreted it) but regarded it as weak in adversity, as amply demonstrated in August 1914: 'Democratic liberty was not able to face the emergency of war and was in effect suspended. This is true in essentials and is worthwhile noticing.' [92] Later he expanded on this viewpoint with a decidedly elitist slant:

> Those who defend present-day 'democracy' in England as a tradition forget that the traditional English democracy was essentially one of the intellectual or politically experienced classes. Now it is mob rule managed by harloting politicians, a Press without any sense of values and this 'democracy' is expected to deal with problems far greater than those which assailed the old 'closed' democracy. Curiously people will not give up their rights to the latter but they will to a dictator. [93]

His belief was that '[d]emocracy is failing because it, like autocracy, is based on a lie, in this case the lie that majorities *ipso facto* are more adequate governors than minorities.' [94] This subsequently took on an even more pessimistic form: 'Only the uneducated or the unscrupulous can be democrats.' [95] Out of this came the following irreconcilable formula: 'I think I believe in the totalitarian state as an economic fact but I also believe in intellectual liberty.' [96] This political outlook culminated in the extraordinary rant Russell committed to his journal in October 1937:

> The real enemies of civilization are England and the U.S.A. whose monstrous political distortion of the liberty of mankind into a deification of vulgarity and a pretence that supreme political power must

---

[90] Diary, 6 June 1932.
[91] Diary, 22 June 1932 & Commonplace book, 10.
[92] Commonplace book, 9.
[93] *Ibid.*, 11.
[94] *Ibid.*, 26.
[95] *Ibid.*, 36.
[96] *Ibid.*, 10.

be in the hands of the stupidest and least educated sections of mankind has done more to destroy human civilized values than anything the world has ever seen. [...] Any revolution whether Fascist or Communist is to be welcomed if it destroys this horror and shows man that true personal freedom is of the spirit and not of his stomach and freedom of the spirit is precisely what modern 'democracy' hates. True political democracy might perhaps return when each man formed part of a community of educated, tolerant, economically free, spiritually-developed men ... [97]

'Regrettable effusion on previous page' he noted five months later. [98]

Though definitely a member of the upper middle class with plenty to lose from any breakdown in the established order, Russell was by no means lacking in a social conscience as the Depression put millions on the breadline, albeit from a somewhat patrician standpoint. 'Saw [Noël Coward's] *Cavalcade* this evening,' he wrote in January 1932. 'It is indeed a wonderful bit of work. But what about 5,000,000 people who are in misery?' Not inconsistent with this outlook was his appreciation of the eternal stoicism of the working poor gleaned from a BBC radio broadcast: 'Listening to a Scots miner's wife's description of how she housekeeps makes one admire the courage and determination with which these people make the best of life and everlasting scarcity.' [99] Russell's passion was for English country life nourished first by the lengthy walks he like many members of the University would make from Oxford to the surrounding towns and villages, and subsequently by his mother settling in an atmospheric old house at North Mymms in Hertfordshire in 1934. His vision of rural life was that depicted by Constable, noting in December 1932 that he '[w]ould give anything intimately to understand the country and not just to revel in its sensation as I do now'. [100] This idyllic interpretation not only provided the setting for his first novel as originally conceived but also underlay the deism he came to espouse as the years passed. Himself a reader of (and correspondent to) the *New Statesman* with its liberal and increasingly appeasing slant, Russell's Oxford diaries are replete with disgust at the urban life of the English middle class and its political masters as variously enunciated in the pages of *The Times*, *The Daily Mail* and *The Daily Express*.

[97] Journal, 2 Oct. 1937.
[98] Journal, 20 Feb. 1938.
[99] Commonplace book, 4.
[100] Diary, 6 Dec. 1932.

Reading the *Labouring Life* — a marvellous transcription of village life in Devon. I see that the reviewer of the *London Mercury* was <u>irritated</u> by the pronunciations in Williamson's book. Can't one just imagine a snotty-minded suburban Londoner faced by something he could never understand — the country as it is and not as it looks from a stinking car, so he called it 'literary weakness' because it wasn't in the heavy mechanical language of *The Times*. When will English literature throw off the manacles of urbanism and urban realism? We want a new Romantic movement to do it alas! [101]

Some of this dyspepsia evidently merged with the frustration of his literary aspirations:

Sunday is made so much more oppressive than it need be by that unhappy memorial of human vulgarity and human stupidity the Sunday newspaper. The less reputable variety with its vast and devastating vulgarity, its synthetic mawkishness and its hungry distortions of truth is sufficient to depress anyone. The 'respectable' variety is not much better. Here is the bank past which flows relentlessly an endless stream of books, second-rate and third-rate, beneath which anything that may be called 'literature' has long since sunk. The hordes of reviewers, long since lost to any ideal they may ever have dreamt of, churn out week by week their flow of words about the books which by next month will have passed into painless oblivion. Anyone who doubts that this is the age of the second-rate has only to read the book reviews, the book advertisements and the books reviewed in the Sunday papers. What a sad vision of thousands of inferior minds extroverting their inferiority in a ceaseless torrent of words! I suppose one day the public worm may turn and refuse to read them any more but I fear by then any aesthetic or even moral ability to discern a good book will have vanished. [102]

'God 'elp me for a snob!' he confessed after sharing a German railway carriage with a garrulous party of Londoners on an escorted tour. [103] One may speculate

---

[101] Diary, 27 Dec. 1932. Henry Williamson, *The Labouring Life* (London: Jonathan Cape, 1932).
[102] Journal, 5 July 1936.
[103] Diary, 26 Aug. 1934.

on its origin, just as one may wonder how well Russell was able to confine this priggishness to his journals, but the realisation that the status enjoyed by his family in New Zealand counted for little in the English society he encountered at Cheltenham — one that required him to change his accent — no doubt contributed to it. Whatever the case, the inherent contradictions in this outlook in a person endowed with his gifts and privilege and in the context of wider social and political developments proved untenable.

*

The other major formative influence was travel, and Russell succeeded in getting away to the Continent during practically every spring and summer vacation between 1931 and the outbreak of the Second World War. His second visit to Spain, a two-month trip in the summer of 1932 during which he took a course at the University of Granada, was initially blighted by illness and loneliness — 'Wish mother was here' — but he soon brightened as Andalusia took him under its spell: first the Alhambra and the Generalife ('Wonderful it is, too') and then the unexpected pleasures of Malaga where he was enchanted by the festivities and watched his first bullfight: 'Very interesting from point of view of old time pageantry but it is a loathsome display of cruelty even if it is clever and exciting.' [104] In the spring of 1933 Russell returned to Spain, this time for study purposes in Madrid; much later he recalled how Andalusia was looked down upon in Oxford in favour of Castile. [105] That summer the focus initially at least was his French studies with three weeks in Strasbourg where he made progress on his Cornish novel followed by a month walking in the Black Forest. Unlike his stay in Madrid this trip left a significant record in his diaries. Russell was much taken by Germany and the Germans, finding the whole very different to what he had been led to expect from the British press. 'Karlsruhe usual up-to-date German city. Everyone seems pleased and they give Hitler salute now instead of handshake'; 'Met lots of charming Germans en route to whom I talked. All very friendly and seemed to be far more intelligent than they would be in England. Hitler is truly Germany whatever one may think of some of [his] politics'; 'Saw one of the voluntary labour brigades singing and happy this morning. One sees the attractive side of Nazi Germany and so far I approve.' [106] Even more appealing to Russell was the Black Forest itself which inspired him to this deistic theory:

[104] Diary, 13 & 24 July, & 28 Aug. 1932.
[105] RSSR.
[106] Diary, 31 July, 2 & 7 Aug. 1933 respectively.

> Have been toying all day with what <u>seemed</u> a great idea. If God is Nature as I believe then God is 'harmony' because perfect harmony is what makes Nature beautiful. Also think that reason is to interpret and give greater value to an emotion and not to be prostituted on impractical abstract theorizing. Perhaps Rousseau was right and to reach a happier state we must construct a life giving at least the equivalent of the fundamentals of life in Nature. [107]

As he added a fortnight later, 'Marvellous time in Forest and the spirit which lives in a place like that is something like the nearest approach to the Supreme Being that man can know, or so it seems to me in the heat of the moment.' [108] The experience was sufficient to bring Russell back to Baden-Baden the following summer though his responses were more muted. Himself in the throes of another unrequited infatuation, Russell again found spiritual peace walking in the Black Forest and reading Nietzsche, noting in his diary that he had 'Seen nothing very detrimental to Hitlerism yet. […] Advantage of Germany is that it has the picturesqueness of foreign parts without the Latin unpleasant traits such as dirt. Hitlerism is at any rate a great self-expression of this agricultural community.' [109] A week later he noted that 'Konstanz is a pleasing place and one sees the German at his best — apparent prosperity, cleanliness, order, neatness, combination of antiquity and modern architecture and the exhilarating effects of the Irredentist revolution', a reference to Hitler's policy of territorial reintegration. [110] Sophisticated though he was at twenty, Russell was able to turn his face away from the ugly realities of Nazi Germany played out in town and city and allow himself to be seduced by the Party's rural idyll with its *völkisch* undertones, a view resonating with his deistic vision and critique of English bourgeois values. This in turn served to validate latent and less than latent prejudices of a kind he committed to his commonplace book: 'One of the chief causes of the Jews' trouble is that they have been arrogant enough to put their religion as noun and country as adjective' adding parenthetically 'but then so have Catholics etc.?' [111] In later years Russell would recall grilling sausages around campfires with the Hitler Youth in the Black Forest and could thunder out the Horst Wessel song,

---

[107] Diary, 20 July 1933. This was later elaborated into a full credo.
[108] Diary, 2 Aug. 1933.
[109] Diary, 7 & 8 Aug. 1934 respectively.
[110] Diary, 16 Aug. 1934.
[111] Commonplace book, 29.

but a remorseful note can be detected in the account of those visits he added to his memoir for 'necrological use' in 1992:

> At first I was rather impressed by Nazi Germany as seen from the Black Forest region but a stay I made in Berlin in 1935 made plain the violence and brutality that was only half-hidden there. I did not go back to Germany after that year, preferring instead to walk in the Austrian or Swiss Alps. [112]

Two incidents during that visit to Berlin had opened his eyes to the dehumanised reality of Nazi regime. The first, which changed somewhat in the retelling, was of 'a blind man with a white stick tapping his way along a pavement which had been fenced off by workmen for some kind of repair. There was a group of soldiers nearby. Russell assumed that they would guide him round the obstruction but they took no notice. The old man walked into it and fell over. "Surely they will help him", he thought. They ignored him. "Then I knew something was wrong."' [113] The second incident, recalled in 1948 and recounted in later years, concerned his witnessing the beating served out to a homeless man by a member of the SS outside the Air Ministry on the Wilhelmstrasse as passersby looked the other way. [114] 'I left Germany the next day.' [115]

In the summer of 1934 Russell was abroad again, fitting in trips to Paris, San Sebastián, Germany, Austria and Switzerland. Here are his impressions of San Sebastián, the first detailed ones for Spain that survive:

> I'm staying in a house, flat of three amazingly ugly and noisy spinsters. Eat in a *pensión* above — a crudish place but amusing — only for the people who are there. The maid might have come out of Ayala's *Consuelo*, so typical is she. However there are lots of fleas, dirt and noise. [...] The sisters Devora, Carmen and Angelita (blotchy face) are full of 'amor humano y divino' and pride themselves on being *inagotables* [inexhaustible]. However I have enormous arguments with them, very good for the Spanish. [...] San Sebastián is not especially interesting.

---

[112] PELR, 2.
[113] Colin P. Thompson, 'Address Given at the Service of Thanksgiving for the Life of Professor Sir Peter Russell (24 October 1913–22 June 2006)', *Bulletin of Hispanic Studies* 84 (2007), 263–5; at 265.
[114] Journal, 4 [Feb.] 1948.
[115] Xon de Ros, notes to the author, 16 Sept. 2020.

CHELTENHAM AND OXFORD (1927–1939)

The two best things are the port and the Basque fish market. The fishing boats have enormous black funnels and there is always a crowd of anxious relations waiting their return — old black-dressed wrinkled women, mothers calmly suckling their children, rather nice-looking young girls and their young fishermen brothers. Awful noises of gossip and howling kids. Great shiny black pop-eyed teeming baskets of sardines, all-pervading smell of fish, blood and sawdust. Spanish girls on closer consideration seem to be very pretty or very ugly — a thing I hadn't noticed before. The boys and youths until about 25 are much better-looking. Delicate and rather sensitive (perhaps sensual) faces and clear fine features. However they soon get coarse and oily — perhaps due to the 'dolor de raza' [Spanish burden; actually from Aeschylus' *The Suppliants*]. The men think nothing of taking off their clothes and bathing from the mole, more or less publicly. Such an attitude pleases me as opposed to the Northern attitude which is always half-ashamed and afraid of anything so frankly physical and sensual as the human body. [116]

Russell had earlier asked himself 'Why do I love Germany and Spain — the most opposed nations in the world? Proud melancholy individualism and proud melancholy (or sentimental) collectivism. Perhaps it's because they're both pagan, idealistic and sad.' [117] It must be supposed that consciously or otherwise he found something of himself and the fulfilment of a need not otherwise accessible in the English-speaking world and in England particularly, latecomer as he was to that society and its mores. On the eve of his 21st birthday he made this profession of faith:

Finally at 21 I believe in myself, in the essential goodness of man and in the absence of evil as a 'free-will' thing. I believe that beauty and harmony and god are one, in the eternity of the soul in Nature (but not in the Romantic way), in the god Pan, in the life stream, in Freud, Flaubert, Beethoven <u>and</u> Wagner, Cézanne, Shakespeare, Verlaine, Valle-Inclán, Cervantes, Zola, Ayala and Herr Hitler. [118]

---

[116] Diary, 21 July 1934. 'Amor humano y divino' is a reference to Juan Valera's novel *Pepita Jiménez* (1874). *Consuelo* (1878) was Adelardo López de Ayala's last play.
[117] Diary, 25 Aug. 1933.
[118] Diary, 23 Oct. 1934.

By the time of the Munich crisis in September 1938 Russell's opinion of the 'half-crazed mystic of Berchtesgaden' had veered round entirely, quite aside from his horror at '[a] Germany filled with reincarnation of Prussian ruthless militarism, suppression of freedom, determined to establish by all means German hegemony in Europe [...] crazed by race madness ... ' [119]

What to make of these youthful attachments, opinions and prejudices Russell set down for his eyes only *avant le déluge* ninety years ago? The commonplace book he kept in the early 1930s in which many of the more extreme opinions were recorded is contemporaneously inscribed 'Ideas, bright or otherwise but original unless the contrary is stated'. Whatever judgments may be applied to them with hindsight, they remain the expression of convictions lying well within the mainstream of contemporary opinion in the context of the time: *autres temps, autres moeurs*. They are also the outpourings of an individual moved to express himself outwardly only in the most intimate, trying or egregious of circumstances, reliant on letting off steam in private while showing his best face to the world — the face described in his poem 'Laughter' (p. 183). Certainly time, circumstance and maturity cured Peter Russell of many though not all of these views under the shifting carapace of his self-described ambiguity, the same as that played out in the confines of his interiorised world where decades of mental anguish awaited. The survival of Russell's pre-war records was providential since they spent the war in his mother's home in Jersey which was first requisitioned by the German military and then looted after their departure: 'I recovered a lot of diaries of mine sporadically kept from 1926 onwards. I must be growing up because they caused me no embarrassment and gave me some interest.' [120] His archive as it was discovered after his death had been purged in the late 1990s yet he never disposed of those diaries and other writings which preserve the raw emotions and experiences of his youth. [121] Indeed, the evidence from his final autobiographical writings and statements is that he had not gone over this material for many decades and the impression at the end of his life is of a man wanting to let sleeping dogs lie, happy to shape or configure his legacy but unwilling to delve too deeply into the past. Writing to the novelist Javier Marías in character as 'Peter Wheeler' in 2002, Russell made these remarks on his recollections of the Civil War which can be

---

[119] Journal, 14 Sept. 1938.
[120] Journal, 4 Feb. 1946. The only diary or journal apparently kept by Russell which has not survived for posterity is that for 1935.
[121] PER to Alastair Saunders, Oxford, 22 Jan. 1997: 'One thing I am doing in a rather desultory way is to go through and destroy files which refer to individuals.'

regarded as doing service for the decade as a whole: 'It was, of course, one of the major events of his youth but one which he remembers, or rather does not particularly want to remember, as an experience befogged for him in ambiguities and contradictions, political and personal.' [122] This together with the nuanced remarks on Germany he set forth in his 1992 memoir may speak for themselves.

*

In the spring of 1935 the award of the De Osma Studentship — for which Russell had the gratifying experience of being toasted by his college in Hall — brought him back to Madrid and to the famous Residencia de Estudiantes, a cultural centre founded under the influence of the philosopher Francisco Giner de los Ríos along the lines of Balliol College in 1910. [123] Here he encountered many of the luminaries of the Second Republic, albeit with mixed success. Among the younger of these were Pablo Neruda and Federico García Lorca (whose impromptu piano recitals in the common room were a feature of life there), though Russell found them annoying and cliquish and there was no significant contact after they ignored him in the garden of the Residencia one day. [124] The diary he apparently kept for 1935 has been lost and the following reminiscence, shared by Russell when he was 'well into his anecdotage', is the sole written record of the trip. It not only gives a flavour of his dry humour and critical eye but also of the air of controlled demolition that was never far from his writing:

> I had first met don Ramón [Menéndez Pidal] in 1933 or 34 [actually 1935] in the poetically famous garden of the Residencia de Estudiantes in Madrid. It was, I recall, not the happiest of social occasions. Also with me was another Oxford undergraduate [Ronald Hilton of Christ Church] who used to cause us considerable annoyance here in Oxford by his unwanted propensity to correct our spoken Spanish. On this particular afternoon the eminent President of the Residencia, Alberto Jiménez Fraud, a devoted anglophile known personally in later years to a few of us still around, told us that there were three distinguished Spanish scholars chatting together in the garden and that he would like to present us to them. The group consisted of Ramón Menéndez Pidal,

[122] JMA, PER to Javier Marías, Oxford, 15 Nov. 2002. 'Peter Wheeler' was the character based on Russell Marías wrote into his trilogy *Tu rostro mañana* (Madrid: Alfaguara, 2002–7).
[123] Diary, 1 Dec. 1934.
[124] RSSR.

Américo Castro, and Fernando de los Ríos, a prominent Republican politician. These three scholarly *grandezas,* as I recall, acknowledged our presence with a fairly perfunctory nod after which we stood politely by while don Ramón continued speaking to his friends. Suddenly my companion from Oxford, a tall man, leaned forward and, extending his finger in the direction of don Ramón's nose, declared à propos of something the latter had just said, 'En castellano eso no se dice.' I rather hoped that this clanger would earn my companion his long-awaited comeuppance but don Ramón, as I recall, paid not the slightest attention to this uncivil interruption nor did his friends and it was left to the distraught don Alberto, always a model of good manners, to apologize for his protégé's behaviour and, no doubt, to wonder whether his decision to offer Oxford students *becas* [scholarships] and accommodation in the residencia had been a wise one. [125]

Expanding on this, and despite the succession of distinguished foreign guests to the Residencia from Valéry and Einstein to Keynes, Russell remarked elsewhere that the outside world held comparatively little interest for Spanish intellectuals of the time, most of them heavily engaged in domestic politics and with French their only foreign language. [126]

After graduating in the summer of 1935 Russell turned to history with the encouragement of Professor Entwistle, a choice which much disappointed his dying grandfather Thomas Russell who wanted him to read law and take over his practice in New Zealand. Years later he explained the decision, one prefigured by Professor Foligno's admonitions to the Modern Languages School as regards Philology in 1930:

> I was by then somewhat disenchanted by the idea of starting graduate research in the Modern Language Faculty and secured a transfer to the Modern History Faculty to work for a doctorate on fourteenth-century Anglo-Iberian history. In those days the Oxford Modern Language School was virtually untouched by the New Criticism or any other

---

[125] 'Reinventing an Epic Poet: 1952 in Context' in *'Mio Cid' Studies. 'Some Problems of Diplomatic' Fifty Years On,* ed. Alan Deyermond, David G. Pattison & Eric Southworth (London: Queen Mary and Westfield College, 2002), 63–72, at 67–8. Jiménez Fraud served as lecturer in Spanish at Oxford from 1938 until his retirement in 1953.
[126] RSSR.

current theoretical notions of what literary criticism was about. Literary history reigned supreme. Undergraduates were not generally encouraged to question but simply to master the conclusions of authoritative critics. Though I had been lucky in having tutors in French and Spanish who, in fact, did encourage some original thinking even they warned one to be very cautious about offering much of it up in Finals. [127]

Oxford, Russell concluded, had no interest in evaluating literary texts as literature, which it reduced to an exercise in chasing sources and could not acknowledge as a serious academic discipline. [128] Nor as it turned out was Mr Russell the only party dismayed at this rejection which offended the better part of the Modern Languages Board and brought a good deal of opprobrium down on Entwistle's head. Already in his inaugural lecture of 1932 Entwistle had deplored 'the divorce so painfully apparent between our schools of modern languages and of history', a statement greeted with consternation by many in his audience. [129] As Russell recalled, the Board 'in those days suffered from a collective paranoia which led them to imagine that the historians were constantly plotting to do their subject down and to kidnap the best graduates from their Faculty', itself a legacy of the prolonged opposition to the establishment of modern languages in the University and the marginal and undepartmentalised status of its components. It was the sort of absurdity which Russell, never one to conform for conformity's sake, delighted in skewering, though the decision no doubt owed much to a concern for professional advancement. [130] In opting to pursue a higher degree he was also part

---

[127] PELR, 2. This point echoes Osbert Lancaster who read English at Lincoln College from 1927–30 and recalled being '[f]irmly discouraged from exercising what little critical faculty one might possess. [...] Personal judgments were not called for; what was required was the largest possible collection of *idées reçues*'; *With an Eye to the Future*, 82. For more on the teaching of modern languages at Oxford in the 1930s, see Russell's 'The *Celestina* Then and Now', *Context, Meaning and Reception of 'Celestina': A Fifth Centenary Symposium*, ed. Ian Michael & David G. Pattison [= *Bulletin of Hispanic Studies* (Glasgow) 78.1] (2001), 1–11, at 3.
[128] RSSR.
[129] *The Scope of Spanish Studies. An Inaugural Lecture Delivered before the University of Oxford on 3 November 1932* (Oxford: Clarendon Press, 1932), 8. See also Russell's 'William James Entwistle (1896–1952)', 6.
[130] An example of this comes in Russell's obituary of his undergraduate tutee Ted Riley in which he alludes to a failed attempt to lure him from literary to historical studies in 1947; 'Edward Calverley Riley', *The Queen's College Record* 7 (2001), 93–5; at 94.

of a growing trend at Oxford which saw an eighty-five-percent increase in the number of research students between 1931 and 1936. [131]

So it was that Russell turned from a sustained interest in drama (chiefly Lope, Calderón, Racine, Ibsen, Chekhov and Pirandello) to begin research on a doctorate on the English involvement in the Iberian Peninsula in the second half of the fourteenth century, Entwistle having first drawn his attention to the subject. He did so under the somewhat erratic supervision of Sir Maurice Powicke, Regius Professor of Modern History, and particularly with the Balliol medievalist and Powicke's successor V. H. Galbraith whom he remembered as 'a brilliant, painstaking and stimulating teacher to whom I owe any competence as a historian that I have'. [132] Much as his research and writing continued until 1940, the outbreak of the Spanish Civil War in July 1936 deprived Russell of the opportunity to work in that country and confined him mainly to the Public Record Office in London, a situation that, together with the onset of the Second World War, imposed a ten-year delay on much of his published output. For now his archival interludes offered more grist for his relentless self-examination and self-criticism:

> My thesis on English Interventions in the Peninsula 1350–1390 progresses and I am putting a great deal of work into it, and interest as well. Working in the Record Office is much less tiresome than I had expected and it is with some disquiet that I find myself getting quite a thrill of pleasure as I encounter some tiny new fact. The bookworm spirit is an undoubted threat I fear. I object on principle because on rational grounds one has no right to exaggerate the importance of finding the little details for their own sake but only when they are really important links in a chain of evidence. The mere satisfaction of facts for their own sake is a sterile emotion, to be eliminated. It is annoying to me that I haven't yet sufficient paleographic skill to be able to read at sight properly. [133]

In the meantime Russell was taking the first steps in his academic career, being appointed a graduate scholar at Queen's (known as a Taberdar) in 1935 with

---

[131] R. B. McCallum, 'The Advance of the Advanced Students', *The Oxford Magazine*, 30 April 1936, 512–4.

[132] PELR, 3.

[133] Journal, 12 July 1936. By 1949 the title of the thesis, now under Entwistle's supervision, was *The English Intervention in Spain and Portugal between 1362 and 1390*.

teaching responsibilities and then to lectureships there in 1936 and at St John's College in 1937; the Queen's lectureship was extended for three years in March 1939 after he served notice of plans to take up a position at the University of Aberdeen. [134] As he noted at the time, 'A semi-inferior academic status of lecturer is something that one's pride and one's sense of one's own worth cannot stomach for long. One would become a hack and so embittered and I am above all determined to do neither.' [135] Whatever troubles assailed him in future years — and there were many — Russell never lost his sense of the superiority of his intellect, affirmed in his inner life and confirmed in his ordinary dealings with others.

Nonetheless, by 1936 Russell's journals reveal an intensification of the depression evident in earlier years and which blighted him for the rest of his life. This particular iteration, set down in a journal entry for 27 June, touches on his loneliness and a degree of resignation at what he regarded as his diminishing career prospects:

> Oxford next year threatens to be very boring without any of my undergraduate acquaintances still being there. Gordon [Robertson] took his departure in the approved English manner and I mine of him in the same but I shall notice his absence quite a lot all the same. Unless the promised posts materialise by this time next year I shall depart myself. Sometimes I almost wish they wouldn't materialise anyway but no other existence that I know of would offer so much freedom from routine and 'superior officers'.

By the autumn of that year this state of mind had assumed a psychosomatic dimension, a trip to Brussels with his mother marred by chest pains and palpitations to which a doctor prescribed a week's bed rest. [136] In his life Russell questioned practically every facet of his existence, his intellectual honesty, the wisdom and value of his career choices and the labels attaching to him, to name but a few. In this case his pitiless critical eye fell on modern Spain and its culture generally on the eve of the Civil War, the world to which he had effectively shackled himself as an academic:

---

[134] The Statutes of Queen's College state that '[t]he eight holders of Open Scholarships who are highest in seniority from the time of their election shall always be called Taberdars.' My thanks to Nigel Griffin on this point.

[135] Journal, 2 Jan. 1939.

[136] Journal, 12 [Sept.] 1936.

I have been reading a somewhat crude and hyperbolical biography of [the novelist] Gabriel Miró, nevertheless interesting. Offers a desperate picture of Spanish provincial and metropolitan life as it presented itself to a talented neurotic. I sometimes feel as if the awful 'abulia' [lassitude] of modern Spain makes it a worthless task trying to interest oneself in them. It might be more satisfying to the spirit if, academically, Spanish studies ceased at 1700 or thereabouts and one was able to avoid the dreary secondrateness of the greater part of Spaniards and Spanish culture since then. Indeed I'm sure that if an opportunity offered for dedicating myself instead to French studies I would take it, if only for the vicarious vigour and intellectual acuteness which one gets from things French even today. Spain attracts as a hobby but I suspect it may not make a satisfying career, however much sheer accidents of fate may drive one towards it. No doubt this mood will pass and some other more optimistic will follow. [137]

It did, but to the end of his life he preferred to be thought of as a historian than as a Hispanist regardless of his attachment to Spain, Portugal and their culture. Not the least attraction of that culture was the revivifying effect it always had on his fragile psyche of which he was perfectly aware as he wrote those lines. Russell was laid up with a poisoned foot at his mother's home in rural Hertfordshire at the time and generally at a low ebb. 'How I am looking forward to some weeks in the southern sun' he wrote. 'I haven't felt properly well for many months.' Still, the utter turmoil in which Spain found herself by the autumn of 1937 reaffirmed his interest in turning to nineteenth-century French literature, a view that had not changed by January 1939: 'As Oxford is at present organized I very much fear that I shall not get much further in the Spanish line. I only wish I could teach French as well which is at the moment my chief ambition and one which I believe I am qualified to carry out as well as most of those who do now.' [138] Nonetheless, these concerns were to some extent allayed once he had been appointed to a second lectureship in 1937:

---

[137] Journal, 2 July 1936. The volume on Miró was presumably José Guardiola Ortiz's *Biografía íntima de Gabriel Miró* (Alicante: Imprenta Guardiola, 1935). The concept of *abulia* first appears in Ángel Ganivet's *Idearium español* (1897), a prominent work in the 'Generation of 1898' canon on which Russell first lectured in 1939. Ronald Truman: 'It signified a radical failure of the will, a response to a felt absence of a much desired sense of value and purpose such as to energize, sustain, and direct the life of an individual person and of society at large.' (Email to the author, 8 Aug. 2020.)

[138] Journal, 25 Sept. 1937 & 2 Jan. 1939.

> I am now lecturer at St. John's as well — this gives me real satisfaction and goes some way to making up for my undignified resentment at not being a full fellow at Queen's. [...] The business of being a Lecturer is not without its compensations but the fact that one is without any permanent status is annoying to one who cannot but feel that his capabilities — even if second-rate — are still superior to those of a number of the full Fellows. I wonder whether I can settle to the idea of teaching indefinitely a subject which is not in itself a fully established one. At the same time I believe that Spanish literature and the Spanish way of looking at life has a proper place in the history of civilization though other people may not yet want to believe that fact. [139]

This also extended to Portugal, and like any non-peninsular Hispanist of the 1930s Russell was fortunate in having practically the entire field for the choosing in all its richness. A case in point was the Portuguese dramatist and poet Gil Vicente (c. 1465–c. 1536):

> I want to write a short story based on the *Barca do Inferno* [play of 1516] of Gil Vicente. Also would like to do an article on him for some English literary review; here he is unknown and yet he is that remarkable if not unique thing a medieval dramatist, and a good one. Also he expresses some important but lesser-known aspects of the medieval mind. [140]

Not the least of the compensations was the discovery that he rather enjoyed teaching:

> Teaching is something I like and I am now sure that I was wise to take it up. I have some 25 pupils and a number of them are intelligent, interesting and pleasant. One would like to make all one's teaching suggestive rather than instructive: I am endeavouring to work out ways and means of applying this — of course it can only be done with the more intelligent ones. I am still so young that I have easy personal connections with them: it is rather sad to think that in [the] nature of things this must end. [141]

---

[139] Journal, 20 Feb. 1938.
[140] Journal, 25 Sept. 1937. There is no evidence that either the short story or the article were ever completed.
[141] Journal, 20 Feb. 1938.

To suggest rather than to instruct was the guiding principle of Russell's teaching style under the expanding mantle of his gravitas, erudition and life experience.

*

In the summer of 1936 Russell made a first prolonged visit to Portugal to visit the Arquivo da Torre do Tombo in Lisbon, beginning with a few weeks in Estoril which provided just the tonic he needed to draw out 'the troublesome metaphysics of the north': [142]

> Here is sun, air and health. Yesterday for the first time for a whole year I lay on the beach in the sun for 4 hours and let the sun sink into me. Sunbathing is an intellectual as well as a physical pleasure of the highest order. The purely physical satisfaction of allowing one's body complete surrender to the sun's rays becomes finally a separation of spirit and body as if the sun had taken one's body to itself and simply left the spirit behind in the delicious warm emptiness to be found by the breeze. Such romantic visions soon retire when night comes and one's crimson flesh is lacerated by the touch of the sheets but it is well worth it. [143]

Here too was blessed relief from the acrid atmosphere of England, a chance 'to put off the Oxford term-time personality and forget academic etiquette and manners', [144] the call of an unselfconscious and deintellectualised life, an invitation, in short, to psychic surrender:

> Writing this in my bedroom in the late evening one notices the essential foreignness of the street and other *moeurs* — frequent shrieking and crunch of tyres being driven too fast around the corner by the hotel, the patter of donkeys drawing carts, rattle of lattice blinds, high-pitched female conversation, unkempt barking of dogs, rattling rustle of wind in palm leaves, shouting of youths and banging of doors, motor engines being raced etc. […] When I lie in bed at night the breeze comes straight off the dark and invisible sea and is deliciously cool. [145]

---

[142] Journal, 28 July 1938.
[143] Journal, 22 July 1936.
[144] Journal, 28 July 1938.
[145] Journal, 23 July 1936.

Russell was *en route* to Lisbon by sea when the Spanish Civil War broke out on 17 July. Nine days later he was in receipt of a week-old copy of *The Times* which served not to enlighten him on that conflict but to sharpen the contrast between the bourgeois English life he despised and the uncomplicated realities of Portugal, however impoverished:

> This wretched business in Spain goes on and the lies pour out in such quantities that one has no idea what is really happening. How odd to receive the *Times* here — all those absurd English religious dog-fights, acknowledgments by the Chancellor of the Exchequer of 'conscience money', stiff notices of London clubs about summer closing of their premises, the heavy and over-prolonged humours of the correspondence columns, the pompous and self-satisfied leader, the subtle 'arrangement' of news in the right direction, all these and many other rather <u>unattractive</u> manifestations of life in England stand out in the freer atmosphere of this little country with its flies, its dust, its poverty and yet its apparent spiritual freedom — even if the latter is nothing more real than a little sensualism and good-humoured contentment sandwiched between a military dictatorship and hunger. Nevertheless the awful dead weight of English 'code life', of English class distinction, of an inane kind of English hypocrisy — or fear of one's self, all these are lifted, and free one's mind somewhat. I believe that one can only retain one's mental integrity by frequent visits to Latin lands, and then only if one makes the <u>effort</u>. [146]

Russell was a severe critic of the Franco regime in later life but his opinions on the Civil War at the time it broke out were in the conservative vein of his earlier years, to which a measure of resignation and indifference was now added:

> All talk here is of the revolution in Spain. There seems to be no proof of any wide popular support for the rebels though they are receiving some. If the news is to be believed at all and the fighting and bitterness is as great as is said then Spain is passing through a very 'tragic' time — not however that it is unexpected. Between [the] two evils of Bolshevism and Fascism I suppose one must plump for the latter and there seems to

---

[146] Journal, 26 July 1936. The Chancellor of the Exchequer was Neville Chamberlain.

be no other choice. The armed communist youth defending Madrid and Barcelona seem courageous, if barbaric, in their behaviour. The real reason why I have a somewhat unwilling desire for the fascists to win is that the Spanish extreme Left is responsible for the division of the land into the state of affairs when Civil War becomes inevitable though God knows Spanish Catholics and the political Right and the aristocracy and lower middle classes are the most stupid, uncultured, avaricious and selfish egoists of their kind, they almost deserve Bolshevism. Anyway the result is by no means clear yet. [147]

Russell surely had in mind the radical violence he had witnessed in Madrid in May 1931 and both there and in Granada in the spring of 1936, fuelled in the latter case by a belief, first asserted during the uprising of October 1934, that only a left-wing government was acceptable in a democratic society. [148]

At home the outbreak of the Civil War not only exposed divided loyalties in British Hispanism but roused a latent prejudice (contributed to in some degree by articles in *The Catholic Herald*) that held Spanish literature to be essentially of interest to Catholic students, eliciting a reaction even among those with private misgivings about Franco and his actions. [149] If these expressions were as Russell recalled less pronounced in the Oxford faculty than elsewhere, particularly at Cambridge where the liberal Professor J. B. Trend and the young don A. A. Parker occupied different poles on the spectrum, at least one member of staff took sides in the conflict, the essayist, historian and literary critic Enrique Moreno Báez having to be removed by Entwistle in September 1938 for delivering pro-Republican propaganda instead of lectures on Lope de Vega. [150] Entwistle himself remained studiously impartial, but Russell, then starting out as a lecturer and always a man very conscious of his image, inevitably found himself questioning his association with the field as a whole, as here in August 1936:

> Sometimes when I think I am in a sense tied to things Spanish I am horrified beyond measure and it is lucky for my peace of mind that it is

[147] Journal, 23 July 1936.
[148] RSSR.
[149] RSSR and Margaret Joan Anstee, *JB: An Unlikely Spanish Don. The Life and Times of Professor John Brande Trend* (Eastbourne, E. Sussex: Sussex Academic Press, 2013), 193.
[150] RSSR and Anstee, *JB*, 154–6. Anstee avoids the subject, but the staunch Catholic Parker left Cambridge to take up the chair at Aberdeen in 1939.

with Anglo-Peninsular historical connections that I look like being connected. It at least provides an escape from the feeling of being chained to a dead animal which I should otherwise have. [151]

Such feelings could only be enhanced in the intellectual hothouse of Oxford where public debate focused on the various initiatives of the OU Spanish Democratic Defence Committee. Russell retained his ambivalence, and in words of characteristic subtlety recalled his reservations at those, mainly sympathisers of the Republic, who despite never having shown the least interest in Spain were ready to take up arms and kill Spaniards. [152] His views hadn't changed much by September 1937:

> There really is so much to be said for and against both sides that a person of reasonably good will must find any cut and dried enthusiasm for either difficult. All the new novels by our young Left-wing novelists now end by the hero going to Spain to fight for 'FREEDOM'. Alas could they both see what freedom of that sort looks like at close quarters they mightn't be so keen. I at least have seen one side. [153]

A visit to Nationalist Galicia the following summer completed the picture. His memoir of 1992 provides the bare context:

> I went to Spain during the Civil War — twice to look after two or three undergraduates who, otherwise, would not have been able to have any on-the-spot experience of the language. We went far behind the lines in Nationalist territory because it was safer. [154]

However, immediacy allowed no such concision. Here are the impressions of Vigo Russell committed to his journal in late August 1938:

> Gradually one becomes aware of the sullen opposition to the régime which exists among all classes except the remnants of the aristocracy and the monied classes. Fishermen, waiters and especially and surprisingly the peasantry are only too ready to express to an Englishman their dislike of

---

[151] Journal, 3 Aug. 1936.
[152] RSSR.
[153] Journal, 25 Sept. 1937.
[154] PELR, 3.

affairs as they are — to them it means that their sons are taken off to fight for a cause which at the best does not interest them. The condition of the Galician peasantry is desperate. The young men are taken off to fight, many have been shot as enemies of the régime, others are still in refuge in the hills and now the old men and the women are forced to struggle with an already poverty-stricken soil to try and maintain their farms. Another trouble affecting seriously the poor here is the lack of clothing. There is no doubt that Franco has shot a great number of people. Here in Vigo in the early days it was a question of self-preservation and the soldiers and Civil Guard forced the revolution as a tiny minority on the mass of the people. The whole town council was shot and every local Left Wing leader within reach and similar scenes must have taken place in many other towns. The Civil Guard certainly took a fearful vengeance for the years of humiliation under the Republic. Up in the Castro [fortress] in the early hours of the morning the firing-squad can still be heard at work, a few weeks ago no less than 28 were shot in a batch. There is no one left to focus the mass resentment and the populace is terrified so there will almost certainly be no successful rising unless a series of defeats rouses the mob and causes sufficient demoralisation among the Army. The general opinion is that the increasing ascendancy of the Phalangistas and the establishment of a Civil Government here have destroyed the hopes which were raised on all sides of the long-awaited Renacimiento. [155]

On his return to England Russell published an anonymous account of the journey in *The Oxford Magazine*, less a travelogue than a penetrating analysis of the sociopolitical condition of Galicia under Franco in what turned out to be the closing phase of the war, this in a country uniformly exhausted after two years of bloodletting:

'Esto no puede continuar.' Whether it was on the deserted quays of a great port, in the greying time-mellowed streets of an ancient ecclesiastical city like Santiago de Compostela, or in the desolate villages of Spanish Galicia, this phrase of impotent war-weariness, constantly repeated, formed the general comment on the war. [...] Civil War is always an abomination, but surely never more so than in Spain now. The

---

[155] Journal, 29 Aug. 1938.

vast majority of her people want to live at peace with each other, and care no longer, if they ever did, for extremisms and alien political creeds. Yet for the moment it is difficult to see any possible solution which Spanish pride could stomach. [156]

If his aim was to nullify a purely binary approach to the war in Spain he succeeded. In its layering, pragmatism and insight this article can in retrospect be reckoned the first time Russell placed the ripening fruit of his critical mind before a broader readership. His concluding remarks were prophetic:

> The attempt by Spaniards to carry out the process of *europeización* advocated by the philosophers of the Republic has not been an encouraging one. Whatever the final outcome of the war it seems probable that Spain will return to her former isolation from Europe for which she now feels a deep distrust. [157]

Sixty years later Russell presented his 'Recollections of the Second Spanish Republic' to a graduate seminar in Oxford. During it he reaffirmed one of his indelible impressions from the years between 1931 and 1936, namely that Spaniards of all political stripes were agreed on one point and one point only: that their country's problems would only be resolved through bloodshed. So it proved, but Russell like most onlookers stood aghast at the atavistic brutality unleashed by the Civil War, one he felt might have been averted had Spain experienced the horrors of mechanised warfare shared by every other major state in Europe from 1914–18.

As time passed it emerged that Russell had been no mere spectator of the conflict but experienced its realities personally. Student exposure to colloquial Spanish and tours of fourteenth-century battlefields provided the ostensible reason for his presence in Spain, but he had, possibly not for the first time, been approached by British intelligence for a task of greater moment. [158] The virtue of

---

[156] 'Spain, 1938', *The Oxford Magazine*, 10 Nov. 1938, 146–9, & 17 Nov. 1938, 179–81; at 148 & 180.
[157] *Ibid.*, 180–1.
[158] Anecdotal evidence suggests that Russell had already been approached by British intelligence, having supposedly fulfilled an assignment in Hungary in the summer of 1935 or spring of 1936 in connection with Jusztinián György Serédi, Cardinal Archbishop of Esztergom and Prince Primate; I owe this memory to Eric Southworth and Nick Clapton. The

these tours, enabled by visas issued by a Spanish agent in London, was that they provided cover for espionage. A first trip to the Canaries in 1937 presented no special risk and has no known intelligence component, but the second to the Peninsula a year later provided the opportunity, among other things, for monitoring the movements of Nationalist warships from Galician ports. These vessels had interfered with the passage of British goods into Republican Bilbao in the spring of 1937 but with the fall of the Basque Country in June of that year were redeployed to the Mediterranean where the Royal Navy was struggling to fulfil its non-intervention patrol duties against the backdrop of operations by declared and undeclared belligerents.

The Hotel Continental in Vigo where Russell dined with officers of the German Condor Legion in August 1938. Author's collection

That Russell's was more than just an *ad hoc* engagement is suggested by allusions in later years to Alan Hillgarth, British vice consul in Palma de Mallorca and subsequently naval attaché in Madrid, as well as other operatives, Spaniards included. The impression is that he had been drawn into Britain's nascent secret intelligence organisation in Spain, albeit at a peripheral level. Whatever the case, the latter assignment, requiring the issue in Vigo of local *salvoconductos* for travel

fact that the archives of MI6 remain closed prevents any link to that organisation being explored. I am grateful to Denis Smyth for his assistance on this topic.

first to the provinces of Asturias and Santander and then to La Coruña and Lugo, almost cost Russell his life in August 1938 when he was arrested by the Guardia Civil photographing the cruiser *Canarias* from the Islas de Cíes in the Ría de Vigo. His position was made the more precarious by the discovery that not only was he sharing the Hotel Continental in Vigo with a rotation of uniformed officers of the German Condor Legion whose presence in Spain was then officially denied, but had photographed and dined with them on at least one occasion. [159] 'I was in trouble if something didn't happen' he recalled. Though facing execution or at least lengthy incarceration following an interrogation by the Falange during which he was accused of being a communist and a spy, he was eventually released (so Russell said) on the orders of Franco himself and with the intervention of the same German officers. [160] After great difficulty arranging exit papers (requiring a letter of recommendation from the British ambassador residing in Republican-held Valencia), Russell made for the border town of Túy with his undergraduate tutee and friend Derek Hamblen. [161] Here in the Civil Guard barracks Russell renewed an earlier acquaintance with the military governor of Galicia who duly expelled him from Spain as a danger to the security of the state.

Their trials were not, however, quite over. Reaching the latticed bridge over the Minho that constitutes the frontier with Portugal they found no means of getting their luggage across so had to traverse it on foot, secure the services of a mule-cart and return awkwardly perched alongside the driver to the Spanish side to collect their things before making good their escape. The incident was not lacking in humour but Russell would recall his progress across the bridge with machine guns at his back as the longest of his life. [162]

Thereafter whenever the subject of Franco arose in conversation he was wont to recall how he owed his life to the Caudillo. By the interposition of such intense personal experiences both physical and psychological were received views

[159] Journal, 5 Aug. 1938 & 21 Sept. 1946. Several of Russell's obituarists (including the author) identify the hotel as the Atlántico as recalled by him in conversation and repeated in RSSR; the correct identification is confirmed in his records including the bill for an eight-day stay ending on 29 August 1938.
[160] Alastair Saunders, email and comments to the author, 29 March 2024.
[161] Journal, 15 Sept. 1938, and RSSR.
[162] Departure from Spain may not, however, have been the end of Russell's trials since he would recount having sheltered in the Escondidinho restaurant in Porto while being pursued by the PIDE (Portuguese secret police) in 1938; see João Gouveia Monteiro, 'Sir Peter E. Russell: The 20th Century in the Palm of His Hand' at <www.brown.edu/Departments/Portuguese_Brazilian_Studies/ejph/html/issue9/html/jmonteiro_main.html>.

and conventional wisdom demolished, a reminder to himself and to others that nothing in this life is either readily interpreted or static in the mind.

Lying between this and his next visit to Spain eight years later was the gulf of the Second World War, the formative experience in Peter Russell's life.

'The longest walk of my life.' The International Bridge at Túy. Author's collection

CHAPTER THREE
S'en va-t-en guerre (1939–1946)

When it finally came in September 1939 the outbreak of the Second World War found Russell as mentally prepared as he could be. Already at the time of the Sudeten Crisis the previous autumn he had recorded that 'a cold shiver of fear passed down my back' as he contemplated the destruction of Western civilisation and all he held dear, writing on 15 September 1938 of 'the horror of this threat in which one's own Mother, family and friends may be blown to pieces or suffocated in one's presence or remain to face untold miseries'. The danger was averted by Chamberlain's first visit to Hitler at the Berghof that same day only to rise again in all its terror two weeks later. After a few days with his mother at her new home in Jersey Russell returned to Southampton to find that the Army had mobilised. In a state of despair he drove to see his closest friend Derek Hamblen in East Grinstead who by contrast he found 'rather elated by the excitement of the whole thing':

> We had a long talk in the late hours of the night and it was with a feeling of almost physical sickness that I thought all the time that it might be the last time that we should talk like that in the world as we know it now, and that a horrible fate might overtake him and all my other pupils, but Derek especially. I do not now mind what happens to me if Mother, Hugh, Derek and all my other friends and pupils are not mutilated or killed or involved in special suffering. How brave they all are! At least this horrific time has revealed to me that we have more moral principles and vastly more courage than I could ever have believed, perhaps partly because we cannot possibly conceive more than a fraction of what threatens.[1]

Not for the first or the last time in his life did Russell find that his heightened perception gave him an insight into permutations of which others for good or ill

---
[1] Journal, 29 Sept. 1938.

remained unaware. Arriving back in Oxford he hastened to the Town Hall to join a throng of people assembling gas masks, three hours during which 'we were able to forget the threat and all its terrifying meaning'. At Queen's he filled out a card volunteering for 'interpreterships, administrative work or anything else here or abroad', believing that the heart murmur diagnosed by his Uncle Gerald fifteen years earlier barred him from any form of active service. To Russell's inexpressible relief news came the following day 30 September of the signing of the Munich Agreement: 'It is as if we had ceased to live at all and had suddenly found our numbed minds and nerves brought to life again. Surely we shall not be thrown into the abyss again after this when so many men are trying to bring into play all that is best in man to save us.'

Still, the threat of war did not recede and Russell proceeded like his forebears on the eve of the Great War to enjoy a social year unmatched since his undergraduate days, aided by the generous set of rooms he inhabited at Queen's: 'There are many sides to Oxford which I am growing to dislike more and more but the social opportunities are [an] amusing relief and whatever their particular defects [the] people concerned are intelligent or at least clever and/or interesting material for dissection.' [2] When the possibility of war again hove into sight in July 1939 it was greeted in a very different frame of mind from the previous September:

> We have become accustomed to the horrifying prospect of a modern intensive war and one's gorge no longer rises as one faces the probabilities and possibilities. A curious fatalism mixed with determination now dominates. Nazi Germany and Fascist Italy are divided from us by an intellectual, moral, political and social chasm too wide to make understanding possible and the thought of living in circumstances such as the German people live in now acts as a focus for our national resistance. [3]

As Russell recalled, 'The general feeling was to end up, if it was to end up, with a complete enjoyment of our last months of peace.' It may have been in this spirit that he set forth on a frantic drive through France to Switzerland on 10 August though it is hard to imagine the risk-averse Russell venturing onto the Continent

---

[2] Journal, 2 Jan. [1939].
[3] Journal, 15 July 1939.

for purely recreational purposes as battle lines were drawn. His 1992 memoir records him as having been recruited for Military Intelligence in 1939 and as in Galicia the previous year he may have travelled on government business and certainly it has no other known purpose. [4] Whatever the case, the trip, which began at Boulogne with stops at Strasbourg, Zürich, Geneva, Chamonix and Grenoble, served to indulge his love of Alpine landscape, the highlight being the Bernese Oberland. 'Tired of motoring and shall be glad to get to Nice. Hitler may make me hurry back' he wrote in Grenoble on the 20th but made his first visit to Provence all the same ('one thought of Cézanne and Daudet and the troubadours'). Ignoring the mounting danger, Russell pressed on for the Côte d'Azur passing countless vehicles heading north away from the Italian border. Only on the morning of the 24th after several days spent along the Riviera did he open a newspaper and, learning of the Molotov–Ribbentrop Pact, decide to join the general exodus and make for Saint-Malo with a view to visiting his mother in Jersey. The drive as he looked back on it in May 1941 was a memorable one:

> It was raining heavily along the road to Avignon and traffic was tremendous as all of the Riviera's holiday crowds fled to their homes while troops — largely black — and guns moved up to the Italian frontier. I remember seeing lorries overturned in what now seem incredible numbers. The stream of cars was tremendous. Eventually I remember getting clear of the Paris-bound traffic and entering the flat plain of Provence near Avignon. I had some idea that the outbreak of war would probably lead to the bombing of the Rhône bridges so crossed to Villeneuve and put up at a curious guest house […] There was an air of near panic among the Frenchmen there but somehow I felt vastly safer with the Rhône behind me. […] In Nîmes I saw the fresh white notices calling out the 'classes' of several years and the streams of men struggling unhappily towards their barracks. The drive northwards after that was through pure Utrillo country and I am now glad that I was bold enough to delay so long to see the real towns and villages and white churches of Provence off the main roads. I had no clear idea of my route except to keep going more or less north-west and eventually got into the Gorges of the Tarn country moving towards Mende. [5]

[4] PELR, 3.
[5] Memoir, 1 May 1941.

At this point Russell's journey met its first obstruction. The blockage of the main road northward forced him into an arduous drive across the Auvergne complicated by a dwindling supply of fuel. At Mende his car was the target of a 'drunken peasant' who shattered its windscreen with a stone, requiring strenuous efforts to obtain a replacement. By the time he reached Clermont-Ferrand in the early hours of the following morning the French government had imposed a blackout and all garages had been commandeered. A few hours' sleep and Russell resumed his journey across the heart of France:

> The next day was the longest motor drive I have ever done but I remember it as one of the most beautiful days I have ever spent in France. As one gradually came into the lovely meadow country of Touraine after lunching at Châteauroux the sky was a deep blue and the sun poured down on the fields and green meadows and grass-edged roads and poplar trees. A country of long flat views to castles really like those one saw on French railway posters and odd remote farm houses or standoffish parks which made one think of Juan Ramón Jiménez. France certainly gave me a grand finale all for my own benefit.

Russell's great love of France no doubt owed much to the memory of this journey which continued through Brittany to Laval and at length to Saint-Malo where he boarded a ship for Jersey. Anxious to get home, Russell lingered only a day with his mother before sailing for Southampton. Here is the Oxford to which he returned in the last days of peace:

> Oxford awaiting the outbreak of war was a typical mixture of wild rumour, apprehension, indifference and sense. For myself I awaited the catastrophe with alarm but also with the regrettable tenseness of excitement. One's reason painted a picture of what would happen to one's life only too vividly but I also felt for the first time the evil thrill of war. Perhaps as excuse one might say one was more afraid of Chamberlain letting us escape again with shame than of war itself.

Hitler having occupied the rest of Czechoslovakia in March 1939, Russell had lost the sympathy for appeasement he had first acquired in 1934. Chamberlain's famous broadcast on Sunday 3 September he missed after being called away to take someone to the Radcliffe Infirmary but the war soon imposed itself all the same:

S'EN VA-T-EN GUERRE (1939–1946)

For the next four days chaos reigned. The Ministry of Home Security descended and occupied a wing of the front quad. The College was filled with shoddily dressed typists and lower grade rude civil servants. The typists spent most of their time, so it seemed, carrying teapots and kettles of boiling water for their frequent libations. One night a mob of unhappy but uncomplaining London mothers and their children descended on the College and we had to bed them down.

Beyond these developments, the first sounding of an air raid siren on 4 September, the removal of the College's books and manuscripts to the beer cellar and the construction of a shelter in the Fellows' Garden, 'life was distressingly normal all things considered'. The salient feature of the Queen's senior common room in those early months of the war was the exhibition made of himself by Provost R. H. Hodgkin:

> We had all our meals in the Taberdars Room as the kitchens were being redecorated. The Provost relapsed with fussy zeal into the mood of August 1914 and was a good deal put out at finding that the same enthusiastic zeal for rushing out and getting killed without training or meditation did not appear as strong in Queen's Common Room in 1939 as it did in 1914. He waited impatiently for a few days and then, finding no one had departed, remarked one day at dinner 'in the last war boys of 16 went off immediately to join up but, of course, they were keen.' Of course no one could go owing to our reservation under the Schedule. This gradually dawned on the Provost, who had been busy sending out unauthorised letters to undergraduates and freshmen telling them to go off as the College would certainly close [...] The curse of dons is that in moments of crisis they tend to become petty.

One who did return to his regiment was Russell's former French tutor Wilfred House, requiring Russell to take over his pupils in that language:

> I was pleased at this as it meant for the first time most of my teaching was in College and I had a wider variety of subjects to teach and, on the whole, a more interesting selection of pupils. [...] [M]uch of it was matter I had not touched since Schools but I managed on the whole adequately — though it was hard work.

One of these students, a brilliant German Jewish *émigré* named Karl Lehmann, was taken away by a detective for internment one morning in July 1940, a victim of the prevailing panic and the corresponding administrative reaction. 'I did what I could to mobilise people to get him out and was eventually successful some six months later.' [6]

Russell also took up Russian, apparently with official sanction, and worked on his thesis in his spare time but otherwise things continued much as usual:

> So we settled down to the anticlimax of the first months of the War. For a while [Wilfred] Harrison [Fellow in Politics at Queen's] and I spent a night a week in the Oxford Air Raid Prevention control room but we fairly soon gave this up, largely because of an unattractive and officious little hunchback who ran it. […] It was a cold and dark winter but we didn't suffer much — far better if we had. One often went for days without realising the final implications of the War, doped most successfully by the complacency of our own propaganda and the mendacity of that of the French. […] I must admit that I had long since ceased to regard the war as anything but a silly annoyance.

Life was even less altered in Jersey where Russell was able to visit his mother over the first Christmas and Easter of the war:

> It seemed as if the war had passed Jersey by even more than it had ceased to affect England. I cannot remember that I did anything unusual except enjoy those domestic pleasures which often then seemed so pedestrian and which even now I cannot realise are cut off from me by a hostile if invisible front line: one's own comfortable bed and familiar belongings; food home-cooked; fire, wash-table and comfortable chairs; the right to come and go as one pleased and do nothing if one did not wish to; Mother's voice calling to meals in that high-pitched call she used for that purpose; her petty troubles with tradesmen and the maid Freda and her pride in the garden. […] We often denounced the comforts and complacency of our bourgeois family life in those days — what fools we mortals etc.

---

[6] Following his release Lehmann went on to a career with the BBC Monitoring Service; he died in September 2022 at the age of 101; <www.leightonpark.com/karl-lehmann-s1939/>.

S'EN VA-T-EN GUERRE (1939–1946)

However, the war was coming closer by degrees:

> Gradually the vast disaster of May–June 1940 began to trace its cracks across the newspapers. [...] Each day the radio and newspapers were more threatening [...] by what they did not [say] as by what they did. At Queen's we spent much time playing bowls on the lawns in the warm summer afternoons. Dunkirk brought a momentary relief and tired undergraduates of the year before returned to Oxford for a few days to rest and wonder at themselves. Gradually it became apparent that France was really down and out. I could hardly believe that Paris was occupied by Germans.

As Allied resistance collapsed in the face of the Wehrmacht Russell's first thought was for his mother in Jersey:

> When Hitler's armies reached Amiens I rang up Mother in Jersey and told her to come over prepared for a long stay. I failed to realise what I was asking nor the supine complacency of the Channel Islands Governments. She was astonished at my suggestion and only agreed to come over for a few days in a fortnight's time. There was nothing I could do but hope the place would not be occupied before then. [...] One day early in June Mother arrived. She brought only three suitcases and said she was only staying for a week or two before returning to Jersey. I put her in Bardwell Court. How to break the news that she was a refugee and that years might pass before she saw her home and belongings again? [7]

In the meantime news that the age of reservation for university teachers was to be raised to thirty in August led to an introduction by someone Russell refers to in his journal as Sinclair to a Major John D. Kennedy of Military Intelligence (Research) — MI(R) — a short-lived division of the Directorate of Military Intelligence (DMI) and forerunner of the Special Operations Executive (SOE) concerned with irregular warfare and subversion under military as against civilian command: 'I went up to see him and thought him charming; he seemed certain he could employ me and spoke of an immediate commission or, at the worst,

---

[7] Jersey was occupied on 1 July 1940.

going straight to an Officer Cadet Training Unit [OCTU].'[8] This contact in early June 1940 coincided with an invitation from the Portuguese government for Russell and Professor Entwistle to attend the celebrations being held to commemorate the eighth centenary of the foundation of Portugal and the 300th anniversary of the Portuguese Restoration War, this as part of a delegation led by the Duke of Kent. The invitation was likely prompted not only by the paper on the court of Philippa of Lancaster as Queen of Portugal Russell and Entwistle had submitted to the related academic congress which opened on 1 July but by the strategic bestowal by Oxford of an honorary doctorate on the Portuguese dictator Salazar in May.[9] Aside from this the British Council had asked Russell to deliver a lecture for them while he was in Lisbon 'and examine Council work there' which may have been code for some dimension of intelligence.[10] By whatever means these arrangements caught the attention of MI(R) whose wheels, however, proved slow in turning:

> I had a first taste of the incompetence of the 'I' section of the War Office. Kennedy procrastinated — one minute holding out the prospect of me as assistant military attaché in Lisbon; the next denying all knowledge of me — the whole in an impeccable accent with heavy layers of charm. [...] Meanwhile I had had more interviews and letters with Kennedy and his partner in incompetence [Maj. Lionel] Kenyon; blandishments, attractive offers of employment, total ignorance of one's existence varied the order. Eventually I got a priority passage on a seaplane to Lisbon after various steamship sailings had been cancelled. The day before I left [i.e. 29 June] I went to see Kennedy for the last time. He wrote out on a sheet of War Office notepaper various questions concerned with the political and military situation in Portugal — this I was to carry with me; the whole affair was a gross

---

[8] Memoir, 1 May 1941. See Malcolm Atkin, *Pioneers of Irregular Warfare: Secrets of the Military Intelligence Research Department in the Second World War* (Barnsley, S. Yorks.: Pen & Sword, 2021).

[9] 'A Rainha D. Felipa e sua córte' in *Congresso do Mundo Portugués: Publicações* (Lisbon: Comissão Executiva dos Centenários, 1940), II, 319–46; on wartime relations between Oxford and the Portuguese government, see Ian Michael, 'Afterword: Spanish at Oxford, 1595–1998', *Bulletin of Hispanic Studies* (Glasgow) 76 (1999), 173–93; at 183–4.

[10] Memoir, 19 Jan. 1941. For the context see Frances Donaldson, *The British Council: The First Fifty Years* (London: Jonathan Cape, 1984), 84–6.

abuse of Portuguese official friendship but in the circumstances of the time perhaps it was excusable. [11]

The 'circumstances' in question related to the imminent arrival in Portugal of the Duke and Duchess of Windsor who had fled Paris on 16 May six days after Germany launched its offensive in the West, heading first to their home on Cap d'Antibes and at length to Barcelona and Madrid where they arrived in a four-vehicle convoy on 23 June. [12] Four days later the German Army reached the Pyrenees making the continued presence of the ducal couple in Spain a matter of grave concern to the British government. After spending much of June at forty-eight hours' notice to travel by sea or air with constant delays and changes of plan — attributable no doubt to the evolving status of the Windsor matter — Russell was ordered to appear at Poole harbour at 5 a.m. on the 30th for the eight-hour flight to Lisbon via Madrid in an Empire flying boat. Among the handful of passengers was the noted figure of Walter Starkie, travelling to take up his position as first director of the British Council in Madrid whose distracting flow of conversation covered, among other topics, the sex habits of Hungarian gypsies and the relationship between music and sexual precocity. [13] The result was anticlimactic. After hours taxiing up and down the harbour in driving rain the British Overseas Airways Corporation abandoned the flight for mechanical reasons and conveyed its passengers to the Royal Bath Hotel in Bournemouth. In the end it was decided that the chances of the plane becoming airborne would be improved by taking only two passengers and, rather to his relief, Russell was not among them. 'I returned to Oxford after a further interview with Kennedy, who had already, as I expected, once more denied knowledge of my existence.' [14]

Russell was no doubt somewhat disenchanted with the workings of British intelligence but though no detailed mention is made of it in his memoirs his service was in fact about to begin in earnest. The arrival of the Windsors in Lisbon on 3 July galvanised the British authorities with well-founded fears of persuasion,

---

[11] Memoir, 1 May 1941.
[12] Michael Bloch, *The Duke of Windsor's War* (London: Weidenfeld & Nicolson, 1982), 76–103. See also Ronald Weber, *The Lisbon Route: Entry and Escape in Nazi Europe* (Landham, Md.: Ivan R. Dee, 2011), 146–51.
[13] Memoir, 19 Jan. 1941. On Starkie see Marina Pérez de Arcos, 'Education, Intelligence and Cultural Diplomacy at the British Council in Madrid, 1940–1941', *Bulletin of Spanish Studies* 98 (2021), no. 4, 527–55, & no. 5, 707–38.
[14] Memoir, 1 May 1941.

inveiglement, coercion or even abduction through German or Spanish channels. [15] Much disgruntled at the treatment meted out to him and his wife by the British establishment after the abdication, the Duke had been an admirer and an appeaser of the Nazi regime as the main bulwark against communism and had latterly become a defeatist. Concerns in London were heightened after the couple took up residence in Cascais at the home of the Duke's friend Ricardo do Espírito Santo Silva, a Portuguese banker with ties to Berlin. Russell's passport shows that he eventually left Poole for Lisbon on 10 July having been drawn into the effort to usher the Duke and Duchess out of Portugal to the Bahamas, over which the former was appointed Governor by a British establishment as determined to keep him out of Britain as it was anxious to get him out of Europe. Meanwhile, German and Spanish agents were putting it about that the British secret services were themselves plotting to abduct the Duke or worse. [16] There is no evidence that the Duke gave much credence to these rumours, or of any traitorous intent for that matter, but Russell would tell how he was under orders to shoot the couple if they threatened to fall into German hands during their nightly visits to the casino at Estoril. [17] In the event, he enjoyed cordial relations with the Windsors whom he found charming and intelligent and in later years would characteristically not brook too much criticism of them. Russell's memory of them equates to that reported by Francine Farkas who knew the Windsors in the early 1970s: 'Her conversation was animated and she could talk engagingly about business or politics and especially food... He was the most charming person with real presence. Though a small man physically, people parted in front of him... People liked being with them.' [18] Russell was back in England by the time the Windsors sailed for Bermuda in the American liner *Excalibur* on 1 August; they reached the Bahamas safely on the 17th. For these exertions on behalf of the Crown he was apparently paid £50 plus £15 in expenses. [19]

---

[15] Michael Bloch, *Operation Willi: The Nazi Plot to Kidnap the Duke of Windsor, July 1940* (London: Weidenfeld & Nicolson, 1984).

[16] Philip Ziegler, *King Edward VIII: The Official Biography* (London: Collins, 1990), 431–2.

[17] Ian Michael mentions being told by Russell that he was accompanied by an armed naval officer as escort; 'Sir Peter Russell (1913–2006)', *Bulletin of Spanish Studies* 83 (2006), 1133–44; at 1136.

[18] Cited in Andrew Lownie, *Traitor King: The Scandalous Exile of the Duke and Duchess of Windsor* (London: Blink Publishing, 2021), 330–1.

[19] Itemised statements of the account held by Russell with the Oxford branch of the Westminster Bank survive, with interruptions, from June 1939 to November 1943. £50 in 1940 equates to approximately £2,300 in 2024.

Russell as the Duke and Duchess of Windsor knew him, from his passport as a wartime intelligence officer.

Russell had been due to start an OCTU course with other MI(R) nominees in late July but 'Kennedy's department made a mess of my calling-up' with the result that he did not report to Ramillies Barracks, Marlborough Lines, Aldershot until 23 August. In the interim, and as the Battle of Britain unfolded in the skies above, he was involved in preparing the contingency plans for the occupation of the Canary Islands in the event Franco invaded Gibraltar or allowed German troops safe passage across Spain to do so. This apparently involved an aerial reconnaissance of Las Palmas during which he noted the topographical inaccuracy of the late-eighteenth century Admiralty charts being used to plan the landings. [20] It was typical of the lack of preparedness that marked Britain's entry into the Second World War and the parade of muddle and ignorance he would have occasion to witness at first hand over the next five years. Of this and Army life generally he soon had the fullest immersion in Aldershot, recalling

> The voice of bull-necked Colour Sergeant Major Guy bellowing 'Get on Parade'. One's days as platoon and company commander, tactical exercises, field firing, cycling in mud and rain, endless cleaning and polish[ing] of boots. […] The ghastly stand-to in full equipment in the early hours of the dawn; frequent bombing one soon learnt to ignore. [21]

After Aldershot came Droitwich in Worcestershire and abominable living conditions ('mud, no water, constipation, damp') in November, the nadir reached when he was transferred to the Barnsley Hall mental hospital in Bromsgrove after contracting pneumonia ('Shut up with lunatics. Bombs every night. Grandeurs and miseries'). [22] In December he was sent home to Oxford on sick leave which effectively marked the end of his basic training. Mistakenly assigned to the Durham Light Infantry, Russell was eventually commissioned a 2nd Lieutenant in the Intelligence Corps on 20 December 1940. Nonetheless, Russell appreciated the order and discipline and in retrospect found his training to have been a positive experience:

> Looking back on this now I think it was very much less appalling than I expected it to be. Ten years of Oxford had given me a suppressed regret I had not done more active things; now I had an active life in all conscience! But I found I was able to become quite a good cadet after the initial bewilderment was over and the technical side of the course was interesting enough. The worst feature was long periods of boredom. But quite a new sort of cameraderie [*sic*] for me made up for this and the pill was sweetened by the belief — quite unfounded in fact — that the Military Intelligence people would not have to do the full 4 months. Haslam, the Company commander, was an amusing wit in a domine's

---

[20] Xon de Ros, notes to the author, 16 Sept. 2020.
[21] Memoir, 19 Jan. 1941.
[22] Memoir, 1 May 1941.

[*sic*] way but unreliable and given to fits of frank sadism. […] It was a hard life — I used to have some idea I had a weak heart but now know this to have been a myth as I could do everything in the training. [23]

Uncle Gerald's childhood diagnosis of a heart murmur had spared Russell the horror of team sports but fostered a more insidious demon in the recesses of his mind, a sense of himself as not being a man of action. This the war only partly dismissed, and asked in later years which book most accurately described life in the wartime services he had no hesitation in citing Evelyn Waugh's *Officers and Gentlemen* (1955). [24]

*

As luck would have it Russell's next posting after a month's leave was to Oriel College where the Intelligence Corps had its wartime headquarters. Early in the new year he was sent to the War Intelligence Course at Smedley's Hydro in Derbyshire following which he returned to Oriel for further training after being earmarked for service in Spain. This phase came to an abrupt halt on the night of 21 March 1941 when the car in which he was a passenger ran into a stationary lorry in the blackout after supper in Burford. Rushed to Oxford, Russell nearly died on the operating table in the Radcliffe Infirmary before spending four or five days unconscious. With severe facial lacerations and fractures of both jaws he was sent to Park Prewett Hospital near Basingstoke for reconstructive surgery by the great New Zealand plastic surgeon Sir Harold Gillies. His brother Hugh, then completing a degree in medicine at St Thomas's Hospital in London, hastened to his bedside to find him drifting in and out of consciousness, recognising their mother but not him. [25] 'Many operations, much pain both physical and mental, the latter when I realise my disfigurement. A month with jaws clamped together so that I can eat nothing. The surgery excellent, nursing poor. Mother stays at Red Lion and behaves wonderfully. Utter boredom as I get better.' [26] This was followed in June and July by convalescence at Harewood House, a period he unexpectedly recalled as 'one of the happiest times of my life' for the friendships he made there before a final round of operations at Basingstoke. Found among Russell's papers after his death was a touching letter from a fellow patient at both

---

[23] Memoir, 19 Jan. 1941.
[24] Alastair Saunders, email to the author, 30 April 2024.
[25] Russell, *One Man's Journey*, 56.
[26] Memoir, 1 May 1941. Rita Russell makes no mention of the accident in her memoirs.

establishments, reporting the medical and psychological progress or otherwise of their number.[27] Though his injuries left him permanently scarred and thereafter required the use of a denture, Russell recounted his sense of shame among the dreadfully disfigured RAF airmen and others with whom he found himself. Out of a trauma he scarcely ever discussed came this untitled poem:

> At last the needle's point pricks
> The quivering bubble of my being
> Slackening the tight harness of pain
> Round the muscles of the mind.
> At last they fade, images
> Of men with noseless faces and
> Burn-stained minds and the starched smiles
> Of nurses mechanically
> Soothing the sick crumpled covering
> Of my fear.
> Under the arc-lights perceptions
> Recede soft-footed down the long
> White corridors of time and I,
> Naked of memory at last,
> Attend your dark voluptuous caresses
> A dying man knowing no answers.

No sooner had Russell been discharged in August 1941 than he was sent to the Paramilitary Training School at Lochailort on the west coast of Scotland. Still recuperating, he was severely beaten by former officers of the Shanghai Municipal Police during the part of his training intended to prepare him for the possibility of an enemy interrogation, part of the regime set up by the notorious personality of William Ewart Fairbairn among other pioneers of Commando warfare.[28] Russell secured his return to Oxford within a week. Between other absurdities and examples of incompetence these experiences no doubt confirmed Russell in his lasting belief, reaffirmed by historical research, in the essential stupidity of institutions and too many of their emanations, counterbalanced by the courage, gifts and humanity to which individuals could occasionally rise when it was

---

[27] Gordon Rimmer to PER, Basingstoke, 25 Sept. 1941.
[28] On Lochailort see Atkin, *Pioneers of Irregular Warfare*, 58–62.

needed most. To this he cleaved to the end of his life, expressed always in a favourite quote from *Celestina*: 'El cierto amigo en la cosa incierta se conoce' (A true friend is known in uncertainty).

Thereafter Russell was transferred to the 5th Battalion of the Bedfordshire and Hertfordshire Regiment in Warwickshire and Litchfield followed by 'the various military hoops required to justify giving one the rank of captain in the Intelligence Corps', chiefly training in field security. [29] Among these was drafting as Intelligence Officer to the 1st Battalion of the Royal Ulster Rifles at Carmarthen in October 1941 followed by an attempt to place him as a 'stooge' in the DMI's administration department, presumably in Oxford: 'After fortnight I protest. I am released from duty to improve my Russian. Go on Foreign Service Course at Matlock.' [30] Russell certainly knew how to get his way when circumstances required it. In late 1941 he was taken on by the Overseas Section of A Division of the Security Service (MI5), becoming in due course one of 330 officers to serve in that organisation during the Second World War, and one of just twenty-seven to operate overseas; among those Russell recalled meeting *en passant* at the War Office in London was a lissome figure with an adenoidal drawl: Anthony Blunt. [31] The following March he was promoted captain and 'rather to my embarrassment' appointed Defence Security Officer (DSO) in Jamaica, after which he seldom wore uniform. In fact, Russell was to fill a yawning gap in British counter-intelligence coverage as perhaps the only MI5 officer with the language skills to operate effectively in the Caribbean Basin (to include German). For now, with the German submarine offensive at its height in the Battle of the Atlantic the voyage to Halifax, Nova Scotia threatened to be as perilous as that of the *Rotorua* in 1917. Russell boarded the SS *Tucurinca* at Newport on 18 March, the ship at length forming part of convoy ON79 which assembled off Ireland to begin the Atlantic crossing under escort five days later. Among the vessels in the convoy was one harking back to another time and place, the SS *Port Melbourne* in which Russell had sailed from Wellington to London in 1926. In no sense a new ship even then, by 1942 she was ancient, her coal-fired reciprocating engines making her the slowest unit in the convoy, dictating its overall speed and roundly cursed

---

[29] PELR, 3.
[30] Memoir, 1 May 1941.
[31] The bare outline of Russell's MI5 career can be traced in the abbreviated notes he added to a journal and memoir in *c.* March 1942 and in the letter sent by the MI5 Enquiries Desk to the author, London, 26 April 2023.

by one and all.³² In later years Russell recalled his alarm when the *Tucurinca*'s officers proceeded to get drunk on the eve of her arrival in Halifax, a release they permitted themselves based on previous experience though hardly appropriate on this occasion. The convoy as a whole got through unscathed but the largely unreported depredations of the U-boats were all too apparent in the shape of wrecked and beached shipping visible on either hand as the *Tucurinca* steamed up to Halifax. Russell had had his first taste of Operation PAUKENSCHLAG ('Drumbeat'), the rapid mobilisation of the *U-Boot-Waffe* to the eastern seaboard of North America and the Caribbean following America's entry into the war in December 1941. The voyage was otherwise an agreeable one and Russell kept the menu of the last meal served to first-class diners before the ship made port. Among the farewell messages left by his fellow passengers is that 'To the Brains Trust Buster of the Atlantic'.³³

On 8 April Russell entrained at Halifax for the US border at McAdam, New Brunswick, from where he crossed to Vanceboro, Maine. That border crossing had been the focus of diplomatic friction since the outbreak of the war and Russell later recounted his experience of it to one of his students:

> In Vanceboro, the US customs agent asked him, PER being in uniform, if he was carrying any firearms. PER said that, as a British officer on active service, he was. The customs man paused, and then informed PER that US law forbade aliens from entering the US while bearing arms. Another pause, and a steady gaze at PER. 'Now, are you carrying any firearms?' To which PER replied, 'No.' 'Good. You are now cleared to proceed. Welcome to the United States of America.'³⁴

Russell stopped in New York in the ten days before taking up his position in Jamaica, and it is here that he presumably had his first contact with William Stephenson, the Canadian director of British Security Coordination later christened 'the Man called Intrepid'. With offices in the Rockefeller Center on Fifth Avenue, BSC was the umbrella organisation for the entire British intelligence effort in the Western Hemisphere and the main liaison with the FBI and the Office of the Coordinator of Information. Nonetheless, BSC's relations

---

³² PER, email to the author, Oxford, 23 Aug. 2002. *Port Melbourne* was launched in 1914.
³³ *The Brains Trust* was a popular BBC radio programme in which an expert panel answered listeners' questions.
³⁴ Alastair Saunders, email to the author, 5 Oct. 2020.

with the London intelligence establishment had come under increasing strain in view of Stephenson's status and influence, with the result that MI5 operatives in the Caribbean were removed from his authority and made directly responsible to London in September 1941. [35] Since then the United States had entered the war and Washington become critical of the poor state of security in the British Caribbean as the U-boat offensive exacted an immense toll of shipping in those waters. Of particular concern was the interdiction of bauxite from British Guiana, the ore of aluminium vital for Allied aircraft construction. It was in this context that the new Defence Security Officer reached Kingston by air from Miami on 19 April 1942.

The Defence Security Officer, Jamaica, with unknown assistant at Kingston in 1942 or 1943.

Though reporting to London, as DSO Russell was, locally at least, answerable to the Governor of Jamaica, Sir Arthur Richards and his successor from September

[35] F. H. Hinsley & C. A. G. Simkins, *British Intelligence in the Second World War*, vol. IV: *Security and Counter-Intelligence* (Cambridge: Cambridge University Press, 1990), 145–6. Further measures to improve security coordination and communication in the Western Hemisphere had to be taken in respect of Stephenson in November 1942, Russell being copied on the instructions; The National Archives, Kew [TNA], KV [Security Service] 4/447, Organisation of and Liaison with British Security Coordination, USA.

1943 Sir John Huggins, to both of whom he acted as Security Adviser. The official report prepared by the Overseas Section in December 1945 on the work of its officers in the late war outlined the responsibilities given to DSOs appointed to the Caribbean colonies:

> (a) surveyance of measures to prevent illicit entry
> (b) declaration and protection of vulnerable points
> (c) arrangements for the prevention of leakage of information in general and in particular regarding shipping and troop movements
> (d) arrangements for the detection of illicit signalling and other communications
> (e) anti-sabotage precautions
> (f) control of aliens in the Colony and any subversive elements whether internationally or locally inspired. [36]

However, together with a coordinating role involving the Colonial Office and the expanding British and Allied intelligence establishment, these duties inevitably turned out to be much more extensive than anticipated:

> Our officers, who were intended primarily for security work and had received careful training courses in London on the difficulties which they might meet in their appointment, as well as individual Charters officially accrediting them to the Governor and Service Commanders of the Colony concerned [...] soon found to their consternation that Colonial administrations had neither the authority nor the personnel to establish and enforce the security recommendations made by them. The only remedy to these short-comings lay in the provision of Field Security Personnel, sent out by the War Office on the recommendation of the Security Service to staff their offices. These men were employed on many and diverse duties such as Immigration, Censorship, issue of Entry and Exit Permits, Frontier Control and general Registration, and although administratively responsible to the Military Commander, received intelligence directions from the D.S.O. This action had the result in some Colonies of the granting by the

---

[36] TNA, KV 4/18, Report on the work of Defence Security Officers in British colonies and liaison with the Dominions, 1945, ch. VI.

S'EN VA-T-EN GUERRE (1939–1946)

Governor to the Defence Security Officer of executive powers under the Colonial government. [37]

Years later Russell explained the nature of some of these responsibilities in a Jamaican context:

> Jamaica was important in those days mainly because neutral shipping from Europe and elsewhere on its way to Latin America was forced to put in there for control of passengers and crews. The passengers had often come from Germany or the occupied countries only a few weeks before their arrival in Jamaica en route for Latin America or the U.S., so that their effective interrogation (my main duty) was capable sometimes of producing interesting results of one sort or another. [38]

On one occasion Russell found himself interviewing a man who weeks earlier had met with Goering in Berlin, the *Reichsmarschall* being susceptible to bribery in return for safe-conduct out of Germany. Mostly, as he recalled in 1948, it was arduous and frustrating work:

> All those hours and hours of patient probing and verification — mostly of trivial personalities whose journey had given them a momentary significance which they had <u>always</u> failed to grasp at the critical moments when a little observation would have been invaluable. [39]

These duties extended to the identification and interrogation of possible German agents and, more onerously, to examining the holds and cargo bays of the ships and flying boats obliged to call at Kingston, a task Russell had at times to perform personally, much to his annoyance. MI5 had also set up a mail interception centre at Kingston in the spring of 1941 of which Russell had charge. [40] He later reported that '[t]his job sometimes took me to Latin America or to the independent Caribbean countries', a statement borne out by the issue of visas for Haiti and

---

[37] *Ibid.*, ch. III.
[38] PELR, 3.
[39] Journal, 15 Feb. 1948.
[40] Bill Macdonald, *The True 'Intrepid': Sir William Stephenson and the Unknown Agents* (Surrey, B.C.: Timberholme Books, 1998), 227.

Colombia (at Barranquilla) in April and August 1943 respectively.[41] What business Russell had in either country is not known, but MI5 was concerned with the traffic of contraband from South America to the Canaries, while the Axis maintained extensive intelligence-gathering networks throughout the Caribbean which the Security Service was responsible for dismantling.[42] However, Russell was also MI6's representative in Jamaica, 'and in this capacity received reports from their representatives in Latin and Central American territories in regard to the impending departure of persons of interest who were likely to transit the Colony, as well as other information obtained from Security Co-ordination in New York having an interest to Caribbean Security as a whole.'[43] No doubt this was among the circumstances that brought him into direct conflict with Stephenson whose zeal to eliminate certain individuals obliged Russell to remind him that liquidation was not within MI5's remit. Russell also had responsibility for the large number of internees held at Gibraltar Camp on the island, one that in due time received German and Italian prisoners of war and enemy merchant seamen, with valuable opportunities to gather intelligence. The other influx into the Colony was that of US personnel in connection with the Destroyers-for-Bases deal signed with Britain in September 1940, under which fifty U.S. Navy destroyers were handed over to the Royal Navy in return for ninety-nine-year leases on British territories scattered throughout the Caribbean and in Newfoundland, in Jamaica's case at Vernam, Port Royal and Goat Island on the south coast. As the Overseas Section's official report explained, this brought problems in its turn 'arising from [...] American civilian and Service personnel with different views and standards in regard to working conditions and the status of coloured workers.'

While not directly concerned with countering the U-boat offensive, that strategic development formed the backdrop of Russell's activities as MI5 station officer in the Caribbean and the Gulf of Mexico where rich pickings were to be had of the poorly organised and as-yet unescorted merchant shipping plying those waters. Russell never yielded much to questioning on the subject but what is clear from the few redacted documents which survive from his Caribbean interlude is that the Cayman Islands lying 200 miles west of Jamaica were a particular focus of his attention.[44] The Caymans, he reported, 'represent one of the best sources of information regarding irregular shipping and passenger

---

[41] PELR, 3.
[42] For contraband traffic, see TNA, KV 4/447.
[43] TNA, KV 4/18, ch. VI.
[44] 'Jamaica & Dependencies', 3.

movements in the Caribbean', Grand Cayman itself being a centre of schooner traffic and the Islanders recognised as 'the best small craft seamen in the West Indies'. As elsewhere in the Caribbean, Russell's other interest in the Cayman Islands was their possible use for the infiltration of German agents by U-boat. The Caymans had been among the many places visited in the summer of 1938 by the German coaster *Æquator* which was known by the British to have reconnoitred the group for intelligence purposes under cover of a shark and turtle fishing expedition. These concerns were heightened not only by Russell's discovery that the coast-watching service supposedly manned by the Cayman Islands Home Guard had been allowed to lapse since the beginning of the war, but by the sighting of a U-boat — probably *U-509* — cruising inshore during his own visit on 9 August 1942. Far from being secret, Russell's tour of inspection to Grand Cayman was the excuse for an outburst of revelry and in early 1948 his mind was drawn back to the enthusiastic welcome he received in George Town (pop. 1,000):

> Somehow while I have been writing this I have been thinking a lot about Grand Cayman — the mosquitoes, the dance given in my honour with the sexes kept in separate rooms until actually dancing, the old-fashioned dances, the crates of whiskey, the sand everywhere, the swamps and (now I have it) the schooner which arrived from the Isla de Pinos [Cuba; now Isla de la Juventud]. [45]

The Defence Security Officer's other area of concern was the Turks and Caicos Islands which he visited via Haiti in April 1943. Occupying a strategic position on the Turks Island Passage, Russell found this territory to have little or no security clearance measures with respect to visitors or shipping. He also discovered extensive smuggling operations and general lawlessness exacerbated by the influence of voodoo practices from nearby Haiti. This was particularly true of the Caicos Islands which had no administrative, judicial or medical presence whatsoever. The government launch had been destroyed by arson in early 1942 and there were rumours the Caicos Islanders engaged in wrecking and had done away with two US airmen after their plane came down off North Caicos in February 1942. Confidential papers removed from the wreckage were recovered but '[s]ome of the Islanders were found to be wearing clothing made from material and articles of clothing carried by the 'plane'. Russell saw to the

[45] Journal, 9 Jan. 1948.

installation of coast-watching stations on Grand Turk though the public order situation made similar arrangements in the Caicos impracticable. Then there was the incident Russell would recall in later years concerning a night spent in a small boat off Cap-Haïtien waiting to pick up a very important passenger from what was presumably a US submarine. [46] Far more than the identity of the agent, the incongruity of the episode never left him.

*

Promoted major in October 1942, in December of the following year Russell was reassigned as Security Liaison Officer to Accra in the Gold Coast which he reached in March 1944, initially via Miami and New York followed by an Atlantic crossing in the liner *Queen Elizabeth*, and ultimately by air from Bristol via Lisbon. The appointment was to a large extent due to Sir Arthur Richards who had exchanged the post of Governor of Jamaica for that of Nigeria and was impressed by Russell's service in the Caribbean, though the latter in fact reported to one of the leading figures in the British security establishment and now Minister Resident in West Africa, Philip Cunliffe-Lister, Viscount Swinton, also based in Accra. Until the disintegration of the Vichy regime in November 1942 the security position of the four British colonies in West Africa (Nigeria and the British Cameroons, Gold Coast, Sierra Leone and Gambia) was complicated by the chain of French colonies with which they shared a frontier of approximately 3,000 miles and the semi-hostile relations prevailing between them. Not only that but West Africa was Britain's chief or only source of large quantities of *matériel* vital to the Allied war effort and much coveted by the Axis, particularly wolfram from the Belgian Congo and manganese from the Gold Coast. This state of affairs, which Russell summarised in a remarkably concise and occasionally pungent official document in October 1944, had required his predecessors as Defence Security Officer to carry out security and counter-espionage activities against Axis agents who were tracking convoys bringing minerals and foodstuffs from West Africa and fomenting sabotage and subversion among the colonised population. Here are some of the requirements of DSOs in West Africa outlined in mid-1942 by a visiting MI5 officer, Major W. B. Webster, one fully borne out in Russell's experience:

> To observe with an eye trained in general Security principles the local targets and the local protective system for guarding them from enemy

[46] I am grateful to Alastair Saunders for this information.

agents. A general knowledge of enemy espionage and sabotage methods would need to be a part of that specialised and extraneous contribution from M.I.5. to West African executive services. The discharge of this function would entail a good deal of travelling for purposes of direct observation. [47]

Although the collapse of Vichy France lessened or eliminated many of these threats, in his capacity as Chief Security Liaison Officer West Africa (which again included representing MI6 and SOE in addition) Russell soon identified other dangers, not least the yawning gap in security arrangements created by the resumption of air traffic from Europe in late 1942:

> During the Vichy period little was done in the way of control of air passengers in British West Africa. When, however, the former Vichy colonies were opened to Allied air traffic and passengers to and from them were carried by British, American, French and Belgian airlines, and an influx of refugees and *évadés* from Metropolitan France into French African territory commenced, it became apparent that certain categories of passengers passing through British territory, as well as all air passengers proceeding to or coming from Lisbon by air, required security attention. British airport security controls began to function regularly in April 1944. [48]

Nor until Russell's arrival was the danger of continued Axis activity in Portugal's equatorial territories including the island of Fernando Pó (now Bioko) fully apprehended:

> During the Vichy period some espionage and attempts at causing political subversion among British African natives had been undertaken by German agents operating in Portuguese Guinea and, more especially, Fernando Poo. As the French brought the security situation in their territory under control these latter operations represented the sole direction from which enemy espionage activity against British territory could be directed. Colonial Governments were slow to comprehend the

[47] TNA, KV 4/18, ch. IV.
[48] 'West Africa', 11.

possible significance of clandestine traffic with suburban Spanish and Portuguese territory — a failure whose consequences could not be rated as serious in view of the steadily diminishing number of security targets in the area. Some military security problems continued to exist while the two West African [army] divisions were being organised and preparations for their departure to Burma were under way. [49]

This appreciation and the measures he implemented in consequence were the result of a series of arduous but fascinating journeys throughout the vast tract of territory that constituted his beat in West Africa and beyond, often alone but occasionally in the company of his friend and fellow intelligence officer Major Jo Heigham. Needless to say, Russell took the opportunity presented by these travels to broaden his mind as much through the historical, topographical, ethnological, natural and other material he gathered for his reports as by the searing mental and physical impact that attended any prolonged exposure to the tropics.

Russell kept few documents on his service in the Caribbean beyond a couple of heavily redacted reports, but this is not true of his service in West Africa which came after the tide had turned against the Axis in that theatre and security requirements been relaxed somewhat. The chief surviving official record of Russell's time there is the collection of geopolitical and security reports he prepared on the Gold Coast and especially Accra where he had his office. However, from a personal standpoint the major sources are the detailed journals he kept of seven journeys across the region in the ten months he was on station. These are of interest not only as a perceptive record of the declining years of colonial rule but also as evidence of Russell's heightened powers of observation and expression together with the devastating opinions he committed to paper. Gone also is the idealism and self-absorption of the pre-war diaries and journals.

The first of these accounts concerns his journey by air from England to Accra via Rabat in French Morocco in March 1944, starting with the physically and emotionally discomfiting night flight he took from Bristol to Lisbon in a Dakota transport plane:

> Long seven hours pull in blacked-out plane over Bay of Biscay. One pays much unwilling attention to the beat of the engines, contemplating the

---

[49] *Ibid.,* 12.

consequences of an attack by German fighters and the coldness of the Bay. Seats which turn into life-rafts somehow do not seem enough. [50]

Ten years earlier in Brussels Russell had declared himself to be 'still adolescent enough to be horrified of death' [51] but the experience of war necessarily hardened him to this harvest and the attendant suffering, in this case at Yundum in Gambia where his plane put down during that first journey to Accra:

> We landed and walked to our tent. Were eating our sandwiches when there was strange noise, American Dakota hit runway by tent, bounced into air for 200 yards and crashed in cut bush stumps. Up in a sheet of flame and black smoke. Pause. Said to be four removed, some burnt with flesh shrivelled off fingers. Three left inside. We eat our sandwiches and watch fire and smell burning flesh. Nothing we can do. [52]

No wonder Russell was keen to avoid aircraft by the end of his war service, even at the cost of prolonged journeys by sea. Contrasting with that clipped report is this description of the denizens of the Medina of Rabat:

> Men in white, striped or ragged soutanes like dressing gowns, naked legs, painted or embroidered slippers on which they pad along their heels showing, red fezzes, white turbans, cowls. Sultan's bodyguard in cerise pantaloons and blouses with worked gilt ribbing, square cerise turbans, desert horsemen, Bedouins, with flowing robes and rifles over shoulder. Women with painted eyebrows and eyes backed in indigo gazing insolently through a narrow slit between veil and hair or cowl. An occasional veil with red pattern makes woman look as if her nose was bleeding. Fine old faces with aquiline noses and black or white beards like models for paintings of patriarchs. This civilization seems aloof, satisfied with itself and utterly unchanged by the European life without. Inside the Medina the French might be a hundred years away. [53]

---

[50] Journal, 15 March 1944.
[51] Diary, 26 Aug. 1934.
[52] Journal, 20 March 1944.
[53] Journal, 16 March 1944.

To Russell's unaccustomed senses much of Africa seemed surreal. An early example came at Port-Étienne in French Mauritania:

> Immense monotony suspends one's soul in its own vital resources. Self-sufficient or you go mad. The pleasure of evacuation on sheltered peak of sandhill. Sherry and cider smuggled across hill. Brazilian brigadier and his elegant officers appalled by primitive conditions. Lie on the camp beds in our common Nissen hut and count the passing of the hours. [54]

Another was this observation: 'One of the basic themes of Africa is the dusty bottoms of small boys. They are never absent.' [55]

The Chief Security Liaison Officer, West Africa Command in his residence and office at 21, Sixth Avenue in the British cantonment of Achimota, Accra, Gold Coast, 1944.

Reaching Accra Russell found evidence of the abject failure of colonial government at every turn, the city 'unplanned, undistinguished, smelly' and awash with prostitutes, the architecture dismal and the houses poorly built, the administration 'tied up in red tape' and 'lacking in loyalty or discipline', the 'bureaucracy inefficient, often insolent and contemptuous', corruption, monopolies, deforestation. This particular fish was rotting from the head, with lacklustre timeserving British functionaries enduring the discomfort of West

[54] Journal, 20 March 1944.
[55] Journal, 27 July 1944.

S'EN VA-T-EN GUERRE (1939–1946)

Africa solely to earn a living, while in London '[t]here are important officials who have done years in the Colonial Office and never visited a Colony'. Here in the European ghetto of Achimota Russell resided and worked with the assistance of a number of secretaries and other staff. This brought its own difficulties:

> One trying feature of life in West Africa to which any officer must resign himself is that a large amount of his time will be occupied every day in keeping the minor administration side of his office and his home functioning. Native staffs have little or no initiative and will take no action in matters affecting the job until they are ordered to do so. Local bureaucracy has a mania for forms and paper generally. Personal intervention and visits will often be found necessary where matters with which an employer would never concern himself in England are involved. [...] No officer or secretary should imagine that the size of domestic staffs in West Africa bears any relation to the efficiency [with] which his home will be run. Constant supervision is necessary since most servants are apt to cheat their employers in any way possible. Cooks can rarely be left to arrange meals according to their own discretion. In dealing with most servants and African workmen generally it will be found that verbal communication, to be intelligible, will have to be at least partially in pidgin English. [56]

Unsurprisingly he lost no opportunity to get clear of the place.

The first of Russell's journeys of reconnaissance took him east to Lagos and Calabar in Nigeria and then to Douala in French Cameroon where the picture of a banal colonial world in full decay revealed itself in a different guise. At Itu in Calabar, site of Mary Slessor's famous mission to the Efik people, Russell found her '[h]ouse falling into decay and natives relapsed. Little sign of long lifetime of work.' [57] On this trip too Russell sighted one of the great landmarks in the early navigation of West Africa, Mount Cameroon rising 13,250 feet to a bare summit above the coastal rainforest. Another crystalline memory of that equatorial summer was the moment he learnt of one of the turning points of the Second World War, the Normandy landings on 6 June 1944, news of which he picked up on his radio set on the beach in Accra. Later that month Russell travelled west to

---

[56] 'West Africa', 9 & 8.
[57] Journal, 27 April 1944.

Freetown, Sierra Leone which offered another study in wretchedness: 'Bum boats, dock rats, thieves, touts, tugs, lighters, launches and hulks. Dead dog in middle of road at 11 a.m. on Sunday still there at 6 p.m. Even the vultures are not efficient in Freetown.' The world, in short, of *The Heart of the Matter* by Graham Greene, MI6's last intelligence officer in Sierra Leone whose responsibilities Russell assumed in due course. [58] After Bathurst (now Banjul), the colonial capital settled on the banks of the River Gambia, Russell proceeded to Dakar in Senegal via Royal Navy motor launch:

> Crew in shorts. Youth remarkable. Engineer's shorts expose black bush. Cast off smoking cigarette. Bright hot day with breeze. We lie on deck and talk. Pass basking sharks, Portuguese men-of-war with pink coral-coloured handles, porpoises, swallows, square sails of canoes, silhouettes of trees on flat coast, damp heat. Little wardroom. Young quartermaster. Lunch of hot spam, mashed potatoes, carrots and tinned peaches. Navy gives thick cups of tea. Pre-prandial gin and warm water on deck. [59]

In the summary of his war service he provided the author Javier Marías as source material for his *Tu rostro mañana* trilogy in 2002 Russell alluded to 'another role' he fulfilled in the former Vichy territory of Senegal. [60] The nature of this duty is unknown but in the same letter Russell mentions lengthy river journeys by canoe, possibly while investigating diamond-smuggling from as far afield as the Congo and Cameroon. [61] In later years he also shared reminiscences of witnessing slavery in West Africa, illustrated by the series of photos (now lost) he took from the branches of a tree in Calabar of chained slaves being led down to canoes for onward shipment to work on the cacao, coffee and timber plantations of Fernando Pó. [62] When Russell wrote of slavery in future years he therefore did so as an eyewitness of the phenomenon.

Russell's next journey which began in late July took him, Heigham and their servant Davis into the interior in a 1941-model Ford. Over the next two weeks the

---

[58] London: Heinemann, 1948. Greene was stationed in Sierra Leone from 1942–3.
[59] Journal, 21 June 1944.
[60] JMA, PER to Marías, Oxford, 4 June 2002.
[61] TNA, KV 4/196-1, Liddell Diaries, vol. 12, 173, 5 March 1945. I am grateful to Nigel West for drawing this source to my attention.
[62] I am grateful to Clive Griffin and Alastair Saunders for their memories and information on this subject.

trail brought them on unpaved tracks to Kumasi and Tamale in the Gold Coast's Ashanti and Northern Territories respectively. Here as elsewhere in West Africa came an assortment of governors, district commissioners, consuls general, legal functionaries and policemen together with their wives, mistresses and children, all bearing the white man's burden. Russell's pitiless critical eye was never at rest:

> We dine with Butler, the Deputy Commissioner and his wife. In their way pleasant people but conventional to a degree. Their social life is set in formalised moulds which require the minimum use of intelligence and provide the maximum of personal cover — bourgeois in the bush in fact. Jo meets an acquaintance there whose only apparent characteristic is clothes-brush hair. [63]

Russell watches as his official car is serviced at Anyinam, 70 miles north of Accra during one of his many journeys through West Africa in 1944.

These minor aggravations apart, not the least attraction of the trip was his developing friendship with the athletically heterosexual Heigham, a Cambridge classicist assailed with marital problems but unfailingly cheerful for all that:

> We walk home in the moonlight. [...] This form of *ménage à deux* is delightful. Tonight Jo propounded theories of time and particularly

[63] Journal, 30 July 1944.

John Donne's until nearly two. It was practically the first time I had had to use my mind seriously since May 1940 [...] Jo appears to be intellectually completely honest, which is something I am not much accustomed to. [64]

Lt-Col Russell seen in the Gold Coast driver's licence issued him on reaching Accra in March 1944, the first surviving portrait photo since his motor accident and reconstructive surgery in the spring of 1941.

[64] *Ibid.*

Heigham also featured in an untitled and unpublished short story Russell drafted in West Africa, possibly the last he ever wrote. Plans to continue to Ouagadougou in Upper Volta were thwarted by mechanical trouble to the Ford which was discovered to have been lubricated with peanut rather than engine oil. They returned to Accra by train. Russell's next excursion, alone this time, was to the Belgian Congo in early September 1944, the capital Leopoldville reached after another grim wartime flight:

> There followed eleven hours on a bucket seat and steadily increasing jabs from innumerable nuts, bolts, knobs and plates. A form of torture in the aseptic twilighted fuselage. A weary and haggard nurse leans on me throughout the night with distressing impersonality. For seven hours we are over the sea, a fact which intrudes an element of tenseness into our weariness. [65]

Russell's arrival coincided with the liberation of Brussels and appropriate festivities among the European population of Leopoldville. Here, however, was a taste of colonialism at its most debased:

> Tonight the natives are to be given free cigarettes and beer to show them they are not forgotten. At the Cercle [club building] last night I saw a steward boy get a tremendous kick in the backside from a member dissatisfied with the service. Nominal penalty here for manhandling is 500 francs. There are two cathedrals here — one exclusively for whites. [66]

Still, it was in the Congo that Russell came within sight of one of the scenic wonders of Africa, the Ruwenzori range on the Ugandan border and the abundant wildlife near Lake Edward:

> At sunset went for drive. Turned off road and went across the plain. Elephant, buffalo and antelope on every side. Came across a very large elephant in bushes about 60 yards away. Left car, put cigarette out and approached stealthily great grey-black beast with big curved tasks

---

[65] Journal, 3 Sept. 1944.
[66] Journal, 5 Sept. 1944.

flicking its tail, trampling about in bushes and tearing off leaves with its trunk. Somewhat anxious moment when elephant came out to have a look at us and showed signs of approaching. Guide clears off to a safe distance but I manage to summon up enough courage to stay and take a photograph. Warthogs dashing through bushes. Sunset after thunderstorm is magnificent, lightning, white clouds round mountains and making grass seem yellower than ever. [67]

A sixth journey, this time with Heigham, took them by road to Togo, Dahomey (now Benin) and Lagos in October 1944. The highlight of the trip between encounters with French colonial officials behind their vast mahogany desks was again the rapport between the two, but poor roads and deteriorating weather brought an early end to the trip:

We returned to the Gold Coast with a certain sense of anticlimax. The road and threatening weather made us turn back from an attempt to reach Keta [on the Dahomey border] after we had driven for some miles by the side of a broad stinking lagoon which turned from time to time into baleful marsh. The road to Accra is in a disgraceful state after the rain and we slip and slide through mud and sand in what must be, even for West Africa, a dreary landscape. Page, who originally invited me to Cotonou [in Dahomey], is in hospital there after going off his head following pneumonia and malaria. Imagine being mad and white in Cotonou! [68]

For all his distaste at the trials of life in the territory, the reigning squalour and bourgeois colonials of every nationality, Russell could not fail to be moved by the overpowering elemental realities of Africa and the elevated sensorium that occasionally resulted:

> Cherry Gardens
> A stiff-necked palm
> Naked in the warm moonlight.
> Like white confetti

---

[67] Journal, 16 Sept. 1944.
[68] Journal, 22 Oct. 1944.

S'EN VA-T-EN GUERRE (1939–1946)

The night falls on the shining grass.
Monotonously
The cicada
Saws the tired silence
And the crouching cabin
Tight-shuttered under a cotton-tree
Turns its back on the night
Hiding
Black lovers striving
Perfumed with the scent of burning wood

Russell's travelling companion Maj. Jo Heigham in a kente cloth at the coastal town of Winneba 35 miles west of Accra in 1944. A photo of Russell taken in identical garb on the same occasion is now lost.

In time Russell came to look on this as his African Arcadia. He and Heigham planned a book of their travels and observations under the tentative title of *Before God's Eyes* and the former drafted a couple of chapters of which one survives in ornate prose, but nothing came of the project despite some encouragement from Faber & Faber. [69] Nonetheless the posting was of immense value to Russell's subsequent research and in his last major work he paid tribute to those who had flown him to and over many of the places which loomed large in the Portuguese reconnaissance of Guinea during the fifteenth century:

> Now is also perhaps an appropriate time for me to acknowledge my debt to the RAF pilots who, in 1943 and early 1944, several times ferried me in stages up and down the coast of West Africa in DC3s flying at altitudes that made it easy to secure close bird's-eye views of many of the geographical features which are mentioned in this book and which Prince Henry's men first saw in the fifteenth century. Though I did not properly realize it at the time, the visual memories of those flights and of the months I then spent in various parts of West Africa long ago were to serve me well when I came to work on the Henrican discoveries. [70]

His subsequent research also yielded a poignant echo across five centuries of Gold Coast history, the Flemish merchant Eustache de la Fosse having been importuned by a prostitute in the same terms in 1479 as Russell was in Accra in 1944: 'choque choque'. [71] In his finest work Russell succeeded in imparting an almost intuitive understanding of his subject matter based on emotional, intellectual or physical experiences and responses at the deepest level. This is nowhere more vivid than in his writing on Africa, published and unpublished.

*

In February 1944 Russell was promoted lieutenant-colonel and on 11 November received word of what would be the last and most significant appointment of his MI5 career, that of Defence Security Officer in Colombo. After a final journey to the Gold Coast hinterland with Heigham in January 1945 Russell flew home for a few weeks' leave during which he visited his mother, now removed to the Isle of

---

[69] The surviving chapter in manuscript concerns Port Etienne.
[70] *Prince Henry 'the Navigator': A Life* (New Haven, Conn.: Yale University Press, 2000), xv.
[71] '*Veni, vidi, vici*: Fifteenth-Century Eyewitness Accounts of Travel in the African Atlantic before 1492', *Historical Research* 66 (1993), no. 160, 115–28; at 121.

S'EN VA-T-EN GUERRE (1939–1946)

Man, and survived a near miss by a V-2 rocket in London. There was also time for a sentimental journey back to Oxford where, oiled by hock and port at Kolkhorst's home at Yarnton Manor, he delivered a slideshow on his African travels to a distinguished but malicious audience including Osbert Lancaster and John Betjeman. [72] Within weeks Russell was flying to Ceylon via Malta, Cairo and Karachi, and by early April was installed at the MI5 station at 78 Turret Road, Colombo while living in the same Galle Face Hotel he had stayed in with his family in 1919.

Russell pays a visit to his mother Rita on the Isle of Man between foreign service postings in early 1945.

Though not lacking in importance, the Caribbean and particularly West African theatres were comparative backwaters alongside South East Asia, where Russell for the first time came face-to-face with the enemy. By the time of his arrival in the spring of 1945 the British war effort in the Far East had taken precedence after long occupying a secondary position in London's strategic planning. In April 1944 Admiral Lord Louis Mountbatten transferred the headquarters of his South East Asia Command from Delhi to Kandy in central Ceylon. Meanwhile, the British Eastern Fleet had in 1943 returned to its main Indian Ocean anchorage at Trincomalee after a long exile at Mombasa. As a result

---

[72] PER to Maj. J. B. Heigham, Oxford, 26 Feb. 1945.

of the breaking of Japanese cyphers, in the autumn of 1944 MI5 had learnt of the existence of an Indian Nationalist agent to whom the British gave the codename CARBUNCLE. CARBUNCLE, who turned out to be singularly ill-suited to the role of a spy, had been recruited to operate in Ceylon by the Japanese in Singapore. Assigned to report on British naval movements in Trincomalee, he was promptly picked up and handed over to MI5. The Security Service initially had difficulty finding a suitable case officer for CARBUNCLE, a point noted in his war diary for 1 November 1944 by Col. Guy Liddell, Director of MI5's B Division with responsibility for counter-espionage. [73] In Lt.-Col. Russell, however, they found their man. Given charge of CARBUNCLE on his arrival in Ceylon in April 1945, Russell proceeded to 'turn' him using the 'Double-Cross' system perfected with German agents in Europe by three distinguished intelligence figures: Col. Robin 'Tin-eye' Stephens, Lt.-Col. T. A. Robertson and a history don at Christ Church, J. C. Masterman. Against the threat of execution the would-be agent agreed to transmit whatever intelligence the British saw fit to provide his controllers. Although this initially consisted of 'chicken feed' — accurate data of limited value or past importance — the opportunity was eventually taken for a major exercise in disinformation which in CARBUNCLE's case consisted in luring Japanese cruisers out of Singapore against reports that Allied supply convoys had sailed from Trincomalee. The bait was evidently taken more than once and though Russell was evasive on the subject these efforts may have contributed to the interception and sinking of the *Haguro* or the *Ashigara* by British naval units in May and June 1945 respectively.

Russell was also responsible, in collaboration with the Ceylon Police, for monitoring the Trotskyist and nationalist Lanka Sama Samaja Party, founded in 1935 as the first political organisation of its type in the Colony but forced underground due to its opposition to the British war effort. [74] However, Russell's papers indicate that there was little in the way of counter-espionage to engage his attentions in what turned out to be the closing months of the war, his time instead occupied with administrative work hampered by a severe shortage of staff and greatly complicated by confusion, incompetence and lack of direction from MI5 head office in London. The letter he wrote to his coordinating officer Col. Alan McIver from Colombo on 7 August summarises the situation and attendant frustrations:

[73] TNA, KV 4/195-2, Liddell Diaries, vol. 11, 215; see also KV 4/196-2, vol. 12, 185, 21 March 1945.
[74] TNA, KV 4/18, ch. XII.

I have not heard a word and have no idea whether I am supposed to be holding down this job until it ceases to exist at the end of the year or will then hand over to a successor. It makes filing and carding and work generally extremely difficult. However, as Head Office have almost given up replying to any letters or reports of mine and usually write nonsense when they do reply, I suppose a policy decision is too much to expect. […] Dixon and I have at present a frustrated indignation over the apparent complete inability of London to grasp our needs and troubles out here. The secretarial position in my Office has been abominable. As you know, I very much doubt whether anyone's interests would be adversely affected if we did not do most of the work we are doing. However, if it is to be done, a proper staff must be provided. […] Elizabeth McKenzie [registry secretary] is still in Kandy where she must remain as long as the Director General [Sir David Petrie] labours under the illusion that an office dealing with Counter-Espionage for the whole of the coming campaigns in South East Asia is adequately staffed by three secretaries. [75]

This frustration evidently boiled over in a communication Russell sent to London which was the subject of a meeting between Petrie and Liddell on 12 September, one recorded in the latter's war diary. The disagreement between Russell and Liddell seems to have focused on the DSO's resistance (supported by the Governor of Ceylon, Sir Henry Monck-Mason Moore) to putting MI5's counterintelligence operation in the colony onto a peacetime footing as part of its expanded directive:

We had a meeting with the Director General today to discuss the rather petulant letter from Russell. DG was rather inclined to agree with Russell's view that Ceylon could be written off as a DSO point in peacetime. I said that I could not see how Ceylon differed from other fortress areas such as Gibraltar and Malta. It had one of the biggest naval bases in the Empire [at Trincomalee] and there was moreover a considerable amount of unrest in the island. DG seemed to think that it was not our business to carry out any investigations into such movements. I made it clear that normally DSOs did not do this but that

---

[75] Col. C. E. Dixon was Russell's counterpart as Defence Security Officer in Singapore.

they did stimulate the local police and on the information they received could make the necessary adjustments and security measures. DG finally agreed that if we were to be only concerned with the security of the naval base he saw no objection to keeping an Assistant DSO. He thought however that it was desirable to get Russell back for consultation. [76]

Russell's aggravation was compounded by an urge to get home and his request on accepting the post in Colombo in late 1944 that consideration be given to the fact that he had already spent three years in the tropics. The dropping of the atomic bombs on Japan and the imperial surrender which followed on 15 August brought an early lifting of many though not all of these burdens but the war had not done with Peter Russell yet, nor with CARBUNCLE for that matter.

In early October 1945 the British reoccupied the Andaman Islands, an archipelago in the Bay of Bengal which since March 1942 had been under an occupation so brutal it eventually accounted for ten percent of the population. In November Russell was ordered to fly to the capital Port Blair to interrogate the most egregious of the 250 war criminals being held there. Interestingly enough, he elected to take CARBUNCLE with him. No explanation is provided for this in his papers but the Andamans had been visited (and renamed) by the Indian Nationalist leader Subhas Chandra Bose in December 1943 and Russell may have imagined that CARBUNCLE had some propaganda purpose to serve there as a Nationalist traitor anxious to save his skin. The scale of the Japanese oppression, punctuated by a series of atrocities which extended to their Nationalist collaborators, had no doubt dampened the enthusiasm of the Andamanese for that particular cause, but Russell subsequently reported in a letter to a colleague in Singapore that 'Carbuncle has at last paid some dividends'. [77] The interrogations themselves revealed the full horror of the occupation:

> The local inhabitants suffered severely from terror and starvation and are now so emaciated as to be unfit for work. They only grow a little paddy and coconuts. [...] Two weeks before the British arrived they took several hundred people to a place called Havelock Island. Could not approach owing to reef so threw them into the sea. Only two survivors. Also shot the entire complement of a number of Burmese

---

[76] TNA, KV 4/466, Liddell Diaries, vol. 13, 199.
[77] PER to Dixon, Colombo, 30 Nov. 1945.

families who had tried to escape from Port Blair in a Jap boat. Taxed with these massacres they express profound regret, blame food shortage, say they were very sorry they had to shoot the women and children but explain by way of complete excuse that they blindfolded them first. [78]

When Russell asked the sadistic Japanese commander Colonel Jochi Renusakai why he had ordered the massacre, he received the indignant reply that this had of course been necessary to ensure sufficient food for the garrison, the Andamans being small and relatively infertile. To this even Russell had no answer.

Meanwhile CARBUNCLE's legal status had for reasons unclear become a matter of interest in London, a development greeted with considerable annoyance by certain MI5 officers in the Far East more keen on disposing of him altogether. As Russell recalled, he had been instructed to settle with CARBUNCLE in whatever way he thought fit and prior to the Andaman trip it was suggested that CARBUNCLE might find a watery grave *en route*, something the latter evidently feared as well. In the event, Russell couldn't bring himself to any such action and when the flying boat in which they had travelled from Port Blair put down at Singapore he disembarked with CARBUNCLE attached to his wrist by means of a pair of handcuffs. Producing a key, Russell unfettered them both and to CARBUNCLE's evident astonishment told him to 'Fuck off!' CARBUNCLE duly took to his heels and disappeared into the crowd. This, however, seems not to have been the last of CARBUNCLE, who was back in the clutches of MI5 by the end of the year, possibly with a view to returning to his family in Ceylon with the assistance of a cover story of Russell's devising. Anxious to please, CARBUNCLE had taken up a correspondence course in road engineering. 'I can only assume that this is a modified form of stone-breaking' wrote one of Russell's colleagues on the eve of his departure for England. [79]

*

Liberated Singapore as Russell found it in November 1945 added to the catalogue of massacre, torture, rape and forced prostitution he had first confronted in the Andaman Islands, aside from the crassness of the newly arrived military administration headed by the supremo of South East Asia Command, Admiral Lord Louis Mountbatten:

---

[78] Journal, 8 Nov. 1945.
[79] Maj. C. T. Young to PER, Singapore, 29 Dec. 1945.

Supremo is rapidly dissipating local goodwill by pouring into this overcrowded and underfed city the inflated HQ [...] and requisitioning all the best accommodation for himself and his officers — all at vast expense to the taxpayer and with the worst possible consequences for the commercial rehabilitation of Malaya. [80]

For all that he recognised Singapore as 'far and away the most impressive place I have seen in any British colony' [81] and quickly formed a great appreciation of the Chinese and their culture, attending a traditional banquet and buying various artifacts in jade, the experience confirmed Russell in what he had earlier recognised as a 'spiritual malaise':

> I realised today I think the reason for the spiritual malaise which has affected me ever since I came to the East. It is the humiliation of the alien conqueror who has brought nothing to India or Ceylon except the power of superior force. What I would like is to be Indian to understand India or Ceylon too for that matter. One is excluded and shut off from understanding except painfully and by hard-won confidence. We are the conquerors who do not believe in conquest. [82]

On 18 November Russell boarded the frigate HMS *Loch Quoich* ostensibly bound for Colombo but promptly diverted to the island of Sabang in the Dutch East Indies to escort the landing ship *Persimmon* loaded with troops to accept the formal surrender of Sumatra. On arrival Russell was invited as the ranking officer to command a landing on a nearby island whose garrison had yet to learn of the Japanese surrender. Unpersuaded that the Platoon Attack component of the OCTU course he had completed at Aldershot five years earlier quite fitted him for the task, Russell politely declined the offer though the incident was one he had much amusement recounting in later years, Lieutenant-Commander J. E. B. Healey taking pleasure in labelling him 'a bloody coward'. With Indonesia restive at the prospect of any restoration of Dutch colonial rule and work piling up for him in Colombo, Russell was forced to take passage in that most uncomfortable of oceangoing craft, a nameless tank landing ship, *LST-3017*. From this he was disgorged at Trincomalee after a six-day voyage across the Bay of Bengal during

---
[80] Journal, 13 Nov. 1945.
[81] PER to Heigham, HMS *Loch Quoich*, Sabang, 23 Nov. 1945.
[82] Journal, 20 Oct. 1945.

which his rank and status counted for nothing and his natural fastidiousness was set at naught:

> I have not written a line for some days because even that effort has been too much in the mental collapse induced by this LST (3017). Owing to a fault in its construction the cabin temperature averages 95°–100° at night from the uninsulated heat of the boilers directly underneath. It is impossible to stay in the bathroom for more than 10 minutes owing to the heat and at times almost impossible to sit on the lavatory seats they are so hot. It has been a question of drugging oneself with print, playing draughts, watching the habits of one's [fellow] passengers and frequently going up on deck for gasps of air. The ship rolls like nobody's business, and even in a fairly calm sea. Yesterday afternoon was obliged by the odour of my own underclothing to do my own dhobying in a bucket in the hothouse-like bathroom. In the evening slept on the boat deck on the captain's camp bed under a swaying belt of stars. This was cool and pleasant until 5.15 when we ran into the northeast monsoon rains and I had to leave. In some ways this trip is fun. There is no place for service or social pretension. We take each other at our own face value and know nothing of each other's background or names. Yet I have never eaten such unpalatable food, been so inescapably hot or worn soiled and sweaty clothes for so long. [83]

On his return to Colombo Russell resumed the lengthy process, finally approved on 5 October, of closing down the Defence Security Office, handing off such responsibilities as remained to Singapore or Rangoon and making preparations for his own repatriation and that of his staff. The task was complicated by further depletion of and personality clashes between his staff together with an exasperating decline in discipline after the cessation of hostilities, a series of drunken accidents culminating in a secretary illegally taking and wrecking his official car. It was the sort of loss of self-control that was and remained anathema to him. Most frustrating of all was a continued lack of communication from London, in this case concerning the custody of highly sensitive material. The letter Russell wrote to the Director General Sir David Petrie a few weeks before his departure on 28 December does not disguise his irritation:

---

[83] Journal, 27 Nov. 1945.

1.   In accordance with your instructions cyphers held by me will be handed over to the Governor's Secretary on 12th December 1945 and files and other material to the Deputy Chief Secretary.

2.   With regard to these arrangements, in so far as they involve the Deputy Chief Secretary's Office, I have already in my letter [...] fully explained to you what I consider to be the security risk involved. I presume that, no doubt, on account of other considerations at the London end you have not felt this point to be of sufficient weight to warrant the acceptance of my alternative proposals as outlined in [...] the above letter.

3.   I should add that Col. Bacon has expressed to me his alarm, from the security point of view, at the prospect of the material concerned being retained in the Chief Secretary's Office, but I have told him that, since the nature of this risk is known to you, he may assume that you have considered the matter fully and decided that other considerations outweigh it. [84]

*

As in West Africa Russell took the opportunity to expand his horizons and between whiles carried out lengthy tours throughout Ceylon and to India, travelling as far as Kashmir (where he spent two weeks in a houseboat on a lake) via Madras, Delhi, Lahore and Bombay and subsequently to Dravidia (now Karnataka) aside from official trips to Madras. India at once fascinated and appalled him much as Africa had done, but where Ceylon was concerned his main interest was to uncover the remains of Portuguese colonisation, most of which had been expunged by the Dutch from the seventeenth century. To this end he not only contacted local historical circles including the Royal Asiatic Society and travelled across the island meeting scholars and viewing private collections, but also took up Sinhalese in an effort to establish how many Portuguese loanwords survived in that language. The architectural remains of Portuguese Ceylon proved to be vestigial but Russell found that a Portuguese dialect had survived as a trading lingua franca well into the nineteenth century and continued to be spoken as a patois in a village near Kandy. Later he immersed himself in Ceylonese civilisation generally and travelled extensively, visiting its major sites including the ancient rock fortress of Sigiriya which he surprised himself by

---

[84] PER to Brig. Sir David Petrie, Colombo, 8 Dec. 1945.

scaling at no small risk. He also experienced the abundant wildlife of Ceylon with its elephants, birds and most consequentially for his highly impressionable mental state its crocodiles, as well as the indignity of a twenty-minute chase after a monkey which made off with his shorts as he bathed in Arugam Bay. Although there was no Jo Heigham to accompany him on his tours of Ceylon, Russell did have an Indian Tamil member of his staff as a guide and for company, one S. Sockalingam. Russell not only taught Sockalingam English but supported him financially and found him employment before leaving Colombo for good. Though Sockalingam was married, an amused Russell reported him — 'a youth with earrings and a sarong' — as having formed 'a violent attachment' to him, a situation reckoned by the largely female staff at 78 Turret Road to be such as to warrant his dismissal. [85] Be this as it may, the touching note Sockalingam left Russell before he departed leaves little doubt of the extent of his gratitude or the generosity extended to him.

On the whole Russell as so often found himself lonely and stifled, particularly once the monsoon set in in late September and the opportunity for travel was curtailed. He was also bored with Colombo, bored with Ceylon, bored with the war:

> Life at the Galle Face [Hotel] is comfortable internment. I never go to the continual dances there as they are Sub-Lieutenant (A) affairs dominated by a conviction that drinking and talking trivialities constitute entertainment — the whole thing merely mechanical. [...] My life is divided between killing time in the office, reading or writing in my room, walking on Galle Face Green in the evening, drinking in the Colombo Club or very occasionally being social. What a life! I have met no one in six months in whom I am the least bit interested. Shades of Jo. Last night I saw the full moon on the beach from my window and thought of those other evenings on a moonlit tropical beach a year ago. [...] Thinking over my life in the Galle Face I have realised that comfortable internment is probably more demoralising than uncomfortable internment. Here one does not have discomfort and hardship to give one something to think about and resist. There is just nothing at all and if I did not have an active mind I too should be suicidal. [86]

[85] PER to Heigham, Colombo, 30 April 1945.
[86] Journal, 20 Sept. & 14 Oct. 1945. 'Sub-Lieutenant (A)' was the rank held by newly qualified Royal Navy pilot officers.

'Even the rain beats time to its own monotony.' [87] As ever he struggled gamely with his depression:

> Before I go I want to go up to India once more. I find India fascinates me more and more though I loathe the dirt and hopelessness of it when I am there. However it is a great place to be in if you are depressed because you know you are surrounded by millions who are even more depressed than you and this acts as a tonic. Instead of being a depressed individual you get assimilated into a continent of Aryan melancholia which has much the same effect as a frenzy of confession. Am I talking rot? Probably. [88]

As his war service drew to a close Russell's mind went back to his early days in the Army and his brief posting to the 5th Battalion of the Bedfordshire and Hertfordshire Regiment in the autumn of 1941 with its congenial officers' mess. This unit was among those transferred to Malaya in time to participate in the Battle for Singapore during which several of his erstwhile messmates were killed and the rest taken prisoner in early 1942. Among the latter was John Crooke whose fortunes Russell was able to follow and whom he met off the liner *Orduna* in Colombo as he was in the course of repatriation to England:

> Today John Crooke who was Signals Officer in 5 Beds & Herts came here from Rangoon. He had been in Siam. Very pleasant fellow who has retained his intelligence and balance to a degree which is astonishing when one thinks of the conditions in which he has lived for the past 3½ years. Went shopping, gave him tea and dinner and a hot bath which I think he appreciated most of all and took him back to the *Orduna* at 9 o'clock. With all these chaps I cannot help thinking that there but for the grace of God [go] I. I wonder how I should have made out? Fairly well if I had had a twin soul or kindred souls, otherwise not at all I suspect. [89]

He no doubt also dwelt, as he continued to dwell, on those who would never come home, particularly a contemporary at Queen's, Lieutenant Norman Brittain, lost in the cruiser HMS *Curacoa* after she was run down and sunk by the liner *Queen Mary* in October 1942, and one of his first students, Harold 'Rollo'

---

[87] PER to Heigham, Colombo, 15 Oct. 1945.
[88] *Ibid.* The trip to India was cancelled.
[89] Journal, 25 Nov. 1945.

Woolley, an RAF Spitfire pilot shot down over Tunis in December of that year. Nor for that matter did Russell forget his academic friends, dispatching packages of good Ceylon tea to ease the rationing in faraway Oxford, now sending increasing intimations of itself to him in the tropics. In May 1945 he had been elected Fellow of Queen's and, at Entwistle's instance, appointed to a University Lectureship in Spanish. The future beckoned but there was one final ordeal, the long voyage home in a crowded troopship filled with the detritus of war, a journey again not materially eased by his rank of lieutenant-colonel:

> We are now 4 days out from Colombo. The ship is small and crowded with 1400 bodies. I have a cabin on the promenade deck which I share with 2 Dutch naval commanders fresh from internment in Java and an old French colonel who led the fighting retreat to Kunming from North Indo-China. We are crowded, unbathed, bored and clad in dirty linen but might be a good deal worse off I dare say. All the majors are on troopdecks. [...] There is no end to the torture to the nerves inflicted by the loud-speakers, either forwarding the ship's orders in twisted vowels or blaring jazz which remarkably few seem to want to hear. [90]

Reaching Liverpool on 18 January 1946, Russell made his way to London to be debriefed by the MI5 hierarchy. Inevitably the subject of the Defence Security establishment in Ceylon argued over in the autumn loomed large in his meeting with Liddell who had earlier blamed the failure of the initiative on what he described as Russell's 'machinations' with the Governor: [91]

> I saw Russell who is just back from Ceylon. I told him that SIFE [Security Intelligence Far East] was now on its legs, that the DSO points at Singapore, Burma and Hong Kong have been set up, and that I felt it was a pity that there was not the same link with Ceylon. He seemed a little astonished that SIFE had really come into being and blamed the position in Ceylon on the Governor. Personally I think that he rather encouraged the Governor to haul down the flag, although there is no doubt that the latter was an extremely timid person, terrified of having anything to do with Intelligence. I explained to Russell that it might well

---

[90] Journal, 1 & 6 Jan. 1946.
[91] TNA, KV 4/466, Liddell Diaries, vol. 13, 1 Oct. 1945, 249.

be necessary for us to know something of what is going on in Ceylon just as much as we may have to have some link with Malta even when the country obtained its independance [*sic*]. It will not of course be possible to have a full-blown DSO, but there are many other covers in which we can have representation. Though Russell is intelligent I do not think that he has much imagination. [92]

Whatever the validity of the assertions, and notwithstanding the recommendations of the Soulbury Commission in connection with dominion status for Ceylon, one may suppose Russell would among other things have viewed SIFE as a matter for the peacetime Service, not for an understaffed hostilities-only officer lacking direction from London and anxious above all to recover the threads of his earlier life. Even so, the interests of HM Government would presumably have been better served had he spent more time on postwar security than beginner's Sinhalese and the vestiges of Portuguese colonisation in Ceylon. His own account of the debrief survives:

> Have seen [Sir David] Petrie, [Jasper] Harker, [Charles] Butler, [Guy] Liddell and [Bertram] Ede — all extremely polite and in varying degrees concealing their ignorance with the exception of Liddell whom I cannot make out — he is obviously highly intelligent but one establishes no relationship with him. Anyway the whole place is in a state of disorganisation prior to the Director General's replacement by new broom. [93]

Russell always took people and institutions on their merits. After a spell of leave he returned to London to sign the Official Secrets Act and was demobilised at Regent's Park Barracks on 20 March 1946. It had been just under five years and seven months since he first reported to Aldershot. 'Back to Oxford by the 4.45 a free man.' [94] The provisions of the OSA he in most essentials respected to the end.

*

Although offered a permanent career in MI5 Russell unsurprisingly had no hesitation in turning it down. Aside from the incompetence he had observed at its

---

[92] TNA, KV 4/467, Liddell Diaries, vol. 14, 22 Jan. 1946, 73.
[93] Journal, 22 Jan. 1946. Petrie's successor was Sir Percy Sillitoe.
[94] Journal, 22 March 1946.

head office in London and in too many of its operatives in the Far East, he regarded it as a professional dead-end: 'I am glad I am leaving them as I see no future for them on present lines.' [95] Subsequent developments both in MI5 and at Oxford proved the wisdom of the choice, but one can't help speculating that the many university committees over which he subsequently presided, together with the waspish discourse of academic life and politics, must often have seemed trivial alongside the harsh realities of wartime intelligence, of death and survival, brutality and humanity, incompetence and intellect. As Russell recalled,

> I am one of those academics of the 1930s who, not without a certain unease of conscience, look back on the Second World War as one of the most positive and creative periods of their lives since it gave them a great variety of new experiences as well as opportunities to discover in themselves talents which would have remained hidden had they not been hauled out of academia. [96]

There was more to it than that. Later he explained in his elliptical way that 'one was not always mainly committed to the job everyone thought one was there to do. Playing for real what were essentially pretence roles always appealed to my penchant for ambiguity.' [97]

Those who came to know Russell in future years immediately recognised some deep wellspring of human experience beyond his natural charm, outward self-assurance and power of mind. Because he rarely gave up other than hints of his wartime past they could not know the origin of it and it has been left to posterity to reconstruct this phase in his formation. Writing to his friend Jo Heigham shortly after his arrival in Ceylon in April 1945, Russell set down these words to live by:

> [I]f one is ever in a position to exercise any power over other people as a necessary part of one's work it is a good thing to study the use of power a bit — most people do not and therefore make a balls of it, or at best do it badly. As I put you and me in the category of potential wielders of power I think we might, therefore, think about it. [98]

[95] Journal, 22 Jan. 1946.
[96] PELR, 3.
[97] JMA, PER to Javier Marías, Oxford, 4 June 2002.
[98] PER to Heigham, Colombo, 30 April 1945.

For all his massive learning and innate humanity there was one experience which perhaps counted for more than any other in the subliminal impression Russell gave to the world after the war, and that was the measured exercise of power when lives and fortunes lay in the palm of his hand. Inwardly, however, Peter Russell was about to confront a challenge more searching and more frightening than any he had encountered in time of war.

CHAPTER FOUR
Dark Tower

Though Russell's achievements as a scholar, teacher and as an intelligence officer would merit a biography on that account alone, it was his power of mind and depth of personality that drew people to him and continue to invite deeper inquiry. To spend time in Russell's company was to form the impression of a man fully equipped personally and intellectually to explore the complex themes which he — and those who knew him — would encounter in the matter at hand and by extension in the business of living. The fount of this gift, shared both directly and in his writing and lecturing, was a humanity and sensitivity which from his earliest years took him on a mental journey more consequential, more searching and more painful than any other experience in his life. It was also one that almost to the end he never revealed to any outside a therapeutic setting, a torment lived almost entirely in the mind.

Any biography of Peter Russell must therefore intercalate the facts of his life and the stages in his personal and professional development with the extraordinary mental and emotional world in which he lived. While that statement could in a sense be applied to any individual, it is the more pertinent with Russell for whom the mental experience was of far greater importance than the external manifestations of his life, career, scholarship and achievements, impressive though these were. It also explains why a highly accomplished man was also an exceedingly private one who chose his company very carefully, avoided administrative entanglements beyond those attaching to the few positions he held in his career and frequently turned down major appointments in Oxford and elsewhere. The pertinence also derives from the volume of intimate information on his psychological makeup contained in his private papers which bear witness to the excruciatingly long and detailed examination to which he subjected himself and also the insight with which it was carried out. It can be said that there was no subject on which Russell expended more energy and intellectual resources than the operation of his own mind, the exploration of which had incidental benefits to others and to the richness of his work but came at such a price to him.

*

'The years of childhood are the formative ones' Russell wrote in his last major work.¹ The context of his life and the milestones of his infancy, childhood and youth have been traced out in earlier chapters but it is the formation of Russell's psyche that concerns us here and there can be no doubt that his mother Rita remained at the centre of his being, the alpha and omega of his personal life. Russell's earliest memory was of the birth of his brother Hugh in Christchurch on 9 August 1916, two months before his third birthday. In 1935 he recalled 'very vividly going into Mother's bedroom at Knowlescourt and seeing Hugh just born lying naked in a cot and bawling hard'. ² What Russell admitted decades later was the disgust and jealousy that rose in his gorge at this intrusion in the exclusive relationship he had hitherto enjoyed with her. It was a feeling that never left him, much as he understood it to be unjust and unreasonable to his brother who was always attentive to their relationship and to their mother and went on to a distinguished career in his own right, the much-loved head of his own family. Another contributory factor, unvoiced this time, was that Hugh Russell *né* Wheeler knew too much of the past.

'[He] did some very odd things about the house.' Bernard Wheeler with his younger son Hugh at the family home on Weston Road, Christchurch, c. 1919. Within a year his marriage was essentially over.

¹ *Prince Henry 'the Navigator': A Life* (New Haven, Conn.: Yale University Press, 2000), 19.
² ALRTP, 10.

Russell's early years were lived against a backdrop of geographical relocations between Britain and New Zealand and the frequent absences of his father first in the war and latterly in an army convalescent hospital following the collapse of his marriage. Of this disintegration Russell was an eyewitness, including the incident of domestic violence related elsewhere, but the account of his childhood he set down in 1935 shows the experience in the way of all children to have been one of intuition as well as observation: 'I was an exceedingly inquisitive child I remember, only too anxious to hear what people said on the telephone or to each other and quick to make deductions from what I heard, deductions which I now realise were usually right.' [3] The reference in Hugh's memoirs to 'another very frightening moment' with his father aside from being threatened with a razor strap and Rita's memory of Wheeler doing 'some very odd things about the house so that I became afraid of what he might do' after the separation indicates that there were dimensions to his behaviour too painful to spell out. [4] Russell reserved his comments on the matter to his most intimate writings.

The dates of Wheeler's departure from the family home and the annulment of the marriage in 1924 are mentioned nowhere in the family papers but the former appears to have occurred around 1920 when Russell was six or seven. It is clear that Russell's grandfather Thomas in particular stepped in to fill the void:

> At the beginning of each month I used to go to Grandpa to collect my monthly 4/- pocket money which I always spent in about a week. Often he would forget and I had all sorts of formulas for tactfully reminding him. Once on my birthday he gave me a silver fob watch which I was enormously proud of and which I still have. One Sunday night when we were taking leave he shook me by the hand instead of kissing me as usual and said I was too big to kiss him now. After that we always shook hands. His moustache was very prickly when he kissed me. [...] Once, when I was in bed for some reason or other, Grandpa brought me a new copy of Hans Andersen's Fairy Tales — I can still see his animated blue eyes and white moustache as he brought it. [5]

Kindly and paternal though he became, Thomas Russell's word was law: 'The only person I was really afraid of in those days was Grandpa and of him I was very much

---

[3] *Ibid.*, 3.
[4] Russell, *One Man's Journey*, 6, & RMR, 26.
[5] ALRTP, 7 & 24–5.

[afraid] though much respect went with it too.'⁶ Aside from the formidable presence of his grandfather, discipline was dispensed by Rita in the traditional manner: 'Mother's theory of bringing-up was affectionate but old-fashioned on the disciplinary side', including wielding the handle of a feather duster. ⁷ On the whole, and without being idyllic, Russell's childhood was lacking neither in love nor in care, comfort, entertainment or stimulation. Among many abiding memories were excursions, the boys' pet cat Basher, a cherished model of a 1913 car kept boxed and wrapped in tissue, Uncle Gerald's tame magpie Jackie and milk dispensed from a dray drawn by a shire horse, all under the aegis of his grandfather and extended family, and against the natural wonder of New Zealand, the streets lined with Monterey cypress, the Canterbury Plains and the towering Southern Alps.

Nonetheless, aside from the divorce and the domestic violence that preceded it a series of indelible traumas were visited on the highly sensitive and impressionable young Peter by the time he returned to England in 1926. The first came during the family's voyage to New Zealand in the *Oxfordshire* in 1918–19. Aside from her civilian passengers the ship was repatriating 1,175 troops of the New Zealand Division, practically all veterans of the Western Front. By the time the *Oxfordshire* reached Auckland some of the soldiers had extended their battle trauma to one of the youngest passengers embarked, not as a misguided prank but in what he interpreted as malevolent anger. Committed to his youthful memoir in 1935, this searing experience lived with Russell for the rest of his life:

> One moment of horror returns. I must have annoyed the men by stepping on them or something and one afternoon two of them held me at an arm's length of the edge of the water from the deck and said they would drop me in. Since then heights have always made me frightened or at least giddy when I look over the edge. ⁸

Another incident never mentioned by Russell but recorded by his brother concerned the occasion he came close to burning down the family home in Christchurch:

> There was one occasion in the Heaton Street house which might have been disastrous. Our house was entirely built of wood, and we had an

---

⁶ *Ibid.*, 3.
⁷ *Ibid.*, 26.
⁸ *Ibid.*, 14–15.

open fire in the sitting-room. Peter had been rather grumpy one evening and told off for it, so he proceeded to build a large fire in the living room fireplace using wood from the wooden boxes which we had to buy petrol for the car. Each box held two tins of, I think, two gallon capacity. There were no petrol pumps at that time. The chimney went on fire and the next thing was the arrival of the fire brigade. Firemen scrambled all over the house and the roof to get to the chimney and the fire was quickly quenched. A chimney fire in a two-story wooden house was a very dangerous occurrence where other similar houses were near, and the penalty for having one was usually a stiff fine. However, the firemen — all of them volunteers in those days — followed my mother into the dining room and each had a dram or two, and we never heard any more about it! Peter, meanwhile had a great fright and shut himself in his bedroom while all the shenanigans were going on. [9]

These traumas were, however, dwarfed by another of Russell's making and characteristic of young children under any circumstances but which in voluntarily separating himself from his mother he later recognised to have touched him at the deepest level:

When I was especially perturbed or annoyed I would do what I called 'run away'. This consisted of putting a few things I selected in a suitcase (I can't remember what things) and then walking off down the road vaguely in the direction of the 'country'. I usually found the suitcase grew too heavy and so would end up in a field somewhere. If it was summer and the grass long I would lie down in it out of sight of everyone and everything. I loved being thus hidden among the thick green stalks, the clover and the hay. After that became boring I would finally return home without being seen, if possible. [10]

Add to this exposure to death, not in adults (which came when his Uncle Gerald, a doctor, died of septic pneumonia in 1925) but among his peers, several of whom succumbed to polio during his childhood. Hugh's memoirs record the imposition of periods of isolation and quarantine when schools were shut and

---

[9] Russell, *One Man's Journey*, 12–13.
[10] ALRTP, 26–7.

children confined to their homes, but the mortality eventually touched Peter personally, a shock vivid enough to be shared with a friend late in life:

> We must have been talking about epidemics, or perhaps vaccinations, when he mentioned that when he was a child in New Zealand he and his brother used to play with two boys who lived next door (or perhaps in the same street). One day they were going round to play with them as usual when his mother stopped them and told them that the two children had died of polio in the night; it made a great impression on him, he said. [11]

The consequences of such events on an individual either at the time or later cannot be gauged or traced without detailed input from them, but by the age of around ten Russell was as he recalled exhibiting signs of withdrawal and emotional upheaval consistent with these and other traumas: 'I was rather lonely and wanted to get inside and read but Uncle Gerald […] used to see that I didn't do so. He used to tell me that I would be "party-faced" if I did so and I used to think that, as he was a doctor, he was probably right.' [12] 'I was' he recalled 'a rather bad-tempered and sensitive child.' [13]

Russell evidently had a considerable ego to go with his superior intellect and physical stature, one challenged, as already noted, by the strictures and society of other boys at St Andrew's College, which he entered at the age of seven in early 1921: 'Though I was as big and strong as the rest I used to hate playing rough games or fight with the other boys as I was afraid of being beaten by them and the humiliation would have been unendurable.' [14] This and the exemption from games which resulted from Uncle Gerald's (erroneous) diagnosis of a heart murmur in 1920 may have been partly responsible for generating another of the millstones that came to hang around Russell's neck, the sense of himself as not being a 'man of action', of being physically inept and incapable which complicated his psychosexuality and marked some of his key relationships, an intellectualised characterisation of the impotence that awaited. To this neurosis was added the experience of corporal punishment which resulted in a premature sexualisation:

---

[11] Clive Griffin, email to the author, 9 March 2020. This episode may date to the spring of 1925 when Russell's school St Andrew's College was temporarily closed due to a polio epidemic.
[12] ALRTP, 17–18.
[13] *Ibid.*, 26.
[14] *Ibid.*, 30–1 & 38–9.

'I was a rather bad-tempered and sensitive child.' Peter Wheeler, 1915.

The boarders were even more under the rule of corporal punishment and it formed the subject of a great deal of their conversation; they would boast of the amount they could stand. I remember the boy Dunnet describing the 'pure blue marks' he was carrying with great pride. Talk of this nature stimulated our adolescent minds at their early stages and we

> would gradually become aware of pleasurable sensations which could be derived from watching other boys who were beaten or examining their wounds. I remember being somewhat worried when I began to grow the pubic hairs and have erections often brought on by contemplation of flagellation — but noticing in [the] changing room that other boys had them too was not greatly put out. [15]

More generally, although Russell recalled feeling a 'sympathetic interest' in the plight of one of his fellows given twenty cuts by a prefect for swearing, in his sensitivity he later regretted not showing solidarity with 'a weak frail boy with a very red face called Neville Lewers, whom I liked but was rather ashamed of so doing as the other boys bullied him as a weakling'. [16] Ten years on it was these memories and sentiments that shaped Russell's concluding remarks on his experience at St Andrew's as a whole:

> I was probably more intelligent than most of my contemporaries but I had the makings of a coward and with lots of others came to get a temporary flagellation complex as adolescence became confused with the frequent sight and talk of thrashings of my contemporaries. [17]

Russell had earlier stated that 'I think on the whole I resented school for its loss of freedom and for the collective air of it all', by which he presumably meant his inability to thrive as an individual in a situation in which, as later, he could neither dominate nor interact normally as part of a group. This cast of mind together with his innate sensitivity amounting to an emotional disorder, especially as it centred on his attachment to his mother, the traumas of his childhood and the austerity he evidently found at Sedbergh School in Westmoreland contributed to the complete mental and physical collapse he experienced within weeks of his arrival there in September 1926, an outcome that kept him out of school for a year.

And so to Cheltenham where Russell gradually found his feet largely it seems on the basis of an immediate assertion of his academic distinction. At an emotional level the single-sex configuration of the English public school naturally served to channel his adolescent inclinations in the direction of his fellow pupils:

---

[15] *Ibid.*, 36–7.
[16] *Ibid.*, 34. Lewers (1913–2009) went on to a distinguished career as a photographer and photojournalist whose work was exhibited in London, Paris and Vienna.
[17] *Ibid.*, 39.

Then there were various romantic but innocent friendships. Now such things are over I look at them with a slight touch of sadness — George Garlick, Bush, the Longdens, Maurice Carter, Seddon and Castle, M[ike] McNeile, though the latter can hardly be styled a 'romantic' friendship. [18]

None of these friendships took on a physical dimension but Russell's journal for 1939 makes plain that his flagellation complex was enhanced by the experience:

[O]ne is amazed to think how much part beating played in one's life then; first interest in its technicalities and in the experiences of those who had recently suffered and their weals; fear of being beaten oneself and at the same time a half-felt desire to suffer for experience and for the interest in oneself it would create; later it came to be associated with more troublesome feelings, the thought of beating someone produced new sensations and the sight of weals on buttocks gave one sexual stimulus at times. Therein lies the real psychological danger to adolescents of beating as understood by [the] public-school system. To some it must have produced a twist which might induce permanent homosexuality and for many it must have delayed the passing of the 'homosexual period' of their adolescence. [19]

The burden of Russell's last sentence is that he had successfully emerged from his own 'homosexual period', but if so this was true only in the sense that his yearnings in that direction had no physical outlet nor in his case could reasonably be expected to do so. It was a dimension of his sexuality destined to evolve through various phases of denial, repression, self-delusion, rationalisation, recharacterisation, admission and acceptance. For now, however, Peter Russell was in every respect ready for Oxford.

*

---

[18] Diary, 20 Sept. 1934.

[19] Journal, 15 July 1939. 'Such a silly vice' he later wrote of flagellation; Journal, 15 Jan. 1948. The same entry, written in connection with his reading of Christopher Isherwood's *Mr Norris Changes Trains* (1935), alludes to Russell's tutor and friend George Kolkhorst's flagellation complex, administered by 'his Corpion'. See Bevis Hillier, *John Betjeman: New Fame, New Love* (London: John Murray, 2002), 287, 289 & 291 for other dimensions of Kolkhorst's sexuality evident at this time.

Imposing, brilliant, charming though occasionally forbidding and reputed to be the handsomest man in Oxford, Russell's private writings and memories, together with the recollections of those who knew him, leave no doubt that he had plenty of admirers of both sexes. The question left unanswered for decades is why that never led to a partnership as most would understand it and what carefully guarded sexuality underlay that outcome. Though Russell was unquestionably attracted both to men and women and clearly appreciated the male and female form in a sexual as well as in an aesthetic sense, there is no firm evidence that this ever extended to a full consummation of relations despite periodic efforts to bring that about. Why this was so brings this narrative to the heart of a psychosexual world as complex as it was private.

Reaching Oxford in 1931, Russell embarked on the first of a sequence of romantic infatuations with men which, with intervals and in many different guises, lasted practically all his life. All of these friendships came in the context of the loneliness and depression which clouded much of his existence and were essentially or ostensibly carried at the level of emotional and intellectual engagement, the desire for an intimate relationship not of the body but of the mind. So far as it is possible to tell, none of these men were other than heterosexual, often avowedly so, and all those for whom information on their subsequent lives is available can be shown to have married and in most cases fathered children.

The first to appear in Russell's diaries was a fellow undergraduate at Queen's College referred to only as Ian, though the listings of the *Oxford University Calendar* would by a process of elimination identify him as Ian Wright Thomson, an Exhibitioner of the College. Theirs was a shared love of the countryside and an appreciation for quiet companionship: 'Ian and I sat in my room after Hall and listened to a very good radio programme. A marvellous evening which gives me faith in friendship if nothing else.' [20] A week later and after two walks to nearby Frilford Russell committed this to his diary: 'God grant this friendship may last. Everything very depressing now.' On New Year's Eve he wrote the following: 'So ends 1932. It has given me advance in work and influence. Crystallization of ideas. Confidence and above all a friendship of the highest importance which I hope may be a life-long thing.' Except for two sad entries in early 1934 this is in fact the last reference to Ian with whom the friendship clearly did not prosper, though a pattern of ecstatic infatuation, nervous anticipation, obsessive commitment and,

---

[20] Diary, 27 Nov. 1932.

in most cases, pained resignation and ultimate disillusionment had been established which was repeated *mutatis mutandis* until long after the war. [21]

The first of these relationships known to have assumed a significant dimension was that with John Hennell, another student at Queen's who first appears in a diary entry for 10 June 1933 ('[w]asted the first part of the morning talking to John Hennell who may or may not be worth bothering about'). Lunch with Hennell and a companion followed at the Criterion Bar in London but the next mention on 4 July was decidedly unpromising, a further example of the haughtiness of which the young Russell was capable: 'Letter from John Hennell who is quite a pleasant person though entirely lacking in intelligence and fairly plebeian.' This letter had reached him in Strasbourg but an exchange of correspondence over the course of that summer clearly put Russell in a very different frame of mind. The development of this relationship and the demise of that with Ian cannot be followed in detail because Russell destroyed all the pages up to and including 8 August in his diary for 1933 and created an expurgated copy in its stead. Nonetheless, the entry he made for the 23rd in Paris leaves little doubt as to the depth of his feelings:

> Life is just bloody. Letter from John who can't come. Nasty feeling when 10 weeks hopes crash like that but somehow I expected it. Also he's fallen in love blast it! Why? Still it's just Hell. As if that wasn't enough to ruin everything Mother and Hugh aren't coming either as Hugh's got to have something cut out of his foot. I sometimes feel just a silly lonely little boy.

The following day came this entry: 'My broken heart (how banal!) has written some decent prose today.' Already in a heightened emotional state ('Wonder if it is possible for [John] to have the same feeling for me inside him as I have for him. It would be nice to think so'), in mid-September Russell suffered some traumatic experience in Paris to which he alludes in his diary but of which no other mention is made in his papers: 'I have left the preceding pages blank as they are not big enough to contain what I might put there and anyway they are going to be black in my mind.' [22] Weeks earlier he had written that '[t]he wheel of life is revolving so fast that I'm wondering how it's going to stop'. Now he had his answer, but

---

[21] Diary, 20 & 26 Jan. 1934.
[22] Diary, 14 & 20 Sept. 1933 respectively.

Russell was destined to re-cultivate the impression of himself as 'just a silly lonely little boy' in all his key relationships. [23]

The return to Oxford in the autumn brought with it a resumption of his friendship with Hennell though for Russell it was one tinged with sadness: 'Wish I wasn't so jealous of John and try too hard to be like him as a result and fail. Still it's all too beautiful for the mere words of a diary.' [24] 'He's too good for a silly ass like me' Russell concluded. [25] All the same, relationships of this sort brought blessed albeit temporary relief from his crushing loneliness: 'Spent one of our glorious afternoons in John's room until tea-time. One is really what one aspires to be for an hour or two and life is worth living.' [26] Among the topics of discussion were 'the usual troubles of continent young men — reaching as obvious no practical conclusions'. [27] Hennell's departure to play rugby in early December left Russell 'feeling lost — but not so much as last time when it was for four months', apparently forgetting the chronology of their relationship. [28] Still, his absence allowed Russell to get on with his novel: 'When John's about I'm living too romantically to want to write.' [29] Russell was therefore left 'very cut up' when plans to spend Christmas with Hennell's strict Nonconformist family in Lincolnshire fell through; earlier he had reported having gone out and 'bought John an expensive cigarette case — not for that but because I'd like to go without things for him'. [30] The only evidence of physical intimacy between the two are the backrubs Russell records giving Hennell, possibly in connection with the latter's exertions as a rugby player, but the expurgation of his diary may tell its own story. By early February 1934, however, Russell had begun to question the wisdom of his attachment:

> Principal event of day has been an attempt on my part to try and put some ideas on the future into John's head and I am going to try and leave him alone for a few days to think it out. I like him so much that I can't bear to see the way he is drifting alone — taking the ribboned cap for the

[23] Diary, 24 Aug. 1933.
[24] Diary, 15 Oct. 1933.
[25] Diary, 13 Dec. 1933.
[26] Diary, 18 Oct. 1933.
[27] Diary, 2 Nov. 1933.
[28] Diary, 2 Dec. 1933.
[29] Diary, 14 Dec. 1933.
[30] Diary, 23 & 14 Dec. 1933 respectively.

halo and the vague emotion for the ideal. I realise what repression in childhood can do now but with help from the Chaos he will turn out all right in the end. [31]

Nonetheless, the prospect of Hennell going down at the end of Hilary term 1934 again put Russell in a state of despair:

Tomorrow term ends. I stay here for a month and John will be gone so that I feel as if the bottom of things is going to drop out in a few hours. Goodness knows how it will end next year when the auditions of schools are dimmed by the thought of what will happen. Besides this time it's only for a month and I mustn't be a bloody fool. [32]

The following month Russell enjoyed a successful stay with Hennell and his family in Lincolnshire: 'Now that I know more of John's background I shall be able to do more to help him.' [33] However, the trip Russell took with Hennell to France, Germany and Austria in the summer revived earlier concerns:

A further cause of trouble for me is the question of John, whom I have liked very much, for whom I am very sorry and who has even been a source of inspiration sometimes. Now I begin to feel the vacuum. I've tried to interest him in things of intellectual value and things worth while, but all to no purpose and he is in danger of appearing to me as a waste of time, because he refuses to bother about the chances and advice (obvious) which is given him. What am I to do? [34]

By 13 August the fantasy had collapsed: 'Picked John up — alas how are great thoughts fallen!' A month later Russell sent Hennell a letter ending their friendship: 'Had letter from John Hennell this morning and it appears he has understood so that is that and never again!' [35] This left the problem of the room they had agreed to share in college for a term. Resolute action was required: 'Why I ever said I would share a room with him for one term I do not know. If it is not

---

[31] Diary, 8 Feb. 1934.
[32] Diary, 9 March 1934.
[33] Diary, 19 April 1934.
[34] Diary, 2 Aug. 1934.
[35] Diary, 16 Sept. 1934.

to be hellish I shall have to crush him mentally at start.' [36] This he presumably did. In the lengthy summary of 1934 he wrote in his diary on New Year's Eve Russell dismissed the relationship with Hennell and presumably that with Ian as 'boyish infatuations', adding that 'apart from my boyish and perhaps regrettable Hennell episode no trouble has come my way either as illness or mental worry'. In fact so great was his embarrassment and annoyance at himself that as with his 1933 diary Russell went to considerable lengths to erase several portions of it in which Hennell was mentioned, a task facilitated this time by his use of soluble ink: '[r]eferences to John make me blush to read yet at [the] time I really thought I meant it.' [37]

As his undergraduate years drew on Russell reached the unhappy conclusion that he was a far more sensitive and introspective individual than anyone he knew, for which together with his career aspirations the only reliable balm was his creative writing and Nature as he understood it:

> Why do some people feel and suffer so much more deeply than others? There are only two things I believe in now. One is love in which I include friendship and the other is the purity of Nature.
>
> How terrible a thing it is to be obliged to think. How can I believe in any hope of mankind after the evil that I have seen in the last few weeks. Either mankind is corrupt and hopeless or there is no such thing as good and evil. Yet there is good untouched by evil (Nature as I know it). So mankind must be externally corrupt and happy [are] those who don't realize it. I must go on and try to find and follow beauty, seeking it in all things and yet believing that I shall probably never find it. God! The deuce theory!
>
> I believe out of the chaos of feelings and ideas something is emerging, which means I shall soon be able to continue my book. Creation is the one sure joy, or perhaps I should include unphysical love too. [38]

Russell came early to the importance of knowing himself and his limitations, though the consequences of this self-knowledge were all too apparent: 'Introspection is dangerous. I am a cynical idealist and the combination is not a

---

[36] Diary, 5 Oct. 1934.
[37] Diary, 7 Aug. 1934.
[38] Diary, 5 Dec. 1932, 21 Sept. 1933 & 18 March 1934 respectively.

happy one.' [39] Equally apparent was the strain of having to maintain a veneer of conviviality, and among the writings which emerged from this realisation was a poem dated Paris, 24 August 1933, the first significant record of a pervasive depression:

> Laughter
> Laugh, laugh like fools but always laugh
> Lest truth us mock and courage fails.
> Avoid dark caverns where peace prevails
> And shrieking choose the easiest path.
> Keep with the mob of grinning faces
> Lest doubts and sorrows burn the heart.
> Thought is pain making a soul smart
> In the still of lonely places.
> Laugh and the world laughs too they say
> But weep and watch it laugh still more.
> God is a clown, and life a bore
> Joy a myth and our bodies are clay.
> So twist your lips in a smile you fool
> (And never worry about your eyes).
> Run from the angry demon who spies
> Your tear and, quickly brushing a cheek,
> Points with a shout 'he weeps the coward!'

In February 1938 Russell revisited this theme with the candour that became the mark of his private writings:

> I am discovering that my own excessive capacity for pity is going to be a great trouble in life. It seems that my strongest and most sincere emotion is just that. I am so sensitive to [the] feelings of other people that I would suffer great annoyance and unhappiness myself rather than cause hurt to anyone's susceptibilities. This is no doubt due to my own neurotic sensitivity. I suffer so much if my own feelings are trampled upon that I can too easily attribute similar sufferings to others. All the same I am not really ashamed of that salient feature of my character though objectively

---

[39] Diary, 19 March 1934.

I regard it as weakness. Yet my own facility and even delight in the malicious gossip and unkind remarks about even my friends, which is characteristic of Oxford Common Rooms, is in no way checked by this feeling of pity which seems to be purely a personal matter. [40]

'Laugh, laugh like fools but always laugh.' Russell c. 1935.

[40] Journal, 20 Feb. 1938.

It was at this juncture that Russell formed another of his close attachments, this time with one of his earliest students, Derek Hamblen of St John's:

> He is intelligent, sensitive and entirely lacking in any form of conceit or affectation. Also has real feeling for music which seems to me to be the acid test of genuine culture and civilization in such a man. Also a little lazy and plays games without having that wretched English worship of them. [41]

As would happen so many times over the ensuing decades, relations evolved from that of tutor and student to one of close friendship, Hamblen accompanying Russell to Paris, Tuscany and Rome in the spring vacation of 1938:

> Derek is a delightful person to have with one on such a trip and the whole thing would have been much inferior if he had not been there to share and enhance the experience. Our relation of tutor and pupil has been wholly destroyed now but a much better one has taken its place; it remains to be seen whether our relationship was artificially created by the surroundings or not. For me I experienced an intimacy of feeling which I have not known since I ceased to be an undergraduate and my friends of that time left. Derek showed me that my childhood days are not yet over and for that alone I am inexpressibly his debtor though he will not know it. Catharsis of repressions of three years. If I can repay him in a small way by helping him to get a 'first' I shall do all I can. He is a gifted being too *comme je n'ai pas connu depuis longtemps*. [42]

As related elsewhere, Russell and Hamblen travelled at some personal risk to Portugal and Spain together in the summer of that year before enjoying each other's company during the Michaelmas term that followed:

> I saw a lot of Derek. Curious what a complete and mutual understanding there is between us as he is nearly 4 years younger than I am. I would give a lot to help him get a 1st so that he would have something really worthwhile to remember me by when the melancholy but I suppose inevitable parting of the ways comes. Oxford will be a very much less agreeable

---

[41] *Ibid.*
[42] Journal, 26 March 1938.

place for me when he has gone. I think our association may be because we are complementary to each other. [43]

There is no evidence that Russell saw or corresponded with Hamblen after the outbreak of war until 1953 but during it he befriended fellow intelligence officer and Cambridge graduate Major Jo Heigham whom he met in Accra in 1944. Heigham was evidently one of the few people in Russell's life in whose company he felt truly at ease, and never more so than on their extended trips through West Africa:

> Maurice [French official] obviously bewildered by the setup between Jo and self. The verbal Nicky–Willy correspondence escapes him which is hardly surprising and merely flatters our sense of *reserrement.*
>
> After we had disposed of Auger we drink whiskey in our bedroom and attain one of our better *entretiens.* These are less and less conversations in the Johnsonian sense and what is actually said is more more like the visible part of an iceberg — its real import does not appear. This is an excellent thing — what Baudelaire would call *correspondance des âmes — avec les autres c'est du théâtre.* This is shameful weakness, writing in French what I think but hesitate to say in English, which can well take such mild statements of sensibility — the bleary stiff upper lip tradition is always just around the corner.
>
> In the evening we retire to our room — our minds sharpened by reflex from the surrounding nullity. What we talk about does not belong here.
>
> Jo and I return to our bungalow more than a little drunk and indulge in one of our more civilised pastimes — getting undressed leisurely. So few people have the art of making getting dressed and undressed and washing something more than a mechanical function. [44]

Nonetheless, the inescapable impression here as elsewhere is that practically all the elevated emotion in the relationship was Russell's, whereas for his counterpart it was simply a matter of close male friendship under stress of war of the kind shown in Heigham's correspondence after Russell left for Ceylon in early 1945.

[43] Journal, 2 Jan. 1939.
[44] Journal, 17, 18, 19 & 21 Oct. 1944 respectively. 'Nicky–Willy correspondence' refers to the messages exchanged between Kaiser Wilhelm II and Tsar Nicholas II prior to the outbreak of the First World War.

In fact, as Russell reported a few years later, the inevitable disillusion had come while he was still in West Africa, Heigham having 'round[ed] on his benefactor' in unexplained circumstances after six months in Accra. [45]

After the war it was the turn of E. C. Riley, one of Russell's earliest and most brilliant students to come unwittingly into the orbit of his infatuation. Here the pattern of former years repeated itself. The relationship was again configured as an intellectual meeting of minds which unbeknownst to his counterpart brought Russell to a plane of obsession and unrelenting introspection that damaged both his mental and his physical health. With Riley away in Cuba and the United States visiting relatives and investigating the possibility of a career in the United Nations in early 1948, Russell was frequently beside himself with concern as to whether his friend would write to him, how he would receive the content of his own letters and whether indeed he was thinking about him at all. The fact that Russell was fully aware of his codependency did not lessen the mental anguish to which he lent himself:

> Thoughts have been rather in the <u>west</u> all day; found myself thinking it was about time I had a letter from Cuba but managed to dismiss at least <u>that</u> unworthy notion; if I reach a stage where I start nagging Ted with my mind then self-immolation will be certainly the only thing left. But I do not think I shall sink to spiritual assassination of that kind at least. [46]

That assassination he instead visited on himself in a series of dreams and hallucinations, possibly exacerbated by medication, which drained his energy and enthusiasm for teaching and work and left him on the verge of physical and mental collapse: 'I have very nearly lost control of the situation — my situation — during the past few days. This is due to excess of work having reached such proportions that I found it impossible to do <u>anything</u> at all.' [47] Anything, that is, except capture his repressive predicament in coruscating prose:

> A wasted day; futility hangs like a sword unseen but casting its shadow which I <u>can</u> see; so all the creative impulses are held rigid by tensed nerves and escape only metamorphosed into idiotic puffs of cigarette smoke. After tea retired to bed to escape from the clutch of the day,

[45] Journal, 5 Feb. 1948.
[46] Journal, 8 Feb. 1948.
[47] Journal, 23 Feb. 1948.

eluding it by doubling away into the blue lands where the several suns of aphrodisiac warmth restore tingling life to the fingertips and flex the muscles into the shape if not the form of creative effort. Then felt better, though resentful. [48]

At this juncture Russell came to the work of the bisexual poet Vicente Aleixandre with its appreciation of the beauty of nature and exploration of failed and ephemeral love affairs:

> I also read some Aleixandre — quite different but very effective — passion which transforms whole universe into reminiscences and suggestions and symbols of the flesh. I did not read much but I thought I had rarely read verse which expressed so lyrically the sensations of overwhelming desire. They read as if they were written when the poet was three quarters of the way to an orgasm. [49]

Out of this came a measure of release: 'Bed last night very difficult. Aleixandre-like frenzies of the flesh, but all too literally *sombras del paraíso.*' [50]

The journal Russell kept of those first three months in 1948 is not only a record of fixation and declining health but is also, as it was intended to be, the release of a torrent of emotions pent up since he and Riley had spent a month together in France and Spain the previous autumn. During that trip a moonlit walk with Riley through the pine and cork woods above the Catalan fishing village of Calella de Palafrugell apparently brought Russell to the brink of suicide over the cliffs. The urge was resisted but something ancient was disturbed and crystallised in Russell's mind which now vented itself in all its anguish and frustration. Past the hundredth page of his journal Russell unveiled what he called his Dark Tower:

> Come; it is the time and occasion to make an effort of will to escape from this debasement; let the *Lebensblut* stream and not into the well-worn utensil set out to catch it but onto the untried smooth surfaces where it may make its unimpeded patterns.

---

[48] Journal, 8 Feb. 1948.
[49] Journal, 14 Jan. 1948.
[50] Journal, 24 Jan. 1948. *Sombra del paraíso* is the collection of poems Aleixandre published in Madrid in 1944.

[...]
You. This is mere playacting. A simulated death lust rubbed by the friction of literary memories. It is without meaning. The reality is too absurd to contemplate, posturing yourself into an eternity of nothingness at the same moment as I have pains in my abdomen which will soon lead to defecation. You cannot make the two ends meet, the corporeal and imaginative. All that happens if you strain them too much is that the content snaps like a worn bootlace and nothing is left. Remember Icarus mid-ocean drowned. It is a child's error to be over-greedy and want to go on eating happiness without ever stopping to digest it. It soon makes you sick. Moderation is feeling emotions as the angels do. Besides what you are feeling is, anyway, not the result of your own playing, alone strumming the keys in a dark room like a deaf man imagining he is playing music dipped in the colour of the sun. The tune is the melody of pipe and flute and without both there could be no poetry. I condemn you for a selfish music-maker, trying to make me play like the orchestra at a ball, left to put on soft hat and worn overcoat over my fine clothes and walk home supperless when the dance is over.

[...]

I know you are right but I resent it, deep inside. You should have allowed me my last deception, allowed me to think I could dance to the sea's tune, aping the perfection of that shape.

What results? People stand sparse and motionless, their feet rooted in the anonymity of the concrete which flows towards their hearts. They stand, meaningless as trees leafless in summertime. Far away in *their* distance, on the seat next to us, the unmarked stranger sits unaware like an empty glass on a ledge. Time, at last compounding his treasons, sneaks off smaller and smaller down the long platform until he disappears hidden by distance and the white tunnel, echoing, leads only back to the dark tower where one watches, thinking of catching with a pin the black eel which lived in the pool in Dog Creek. Was it really better to have stood on the platform than to have decapitated the future with the sharp edge of one's will? [51]

---

[51] Journal, 31 March 1948. Measuring up to five feet, the longfin eel (*Anguilla dieffenbachii*) is endemic to New Zealand's lakes and rivers.

Dog Creek, or Dog Stream as it is better known, flows near Hanmer Springs in New Zealand where Russell's father was in convalescence for shell shock after the Great War. Russell can scarcely have imagined that the love of beauty to which he had wedded himself fifteen years earlier should come to this tragic pass in his own mind.

Russell during his visit to Calella de Palafrugell in Catalonia with Ted Riley in September 1947.

This declaration, heavily influenced by the language, sentiment and rhythms of Swinburne, Rimbaud, Eliot, Auden, Aleixandre, *Ulysses* and *Finnegans Wake*, was followed by a longer and even more esoteric piece of writing, the Calella Eclogue mentioned in it and throughout Russell's journal as fermenting in his mind, the last outpouring of his literary yearnings. Once again, there is no evidence that Riley had the full measure of these perturbations until Russell shared his diary of their journey to Spain the previous year and particularly this latest journal on Riley's return from America in April 1948, part of an agreement to exchange the writings kept by them while they were apart. Russell's autumn 1947 diary including his account of their walk and his near-suicide above Calella moved Riley to tears when it was shown to him on his return, but the successor journal kept by Russell while his friend was overseas received this in reply:

Peter, I don't know how to begin to say this. It is about the most difficult thing I have ever had to put into words in my life. So I beg you to take as charitable a view as you can, if I put it clumsily and ungracefully. I nearly told you when we walked through Mayfair back to the hotel last Thursday night. I tell you now because — no secrets. I read your diary — this one (and I don't think I am under any vain illusion) — and I remember the end of the last one. Peter, don't ask for everything when I am not <u>able</u> to give it. Believe me, I am not (for once!) holding something down and keeping something back. I cannot help it and I loathe saying it, but I'm just not able to respond in like manner. Not the whole way. The limit of my <u>capacity</u> is to go part of the way. I don't quite mean that either. In other senses I can go all the way and I would rather die than have that altered. But I cannot make an ocean where there is only a lake, and Peter I have to tell you that. Don't, don't, don't let anything be changed, but don't ask me for what I cannot give. Oh, I know you never <u>have</u> asked anything, but nothing could be more exacting than your wonderful non-exactingness. If this is going to make any big difference, any difference that <u>matters</u>, I shall blame myself for the rest of my days for not having kept quiet. And I am scared to death at what your reply is going to be. But it is better to have said this nevertheless; and I expect I am making mountains of molehills. There was repression, of course, but it was repression of the act of living a lie. The hot flesh and blood, in any case, as you once said, does not signify. There's nothing terrible about this, in the least. I've no right to ask you to play down to my lower key, if I am unable to attune myself to yours. But there is no reason why, in that case, there should not be harmony, and the music need never, shall never stop. [52]

His own feelings aside, Riley was plainly unable to square the homoerotic overtones of Russell's Dark Tower declaration with the latter's stated abstention from 'hot flesh and blood'. No response from Russell is on record but the depth of his pain at this rebuff is to be imagined, one astutely anticipated by his confidant George Kolkhorst the previous autumn. [53] The outcome had in its way been prefigured by Russell in his Dark Tower: 'You cannot make the two ends meet, the corporeal and imaginative. All that happens if you strain them too much is that the content snaps like a worn bootlace and nothing is left.'

---

[52] E. C. Riley to PER, Swindon, 15 April 1948.
[53] Kolkhorst to PER, York, 1 Oct. 1947.

Russell's student and friend Ted Riley with the Alhambra as his backdrop during the trip they took through France to Spain in the autumn of 1947.

Nonetheless, in July 1948 he saw to Riley's award of a Laming Travelling Fellowship at Queen's, the receipt of which presumably contributed to saving him for scholarship rather than some facet of international relations. Ten years later Riley, by now a lecturer at Trinity College Dublin, turned to his old tutor for advice on the publication of his seminal study on Cervantes' theory of the novel.[54] Russell was instrumental in securing its acceptance by the Clarendon Press, but the easy-going rapport of their earlier correspondence is now replaced by something closer to the respectful though amicable student–tutor relationship in which it had originated.

The economist and Fellow of Queen's Charles Kennedy, c. 1949.

On Riley's departure to take up his lectureship in Dublin in 1949 his place as the focus of Russell's emotional attention was filled by the economist Charles Kennedy who had been appointed to a fellowship at Queen's in 1948. Kennedy was the brilliant product of a gifted family on the fringes of Bloomsbury, his architect father George a close friend of J. M. Keynes and the artist Henry Lamb and his mother Mary reportedly a model for Virginia Woolf's Mrs Ramsay. This relationship, which from the available evidence had a less intellectually intense but an even more possessive dimension than those that preceded it, is more

---

[54] *Cervantes's Theory of the Novel* (Oxford: Clarendon Press, 1962).

sparsely documented from Russell's side, though in later life he reported having had a sexual encounter of some kind with Kennedy, one he deeply regretted. Even so, the surviving correspondence received from each of these three men — Heigham, Riley and Kennedy — bears out the disproportionate nature of the emotional engagement, treated on the one side as an easy if occasionally speculative communication between close friends, but configured on the other as an overwhelming emotional journey yearning to escape its mental confines. And with all these figures Russell maintained a friendship sundered only by death, fated to compose obituaries for two of them and be outlived by the other.

*

Although he spent his life at Oxford surrounded by gay friends, colleagues and pupils, Russell never sought the company of homosexual men on that ground alone and privately confessed to finding the modes and promiscuity of gay society unappealing; nor did efforts to introduce him to the outward expressions of gay life enjoy any success. In the first instance any association might in the ordinary course of events lead to the suggestion of corporeal relations and this for reasons that will become apparent Russell was not prepared to contemplate. Nor it seems was homosexuality a topic Russell ever found himself willing to discuss in other than philosophical terms. A case in point comes in February 1948 when he was visited at Queen's by Riley Workman, a prewar student who had decided to make a career of the Army after the cessation of hostilities. Workman had married but was bisexual and throughout his life indulged in illicit affairs and trysts which may or may not have had a bearing on his notorious murder at home in Hertfordshire in 2004. [55] In the context of 1948, however, his visit to Queen's was one Russell viewed with some trepidation:

> I sense a problem. He is agreeable but not clever and seven years in the Army have not polished his wits any more. I find I respond little these days to agreeable people who are unintelligent but Riley is, I suppose, a link with the pleasanter past. Perhaps that is why I half resent his arrival. Also there is that Fitzroy Tavern side. [56]

---

[55] 'Colonel Riley Workman Murder: Former Gamekeeper Guilty', 5 Nov. 2012; <www.bbc.com/news/uk-england-beds-bucks-herts-20151531>.
[56] Journal, 7 Feb. 1948. A centrepiece of Bohemian London, the Fitzroy Tavern was known as a gay meeting place from the 1920s.

Russell's intuition proved correct. His description of the occasion provides, among other things, a demonstration of his lifelong preference for silence over bromide:

> Riley to dinner. Afterwards, as I guessed would happen, he began to talk of the problem I guessed he had. Poor Riley! I was obtuse — I could not be anything else and because of this I felt a cad — it would have been possible to say something more helpful at least but truth to tell I was in a panic lest he should reveal more because then obtuseness would not have been enough and one might have sought escape in hypocrisy which would have been revolting. [57]

How, then, can this aversion to the lineaments of homosexuality in general and sexual relations in particular be explained — even, as here, in the privacy of his journal? The answer, as ever, is complex. To begin with Russell was as keenly aware of his own beauty as he was of his intellect; there is an extent to which the two went together in his mind as part of a narcissistic personality trait, the likely result of love withheld from some essential quarter. This awareness is never stated in as many words where his looks are concerned but the frequency with which his journals and occasionally his correspondence insult and dismiss others — both male and female — for their unprepossessing appearance or downright ugliness captures the sense in which he regarded them in contraposition with himself. Though set down while Russell was in a highly agitated state, the most savage example of this comes in his journal for February 1948:

> The Chaplain called me in the morning and asked me to tea. Not being able to face the thought of tea in that pokey little warren I asked him and his wife here. They ate everything I had and more. She swollen with a lusty foetus hung onto the tablecloth to retain balance when reaching for her cup. He really is of phenomenal ugliness — Gide would say something effective on this. It must be awful to be undistinguished — ugly. [58]

This self-appreciation never entirely left him, and as late as 2004 Russell felt moved to recall Professor Entwistle's 'slight physical ungainliness' in the entry he prepared for him in the *Oxford Dictionary of National Biography*. [59] As for his

---

[57] Journal, 15 Feb. 1948.
[58] Journal, 7 Feb. 1948.
[59] 'Entwistle, William James (1895–1952)', *Oxford Dictionary of National Biography* (at

intellect, the inferences are frequent though never stated as bluntly in respect of others as in the letter he wrote to Jo Heigham in April 1945: 'I must admit that being rather more intelligent than most is one of the things that gives the most satisfaction in life.' [60]

Whatever it may say about Russell, this dual assurance and the narcissism that underpinned it no doubt constituted the basis of his own aesthetic values, easily offended by the intrusion of ugliness and unshapeliness on the one hand or by idiocy or lack of acuity on the other. He was, as Kolkhorst reminded him in 1951, 'the expert in stupidity'. [61] Where his aesthetic sense of beauty was concerned it was of a type that soon drove him away from Parson's Pleasure, the secluded male-only bathing spot on the Cherwell which Russell will presumably have visited clad in a period swimming costume but which was also known for naturism ('Went to Parson's Pleasure this morning and found it good before the droves of ugly white nakednesses arrived'), years later recalling 'those pale, fat, misshapen naked bodies of the old men who used to be seen exposing themselves at Parson's Pleasure in the days when I used to go there'; '[n]akedness on bulls may be beastly but not wrong.' [62] If Russell was no adherent of gymnosophy he nonetheless had little difficulty appreciating nakedness under the Mediterranean sun and his diaries contain many references to frolicking youngsters both in Spain and Portugal and in Africa, in this case at Estoril and Caparica in 1936:

> Sun-bathing and walking long distances in forests and alpine valleys are two of the major joys of life. Sea-bathing is purely physical like sexual intercourse and hence has similar limitations — the pleasure can't continue for long for instance — but it is one of the best of physical amusements and the only form of exercise that I can indulge in, apart from walking, with any pleasure and unselfconsciousness. [...] The brown and black litheness of the bodies of the boys and youths and the dark neatness of the young women appeals to my sensual mind when I see them all on the beach, lying in the sun or disporting themselves together in the water. Latin bodily pride is a tonic to repressed Northerners.
>
> Yesterday being Sunday the popular element was dominant and as we sat on the beach for a few minutes male buttocks and female breasts and

<doi.org/10.1093/ref:odnb/33024>; revised version, 25 May 2006).

[60] PER to Major J. B. Heigham, Colombo, 30 April 1945.

[61] Yarnton, 20 Feb. 1951.

[62] Diary, 16 June 1932, Journal, 15 Feb. 1948 & Diary, 25 May 1933, respectively.

other parts of the human body were to be seen unashamedly on all sides as men and women changed unconcernedly on the beach. I like such unashamedness really though it was a little remarkable at first. However I am a person who enjoys such popular scenes as Caparica beach on Sunday more <u>afterwards</u> than during the actual event or rather the actual seeing. [63]

Russell was on the whole extremely tolerant where sexual orientation was concerned, albeit with scant patience for the formalities of heterosexual relations. What really roused him to indignation was anything that smacked of a moral squint, as here in 1936:

I like Rosamond Lehmann's *Dusty Answer* [1927] which seems to me to be both original and well-written. The reason I hadn't read it before was that I once asked one of my friends what it was like and got the reply that it was 'about Lesbians'. What a mealy-minded repressed people the English really seem to be — that is certainly an answer my own intelligence ought to have told me was merely prurient. [64]

In the same year his ire fell on an apparent display of homophobia by one of his students:

Hoare rather dislikes the Portuguese apparently because of the fact that the local youths sometimes walk about arm-in-arm. A typically idiotic English reaction to an entirely natural and normal occurrence of social intercourse of any affection with female or male. The English is really disgustingly prurient about anything where he suspects sex to exist. [65]

Russell may have subscribed to these views in private but characteristically seems only to have deployed them in confidence. Twelve years later and not without humour he took up the cudgels with Ted Riley over the moralism Russell found in Aldous Huxley's *Point Counter Point* (1928):

---

[63] Journal, 22 July & 3 Aug. 1936.
[64] Journal, 23 July 1936.
[65] Journal, 14 Aug. 1936.

I was moved to intense and indignant loquacity by Ted's quotation of those cheap remarks of Huxley's on lyric poetry as the product of deliberate idealisation of the unpleasant facts of sex. Really too silly. The notion that the facts of sex are <u>unpleasant</u> is a purely modern one; moralists medieval and later never said sex was <u>unattractive</u>; they said it was sinful and never tired of pointing out that its attraction was false. Some said it was revolting <u>because</u> it was wrong. The Huxleys of this world think the thing in itself revolting — thus perhaps a really decadent symptom — but there is no evidence at all for supposing the Elizabethans felt the same way. I'm bloody sure they never looked at it that way at all. [66]

Whereas Russell could find amusement in his wartime driver's habit of making unheralded stops at the house of a female acquaintance for a moment's refreshment in Accra, he regarded amorous relations of a public kind with at best ridicule but more usually a measure of distaste. An acute and practised spectator of human behaviour and rarely himself a participant, here is his memoir of young love in wartime Colombo:

> Dinner in the Galle Face quite amusing for the observer. The parties of young officers with their W.R.N.S. give an astonishing picture of the immature sexuality of the English male and female. Most of the time they simply sit and make obviously trite conversation. Sometimes even this fades away before the sweet and they just sit. The men do not seem to be able to say the things one should say to put the girls in the right frame of mind and the girls are painfully amateurish in their efforts to captivate. No wonder most unmarried fornication among the English takes place only when both parties are half or wholly tight. [67]

The most flagrant example of this and of his tendency to extreme misogyny under emotional and physical stress came on the journey home from the war in the liner *Antenor*.

> The 150 women are gradually increasing the sexual pressure on the males. The more attractive are already paired off with officers, the bitches

---

[66] Journal, 23 Jan. 1948.
[67] Journal, 20 Sept. 1945. W.R.N.S. refers to the Women's Royal Naval Service.

are to be found holding hands through alleyways and doors leading on to the troop decks. In between these are those as yet unwanted but by now sexually alert and watchful. […] Promiscuity becomes more blatant daily now much aided by the fact that a blanket as covering when lying on deck is not now unreasonable. I must say I think this mass display of cold-blooded sexual concupiscence is rather objectionable. [68]

More private alfresco congress on the shores of the Mediterranean was however quite another matter:

> How attractive are the youthful peasant-boys bathing with their girls on Sunday morning. Walking among some low rocks I came on one tumbling his girl on a tiny beach. All they did was to grin and go right on with the matter in hand, which it was. I was delighted at the appropriateness of the picture though its effects were perhaps diminished a little by the knowledge that Lord [a friend] with an ice-box and cocktails was waiting only 200 yards away. [69]

*

Contrasting with these overt displays and his response to them was Russell's own veiled sexuality which he knew to be the subject of speculation, assumption and rumour all his adult life. Though questions would inevitably present themselves the topic was an unbroachable feature in all his friendships, the sense imparted of a private hinterland never to be violated, a line of inquiry not to be pursued on any account. The closest Russell ever got to making a public utterance in respect of his own sexuality came in the memoir he deposited for posterity with the British Academy in 1992. Russell was a master in the use of coded language and rarely deployed his gift more adroitly than in that context. It appears in the description he provides of his first visit to Spain in 1931:

> I found travel alone in Spain rather intimidating but I visited Granada and was captivated by its magical quality, though also, I recall, baffled by the displays of what I thought of as inexplicably enthusiastic friendliness I received from some of the Spanish and foreign men I met there. [70]

[68] Journal, 3 & 6 Jan. 1946.
[69] Journal, 19 Sept. 1948.
[70] PELR, 3.

Russell in Spain c. 1935, apt in earlier years to be 'baffled by the displays of what I thought of as inexplicably enthusiastic friendliness I received from some of the Spanish and foreign men I met there'.

Some colour is added to this in an exchange in the early 1980s recalled by a graduate student, Colin Wight. The scene is Russell's Spanish graduate seminar which met weekly at 65 St Giles' when the University was in session:

> On one occasion a fellow postgrad was blathering on about Lorca, and how difficult it must have been to be an 'out' homosexual in the 1930s, etc. Peter Russell waited for a few seconds, then said, with that characteristic wry smile, 'I think I am correct in saying that I am the only person in this room who knew Lorca, and I can assure you that being a homosexual in Spain in the 1930s was not a problem.' There was no coming back from that. [71]

---

[71] 'Don Javier Marías Franco', 21 Feb. 2019 at <colinwight.blog/2019/02/21/d-javier-

More than once he took trouble to recount the occasion when he turned on his heel and walked out of the gay bar in Madrid to which he had been brought by his successor in the Oxford chair Ian Michael in the 1980s. At the end of his life he declared himself to be against gay marriage but could not, or would not, say why, the veneer of his privacy left inviolate.

The prevailing impression of his sexuality among Russell's circle is captured in Javier Marías's novel *Todas las Almas* when Professor Toby Rylands, the character he based on Russell, is being discussed:

> 'So is Rylands homosexual?' I asked. 'Oh, I really couldn't say. He's been alone for as long as I've known him and he doesn't talk about such ungentlemanly things. Taken all around he seems asexual.' [72]

Insofar as he identified with any particular orientation Russell preferred for reasons of convenience to be regarded as heterosexual, or at least to have the question left open as a private matter. The 1992 citation above is in fact one of only three references in Russell's surviving writings to his being importuned by men, whereas propositions from women frequently appear in his diaries and letters, ranging from his Danish undergraduate contemporary Countess Benika Reventlow ('Am still wondering what Benika was trying to do last night but no doubt it was all for the best') to an assortment of chambermaids and fellow passengers and hotel guests, all of whom were brushed off, ignored or treated with incredulity. Almost as frequent as the rebuffs and dismissals recorded in his journals were the excuses and rationalisations offered up for not taking the opportunity. Overtures by a fellow resident of his *pension* in Strasbourg failed 'because she's been a consumptive'; when a maid proffered her services in a Stuttgart inn for two reichsmarks a few weeks later in 1933 he declined 'as she wasn't pretty enough. If she had been it might have been different!'; in Estoril in 1936 he lamented that lack of money would make him unappealing to 'a really attractive girl'; two years later in Lisbon he fended off a chambermaid 'owing to company [Derek Hamblen] and to a dislike to risk syphilis'; in wartime Leopoldville an invitation from a Scots girl to make her a bad girl was declined at 4 a.m. because 'I did not [...] feel like being an instructor at that hour and anyway I resent the Scots'; in 1946 he passed up the chance of an encounter with a fellow

marias/>. For another account of the same incident, see José Luis Giménez-Frontín, *Woodstock Road en julio: Notas y diario* (Pamplona: Pamiela, 1996), 69.
[72] Barcelona: Anagrama, 1989; 2nd ed. (1998), 204; my translation.

guest at his mother's hotel in Jersey since 'the consequences of discovery would appall Mother'. [73] Then there were the amorous widows and the 'elderly nymphomaniac' pestering him in the Galle Face Hotel in Colombo ('it really has been too revolting'), an episode that had a lasting impact on him. [74] In later years he would beguilingly report apropos of nothing how this or that woman had 'set her cap' at him but offer no comment in addition.

What these and other expressions reveal is that Russell could not cope with women as active and independent sexual agents. Thus when an Uxbridge prostitute invited him to 'buy her' in December 1933 'that pretty well finished the evening for me. Awful!' [75] A visit to a favourite bar near Valencia in 1948 found it to be under new management, 'the place run by an immensely fat, tight-eyed bawd in black. The dancing was really stomach and pelvis and very little covering or pretence. Fatal for me as always. [...] Cock-teasing of that kind always ruins me.' [76] No surprise since not even Josephine Baker performing at the Casino de Paris in 1933 could move him: 'I dislike nude women as well as clothed ones.' [77] The acme of this came in Madrid in September 1948:

> Next to my table was a middle-aged man with the most sexual girl I have ever seen. She was simply built around a cunt and had no existence apart from it so that even her mouth had the appearance of a subsidiary one and it didn't look like a mouth at all. The man, worn-out, could not keep his hands or shoulders off her and she fed him with olives on a fork because he lacked the energy to feed himself. [78]

Still, Russell found himself drawn inexorably if reluctantly to the anonymity of paid sex though the endeavour enjoyed no better success at meeting his needs. Far from lust, the overriding impression is of a hurdle to be surmounted, some anguish needing palliation. A failed attempt to pick up a prostitute in London in November 1933 was followed by a second effort a month later:

---

[73] Diary, 11 & 31 July 1933; Journal, 23 July 1936, 28 July 1938, 6 Sept. 1944 & 8 Feb. 1946 respectively.
[74] PER to Heigham, Colombo, 10 Sept. 1945; Journal, 19 Aug. 1959.
[75] Diary, 11 Dec. 1933.
[76] Journal, 18 Sept. 1948.
[77] Diary, 20 Aug. 1933.
[78] Journal, 7 Sept. 1948.

John [Hennell] and I went to the Varsity match and saw Oxford win a bad game. After that we came back here and drank then met a large number of the College bores at the Brasserie. I got fed up and picked up an appalling female in Piccadilly to whom I gave a drink and got some reforming instinct. After that went to *Gay Divorce* with the others. [79]

The scene was repeated in February 1945 when Russell, apparently at Jo Heigham's urging, again engaged the services of a prostitute in London, reporting that 'I did the buying but the goods (when put on the counter) were so dreadful that I left them where they were. I now think that an effete thing to have done.' [80] A year later he noted in his journal that '[c]oldness of weather and utter drabness of available ladies drove me to cinema'. [81] Other failed *tentations à la débauche* are on record, the memory of these dispiriting episodes among the reasons Russell so disliked London. Even so, he retained his interest in the *demi-monde* in an observational capacity and his journals are notable for the reliability with which reference is made to prostitutes and speculation on the prevalence of VD during his far-flung travels in the 1940s. Much later in life Russell, now acknowledging his long-repressed homosexuality in the most trusted company, reported having been badly hurt in a failed relationship of some sort with an Italian waiter he met at a favourite Oxford restaurant in the 1990s, the Luna Caprese on North Parade. [82]

In the context of the post-war years, however, this of course left the option of marriage, one long pressed on him by an unwelcome succession of would-be matchmakers and prodders over whom his mother towered. Part of the brotherly advice dispensed by Jo Heigham for improving Russell's sex life during their lengthy talks in West Africa was the need for him to find a wife. Russell therefore took the opportunity between his Accra and Colombo postings of arranging dates in London with 'pre-1941 girlfriends' as well as an acquaintance from the Caribbean. Here is the report of the latter occasion he sent Heigham, an example of the formulaic way in which he and society at large conceived such partnerships:

I bloody nearly popped the question at lunch on Saturday to one Phyllis Roberts whose picture you saw sitting on the beach in Jamaica. However

---

[79] Diary, 12 Dec. 1933. *Gay Divorce* was a Cole Porter musical.
[80] PER to Heigham, Oxford, 6 Feb. 1945.
[81] Journal, 12 March 1946.
[82] Clive Griffin reporting comments by Fred Hodcroft, email to the author, 15 March 2020, and by Ian Michael in conversation with the author, 13 Feb. 2020.

you said you didn't like the look of her and so when she remarked 'Peter, don't you think it was time you were married' I replied 'no' and became courteous and that is the end of that one. There are other possibilities but as I am leaving this benighted country again in the early days of March I imagine I shall be free when we next meet. [83]

'The war' he wrote 'seems to have drawn off the last of the already meagre stock of passion.' [84] A general lack of enthusiasm aside, exposure to British women during the war, mainly in the form of his Roedean-educated MI5 secretaries and an assortment of what through the prism of his misogyny he regarded as oversexed WRNS and FANY nurses, had left Russell disenchanted at the offerings in that quarter. [85] In a subsequent letter to Heigham he stated that 'The more I hear about this marriage business, without your insidious murmurings around, the more I think one should only marry seriously if one is totally lacking in imagination, very rich or orphaned on all sides.' [86] Much later he would without elaboration declare that any woman he had been interested in had been lured away by the actor Ronald Colman (1891–1958). [87] The point of course is that Russell recognised marriage as an estate to which he was signally ill-suited on more than one ground, including negligible interest in children, but characteristically blamed the aversion on circumstances, a lack of suitable partners and the shortcomings of the institution itself. [88] 'The height of flattery' he had described it as in the early '30s. [89] Nonetheless, he fell back on a plan first mooted in his journal in June 1936, that of finding a Latin wife: 'Next year I shall have to look for some suitable female, Latin for preference.' [90] This strategy he revisited shortly before leaving Ceylon, planning a post-war visit to Spain 'for professional reasons and to find and possibly marry my Fate'. [91] The visit finally happened in August 1946 and during it Russell spent time with the family of a

---

[83] PER to Heigham, Oxford, 6 Feb. 1945.
[84] PER to Heigham, Oxford, 26 Feb. 1945.
[85] Women's Royal Naval Service; First Aid Nursing Yeomanry.
[86] PER to Heigham, Colombo, 30 April 1945.
[87] Alastair Saunders, comments to the author, 8 July 2024.
[88] JMA, PER to Javier Marías, Oxford, 24 July 2002: 'Not that I have ever consciously wanted children of my own.'
[89] Commonplace book, 34.
[90] Journal, 27 June 1936.
[91] PER to Heigham, Colombo, 5 Aug. 1945.

fellow intelligence operative he had met during the Civil War, Baltasar Márquez. Among Márquez's many sons and daughters was Piedad with whom Russell struck up a long friendship involving visits by her to England from at least 1956 culminating in her settling for a time in London. In later years Russell recounted having become engaged to Piedad, a forceful personality in her own right, but the relationship ended after a visit to his home at Belsyre Court in about 1960 during which she went round the flat pointing out items that would have to go once they tied the knot. The result as Russell recalled was that she went. [92]

Whatever the precise circumstances of the demise of this relationship and his responses to women, the inescapable fact is that Russell recoiled from full sexual intimacy, something he is not known to have consummated with either gender in any setting. In fact, the obvious conclusion to be drawn is that Russell was like so many of his class and generation ignorant of sex by lack of familiarity. Already in February 1948 he had seized on a citation dug up from the dramatist and poet Paul Géraldy advancing the notion that sexual consummation with a woman was in any case likely to be draining, unfulfilling and even repulsive for the male partner:

> 'La volupté satisfait la femme et l'exalte. Elle assombrit et déçoit l'homme. L'homme a besoin d'un paradis plus difficile.' This is a very profound remark which states a truth I have never formalised myself — the woman glowing with satisfaction of fulfilment, the man gloomy, flat, disappointed at loss of desire and, in some cases anyway, revolted by the whole performance. [93]

At an intellectual level the bottom had been reached but from a psychological standpoint much worse lay ahead. In fact the long-delayed reckoning was at hand. Drawn as he was both to men and women (albeit in quite different ways and under different circumstances), Russell's inability to enjoy a partnership with either responds to the fact that his deepest emotions were linked to one person and one person only: his mother. [94]

---

[92] Russell remained close to the Márquez family for the rest of his life and his diaries record a meeting with Piedad in Madrid in September 1976. Piedad Márquez Cano died unmarried in January 2016.
[93] Journal, 11 Feb. 1948.
[94] The only incident of sexual arousal recorded by Russell in connection with a person of either gender comes in his journal entry for 11 Jan. 1948 while reading the concluding episode of *Ulysses* describing Molly Bloom's stream of consciousness as she lies beside her husband.

*

Rita Russell was the emotional centre of gravity to which her son was drawn but from which he found himself repulsed, a product both of her character and the irresoluble nature of his own needs. Much as this was the dominating reality there can be no doubt that her strength, resourcefulness, generosity and willpower and her undoubted love for her sons made her in many respects a highly effective parent. Laid low in Granada with diarrhoea and sunburn in 1932, it was she Russell missed most: 'What can be worse than feeling ill so far away from home and Mother.' [95] 'My God she's a good woman!' he wrote on receiving a letter from her in July 1933. [96] However, his emotional needs were by no means met and in March 1934 comes the first indication that Russell was trying to bridge a gap in their relationship: 'Posted letter to Mother. So difficult to try and show her how fond I am of her and yet not seem sloppy'; 'Thinking of mother receiving my letter this morning I began to hope that she would understand it as I mean it.' [97] There is no indication whether she did, but it is clear that the immovable and unresponsive quality of her personality became less and less acceptable as time passed:

> Mother doesn't seem to get any older and is as active as ever. It is hard now to reach anything like community of interest on any subject and one is left with the ordinary natural affections — very strong in my case. I suppose it's the same with most parents and children. In any case she has been as good a mother to us as any woman has the power to be. It creates an almost embarrassing sense of debt in one. [98]

Indeed, the ties of love were as strong as ever:

> I left mother and Hugh in London at Waterloo with those usual strong if absurd feelings of distress which I always feel when leaving another and which start with a room or even a seat in a train and increase in intensity to culminate — more naturally — in those one loves for reasons of blood or sex. [99]

[95] Diary, 18 July 1932.
[96] Diary, 25 July 1933.
[97] Diary, 18 & 19 March 1934.
[98] Journal, 27 June 1936.
[99] Journal, 17 July 1936.

'We don't connect at all on my terms and I cannot accept hers.' Rita Russell disembarking at Sydney during one of her trips to the Antipodes, c. 1955.

One difficulty with Rita Russell was that, much as she was a 'lady' in the conventional sense of that word, she had an alarming tendency to state precisely what was on her mind to anyone at any time. This extended from berating doltish maids or tradesmen to commenting publicly on her former brother-in-law Admiral Teddy Evans's latest effort to colour his hair — and plenty in between. To this Russell himself had ample exposure, not least the occasion after the war when Rita loudly remarked on his bachelor status at a guest night in the Queen's senior common room, mortifying her son and leaving him suffused with anger and frustration. Hugh summarised this side of her personality in a letter written to his brother while Rita, then aged sixty-three, was staying with her surviving sister in New Zealand in 1951:

> The family's opinion of mother as expressed to me by most of them was that she has lived alone for too long, and has got into eccentric ways. I have noticed myself that dear mother seems to be quite unaware of the depth and degree of offence she gives to others including her own immediate family when she points out cobwebs to them, or ignores their guests, or says exactly what she thinks of New Zealand and New Zealanders — which, by inference, includes themselves! [...] There is nothing that we can do about it, I'm afraid. One of the difficulties is that she has no roots anywhere now, and consequently very few real friends, but a host of acquaintances only. [100]

Curiously enough Russell seems not to have had his epiphany until he met some of his mother's old Cheltenham friends in 1946:

> One remarked on Mother's force of personality — it never occurred to me to think of her that way but I daresay she could be described as having a forceful personality. She's not a good listener, perhaps that is why. [101]

Not only that but Rita was probably the most hard-boiled person her son ever knew. She had to a supreme degree the quality Russell most admired in others and most missed in himself: the ability not outwardly to be perturbed about

---

[100] Hugh Russell to PER, London, 24 Feb. 1951.
[101] Journal, 22 Feb. 1946.

anything very much at all. In October 1949 he learnt of the destruction of the bulk of her possessions together with many of the boys' childhood things in the famous Le Gallais depository blaze in Saint Helier along with a vast stock of irreplaceable Jersiaise furniture and artworks. In later years Russell would recount how he had steeled himself to make the phone call breaking this ghastly news to his mother but that it left her practically unmoved: 'she never turned a hair'. Although endless trouble was gone to when the boys were unwell and to ensure that they had everything they could possibly need from a material standpoint, Rita Russell had scant capacity for emotional delivery between her sledgehammer personality and Victorian induration in colonial New Zealand. Later her son understood how these traits affected him and how little his deepest needs were met by her:

> We don't connect at all on my terms and I cannot accept hers. She is a true extrovert I think and she, poor dear, has no capacity for understanding what makes me go on like this. She is brave and believes in her own capacity to deal with difficulties and she is interested and stimulated by external things and people. I suppose it has always been like this and I have always wanted to make her different — understanding, dedicated to me, soothing, a listener rather than a talker, intellectual and so on. [102]

However, his difficulties with his mother ran much deeper. By the mid-1930s Russell had begun to read Freud and identify his own psychosexual makeup in the analytical construct he found there. A journal entry in February 1938 provides a first indication that he had recognised himself as having the Oedipus or Hamlet complex. [103] As related above, within a few years of the war Russell's asymmetrical relationship with Ted Riley had reduced him to a psychotic state and brought on what was probably a stress-related duodenal ulcer. In late 1949 Russell experienced a collapse and was obliged to take sick leave in Hilary 1950. [104] Before long he was seeking professional assistance and by January 1951 was under psychoanalysis by Dr Oliver Lyth in North Oxford, practitioner in a field then still widely regarded as semi-scientific. Russell continued to see Lyth (with intervals) until 1965, but no detailed information is available on his condition until the

---

[102] Freudian journal, 13 July 1958, 79–80.
[103] Journal, 20 Feb. 1938.
[104] OUA/FA 9/1/265 PEL Russell, 1945–53, PER to Secretary of Faculties (K. C. Turpin), Oxford, 21 Dec. 1949.

summer of 1955 by which time he had exchanged the depression and psychotic hallucinations of the post-war years for a profound anxiety disorder. [105] Gone is the bristling though fragile don of 1948, the person who could write of Jung's *Psychology of the Unconscious* that 'I suppose such information may be useful for those who don't know what they are really like — at least I do not need information on that subject.' [106] The picture now is of a man utterly overwhelmed: 'My own lack of interior resources in this sort of situation disturbs me; I'm without any real interest to occupy my mind and find anxiety easily creeps in to fill vacant spaces.' [107] In later years Russell told how anxiety caused him to spend the latter part of that decade and the early 1960s confined to Belsyre Court while under Lyth's prescriptions of the sedative hypnotic barbiturates Seconal and Nembutal, now reserved for assisted suicide and euthanasia respectively. Surviving correspondence shows that his condition (if not the cause of it) was known to his colleagues and friends by early 1957, eliciting their concern and sympathy at what he confessed to be a complete nervous breakdown which saw him admitted to the Warneford psychiatric hospital in Oxford in June 1958. [108] Two months later a well-intentioned Civil Service friend in whom he had confided, Pauline Parry-Jones, wrote to him in terms that show how far his self-esteem had disintegrated:

> Are you worried by the fact that you are 43? Is it the fear of growing old, or the feeling that life is passing by at a greater speed than you care to think, that you dislike? Or, again, the fact that you are an unwilling

---

[105] Russell told Kolkhorst he was undergoing psychotherapy in April 1951. Practising from Lathbury Road, Lyth was a student of the pioneering psychoanalyst Wilfred Bion (1897–1979) who had graduated in History from Queen's in 1922. Lyth appears to have charged £4 4s. per session, approximately £150 at 2024 prices. His future wife Isabel Menzies (1917–2008) was another prominent British psychoanalyst, a founder member with Bion and others of the Tavistock Institute of Human Relationships in London and follower of Melanie Klein and Donald Winnicott. Menzies practiced from Church Way in Iffley after her marriage to Lyth in 1975; Lyth, who was on the editorial board of *The International Journal of Psycho-Analysis*, died in 1981.

[106] Journal, 15 Feb. 1948.

[107] Journal, 2 Aug. 1959.

[108] José Ángel Valente to Natalia Cossío, Geneva, 30 June 1958, in *Alberto Jiménez Fraud: Epistolario, 1905–1964*, ed. James Valender, José García-Velasco, Tatiana Aguilar-Álvarez Bay & Trilce Arroyo, 3 vols. (Madrid: Publicaciones de la Residencia de Estudiantes, 2018), III, 407–8.

bachelor of that age? [...] Do you remember a conversation we had some long time ago about this English system of upbringing and its effects, as compared with the hysterical outbursts of so many of the Continental people? I remember you saying then that it was the British who broke down, i.e. nervous breakdowns, whilst the Continentals got it out of their systems then and there. [...] [P]lease do not feel that you are useless, childish or a bore, as it simply is not true. Peter, my dear, you have a fine and true character — what you are suffering at the moment is, I am quite sure, merely a testing time of temporary duration, and I have boundless faith in your ability to overcome it successfully. The fact that you acknowledge what has happened to you during the last six months — i.e. your relapse into a limitless selfishness, etc., proves that you are well over the worst of the attack. If you were not, you would be completely unable to put the affair into any sort of perspective. Make no mistake, you are well worth knowing, as it is, so you must not feel that people may not find you so. [109]

In fact the nadir seems to have come that autumn of 1958 during the cruise of the Atlantic and Mediterranean he took in the liner *Iberia* with the encouragement of his friend Charles Kennedy, by which time he had taken a sabbatical year. He even reached out to a former master at Cheltenham, one C. T. Priestley who replied in September telling him 'I really am distressed that you have had a breakdown — though I am afraid that you always did overwork and your "recluse mind" of great acuteness has been driving you too hard'. [110] The following summer, and against his better judgment, Russell embarked on a further cruise intended to improve his mental health, this time to the Caribbean, Mexico and the United States, for which a journal was kept, the first to survive since 1948. Six days into the voyage Russell suffered his first anxiety attack:

> It is really too bad; another bout of acute anxiety descended just after breakfast. Has all the effort of the last 3½ years really gone for nothing? None of the interpretations seem to work in practice. There is, of course, nothing objective to cause acute concern but I see an endless

---

[109] Oswestry, 5 Aug. 1958. Russell was in fact forty-four years old at the time.
[110] C. T. Priestley to PER, Cheltenham, 24 Sept. 1958.

series of enormous imaginary barriers ahead [...]. What a fool! Yet nothing seems to bring these anxieties into contact with reality. On one hand a little boy who has run away from mother to show his independence and finds absence of maternal security almost overwhelmingly frightening; on other what is left of adult me. One wants to cut and run for hours; the other to see, learn, mix and exchange at all levels. The gap is occupied by fear and from, or as a consequence of, fear, loneliness. The only answer for the moment is Seconal and that, each time taken, leaves a sense of defeat; besides it won't last forever. Where is conquering strength of adult personality to come from? I have about a week to find out. [111]

'Only the sea retains its integrity untarnished' he had written over twenty years earlier, but now found himself confessing that 'it is a sad distance from the days when there was nothing I liked more than the thought of, or the fact of, getting on a ship'. [112] Two days after a second anxiety attack in Xalapa in the state of Veracruz Russell succumbed again in Mexico City, this time turning to a local doctor for help and questioning his ability to continue to New York:

It doesn't seem, to tell the truth, that the treatment of the last four years has made me a person able to travel or venture far from home. This will have to be thought about and decisions made when I get back. In the meantime I keep going partly by will-power and more by Seconal and my return will have to be fixed in accordance with the amount of the latter I have. [...] There is so much I want to see but the effort is so great that I don't know how I am to do it. But perhaps this crisis will pass soon and freedom to behave like an adult person will return. [...] It is all a problem of accepting the fear as an absurd attempt by my surviving infantile self to dominate my present life. But how to do it? [113]

The same day he received a cheery letter from his mother wholly unconscious of her son's afflictions, a painful reminder of the one who mattered most yet could never truly be reached, an unwitting intrusion of the type usually played out by phone at Belysre Court for as long as she lived; 'Dies irae' he noted in his pocket

---

[111] Journal, 6 Aug. 1959.
[112] Journal, 19 July 1936 & 3 Aug. 1959.
[113] Journal, 22 Aug. 1959.

diary. Only with the greatest difficulty and the aid of another medical consultation did Russell complete the trip, hastening home Gilbert Pinfold-like by air from New York. In November of that year he ventured forth to deliver a lecture in Lisbon where he was stricken once more:

> All went fairly well in train and during lunch but about an hour ago was assaulted by a straight attack of inexplicable fear which literally knocked me out — more or less. Whatever for? And whatever of? [...] Where did that all come from? Is it desolation converted to fear by some neurotic process? Or anger, similarly converted? Or forces denied having their revenge? [114]

Under Lyth's crushing pharmacopoeia Russell's trembling hand kept a journal of his long and harrowing therapy by which the dimensions of his condition can be traced. In fact the whole course of his life as described in the opening chapters of this biography together with the early traumas enumerated above is revisited in the context of his Oedipal disorder and its consequences, extending from his jealousy towards his brother Hugh, the trauma of being hung over the side of the *Oxfordshire* in 1918 or '19, the terrors of St Andrew's College in general and of gym and team sports in particular, the occasions he ran away from home, his cowardice summoned in the refrain 'cowardy cowardy custard', and on to his heart murmur diagnosis and its consequences, his flagellation complex and memories of his mother's presumed lover 2nd Engineer Anscombe in the liner *Port Melbourne* in 1926.

There were terrors old and new, of caged rats and above all crocodiles, the legacy of a reptilian encounter at Montevideo in 1915 and the moment in deepest Ceylon when he found himself being watched by a large specimen, together with two haunting memories of victims, a boy called Wood shut into a lavatory at St Andrew's and his friend Norman Brittain drowned in the Atlantic in 1942. The greatest terror of all, however, was the realisation of his powerlessness in the face of a mental state capable of distorting his perception of reality:

> Today all was well until after breakfast when I again saw room clearly, and not filtered through my own special means of seeing it inside. Terrifying. The chasm makes me hold my head. Objective reality is there

---

[114] Journal, 9 Nov. 1959.

and it's not under my control, like when soldiers held me over side of ship and I didn't know they weren't going to drop me. [I] lie on my bed and see things in it as if for the first time — what my dressing-gown really looks like hanging on door, carpet with light making its various areas look different. All these things around me exist as realities and are quite independent of me. This is a matter of feeling. I'm cut off from everything. I can see as from a glass prison but I'm not in <u>contact</u> with anything except this feeling that I am not in contact. It's appallingly depressing as if greyness of day had entered me. [115]

The journal sheds light on Russell's relationship with his parents, on his speculations as to their intimate relations, on the rages of his father of whom he records being the victim of sexual abuse, apparently in a bathroom during the voyage in the *Oxfordshire*, and on the pain of his mother's rejection of his plaint, dwelling on these circumstances and all their labyrinthine implications for his psychosexuality extending to Lyth himself. Also laid bare in the entries is the cause of the episode of catatonia at Sedbergh in 1926 and his confinement in Belsyre Court in the late '50s and early '60s:

Fear is fear of depression because depression arises from the fact that I never have succeeded in being truly independent from moment of walking. Empty gesture of independence carried on all through life against realisation [I] want Mother. Why worry if cannot go out as long as this is seen as statement of independence which is false. Naturally legs give way because that is true relaxation …. [116]

Towering above everything is his irreconcilable regressive fixation with his mother, the essence of which comes in an entry apparently set down in June 1958. It is unusual in being written in the second person:

It's not the actual emission itself [i.e. ejaculation]. This can not have the effects you attribute to it. The feelings and consequences are those of the other acts you associate with it. These are [a] violent casting out of Mother — breast and bottle — on which you believe you are utterly

---

[115] Freudian journal, 12 July 1958, 76–7.
[116] Freudian journal, 1 July 1958, 92.

dependent for strength and life — even existence. Sexual urges, therefore, come to mean destruction of any real sort of life. Must be suppressed, denied, minimised and — at worst — distorted to keep yourself going at all. No alternative object allowed when it comes to [the] point. Avoidance of any replacement of Mother. Weakness equals [*added:* partial] proof that I cannot do without Mother. Sham existence is assertion to contrary, knowing it not to be true that something vital is missing in the assumed position. You must believe that actual emission itself is not [the] cause of these feelings because in any direct physiological sense it is clearly not. Dare I believe this? [117]

Not for a long time did Russell entertain any such belief and on this kaleidoscopic torment rested his inability to conceive of sexual relations on other than an intellectual level, the deadening practical effect of which he always referred to as *abulia* (lassitude), a concept employed by several of the 'Generation of 1898' writers and adopted by Russell in the 1930s as a metaphor for sexual impotence in light of his Oedipal fixation. [118] It also explains his sexual issues with women and the misogyny that was never far from his personal writings until the 1950s: 'Bloody women expose me as impotent.' [119] As with his political views a generation earlier, Russell abjured much though not all of this prejudice, forged as it was in the fires of his private misery, but for now he remained consumed by the greater malaise, and any who saw and felt him recoil as they reached out to shake his hand in later years or tried to express their affection physically was witness to an affliction that never left him.

For many years Russell kept an allotment in Oxford for therapeutic as well as horticultural purposes and one day in the summer of 1958 had the misfortune of finding a thrush caught in the netting covering his strawberry bushes. The symbolism was shattering, the identification with himself complete, the permutations endless: 'Instead of being frightened of that thrush in that cowardy [*sic*] way should have killed it at once if I couldn't free it properly. It was, after all,

---

[117] Freudian journal, 22–3.

[118] The concept of *abulia* first appears in Ángel Ganivet's *Idearium español* (1897): 'It signified a radical failure of the will, a response to a felt absence of a much desired sense of value and purpose such as to energise, sustain, and direct the life of an individual person and of society at large'; R. W. Truman, email to the author, Oxford, 11 Aug. 2020. Russell was still using this term to describe himself late in life; JMA, PER to Javier Marías, Oxford, 30 Jan. 2002.

[119] Freudian journal, 18 June 1958, 25.

only a frightened little bird and I had put it in that position. What I did was to become as frightened as the bird so we were both useless (impotent)'; in short '[t]he most awful morning of my life'. [120] 'Cowardy cowardy custard' revealed in its fullness, on account of a bird.

This is not perhaps the place for any further anatomised elucidation of Russell's complex as it is laid bare in his journal, especially concerning his parents. That his was an extreme and evolved form of the condition is in little doubt, one complicated by his homosexual inclinations, by the duality he recognised in his psychosexual makeup, by his need for control, not least of his own impulses. Suffice to say that by February 1960 Russell again professed himself to be suicidal in words that give an insight into the relentless circularity of his condition:

> I told Charles [Kennedy] I'd go away — and I meant suicide — if I wasn't enmeshed in obligations not to hurt others. But — probably — if I wasn't enmeshed in these obligations I wouldn't want to commit suicide. Anyway that's just talk. Or is it? If I thought there was no hope of company again, no love, no freedom from anxiety again and no obligations I could see no reason for abstaining from suicide. [121]

Russell was at war with his super-ego, drawn into a prolonged psychomachia that threatened to destroy him. Against this fate he struggled with all his might and intellectual resources, applying his tireless curiosity to the problem with recourse to external support both directly and indirectly. As it was, conventional wisdom and learning too often counted for nothing where one's own troubles were concerned. As he noted in the review article he produced under the poignant title of 'The Nessus-Shirt of Spanish History' at the height of his climacteric in 1959, auto-analysis is 'a form of treatment unlikely [...] to lead to an admission of all the relevant facts and still less to their correct interpretation'. [122] In an unpublished lecture he delivered after completing his edition of the *Celestina* in 1991, Russell passed again over this ground in the context of the culminating scenes of that work:

> Melibea, in her final speech, makes the point, based on the experience she is at that moment undergoing, that she has discovered that it is

---

[120] *Ibid.*, 23 & 28–9.
[121] Freudian journal, 28 Feb. 1960, 69.
[122] *Bulletin of Hispanic Studies* 36 (1959), 219–25; at 220.

useless to memorize a lot of adhortatory maxims on the presumption that they can be turned to for help and guidance in times of trouble; the reality is that, when one is under strong emotional stress, the accompanying disfunction of the memory means that it is impossible to recall what one has read in books. [123]

Aside from his course of psychoanalysis, lengthy exploration of his mental afflictions made him a keen and lifelong observer of those he regarded as capable of operating physically free of apparent mental constraint and who were yet intelligent, adept individuals. It was one of the reasons he always craved the company of young people with their reserves of energy and insouciance, an opportunity for vicarious mental renewal and refreshment while sharing nothing of his own predicament, even analogously. This quality, which in a more general sense he identified as characteristic of Spanish culture, was one of the features that drew him to that field, as expressed here in 1938:

> The attraction for me is at any rate a genuine one — possibly my own intellectualized *abulia* is attracted by the spectacle of men acting and men allowing full sway to their passions without the Hamlet complex intervening. My own mental state is unfortunately one of great admiration for action and the active life in conflict with a mental scepticism which prevents me really doing anything at all creatively in any active (i.e. non-intellectual) way — nor is there any way in which I could do much in the sphere of non-intellectual activity. My own interest in literature is psychological anyway. [124]

This deficiency he saw in himself, rooted in his psychosexual construct, was only partially mitigated by the exertions of his war service, leaving Russell to channel his energies into his teaching, his scholarship and his friendships, so that at the end of his life he acknowledged never having known physical passion as one of his greatest regrets, the one experience that had never touched him nor he it. It was a facet his confidant George Kolkhorst, who perhaps knew him as well as any, unerringly identified in the context of their wider circle:

---

[123] 'Some Thoughts After Editing *La Celestina*', unpublished printout, c. 1992, 25. Russell is referring to the closing lines of act 20, scene 3, 589–90 in his edition.
[124] Journal, 20 Feb. 1938.

John B[etjeman] unlike poor (& dear) Russell — has no European Culture. He is allergic to Europe. On the other hand — also like dear (& poor) Russell — he is taut with Insular tensions. [125]

*

This chapter has concerned itself with Russell's inner life but his swirling mental construct of course found some of its fuel and expression in his scholarly relations and output. It was something else Kolkhorst had recognised in his inimitable style as early as 1947:

> But how much clearer, how much more lucid you are (you <u>are</u> lucid) when you hate. Love seems to have the effect of plunging you into a vortex of crazy — Ectoplasms; whereas as soon as <u>Hate</u> comes on the *tapis*, half-lights, nebulosities, vagaries, crackinesses, nervous-systems, dream-anarchies and world-upside-down-y-diddle-dums cease, and we are <u>instanter</u> as clear and as uncompromising as Daylight. No wonder you write well on your subjects. I have always advocated hatred of one's subject; — it helps. Love does <u>not always</u> serve the best interests of Art. [126]

The first demonstration of this came in 1952 when Russell published a landmark article demonstrating the great epic of Spanish medieval poetry known as the *Cantar de Mio Cid* to have been composed not by a minstrel as previously thought but by a poet with legal training writing up to a century later than was universally accepted. [127] These conclusions were, as they were intended to be, a direct attack on the leading Spanish scholar of the age and the chief explicator of that country's literary and linguistic past, Ramón Menéndez Pidal. The article caused a *frisson* both in Spain and Oxford where greatly to Russell's annoyance Professor Entwistle sent an apologetic letter to Madrid on behalf of the publishing journal explaining that it should not be regarded as endorsing the case he had made. For years Russell awaited a riposte, endlessly examining his adversary, his own motives, his conscience and himself. The lines Russell dedicated to the

---

[125] Kolkhorst to Charles Kennedy, Yarnton, 11 June 1949, at the Taylor Institution Library, Oxford, MS.Fol.E.20, and in I. D. L. Michael's unpublished edition of that correspondence [GKCK], 10.

[126] Yarnton, 23 Nov. 1947.

[127] 'Some Problems of Diplomatic in the *Cantar de Mio Cid* and Their Implications', *Modern Language Review* 47 (1952), 340–9.

matter in his journal in 1960 bring us face-to-face with the dimension of his ego and the magnitude of the conflict created by it:

'Menéndez Pidal is such a worry.' Ramón Menéndez Pidal, c. 1920. Library of Congress

Menéndez Pidal is such a worry — he's 92 and I still cannot be sure my reasons are as good as they seem and his arguments sometimes as weak. Never met him yet urge to demonstrate [him] wrong is enormous. It's too easy. Facts and prejudiced hypotheses all mixed up, yet I don't approach matter correctly either as I have the prejudice of wanting to prove him wrong. But say I do and he either concedes defeat or is shown by others to be wrong, then what is gained? How would I feel? Not triumph but sorrow. At that moment [I] would switch sides. If I went to Nottingham as defender of Menéndez Pidal in public that would be the change I think is necessary — freedom from conflict. But I cannot do this because my insight into the errors is basically correct and I would be just becoming another disciple. How did I start this conflict anyway? Well, it started — I suppose — by [a] feeling of hostility against authority and adulation which caused me to see through weakness in argument others had not seen. But whole quarrel is absolutely sterile anyway. I'd be much better getting away from it on to something different. [...] Yet fact is he's far too old and too certain of himself to be worried by me or care. The trouble with Menéndez Pidal is he will not even say when he's wrong. He surreptitiously glosses the wrong or exaggerated statements in a new edition. He despises his critics. Yet — in all this — my own fight is a phantom one too. I'm against all authority. Yet I want to impose my own authority — by yelling, really. Yet I don't want authority because I'm aware of my weakness. What is worse than a weak dictator? Power drive where the power is bogus. It still remains true that if I didn't concentrate so much of my life on trying to dethrone Menéndez Pidal I'd be much better. [128]

Much to his disappointment his prediction that Menéndez Pidal would never rise to the bait was borne out, the topic left unbroached when the two met in Oxford in 1962 and at the time of Don Ramón's death in 1968. Years later Russell referred in a letter to Javier Marías to 'my difficult relationship with Menéndez Pidal', and those who organised the symposium held in Oxford to celebrate the fiftieth anniversary of the publication of his article in 2002 can hardly have imagined how emotive a subject it was for him or in what frame of mind he must have penned his own wry contribution to the occasion, practically his last published work. [129] In this Menéndez Pidal occupied that part of Russell's mind he reserved mainly for his mother. As in all his obsessive relationships the difficulty seems to have been one-sided.

In the meantime Russell had in February 1960 asked himself in his journal what had been accomplished by his lengthy psychoanalysis. To this no answer was forthcoming either, but decades on he reported having given up Lyth's services after he started increasing the fee for each session, presumably as a ploy

---

[128] Freudian journal, 28 Feb. 1960, 68–73. Menéndez Pidal (1869–1968) was in fact ninety at the time.

[129] JMA, PER to Marías, Oxford, 24 July 2002; 'Reinventing an Epic Poet: 1952 in Context' in *'Mio Cid' Studies. 'Some Problems of Diplomatic' Fifty Years On*, ed. Alan Deyermond, David G. Pattison & Eric Southworth (London: Queen Mary and Westfield College, 2002), 63–72.

to wean his patient off the therapy after fifteen years during which they had at intervals met three, four and even five times a week. [130] Within three months of his last recorded session with Lyth in March 1965 he had taken up with another Oxford analyst in the shape of a Mrs Schiele of Headington whom he had first met in 1959 and continued to see until at least 1977. Years earlier he had read approvingly in Gide's journals that 'the habit of asceticism was such that in the beginning I had to force myself toward joy':

> How profoundly true! We are all instinctive ascetics, if we are Anglo-Saxon anyway. It is so much safer to be ascetic because you can never be <u>wrong</u>. The Christian legacy. This is the probable answer for the problem. [...] It takes courage not to be ascetic — the effort of will needed for that is greater than that needed for the will <u>not</u> to do. One is creative, the other negative. [131]

A long recovery of sorts was in progress.

*

Quite aside from the psychosexual issues assailing him, Russell never subscribed in adulthood to any value system or way of living he could not construe as entirely his own or of his own choosing, a circumstance that barred any form of intimate emotional delivery or cohabitation as would put him on an equal footing with another. The price was loneliness, frustration and torment in the central regions of his life but the conclusion of Russell's long and painful introspection had shown this to be the only and inevitable course, the 'necessary end' as he described it in another context. [132] The fact that his personality and interests lent themselves to a solitary existence did not make the sadness any less protracted even if the breadth of the man emerges clearly enough from the predicament allotted him by time and fate. When it was all over, when all the experiences and reflections had been stilled to leave only rumour and speculation, there turned out to have been nothing that was not in the mind.

---

[130] When it was reported to Russell some time in the 1970s that Lyth had asked after him he responded by asserting that he had met with him but once. I am grateful to Daniel Waissbein for this memory.
[131] Journal, 20 Jan. 1948.
[132] 'Prince Henry and the Necessary End' in T. F. Earle & Stephen Parkinson, eds., *Studies in the Portuguese Discoveries*, I (Warminster, Wilts.: Aris and Phillips, 1992), 1–15

CHAPTER FIVE
Master of Studies (1946–1987)

In May 1945 Russell had while still languishing in the tropics been elected Laming Resident Fellow and Praelector in Spanish at Queen's (making him the first holder of a tutorial fellowship in that language in any Oxford college) and appointed to a University Lectureship. With Japan as yet undefeated the prospect of taking up these appointments must have seemed distressingly remote, but events proved otherwise and as the troopship *Antenor* neared Liverpool in mid-January 1946 Russell paused — not for the first time — to consider all that lay ahead: 'It is exciting to think that the day after tomorrow is the first stage in my freedom from military bondage and the start of a life in which all the chances are available if I have the will and sense to use them.' [1] Russell was looking forward to resuming his academic career in the austerities of post-war Oxford and confessed shortly before leaving Ceylon that 'I still have a tremendous nostalgia for Spain'. [2] Now in the intervals of damning most of his fellow passengers in his journal he plotted the way forward, all earlier qualms as to his choice of field set aside. He was also painfully aware how much time had been lost and how much had to be done to recover his position:

> I have been considering what I must now do to ensure that the mixture of determination on my part and good luck which has got me my fellowship is a success from my point of view and from that of those who elected me. Obviously there can be no more doubts about Spain as my subject so that to that extent one's task is simplified. I must try to spend two months there in the summer at least and also finish my book on John of Gaunt before the end of the year. That will cover a fair start on the academic side. It will also be necessary to take some action on the social side of this academic life i.e. Anglo-Spanish Society, contact with Embassy and Spanish academic life. Must also try to get into circle of reviewers of books on things Spanish not only for *Oxford Magazine* as

[1] Journal, 17 Jan. 1946.
[2] Journal, 19 Dec. 1945.

before but for other and more widely circulated reviews — *Times Literary Supplement* etc. All this will require some careful development and use of contacts. One has lost six years so that ambition cannot be left to flower without some planned gardening! But it must be well concealed! I resent the fact of having to take steps to 'get on' and it would be appalling if one was detected in the act. ³

Russell back in Oxford from the War, June 1947.

³ Journal, 7 Jan. 1946.

His arrival in Oxford a week later was marred by a bout of toothache requiring immediate intervention, but what awaited at Queen's was otherwise a mixture of the familiar and the unexpected:

> As before none of the Fellows who have been here throughout appreciate in the least what it means to have been away for six years and those of us who have been away find it very difficult. The College is very cold but food not at all bad. Contrary to expectations the returned officers are working well and quietly which is not really surprising — the fears were based on last war experiences which were entirely different as regards individuals' nerves and economic position. [4]

Russell soon found himself drawn back into the arcane and occasionally astringent life of the Queen's Senior Common Room, the classicist and papyrologist Edgar Lobel 'giving me a discourse on the etymology of the popular terms of the private parts and sexual aberrations' within half an hour of his arrival, the Praelector in French Iain Macdonald complaining at his failure to be appointed to a fellowship on the ground of his weakness for drink, and the aged Homeric scholar T. W. Allen (elected Fellow in 1890) developing a taste for Australian port as he slipped into senility:

> On the whole I am pleased to be coming back. The conversation in Common Room is better than I thought and the atmosphere of tradition-illuminated continuity is a settling factor which cancels out or reduces in scale many problems which otherwise would remain as skeletons looking for a cupboard. It is very soothing to hear the bells and chimes of Oxford again as a proper background to one's daily existence and not heard with the novel and picturesque delight of a tourist. [5]

There were also visits to old friends in other colleges, beginning with the noted and highly eccentric archaeologist and scholar of classical and modern Greek R. M. Dawkins at Exeter:

---

[4] Journal, 28 Jan. 1946.
[5] *Ibid.*

There was a tremendous rustling of papers after I had knocked and when I eventually got in the old man was hastily locking a deed box. He looked more like a grandfatherly but amiable spinster than ever but otherwise unaltered and shrilled the latest gossip to me in excited shrieks. [6]

Invited to dine at Exeter by Dawkins a month or so later, a fellow guest was another pre-war friend, the Chaucerian scholar Nevill Coghill who 'looking as much like an intelligent schoolmaster as ever told me my greying temples left me as handsome as before.' [7] Balm for Russell's injured vanity in the wake of his accident and convalescence in 1941. There were also memorable visits to Kolkhorst at Yarnton Manor, lacking the Colonel's antebellum complement of servants but garnished among other things by a rare commodity in the reigning austerity: real cream. On 21 March 1946 Russell celebrated his demobilisation with another dinner at Yarnton: 'John Betjeman was there and we had an uproarious evening in the best Yarnton tradition. The Colonel produced 1928 vintage champagne and we were as offensive to him as only his friends can be.' [8]

To that extent at least life was largely unaltered but at Queen's particularly change was afoot. A lunch for undergraduate members of the college returning to complete their truncated studies impressed on Russell the shared experience which as with their predecessors of the Great War created an unspoken bond of affinity: 'It is strange to realise that we all now have our separate worlds of a far more intense and dramatic significance than in normal times and yet can meet and associate again in College as if we had not.' [9] This distinction extended to the Senior Common Room where Russell noted 'a curious cleavage between those of us who have been away at the War (led by [G. E. F.] Chilver) and those who have been here (led by [T. E.] Wright) on the subject of getting on with the business of refurbishing the college to meet present needs'. [10] On 6 March 1946 Russell was formally admitted a Fellow of Queen's after being sworn in by the outgoing and outmoded Provost R. H. Hodgkin at a Governing Body meeting. His successor Oliver Franks, a former scholar of the college, late Permanent Secretary to the Ministry of Supply and senior advisor to the Attlee government, occupied the opposite end of the spectrum, an appointment inspiring fear and

[6] *Ibid.*
[7] Journal, 7 March 1946.
[8] Journal, 22 March 1946.
[9] Journal, 28 Jan. 1946.
[10] Journal, 16 March 1946.

anticipation in equal measure. Russell was suitably impressed when Franks was first introduced to the Fellows at an informal meeting on 16 March:

> Franks is going to be a man of very different calibre to the present one — he is a formidable first-rate brain, concise and somewhat intimidating of mien and manner. He will be excellent for the College as long as the Fellows don't allow themselves to be intimidated by his reputation. Decided to accede to Attlee's request to appoint a pro-Provost for next term.

The Provost and Fellows of The Queen's College in May 1946, early in Oliver Franks's tenure. Back row: J. A. W. Bennett; Russell; D. E. Nineham; J. O. Prestwich; A. Bridges; A. D. Woozley; J. Boyd; W. Harrison; S. Chapman; B. G. Gunn; front row: J. W. Jones; G. E. F. Chilver; E. Lobel; C. W. Carter; Franks; C. H. Thompson; T. E. Wright; U. S. Haslam-Jones; C. J. Hitch.

With his innate distrust of authority and the uses to which it might be put Russell for some time treated Franks with a measure of caution. He had in any case to give his full attention to his teaching and the duties of Dean of the College which he assumed in Michaelmas 1946. This onerous position placed him as the chief point of contact between the Senior Common Room and the student body to which disciplinary responsibilities were added that might have him up at all hours of the night. The office of Dean also had a certain formal dimension the most memorable exercise of which during Russell's tenure came on 24 October 1946 when King George VI visited Queen's after opening the New Bodleian Library. The latter event was a fiasco as the ceremonial key handed the King to unbar the door snapped in the lock requiring an undignified scramble before it was opened from the inside. It was therefore a rather disgruntled monarch whom Russell received at the gates of Queen's, his mood not improved by the aspersions against the German heritage of the Royal Family cast by T. W. Allen from behind a book press in the college library.

More consequentially, Russell had resumed his teaching activities. He was still in Ceylon when Professor W. J. Entwistle had written placing him at the heart of an ambitious programme to improve the low standard of the Oxford curriculum in Hispanic studies and with it the degrees earned by its students, one Russell discovered was shared by the Modern Languages School at large:

> We are going to have a new plan here someday, with more space allotted to *realia* — history and institutions of the sixteenth century, War of South American Independence, special subjects to be lectured on, and possibly changed from time to time. When you get home and are refurbished I want to have a conspiracy and to divide the job. I also want to put a bit of a screw on the young who have discovered that they can get Thirds from their School Cert work. They pay little or no attention to what the University has to offer. We shall have to come to an arrangement to make the Final Honours much more tricky for them. The war has sunk us pretty low. [11]

The evidence is that this state of affairs actually predated the War with elementary questions apt to be posed in Final Honour School examination papers. [12] Although readily explained by the exigencies of war service, only fifty students graduated in Modern Languages in 1945, thirty-five of them women, and just nine in Spanish. Nonetheless, Russell reported himself to be in full accord with this plan and Entwistle got things off to a promising start by installing as visiting professor for Michaelmas 1945 the great French scholar Marcel Bataillon, formerly

---

[11] W. J. Entwistle to PER, Oxford, 19 Nov. 1945.
[12] *Oxford University Examination Papers. Second Public Examination. Honour School of Modern Languages* (Oxford: Clarendon Press, 1932–5).

of the Sorbonne but now of the Collège de France, whose account of the reception of Erasmus in sixteenth-century Spain had opened a new era in the study of Spanish religious and intellectual history. [13] Russell was closing down his MI5 office in Colombo at the time and did not meet Bataillon until later, but the workload that awaited him with an influx of demobilised students on his return in the spring of 1946 was heavy: he was required to give three lectures and up to twelve tutorials a week in Spanish and possibly French if student numbers in the former language were lacking. Russell had already sounded the alarm in a cable he sent from Ceylon in June 1945, and the issue of his teaching load dominates his official record into the 1950s. [14] Teaching aside, this in practice required no less than sixteen lecture series to be written over the next eight years in addition to his responsibilities for electing and supervising the Laming Scholars and those of Dean which he assumed for the first time in the autumn of 1946. For now Russell drew up his teaching strategy as the troopship *Antenor* steamed through the Red Sea:

> I have also been thinking about teaching as it affects me and have come to some rough and ready conclusions: 1) Start with freshmen right away and make it clear you will not put up with any rehash of schoolboy work. Preliminary exams give time to look around and find feet. 2) Insist on competence in the language. Explain what is meant by 'literature' in the Oxford context and insist that no one is capable of studying literature unless he is interested. Give him his chance at history or linguistics if he is not likely to care for literature. 3) Compel attendance at lectures in 1st year and 3rd year. In 1st year require to be made to put something on credit side during settling down process. In 3rd year must be forced to fill in gaps and gain extra tips. But in middle year he should stand on own feet and be able to work for himself in his own way. 4) Urge study of outside subjects and interests suitable to the individual. 5) At all times urge, compel and bully them to understand that the subject of any university subject is never to be regarded as an end in itself. [15]

Russell's journals record him preparing lectures on the translation of Golden Age verse in February 1946 and the poet Góngora the following month, the beginning of a range of academic responsibilities made more burdensome by his

---

[13] *Erasme et l'Espagne: Recherches sur l'histoire spirituelle du XVIe siècle* (Paris: Droz, 1937).
[14] OUA/FA 9/1/265 PEL Russell, 1945–53.
[15] Journal, 7 Jan. 1946.

declining mental health. By January 1948 the resumption of his Oxford journal not only finds him at a low ebb both physically and emotionally but dreading the return of the student body for the start of Hilary term 1948: 'Oh dear! Only 2 days before <u>they</u> return. I couldn't want them to less — total disinterest is the most friendly reaction I can produce.' [16] Three days later he was at his wit's end: 'Morning seeing pupils. I'm obviously not cut out for this job; I could not get up the least interest in most of them. I quite like seeing Stubbs and Whitaker but the rest are just faces to which I'm quite indifferent.' [17] Another few days, however, had brought an adjustment to his teaching strategy: 'Started teaching this morning. I have a new idea which is to give the first year people half an hour's prose each alone. Apart from being quite good for them it saves me the tedium of having to correct the things beforehand.' [18] As in other areas of his life Russell's sanity as a teacher was often saved by his ability to find the humour in utter absurdity:

> Difficult session with Fleming — a pleasant but stupid moustache from Keble — who denounced Garcilaso for his unmanliness in making such a fuss about love and thought it all very unlikely. Eventually I suggested he had never been in love — he took this very ill but was mollified when I said I meant he had never been <u>unsuccessfully</u> in love! [...] Then an appalling pupil called MacArdle appeared — a borderline 3rd/4th — who said he wanted to stay up an extra six months. I asked why. He said 'to give himself a proper chance of getting a <u>first</u>'. I told him the truth about himself. [19]

Although of a forgiving nature Russell was formidable when his patience was tried overmuch. A rambling six-page *apologia pro vita sua* sent by one of his students at Queen's ended by thanking him for his forbearance while admitting that '[a]ll this should have emerged before but I am too daunted by your "presence" usually to be capable of putting it across even this coherently'. [20] Some students, however, were quite beyond redemption:

> Mathieson descended on me at 10 p.m. Saner than usual but desperately anxious to be given a chance to describe his love life. He didn't get it.

---

[16] Journal, 13 Jan. 1948.
[17] Journal, 16 Jan. 1948.
[18] Journal, 19 Jan. 1948.
[19] Journal, 27 Jan. & 5 March 1948.
[20] Richard Grundy to PER, undated but Oxford, *c.* 1950.

> [...] Mathieson arrived as I was making tea (for a tutorial). 'Have some tea,' said I. Naturally he said 'I have not been to bed since Saturday [three days earlier] and have not had the inclination to eat since last night.' I took no notice but nothing will stop him posing though he has enough decency to realise I don't trust him after his efforts to make trouble last term. [...] [E]xhaustion and much time wasted on trivialities. Among these Mathieson who telephoned me on Tuesday at 4 to say he would not be attending his tutorial as he was too drunk to do so. I then had the job of sending him down. Miserable creature; I can understand why I found Raskolnikoff boring — there is nothing more tedious than a nonentity aping the grand manner and thinking he is taking in anyone except himself. I'm told he now walks about Oxford in a drunken stupor hoping for a chance to attack me. [21]

Even here it had been possible for Russell to draw inspiration from a situation that presented itself:

> Mathieson for tutorial. I spend ¾'s of an hour elaborating the way the *mythos* theory might be applied to *Don Quixote* to explain its appeal without making Cervantes understand it, consciously. Mathieson had said one couldn't identify oneself with Don Quixote or Sancho because they were both too far away from one's own imagination and experience (at least that is what he meant to say). [...] Mathieson very surprised I was not concerned about the badness of his collection; did not realise I was pleased because it had stirred me to worthwhile thoughts — I think. [22]

Equally, Russell was sensitive to the plight of his most vulnerable charges:

> Keighley — quite a nice lad — is in a psychological decline from which nothing seems able to save him; before long he will probably do himself an injury. The difficulty is that I know what is the matter and might be able to help but on the other hand the effect on him of finding out that someone else knows what his trouble is might be too great. [23]

---

[21] Journal, 29 Jan., 3 & 19 Feb. 1948 respectively. Russell had been reading *Crime and Punishment.*

[22] Journal, 20 Jan. 1948.

[23] Journal, 4 Feb. 1948.

It says much of his state of mind at the time that he should add 'Anyway I really haven't the inclination'.

Russell makes little reference to his undergraduate lecturing in his private writings but the few mentions that survive reveal both the pitfalls and more particularly the degree of preparation that went into the finished product as it reached his audience:

> My opening lecture on Garcilaso [de la Vega] was, I thought, very good indeed though perhaps it <u>wasn't</u> altogether the thing to describe Garcilaso as an 'enthusiastic amateur', though it sounded unpremeditated enough. Nor was my reading of [Valencian poet] Ausías March altogether well chosen as the word 'fire' occurred far too often — *foch*, pronounced 'fuk'; some of them lost control of themselves in a rather embarrassing way. [...] Lectured well on Garcilaso, though I'm not saying nearly enough about him as a writer of poetry. Still, I made them see the funny side of the Second Eclogue. Yet how monstrously one play-acts in these lectures; the rehearsed tone, the planned joke, the carefully prepared peroration. The fact is these all go over much better when they <u>are</u> prepared. [...] Preparing a formal lecture on Garcilaso tonight suddenly realize that I have hitherto quite failed to grasp the obvious fact that the most marked quality of his poetry is <u>loneliness</u>, perhaps the most significant of the discoveries of the Renaissance.[24]

Russell's first undergraduate lecture series in Hilary 1938 had concerned the Generation of 1898, followed next term by another on the novelist Benito Pérez Galdós (1843–1920).[25] Michaelmas 1938 saw the first outing of the most enduring series in his lecture canon, 'Intellectual Movements in the Golden Age' which after the war became 'Thought and Taste in the Golden Age', delivered on three occasions in sets of sixteen lectures but more usually eight. This was followed in Trinity 1939 by 'Problems of Mediaeval Spanish Literature'. Within a few months of his return from Southeast Asia in early 1946 Russell was delivering the first in another notable course, that on Góngora, as well imparting the classes on Composition and the *Oxford Book of Spanish Verse* edited by James

---

[24] Journal, 19 Jan., 9 Feb. & 7 March 1948 respectively.
[25] For a full list of lectures imparted see Appendix IV.

Fitzmaurice-Kelly he had first received from Kolkhorst in 1931. By 1953 he had at different times lectured in addition on Spanish etymology, the *Cantar de Mio Cid*, the thirteenth-century *Primera Crónica General*, the fourteenth-century *Libro de buen amor*, the *Celestina* (with slides), chivalric and pastoral romance, sixteenth-century literary theory, Garcilaso, *Don Quixote* and the sixteenth-century novel, seventeenth-century Spanish verse, the poet Gustavo Adolfo Bécquer (1836–70), and series on Ganivet (1865–98) and Unamuno (1864–1936) as well as leading a class on Azorín's *Una hora de España* (1924) and others on translation. Subsequently as professor he extended his repertoire to literary and textual commentary, philology and linguistics, Alfonso the Wise (1221–84), a much-admired series on Spanish ballads from 1963, Galician-Portuguese *cancioneiros*, Portuguese fifteenth-century chronicles, Spanish romances, pastoralism and Petrarchism in sixteenth-century Spanish poetry and Golden Age balladry, together with a seminar co-hosted with Cyril Jones of Trinity on the Spanish Renaissance, and finally a post-graduate seminar on problems of research in Spanish literature which, with a precursor in 1957, first met in Hilary 1964. There was even a one-off series on Ramón Pérez de Ayala's novel *Tigre Juan* (1926) in 1960. If this listing displays some though not all of Russell's range as a scholar (lectures in history were restricted to chronicles) it also bears witness to the steadfast commitment to teaching he maintained throughout his tenure, one well in excess of his statutory responsibilities.

Though never a keen conference-goer, Russell enjoyed giving scholarly papers and most of his seminal articles were first ventilated in this format. He was a notable lecturer, clear, coherent, engaging and always grounded in wide reading, research and deep thought, the material delivered at a high intellectual pitch, in an elegant patrician drawl and in long balanced sentences whose unusual *conceptista* syntax lent weight and force to the content.[26] Once again, the preparation of a paper was in the first instance a matter for rigorous self-examination, here in 1948:

> Began this evening to write my lecture for London next week. It is a tremendous bother composing a script which will take an hour to read especially as the audience for such a theme cannot very well be more than two or three dozen. However it will clarify my ideas on a subject which has to be dealt with in the John of Gaunt book. I find it difficult, knowing

---

[26] Russell's lecture style is preserved in a recording of the talk he gave on 'Spanish Fiction from the Romance to the Novel' on BBC Radio 3 on 27 March 1977.

it is a lecture to be read by me, not to give far too much weight to the <u>script</u> aspects of what I am writing — to the business of acting the lecture; this makes me want to treat it ironically or maliciously and insert things which I can say in an effective manner — not very good for scholarship. [27]

In the event the lecture was not only attended by his friends Charles Boxer and Edward Wilson (both professors at King's College) as expected, but also by the Portuguese ambassador and a fair number of his staff. Russell recorded finding his effort to be 'rather dull'. [28]

Aside from his mind and erudition, the basis of Russell's success as teacher, lecturer and scholar was the silent self-criticism which remained an unalterable facet of his work as of his life generally, relentless in his detached observation of himself and his output, ever ready to rein in his ego and rebalance the scales of his judgements and opinions by making himself the first target of his objurgation. A poorly delivered paper on Walter Pater he attended at Queen's in 1948 'reminded me of a lecture by me at my most instructive and least human'. [29] The primary task was to guard against any sense of personal exceptionalism to which he no doubt felt prone: 'How ridiculous in the light of everyone's obvious and everyday experience to talk of "personality" as if such a thing existed free of time and varying circumstance' he noted in his journal in 1936. [30] The next was somehow to balance the competing claims of posterity and pleasure. Russell's reading of the Goncourt Journal brought him to the heart of the matter:

> '[T]hose who create must not live. Regular, calm peaceful days, a bourgeois smugness, a cotton-nightcap composure are necessary for the creation of what is grandiose, turbulent, dramatic. People who <u>expend</u> themselves in passion or in the jolts and jars of a restless life will leave nothing to posterity and will exhaust their life <u>in living</u>.' [...] Yet it is possible to exhaust one's life without living. That is far worse; I cannot believe posterity is really important. It seems lacking in proportion to want to stretch one's personality out in front of a million million spermatozoa. [31]

[27] Journal, 16 Feb. 1948.
[28] Journal, 28 Feb. 1948.
[29] Journal, 3 March 1948.
[30] Journal, 2 July 1936.
[31] Journal, 4 Feb. 1948.

Russell soon lighted on an answer of sorts in the context of his obsessive relationship with one of his most brilliant undergraduate students, Ted Riley:

> Last night wrote to Ted at length. This morning thought it not good enough and wrote whole thing again. Does this mean that second letter was insincere (<u>artistic</u>?)? That would be very serious. If I'm insincere then there is no hope for me. But I didn't feel insincere so guess I wasn't. Merely, perhaps, the discipline of a demand for the best one can do and not less. [32]

Whatever the emotional labyrinths here portended, the practical outcome of these convictions where his academic endeavours were concerned was an unshakable sense that only the highest standards would do as called forth by the nature of the subject matter and the predispositions of his audience. In this perhaps the most refined pleasure was that to be had in tutoring bright and engaged students, though even that carried dangers to be guarded against:

> I have been thinking that the tutorial system, whatever its merits for undergraduates, is very bad for the tutors who have, by it, an instinctively destructive approach to all intellectual problems. It is their part to criticise and attempt to undermine arguments presented — soon they become automatic and as a result one becomes able at negation but has very little practice at creation. [33]

Russell had occasion to try these ideas out on an especially gifted crop of undergraduates in the late 1940s: Keith Whinnom, Douglas Gifford, Robert Pring-Mill and Gareth Davies together with Ted Riley, all of whom in due course became distinguished scholars. Alan Deyermond, himself destined for a professorship and a fellowship at the British Academy, joined their number in the winter of 1950 though he did not come under Russell's supervision until after he graduated in 1953. These dimensions are all explored in the journal Russell kept in early 1948 and never again in his writings are his opinions of his charges made so explicit as in the record he kept of those months. His friendship with Riley, among the most intense of his life, has already been treated but it is doubtful

---

[32] Journal, 5 Feb. 1948.
[33] Journal, 9 Feb. 1948.

whether Russell (still only thirty-four) ever had (or found) a more challenging undergraduate than Robert Pring-Mill, recently demobilised from the Army and then in his first year at New College:

> Pring-Mill in an essay tonight — an essay which was <u>sickeningly</u> brilliant — attempted to convince me that there are four fundamental themes of aspiration in the human mind — love, war, the chase and the pursuit of the unknown; I suggested that this meant that the fundamental aspirations of the human mind, were, in three out of four cases only to be achieved in association with or through death. He didn't like that. [...] Pring-Mill makes faces in my lectures when I say something with which he doesn't agree. This irritates me intensely. [34]

Curiosity no doubt drove Russell to invite Pring-Mill to an evening at the theatre. The occasion was not an unqualified success:

> Went to see a play, *The Voice of the Turtle* [by John Van Druten], with Pring-Mill and brought him back for a drink here. Surprised to find that one so intelligent would be such <u>dull</u> company. He needs a mistress who has bad taste. He told me Entwistle had asked him to call because 'he was sure they had many things in common'. What is the meaning of this? Pring-Mill agreed with my comment that it was not exactly a clear compliment. [35]

Pring-Mill was in fact too much Entwistle's creature for comfort, particularly as Russell's patience for the latter began to wear thin, too apt now to be regarded by his former protégé as the relic of an earlier age of scholarship: 'Pring-Mill, now very much in demand by Entwistle, was informed by the latter yesterday it was essential he should read Aristotle "to find out how books are made". Incredible to discover he thinks one has to learn even that out of a book.' [36] By the summer of 1948 Russell was trying to hand off Pring-Mill, now privately christened 'Prigg-Mill', to Kolkhorst for tutorial supervision, a move the latter fended off in one of his epistolary fireworks. [37] Robert Pring-Mill, it should be added, became a

[34] Journal, 11 & 12 Feb. 1948.
[35] Journal, 16 Feb. 1948.
[36] Journal, 19 Feb. 1948.
[37] Kolkhorst to PER, Yarnton, 28 June 1948.

mainstay of Spanish and particularly Latin American studies at Oxford which he helped to include on the syllabus in 1960, a scholar with a range comparable to Russell's own including, among others, the Majorcan philosopher Ramon Llull, the Spanish Golden Age dramatist Calderón and the contemporary Latin American poets Pablo Neruda and Ernesto Cardenal; a fellowship at the British Academy awaited. Still, and no doubt in part because of his standing, Pring-Mill never ceased to elicit Russell's adversarial side. When in later life Russell shared his views on the ephemeral value of scholarly output with Pring-Mill he reported himself as 'astonished to find that he [Pring-Mill] utterly and angrily rejected the notion that his criticism of Calderón would not endure for ever because it was right.' [38]

The next student to come under assault in Russell's diary was Douglas Gifford, one extended to his wife:

> Had the Giffords to tea today. It is remarkable to me that the girl, who is obviously intelligent in an Extra-Mural way (one I don't like much) should have married a person who is I think the most 'little-boy' man I have ever come across — very agreeable but I find myself treating him like one treats a schoolboy out for the day. [39]

Apparently unaware of how intimidating he could be (apt 'with your basilisk gaze [to] reduce to cinders and to ashes' [40] and allowing for the psychological and physical circumstances under which his journal was kept in early 1948, Russell expressed in it a degree of opprobrium for an unusual undergraduate, Alan Eaton Davidson, which eventually — and unusually — escaped the confines of those pages. If nothing else these entries exhibit the extraordinary degree of engagement of which, largely unbeknownst to them, Russell was capable with his students, even when he wasn't in such a fickle and competitive frame of mind:

> Tony [unidentified] talked to me about AED whom he considers quite intelligent and a possible first. I discovered he talked to me about Alan because he thought I was a friend. I didn't commit myself. Am I? I suspect that will depend entirely on any signs of melancholy I may discover in him next term. [...] I dreamt of AED. I cannot remember

---

[38] JMA, PER to Javier Marías, Oxford, 28 Feb. 2001.
[39] Journal, 19 Feb. 1948.
[40] Kolkhorst to PER, Yarnton, 27 Nov. 1945.

any reaction except that I was watching him in the expectation (and hope) of catching him out in some way. Wretched youth. [41]

Professor W. J. Entwistle photographed by Walter Stoneman in 1950. First a mentor then a source of resentment but remembered by Russell at the end of his life as 'the last of the polymaths I have known in Oxford'. National Portrait Gallery

Russell could indeed be mollified, especially when signs of depression became apparent:

> I was sorry for AED who found his way in Hall to the seat where Ted and he used to sit and was very obviously feeling lost and solitary among

[41] Journal, 9 & 11 Jan. 1948.

strangers. A strange youth. He went out of his way to avoid meeting me in the quad this morning — I dislike being made to feel like an admiral appearing on the quarterdeck — I shall ask him to tea. [...] Not fair to let him think he was <u>certainly</u> only *persona grata* to please Ted — not entirely true either. [42]

So invite him he did:

> AED to tea. How curious a case that is! He was charming, well-mannered and talked intelligently and sometimes amusingly but when he had gone one realised he might as well never have come for all the impression which was left. He gives one nothing to hang on to. It is not so much that he has no personality as that he gives you the impression that <u>you</u> have none. Yet he talks cleverly about Kierkegaard whom he is reading. The tea was like a business lunch. Must ask Ted about this; he should know the answer. I want[ed] to say something really obscene and did, putting it quite untruthfully in the mouth of old A. T. Carter who is dead enough not to be harmed. But he didn't react in any way at all. I am baffled but not moved to enquire further. [43]

Russell later expressed relief when others shared his ambivalent view of Davidson while telling himself that 'I must stop an excessive tendency to persecute him mentally'. [44] In fact, as anticipated Russell took it too far by sharing his opinions on Davidson with Riley in a letter, an action he much regretted even though his correspondent found the accuracy of the portrait highly amusing: 'I don't know how you manage to be so nice to him and so unkind to him all at once.' [45] Russell was contrite in his journal, acknowledging a possessive dimension in respect of Riley's friendship with Davidson which harks back to the psychosexual issues described elsewhere:

> I wish I had not made that unpleasant reference to AED in my last letter to Ted. Even if I thought it true, which I did, it is not decent to <u>insert</u>

[42] Journal, 15 & 19 Jan. 1948.
[43] Journal, 24 Jan. 1948. Albert Thomas Carter KC was a recently deceased honorary fellow of the College which he had joined as a scholar in 1884.
[44] Journal, 2 Feb. 1948.
[45] E. C. Riley to PER, Havana, 2 Feb. 1948.

oneself into one's friends' relationships, even if one is Ted. That is being possessive — an emotion best left to mothers-in-law and grandmothers. I am really very much ashamed. [46]

Guilt and shame no doubt prompted Russell to make a further effort with Davidson:

Took AED to dinner at George [restaurant] today. Highly successful. For first time I saw the point. Alan charming and without the usual affectation. Success has done the trick. We drank Grand Marnier at vast expense and I told him a lot of stories after which I went to his appalling squalid little room, where he gave me a glass of port and revealed secrets of his *vie amoureuse* — as far as it goes. [47]

Complex relationships, in one direction. A picnic with two of Russell's students at Queen's, Gareth Davies and Douglas Gifford, c. 1949.

As Kolkhorst told him, 'You are, my dear Russell, for one so susceptible, very stern with the heart!' [48] Alan Davidson took a double first in Classical

---

[46] Journal, 15 Feb. 1948.
[47] Journal, 15 March 1948.
[48] Yarnton, 29 Oct. 1949.

moderations and Greats in 1948 and went on to a distinguished career as a diplomat and food writer. A year later the same degree of emotional engagement had helped bring Russell to the point of collapse, requiring him to take sick leave in Hilary 1950. [49]

Despite these early missteps and the power of his ego, in this area as in so many others Russell was an innovator who drew as deeply on his humanity and personal experience as on his intellect. A pattern was established which traces its origins to his pre-war teaching style and was refined after it: tutorials were conceived as a meeting of minds; any bright or promising student who was also personable was not simply to be afforded the finest lecturing and tutoring it was in his power to prepare and impart; he — and eventually she — was also to be the recipient of Russell's sympathetic interest and in due course admitted to the first atrium on the spectrum of his friendship. Not for him the intellectual conceit or rebarbative put-down that blighted many student–tutor relationships. His aim was to get under the carapace of the more withdrawn student and harness the energies of the most thrusting. The best way of doing so in either case was to alter the setting. A tutorial might therefore be reconfigured as tea in his rooms or a meal in a fine restaurant, or scholarly formality removed altogether in favour of an outing or trip of some sort, sometimes abroad, a situation in which one could be recognised as having something special to add. In their work students were coaxed to reach for the outer limit of their capabilities, a mixture of close reading of the text or the sources along with full engagement of their critical and analytical powers, with encouragement to question the conventional wisdom and attack prominent scholarship — eventually even his own. Academic life and the scholarship that emerged from it was first and foremost interpreted as a civilising human activity. Fate and shared tastes had brought Russell and his students to the same vineyard; studying the literary heritage and historical events, and the texts, documents, processes and phenomena to be found there, placed each in a position of equality with the other; resting within these various expressions of human endeavour were intimations of beauty, wisdom, tragedy and corruption that were not only life-enhancing or instructive in themselves but capable of elucidating the human condition — one's own condition — like no other exercise. The ultimate goal was not so much to learn but to learn to think, and in thinking to discriminate, avoiding at all costs the temptation to craft some private language. Most of all, Russell never made the mistake of believing his students to

---

[49] OUA/FA 9/1/265 PEL Russell, 1945–53.

be cast in his own mould. In Kolkhorst's words, '[y]ou have the tutor's greatest gift; you bring one out. Wherever you settle, you immediately act as a poultice. People love being brought out, because that is life. A poultice is a stimulant.' [50] That was Russell's Socratic teaching philosophy as it was shaped and reshaped in his seventy years as teacher and mentor, the fount and conduit of his erudition and his friendships, the salve for many of his deepest sadnesses.

*

The intellectual pleasure of teaching these bright young things and observing their quirks of personality remained one of the most rewarding dimensions of Russell's chosen profession, but by early 1948 other aspects of his job and a deterioration in his mental and physical health were making him question his position at Queen's. In the first instance Russell found himself overburdened with his teaching, administrative and decanal duties on what he reckoned to be the comparatively low and heavily taxed salary of £850 per annum, this as Queen's tightened its belt due to the loss of much income-bearing property in the blitz of Southampton. [51] A particular aggravation was the parade of inconsequential business that filled his days:

> How I am engulfed in trivial minutiae and the hundred entangling trivialities of everyday life in this place. I spent an hour this afternoon with the Steward visiting electricians' shops to try and find some way of improving the lighting in the Common Room; I discussed the way to make coffee with the chef. I listened to discussions about the College Statutes. How tiresome it all is. [52]

So begins Russell's journal for Hilary 1948. To this add his disciplinary responsibilities; a man who never raised his voice under ordinary circumstances now found himself haranguing a group of freshmen just back from the Christmas vacation. A month later he had in his capacity as Dean to receive 'an "official" deputation of undergraduates to complain of the Chaplain, whom they accused of listening at keyholes'. [53] The office had become burdensome to him:

---

[50] Yarnton, 20 May 1947.
[51] £850 in 1948 equates to approximately £25,000 in 2024.
[52] Journal, 9 Jan. 1948.
[53] Journal, 19 Feb. 1948.

> I very much dislike this Dean business in many of its aspects though I suppose things could hardly be quieter if the College was empty. One is constantly made aware of the less pleasant sides of life, usually in the form of other people's troubles and I feel I have really had about enough of them e.g. finding out Ruffell is a thief and then trapping him into admitting it. [54]

Next was his teaching load which though comparatively light by later standards he deemed excessive at seventy-two lectures or classes per year:

> Thursdays are ghastly — a lecture and translation class in morning and prose in evening for 15 bodies. Feel like a psychopathic case as a result by the time evening comes. Not enough sleep and nothing in exchange. Last term I often had very little sleep but life was stimulating and exciting and one never doubted the losses of sleep were more than worthwhile. [55]

And not just Thursdays. Here is Russell's agenda for Tuesday, 2 March 1948:

> Teach 3 hours
> Dictate 4 letters
> Lunch
> 2 p.m. Dentist appointment
> 2.30 p.m. Watch hockey
> Attend vast tea party in Hall
> Teach 1 hour
> 6 p.m. Sherry party at Austen's at far end of Banbury Rd
> 7 p.m. Colonel [Kolkhorst] to dinner
> 8.15–11 p.m. Meeting of College poets in my room [56]

Small wonder trouble was in store. In the report he prepared for the Faculty Board on his duties as University lecturer in December 1949, Russell dilated on the increasing workload he had shouldered since returning to Oxford after the war which had contributed to the breakdown he experienced that month:

[54] Journal, 23 Feb. 1948.
[55] Journal, 29 Jan. 1948.
[56] Drawn from Journal and pocket diary, 3 March 1948.

I have given about eighteen tutorial hours per week since 1946. Some nine of these have been in connection with my Fellowship at Queen's; the remainder for undergraduates in other Colleges. This latter demand has gone on increasing throughout the period under review. I have recently had to refuse a considerable number of requests for tuition from other Colleges even though it has been represented that the persons concerned could not obtain tuition from any other source. I intend to reduce the number of such hours still further on my return from sick leave. The demand situation in <u>all</u> possible papers for each individual tutor seems to be a particularly exacting feature of tutorial work in Spanish. [57]

For now at least, although Russell was usually on his last nerve by the time he made his nightly diary entry, life at Queen's was by no means all bad nor can the pall cast by his fragile state of mind be overlooked. For one thing he was much in demand as a speaker at the various college sporting clubs which he would otherwise by inclination have given a wide berth:

> It seems I rather overdid my oratory at the Boat Club dinner on Wednesday as it has been immediately followed by requests to attend and speak at the other dinners. I shall go only to the Hockey Club as it is the one which contains the most sympathetic members — besides I have seen their games to date and still know nothing about the game. When I have finished with the Boat Club on Wednesday I had immediately to go and drink with a collection of boxing blues — they were <u>most</u> gentlemanly. [58]

As so often Russell contrived to give others the impression of a man perfectly content with his lot. The truth was otherwise:

> Lunch. Everyone says I am unusually witty this term. This is relative and must be judged in relationship with their dullness. Not really wit at all. Merely cocking a snook like [François] Villon — no humour there. I'm cut off from the consolations of the Church. The temperature is always 70° — warm only. [59]

---

[57] OUA/FA 9/1/265 PEL Russell, 1945–53.
[58] Journal, 20 Feb. 1948.
[59] Journal, 24 Jan. 1948.

'I'm sick of their faces' he wrote later. [60] The nadir came a few days later on 17 March:

> In a poor way this evening. I have a cold. I have spent a large part of yesterday and today interviewing entrance candidates and marking their papers; this has brought me right up against the stark fact that I ought not to be here at all — the whole thing seems absurd to me when I am expected to take an interest in such goings-on.

Even the splendid Baroque fabric of Queen's incurred his dissatisfaction, Russell finding it 'architecturally very undistinguished when one gets down to details'. [61]

His disillusionment was deepened by the upheaval caused by Franks's decision to take up the office of British ambassador in Washington after just two years *en poste* and the ensuing cabals and intrigues centred on the appointment of a successor. First came the drama of his resignation:

> What seemed to me an absurd scene this afternoon at a Governing Body meeting. The Provost announced his intention of resigning and going to Washington. He did this in a firm voice at the start but suddenly began to falter, lost control of his lower lip and stopped in the middle of a sentence. There was then a long silence after which he finished off what he had to say in a quavering voice and rushed weeping out of the room saying 'I don't do this out of foolishness or disloyalty.' It was both impressive and rather disgusting, like suddenly perceiving a deformed limb on an otherwise impressive-looking body. I cannot imagine getting attached to an institution — particularly this one — in such a way though I can well imagine undergoing such a collapse if I were being separated from a person or people of whom I was fond. But he is not that fond of anyone here — it is merely the place. […] However the others — except Iain Macdonald — were tremendously impressed and they nearly broke down too. [62]

Then came the endless discussions regarding a successor:

---

[60] Journal, 13 March 1948.
[61] Journal, 25 Jan. 1948.
[62] Journal, 28 Jan. 1948.

MASTER OF STUDIES (1946–1987)

A ridiculous 'unofficial' meeting to discuss a new provost took place before lunch. The capacity for human self-deception among dons must be unequalled except among clergyman and Cabinet Ministers. They all claim to be 'for' or 'against' the possibles on profound intellectual moral grounds; yet in each case the reaction was really (obviously) dictated by purely egotistic grounds. What does it matter, anyway?

Still it creeps in. Governing Body this morning. All sitting there in their public faces like masks made of too-transparent material, like stereoscopic prints incorrectly focused so that one can see blurred outlines of two separate images, the hidden face and the social face. Neither excite one's interest. I am tired like a player in a repertory company must be tired of playing all this succession of parts, always forcing oneself to be someone else. [63]

By the time an appointment was made Russell had done with the whole affair which seemed trivial in the extreme alongside the onset of the Cold War:

Today a wasted morning while final negotiations on the new provost were carried on in a meeting. It was too silly. Keir was produced at dinner tonight having come from Belfast for the purpose. Seemed to me a rather dull and unimpressive figure. I refused to vote; after hours of bickering it was decided to offer it to him by a majority of 10 to 3 with 4 abstentions. Such a ridiculous occasion — the self-importance of all these people is unbelievable and I think none have the least realisation we may all be blown up in a matter of months, if not weeks. I am weary of the whole pretence. [64]

Here we come to one of the defining characteristics of Russell the academic who never lent himself to political intrigue in furtherance of his own ambitions and involved himself in those of others only where they concerned him directly, endorsing or scotching the claims of this or that candidate in a well-timed intervention. The world of C. P. Snow's *The Masters* (1951) was certainly not his.

[63] Journal, 8 Feb. & 13 March 1948.
[64] Journal, 29 March 1948. The candidate was presumably Sir David Lindsay Keir, then President and Vice-Chancellor of Queen's University, Belfast; the new Provost would in fact be John Walter Jones.

Despite Russell's pervasive cynicism and reticence Franks had evidently noted something in his young Spanish don and one day in January 1948 took counsel of him regarding his appointment in the United States:

> In Common Room the Provost asked me to tell him what my own unbiased and disinterested view of the Washington business was. I realised he only wanted to talk about it and so carefully avoided answering the query; and he did only want to talk. [...] At least I wonder; he asked me when John of Gaunt [Russell's book] would be out of the way and has been very friendly recently. Is he looking for a personal assistant or something there? Not for me. [65]

Oliver (later Baron) Franks is remembered as one of the great British civil servants of the twentieth century and an architect of the post-war world, one of the founding fathers of the North Atlantic Treaty Organisation and chairman of the Organisation for European Economic Cooperation to administer the aid dispensed by the Marshall Plan. Guarded though Russell was in his company in 1948, Franks joined the ranks of his friends in the upper reaches of the university on his return to Oxford as Provost of Worcester in 1962, one delayed by his failure, adroitly engineered by Professor Hugh Trevor-Roper, to be elected its Chancellor in 1960. This association not only gave Russell a private insight on the Commission of Inquiry into the organisation of the University chaired by Franks from 1964–5, but also the other bodies in which he was involved, notably the inquiry into the events leading up to the Falklands War in 1982. For now, and unbeknownst to any but himself, Russell had begun formulating his own strategy for exiting both Queen's and Britain having resolved to pursue his academic career in the United States, the irony of which was not lost on him during his conversations with the Washington-bound Franks. Contributing to this decision was his distaste for the egalitarian and nationalisation policies of the Attlee government:

> Was meditating this evening on what I should say to any American interviewing body which asked me on what grounds I wished to leave Oxford and take a position there. I suppose one would say that it is possible these days to find that ideological barriers between people of the same nationality are greater than the emotions which formally

---

[65] Journal, 21 Jan. 1948.

united them and that, since I do not believe in the social and political ideas which now rule here and will continue to do so and think that they would ultimately deprive me of all stimulus to work or create, I find it more necessary to live in an atmosphere of intellectual and individual freedom in reliance on one's own efforts than I do to respond to the obvious attractions of continuing to live among familiar faces and people. I wonder how they would take that. I think, anyway, it is true. [66]

Despite the war, or perhaps because of it, Russell was still a man who confined his 'socialism' largely to a rustic setting. The journal he kept in the autumn of 1948 is the last of its kind to survive until 1959 so information is lacking on what steps if any he took in pursuit of these transatlantic aspirations or how, when or to what extent his disgruntlement worked itself out. Doubtless the surrendering of his decanal duties at the end of the 1949 academic year lifted much of the administrative burden off his shoulders leaving him to focus on his lecturing, teaching, research and writing, but the experience added another facet to the part of his personality which resisted being stereotyped or perceived as other than exceptional, the man who in later life never wished to be regarded as a New Zealander, a Hispanist or even especially as a don as that term was understood in Oxford.

Aside from his publications, on which more elsewhere, Russell also made the first of his occasional broadcasts on the BBC with a twenty-minute piece on the Third Programme titled 'The Spaniards in Their History', a review of Américo Castro's recently published *España en su historia* aired on 14 July 1950. [67] This was followed by 'The Dilemma of Modern Spain' broadcast on 20 February 1951 in which Russell 'contrasted the vitality of the Spanish people and the inertia of their governments in the face of Spain's internal problems' taking Gerald Brenan's *The Face of Spain* and the memoirs of the exiled Republican leader Julio Álvarez del Vayo as his texts. [68] On 18 December came a broadcast titled 'Spanish Writers and British Critics' consisting of a discussion of Brenan's recently published volume on *The Literature of the Spanish People* and the reception of Spanish literature in the British Isles which in turn provided the subject of one of Russell's

---

[66] Journal, 1 Feb. 1948.
[67] First published in 1948 but subsequently revised; the *Radio Times* erroneously described the author as Ramón Menéndez Pidal.
[68] *The Face of Spain* (London: Turnstile Press, 1950), and *The Last Optimist* (London: Pittman, 1950).

early articles.⁶⁹ Two years later he was back to give another short talk on the Third Programme, this time on the Black Legend of Spanish cruelty broadcast on 30 January 1954.

*

On 13 June 1952 Professor W. J. Entwistle collapsed and died on the steps of St Edmund Hall at the age of fifty-six. Severely wounded during the Great War, his health had been overtaxed while serving as visiting professor at the Universities of Pennsylvania and California in 1948–9 during which Russell had lectured for him in Oxford. The King Alfonso XIII Chair of Spanish Studies he had occupied since 1932 therefore fell vacant and steps put in train to elect a successor.⁷⁰ The electoral committee consisted of Maurice Bowra, Vice-Chancellor of the University, in the chair, Eric Barber, Rector of Exeter College (*ex officio*), Xavier de Salas, Director of the Instituto de España (subsequently Instituto Cervantes) in London representing the Spanish government, Idris Ll. Foster, Professor of Celtic, Alfred Ewert, Professor of Romance Languages, Sir Cyril Hinshelwood, Dr Lee's Professor of Chemistry, and the historian J. R. H. Weaver, President of Trinity and a noted photographer, particularly of Spanish architecture. The nine original candidates were Walter Starkie, Director of the British Council in Madrid (already an unsuccessful candidate in 1928 and 1932 and supported this time by Ramón Menéndez Pidal and Dámaso Alonso), A. A. Parker, Reader at the University of Aberdeen, Professor William Atkinson of the University of Glasgow, Edward Sarmiento, Reader at the University of Durham, Joseph Manson, associate professor at the University of Birmingham, Professor George E. McSpadden of the University of British Columbia, and finally three Cambridge scholars: Harold Livermore, Inez Isabel Macdonald and Alan Ray Milburn. The process was complicated by the concurrent election to the chair vacated by Professor J. B. Trend at Cambridge, to which five of the Oxford candidates (though not Russell) had also applied.

As Russell recalled, he only entered the lists at the urging of Bowra, the determined enemy of academic hypocrisy, pomposity and mediocrity who was

---

⁶⁹ Cambridge: Cambridge University Press, 1951; the article was 'English Seventeenth-Century Interpretations of Spanish Literature', *Atlante* 1 (1953), 65–77. The talk was rebroadcast on the Third Programme on 7 May and 10 Oct. 1952.

⁷⁰ See OUA/UR 6/SPC/1B, file 2 for the documentation concerning the election. I am grateful to Alice Millea of the Oxford University Archive for kindly making this file available to me.

unimpressed at the strength of the field and recognised the pervasive influence for good of a successful appointment. The invitation was apparently issued during a chance encounter on the High after the application deadline had closed on 22 January 1953. A meeting of the electors on 3 February resulted in a shortlist of Starkie, Parker, Atkinson and Russell, proceedings being adjourned for three weeks to allow the latter to forward the names of three referees. In fact, Russell only wrote officially declaring his candidature and submitting his application on the 8th, and it is hard to avoid the conclusion that Bowra shaped the process to facilitate his cause. [71] Whatever the case, Russell had now to scramble to find referees, noting that 'those who know my general work in Spanish best are themselves candidates or cannot be approached for reasons of etiquette'. Letters were nonetheless promptly submitted on his behalf by the historian of medieval England Austin Lane Poole, President of St John's, Evelyn Procter, historian of medieval Spain and Principal of St Hugh's, Provost John Jones of Queen's, and by Professor Edward Wilson of King's College London, who according to Russell 'knows something of my work and would doubtless be willing to speak if he is not ruled out by the fact that he may be committed to another candidate'. The first two attested to his strengths as a scholar, Poole remarking on the ten years' research in Spain Russell had been denied by war but reporting favourably both on his forthcoming book (which he had seen in typescript) and on his capacity as tutor and lecturer since 1937, while Procter underlined his intimate familiarity with the 'scope and needs of Spanish Studies in Oxford'; Jones wrote of his conspicuous success as Dean and Laming Resident Fellow, reporting four of his students as having gone on to university appointments in Spanish. [72] As Russell suspected, Wilson had his own horse in the race, asserting that '[a]lthough I consider Mr. A.A. Parker the most important British Hispanist now living, Mr. P.E. Russell seems to me to be a very considerable one', and moreover that 'I consider that his small output of published work is a testimony to his scrupulousness.' [73] That bibliography — 'such as it is' noted Russell with the self-effacement which characterises his application — consisted of just five scholarly articles (two of them in press), a couple of review articles and the pre-war lecture

---

[71] *Ibid.*, PER to Bowra, Oxford, 8 Feb. 1953.
[72] *Ibid.*, Poole to Bowra, Oxford, 9 Feb. 1953; Procter to Registrar (Douglas Veale), Oxford, 18 Feb. 1953; Jones to Veale, Oxford, 16 Feb. 1953. Those appointed to lectureships were Ted Riley (Trinity College Dublin, 1949), Gareth Davies (Leeds, 1952), Robert Pring-Mill (Oxford, 1952) and Keith Whinnom (Hong Kong, 1952).
[73] *Ibid.*, Wilson to Veale, London, 17 Feb. 1953.

published under the title *As Fontes de Fernão Lopes* at Coimbra in 1941.[74]

No details of the selection process survive in Russell's own papers but on 14 March he received official word from the University Registry of his appointment to the chair, to take effect from 1 June. Russell received what was apparently a fairly perfunctory letter of congratulation from Atkinson to whom he sent a polite note of acknowledgment. This was intercepted by Mrs Atkinson who by way of reply posted him a splenetic epistle on the machinations of the electoral committee which had dashed her husband's hopes, inveighing against Wilson, Trend and Salas and generally bemoaning their fate as a family, Atkinson having also been an unsuccessful candidate at Cambridge.[75] She herself, so it was rumoured, had already gone to the trouble of measuring a house in Oxford for curtains. Much the greatest umbrage, however, was taken by Starkie, with whom Russell had hitherto enjoyed cordial relations, attentive during his monologues at Poole in June 1940 and dining with him in Madrid in August 1946 when he received many courtesies from a man of some influence but who never communicated with him again. The crushing review Russell produced in 1955 of a translation of *Don Quixote* by Starkie notable for its excisions cannot have helped.[76] Years later Russell gave this explanation for Starkie's failed candidature in responding to an official enquiry from the University:

> Dr. Starkie, when he became a candidate in 1953, had been too long in Spain and as a result had, I think, forgotten that these matters were not gone about in a place like Oxford as they would be at a Spanish university. He thus got the Spanish government officially to sponsor his candidature. This was not, in the circumstances of the early 1950's, a move calculated to help his case in a place like this. He also made the mistake of coming to Oxford and calling on each Elector to introduce himself which again must have been a decidedly counter-productive action. I think that Starkie did not understand the changes which had come to Spanish studies in British universities in the ten years he had been away from England. My predecessor [Entwistle], for example, was a brilliant but austere scholar who had established here a tradition of

---

[74] Transl. A. Gonçalves Rodrigues (Coimbra: Coimbra Editora, 1941).
[75] Evelyn Atkinson to PER, Bearsden, Glasgow, 23 March 1953. Information on the election is contained in a letter from Trend to Jiménez Fraud, Cambridge, 17 Feb. 1953, in Jiménez Fraud, *Epistolario*, ed. Valender *et al*, III, 47.
[76] *Bulletin of Hispanic Studies* 32 (1955), 53–4.

almost Germanic scholarship which was far removed from Dr. Starkie's way of looking at things Spanish and the same had happened in other British universities. [...] I am not sure (though I would certainly not wish to be quoted to this effect) whether his interests and character ever made him particularly suited to an academic career. [77]

In fact these developments together with the death in 1952 of Edgar Allison Peers, Gilmour Professor at Liverpool, and the retirement of the musicologist Trend, both of whom had come late to the field as gifted amateurs, represented a changing of the guard in British Hispanic studies. Succeeding them were Albert Sloman at Liverpool, Wilson at Cambridge, with Parker following Wilson at King's and J. W. Rees becoming the first Professor of Spanish at Manchester, all in 1953. Nonetheless, even with the steady professionalisation of academia after the war Russell's opportunity might never have come had Gerald Brenan accepted the entreaties of three Oxford scholars to get him to stand: the anthropologist Julian Pitt-Rivers and the historians Raymond Carr and Hugh Trevor-Roper.

Frustrated ambitions aside, the election of a scholar not yet forty and with only one slender volume in print was not without controversy; Wilson, whom Russell later counted as one of his closest friends in academia, was allegedly heard to say that Oxford had decided to 'chance Russell' who proceeded to hold the chair together with the office of Director of Portuguese Studies (until 1976) for the next twenty-eight years. The appearance of *The English Intervention in Spain and Portugal in the Time of Edward III and Richard II* in 1955 settled any remaining doubts as to the wisdom of the election. [78] 'The rest', as Russell later put it, 'is on public record' though it characteristically rankled with him in private that no invitation ever came to deliver an inaugural lecture. [79]

*

---

[77] PER to Ann M. O'Sheehan, Oxford, 19 Sept. 1978. Starkie had died in November 1976. Russell's concluding remarks are borne out by memories of Starkie's intermittent tenure at Trinity College, Dublin from 1926–47; J. L. Brooks, 'Walter Fitzwilliam Starkie (1894–1976)', *Bulletin of Hispanic Studies* 54 (1977), no. 4, 327. Bowra's ongoing rivalry as Vice-Chancellor in the matter of University appointments with Starkie's sister Enid, Fellow of Somerville College, may also have helped seal his fate.

[78] *The English Intervention in Spain and Portugal in the Time of Edward III and Richard II* (Oxford: Clarendon Press, 1955).

[79] PELR, 4.

Russell's election to the professorship of Spanish at Oxford in 1953 obliged him to move out of Queen's but not correspondingly to rooms in Exeter College to which the chair was attached. As he noted in later years, Exeter 'had long made it a rule never to pay any particular attention to the subjects professed by any of the professors attached to it by university decree.' [80] Of this situation Russell was of course fully acquainted through the experience of Kolkhorst whose university lectureship was attached to Exeter but which steadfastly refused to make him a Fellow, even after he became Reader in 1931. Accommodation facilities were in a similar vein of restriction. Madariaga had fled to the Randolph Hotel after a few days in residence in January 1928, defeated by bitterly cold rooms and the long trudge involving a second staircase to ablute. [81] Correspondence between Russell and Exeter in 1953 and 1956 makes it clear that only temporary accommodation would be made available to him, and then against payment of rent. [82] Russell had therefore to set up what was his first private home, which he did in a flat at 121 Woodstock Road in North Oxford. On returning from the war he had begun purchasing antique furniture, rugs and ornaments which, considerably augmented with the benefit of a professorial salary of £4000 per year, formed the basis of his décor first there and then at his final residence, Belsyre Court, to which he moved in the summer of 1956. [83] Owned by St John's, named for its first president and showing a colonnaded frontage on Woodstock Road, Belsyre Court is an imposing U-shaped block of apartments designed in the 'Jacobethan' style and erected in 1936 as the first building of its kind in Oxford. No. 23 which he leased in 1959 after occupying another unit in the building (No. 28) was a spacious balconied two-bedroom flat looking south across a courtyard giving onto Observatory Street but also lit from the north on which side the property as a whole backs onto St Bernard's Road. In Russell's time the prospect south towards central Oxford was partly obscured by the bulk of the now largely demolished Radcliffe Infirmary but sight was also offered of James Wyatt's eighteenth-century Observatory. Belsyre Court was much favoured by wealthier members of the Oxford academic community and among Russell's immediate

---

[80] 'Ian Michael: A Personal Appreciation', *The Iberian Book and its Readers: Essays for Ian Michael*, ed. Nigel Griffin, Clive Griffin & Eric Southworth [= *Bulletin of Spanish Studies* 81] (2004), no. 7–8, vii–x; at ix.
[81] Madariaga, *Morning Without Noon*, 124–5.
[82] Exeter College Archive, Russell Letters, LIV 6. I am grateful to Victoria Northridge of Exeter College for making this information available to me.
[83] £4,000 in 1953 equates to approximately £92,000 in 2024.

neighbours and friends in later years were the art historian Edgar Wind and his wife Margaret, the classicist Donald Russell and Sir Dimitri Obolensky, Professor of Russian and Balkan History. With neither Exeter nor the University providing any facilities for teaching, it was here that Russell conducted his tutorials and imparted some of his classes and where he kept his study in a third room at the rear of the suite. It was here, too, that for nearly half a century he presided over the circle of friends, scholars and writers which made Belsyre Court an international centre of Hispanic studies, a status that along with its furnishings and the persona of its resident earned it the sobriquet of *palacio* among his friends. [84] Together with Knowlescourt in New Zealand it is the place most intimately associated with him and the destruction of the former in 2011 leaves nowhere offering such powerful reverberations of his life.

Belsyre Court in 2023. Russell's Flat 23, which he occupied from 1959 to his death in 2006, included the second-floor bay window in the centre of the photo and the adjacent balustraded balcony to the left of the entrance. Author

---

[84] Another more mischievous appellation was Clarence House, in allusion to the Queen Mother.

In later years Russell would describe himself as a furtive figure who spent the late 1950s and early 1960s largely confined to Belsyre Court, emerging to deliver lectures or transact other essential business before retreating to that sanctuary. What he would imply to have been a lengthy episode of agoraphobia can now be identified from his journals as the profound psychotic anxiety disorder discussed elsewhere. These miseries did not however restrict him from travelling, which he continued to do on at least a yearly basis both for scholarly reasons and also for pleasure as one of his chief recreations. Russell's heavily stamped passports show that most of these trips were to the countries to which he had dedicated his professional life, Spain and Portugal, particularly the former with whose culture and people he had to reacquaint himself after an eight-year absence during which the Franco regime had been imposed. Although Russell continued to visit Spain most years for over half a century after the war, only the three trips he made in 1946, 1947 and 1948 are recorded in his journals, each carried out under the strict exchange controls and tax regime imposed by the British and Franco governments respectively.

Russell's first post-war visit to Spain came in August 1946 when he boarded Iberia's inaugural Douglas C-54 Skymaster service from Croydon Airport to Madrid. The flight gave him an unexpected impression of the land he knew so well:

> Saw very little owing to clouds until we were over Castilian plain — then many things I had forgotten, barren terraced mountains with the mark of centuries of erosion, the rivers lined with poplars, brown and yellow fields with stooks of corn, remote villages each surrounded by white patches which must have been the 'eras' or threshing floors. Seen from the air Castile is crossed right and left and in all directions by country roads and tracks joining up these forgotten and unvisited villages, tracks which wander over dried up empty land. [85]

On arrival in Madrid ('[h]ad to give five pesetas to porters at Barajas [airport] which shows how times have changed') he made his way to his *pensión*:

> Pensión Isamar, Jorge Juan, 32. Typical Spanish *pensión*. Room small and tastelessly furnished in Spanish bourgeois style but hot and cold running water. I had forgotten the perilously-fixed lighting

---

[85] Journal, 8 Aug. 1946.

arrangements of these places. [...] Usual servant, Elisa, working all day and most of the night. [...] Dined well on salty soup, salad, macaroni. Curious collection of guests at their separate tables each with air of personal aloofness and concern with own affairs that only Spaniards can achieve in such circumstances. One has the impression that the others could never find out what lies inside the limits of that battlemented circle of personality within which each seats himself. One I should say, from his popping anxious eyes and ill-looking face, has either been in gaol or fears to go there. After dinner (11.30 [p.m.] or so) retired exhausted to a hot bed where radio continued to blare in block of buildings on to which I look until I fell asleep.

Outside he found a mixture of old and new together with the labile combination of rigidity and informality characteristic of Spain:

After this went for a walk up Alcalá, Gran Vía. Shops there seemed full of luxury and other goods but at tremendous prices. [...] Various smells came back to me — *cigarrillos negros*, lottery sellers, canopies in front of shops so low that I have to bend to get under. Went into Espasa Calpe — full of books. Certainly in the last ten years book production has enormously improved here and quality has improved too. I had an unsolicited testimonial from the police. The business of crossing the streets here is tremendously disciplined now — one can only cross when policeman blows whistle. I didn't know this and a policeman began ticking me off. I explained my ignorance but he insisted in thinking I was Spanish until I explained I was English when he embraced me and was most affectionate, much to the surprise of the onlookers who expected an altercation. [86]

There were old friends and new acquaintances to meet, all disproportionately marked by the passage of years. One such was Father Pedro Longás, Librarian of the Instituto de Valencia de Don Juan, whom Russell had met during his first visit as a De Osma Student in 1935 and now found reinstated to his position after being dismissed and detained in Valencia during the Civil War. Others were the granddaughters of the nineteenth-century Cervantine scholar and bibliophile

[86] Journal, 9 Aug. 1946.

José María de Asensio y Toledo living in reduced circumstances on the Paseo de la Castellana:

> They showed me their grandfather's library which they want to sell — one of the finest Cervantine collections in existence, some 225 editions of *Don Quixote* including 1605 and 1615 editions, Avellaneda's [version of the Quixote], *Persiles, Ocho Comedias*, first edition of *Perfecta Casada* by Avellaneda, Herrera's [*Comentario a*] *Garcilaso* and so on. I wish I had some money to get hold of some of it. All this, and some good-ish Murillos, in a typical, overcrowded Spanish middle-class flat. I think they are very hard-up and will be very sorry to sell. Their young brother was murdered at 20 — this is the old story of so many. [87]

There were also fellow scholars in the offing, not least the irrepressible figure of Ruth Lee Kennedy of Smith College, Massachusetts, a specialist in Golden Age drama who had lectured at Oxford in the spring of 1946:

> Went along to Biblioteca Nacional this morning and got in without much trouble for [a] month. Had a look at the procedure for withdrawing books and then went to Sala de Manuscritos [Manuscript Room] for an hour or so. To my alarm found there Miss Kennedy, the American professor whom the Entwistles couldn't get to leave. However she was quite useful about finding one's way about the Sala. [88]

Despite his carping Russell plainly got on quite well with Kennedy but her reputation for loquacity was confirmed in no uncertain manner during an unplanned joint visit to Segovia:

> Got to [Estación del] Norte by taxi. More queueing at booking office and there found the Kennedy awaiting. Got into train feeling pretty tired and she then started talking and never stopped whether the noise of the train made her inaudible or I appeared asleep or anything at all occurred designed to stop a person asking foolish questions. [89]

---

[87] Journal, 16 Aug. 1946. Russell later learnt that the collection had been sold to the Biblioteca Nacional for 1.5 million pesetas; Journal, 8 Sept. 1948.
[88] Journal, 10 Aug. 1946.
[89] Journal, 17 Aug. 1946.

This unlikely pair proceeded to tour the architectural wonders of Segovia in a torrential deluge of rain and blather by R. L. Kennedy:

> All the foregoing is very fine but omits the picture of myself walking along these deserted lanes getting wetter and wetter and angrier and angrier with the K., hair all over her face, stumbling over the cobbles, talking all the time, sometimes breaking into her fluent Spanish with its odd nasal grind.

Worse awaited in the train back to Madrid: 'Sitting in carriage the Kennedy embarrassed me beyond endurance by starting to read an enormously long pamphlet in Spanish and going on for ten minutes or so to the astonishment of our fellow passengers.' Russell could see the humour in the situation but it was somehow typical of Spain with its inexhaustible supply of surprises cultural and anthropological:

> What a curiously intimate connection this city [Madrid] has with the country. Just up the street from this building [on calle Jorge Juan] is a byre with about half a dozen Friesians eating hay. This afternoon on my way to the Castellana I passed a herd of goats, about 60, walking along tramlines. [90]

Two years later, and already in the grip of the psychotic disorder which would assail him for the next decade or so, Russell paid a visit to the palace-monastery of El Escorial outside Madrid:

> I was sitting on rather unkempt terrace with formal myrtles thinking the building was really rather a monument of failure — it totally lacks <u>finesse</u> — but this is land of unexpected. Five stories up in one of the towers window opened and a youth climbed out along the parapet, collected a tin kettle placed there and returned perilously to the room. High up on top of central dome some workmen were erecting a wooden scaffolding; suddenly one of them began to sing a wailing *cante jondo* about a gypsy girl which came sliding incongruously down the immense shadowed wall in thin trickles of yellow sunlight. Philip II and *cante jondo* and a tin

[90] Journal, 12 Aug. 1946.

kettle. Very good lunch but surrounded by sagging and over-jewelled bourgeois wives and old spinsters and widows their bodies and minds wizened and raddled by years of imaginary masturbation with the masculinity of Christ. [91]

The greatest discovery, however, was the grim reality of the Franco regime as experienced by ordinary people. Russell had gained some inkling of this in Madrid and elsewhere on his first post-war visit in the autumn of 1946 but the full revelation awaited on a night train journey from Barcelona to Miranda de Ebro in Castile towards the end of that trip:

A night of horror. Yesterday I went to the station at 4.30 [p.m.] and found myself in an ancient second-class carriage already full — a wireless operator from the [SS] *Magallanes*, a labourer with an enormous wife and a filthy dirty and pestilential little boy, a railway official and, as it later turned out, a smuggler, a stoker from the *Magallanes* and an Asturian fisherman. The seats were hard as hell, horribly close together and generally filthy. Shortly before we started a worried-looking youth put some luggage down and dashed off. The wireless operator read out an article published in all the papers today by one Halliday Sutherland described as a member of the Labour Party and a Catholic to the general effect that he sees spectacular social progress here, laments Communist attacks from Russia, England, France and America, thinks Government has similar aims to that of British Labour Party, social justice, visited prisons which he found clean and with more personal liberty than in English prisons, good relations between guards and prisoners, lamented high price of food but noted England to have black market. The reading of this article by the wireless operator caused an uproar and all agreed what turncoats the English were. Stated that now no one listened to the BBC except the newspaper commentaries. All the company, without the slightest care, then began to denounce the regime — lack of food etc., prices, inability to live without black market and without playing one's part (one was smuggling oil up and down railway lines, woman black-marketed in flour, [railway official] in imported goods smuggled in), rule by priests — annulment of

[91] Journal, 8 Sept. 1948.

Republican divorces, prohibition to recognise one's illegitimate children, 12 years for having belonged to a masonic society, no lay education, nuns teaching little children to raise right arm, evils of syndicates. All this was eye-opener to me — these people are dominated by problem of feeding themselves and corrupted by black market. They are anti-Russian, anti-politician. Meanwhile got filthier and filthier and more and more uncomfortable. Dinner was a relief. Found myself sitting with wireless operator and a Basque and Englishman. After dinner we went to their sleeper for two hours and smoked a cigar while wireless operator told a couple of stories [...]. A dreadful night. I didn't sleep at all. The corridors were full of nuns and people without tickets, the filth was indescribable. At Castejón [in Navarre] two civil guards appeared, turned on the lights and in the absence of the railway official who was on the platform by foresight or accident, removed the jar which it afterwards turned out contained a gallon of oil. There was no enquiry — it was simply removed with the remark that the owner could claim it from the Civil Guard in Castejón. Tremendous indignation in the carriage — there is our personal liberty etc. — though they had all been denouncing the black market. The truth is it is everyone's livelihood just now. [92]

On a future trip Russell had the opportunity to meet André Lambert, a talented French etcher settled at Cap de la Nao in Valencia, the Italian translator and poet Esther de Andreis in Barcelona, and the eminent Catalan librarian and philologist Jordi Rubió i Balaguer living in semi-exile at Sant Boi de Llobregat outside that city. To Russell these were oases in the cultural desert created by the dead hand of state-backed clericalism:

> More than ever this time one is conscious of the shifting effect of clerical reaction on life here. At every turn, material or intellectual, one is confronted by an ignorant, aggressive and uncharitable priest. Here there is nothing of the intellectual clarity and vision of the best French Catholicism but only a lust for power and a narrow-mindedness which seeks not to convince but only to overwhelm by endless and ridiculous

---

[92] Journal, 8 Sept. 1946. The physician Halliday Sutherland (1882–1960) was a prominent opponent of eugenics and birth control.

emotional invocations of the past which certainly never existed. Hence creation of an intellectual kind barely exists — good for research but what value has research in an intellectual Sahara? Yet behind this official façade of rhetorical religiosity and traditional piety there is nothing except an unbridled materialism practised precisely by the bourgeoisie which alone responds to this religious appeal. [93]

When not in Spain Russell was able to keep up with Spanish affairs thanks to the latest in a succession of powerful shortwave radios:

> As I begin to write the Spanish news announces that the Duero at Zamora is 18' above its flood level and that all the rivers in the country are in flood; hard to imagine so much water over all those parched plains. How astonishingly provincial the Spanish news sounds — Virgins congratulated, a civil governor given a new car, a Mexican bishop on a tour, an increase ('desde luego' [of course]) in the circulation of the Catholic Press in the USA. [94]

Russell never worked in contemporary history but much of the critical zeal he deployed in his published work over the ensuing decades was driven by a profound distaste at what he referred to as the 'hatefulness' of the régime and the patterns of thought promoted by it both in Spain and Portugal under Franco and Salazar. [95]

*

Appointment to the chair of Spanish Studies in 1953 freed Russell from the burden of tutoring undergraduates and where lecturing was concerned imposed no duties beyond delivering sixteen a year. Nonetheless, he continued to see gifted students for final honours throughout his tenure, some of whom he later supervised as postgraduates for the degrees of D.Phil., B.Litt. and B.Phil. (see Appendix III). His first priority however was to increase the roster of teachers of Spanish in the University which at the moment of his election consisted of himself, Kolkhorst (Reader at Exeter) and Cyril Jones, who had been appointed a University Lecturer in Spanish at Trinity in 1948, this at a time when over 100 undergraduates were reading Spanish and fifty or more students might attend

---

[93] Journal, 24 Sept. 1948.
[94] Journal, 31 Jan. 1948.
[95] Journal, 28 Sept. 1948.

lectures on compulsory papers.[96] In doing so he took full advantage of the expansion of British university life which began after the war and by degrees turned the somewhat amateurish arrangements for the teaching of Spanish, not least the spoken language for which little provision was made until 1951, into a serious academic sub-faculty. In this way the diet of schoolmasterly dictated notes and droning line-by-line textual analysis that characterised the pre-war and immediate post-war course of study was replaced by stimulating, contextualised and iconoclastic lectures and the Socratic tutorials for which he had set the standard. His first additions as University Lecturer were his former student Robert Pring-Mill of New College and Frederick Hodcroft of the University of Manchester, both in 1953, and both veterans of the war in Southeast Asia, Pring-Mill as an intelligence officer in the Black Watch and Hodcroft as an RAF navigator in Beaufighters. Hodcroft, born into a working-class family in the Manchester suburb of Stretford, had travelled down for the interview without the slightest expectation of being selected but went on to give thirty-seven years to the University, one of Russell's most inspired appointments. Russell's vacated Fellowship at Queen's was filled by W. Gordon Chapman of the University of Aberdeen in 1954. These supported by a number of lecturers holding tenure only briefly bore the brunt of teaching in Spanish into the early 1960s by which time a rise in student numbers was making the strain intolerable. To this was added a disparity in status and pay between those holding tutorial fellowships and those serving as university lecturers. Russell spelt the problem out in a letter to *The Oxford Magazine* in June 1961:

> Comment on the question of differential stipends has tended to assume that this particular problem, and those of status and emoluments raised by it, only concern the position of scientists. This is not the case. To give the facts about one arts subject, with which I am connected: there are now about 110 undergraduates reading Spanish here. There is one tutorial fellowship in the subject. Most of the tutorial teaching for colleges depends, therefore, on four full-time university lecturers, some of whom are persons of considerable seniority, and whose prospects of securing tutorial fellowships are, inevitably, uncertain. Their position is, indeed, rather worse than that of scientists similarly placed since most arts teachers have no departments to urge their claims. If it is impossible

---

[96] OUA/FA 9/1/265 PEL Russell, 1945–53, Report to the Faculty Board, Oxford, 29 Dec. 1949.

for colleges to offer prospective fellowships in these cases, the practical reasons for which are quite well understood, there is surely a very good case in equity for taking advantage of the [University Grants Committee]'s offer to compensate some of those affected, at least for the financial disability under which they may be placed compared with their more fortunate colleagues doing similar work. Unless something of the sort is done I do not see how we can expect either to secure or retain here the services of the best teachers in the subject, especially as one effect of the present discussions has been to make widely known details of the disparity in status and emoluments between those who hold tutorial fellowships and those who do not. [97]

Perhaps it was this state of affairs that renewed in Russell's mind the possibility of his leaving for the United States, one strengthened by a visit to Harvard and Dartmouth College in connection with the University Grants Committee for Latin American Studies in the spring of 1963. [98] That his disenchantment at Oxford had become known is shown by the invitation he received to apply for the office of Vice-Chancellor of the University of Exeter in 1964. [99] The invitation was declined, not least one imagines because change was afoot in Oxford where Russell proceeded to secure the creation of tutorial fellowships or the equivalent at Christ Church (1963, filled by Ronald Truman), Trinity (1964, Cyril Jones), St Catherine's (1965, Robert Pring-Mill), St Cross (1965, Fred Hodcroft), St Antony's (1965, John Rutherford), Magdalen (1969, David Pattison), Wadham (1969, Philip Lloyd-Bostock) and St Peter's (1972, Eric Southworth from Cambridge), together with their successors *en poste*: John Rutherford at Queen's from Gordon Chapman's death in 1968, David Gallagher at St Antony's as the first University Lecturer in Latin American Literature from 1968–75, Clive Griffin at Trinity in 1975 in succession to Cyril Jones (d. 1974) and supported by numbers of college lecturers and two devoted librarians — Archie Seldon (1961) and John Wainwright (1969) who with Russell's encouragement built up and maintained the rich holdings of the Taylorian for over thirty-five years. There was also an extremely gifted line of *lectores* and *lectoras* from Spain including the poet and essayist José Ángel Valente (1955–8),

---

[97] 'Flexible Stipends', *The Oxford Magazine*, 8 June 1961, 401. It was among the matters addressed by the Franks Commission in 1964–6.
[98] R. O. Jones to PER, Dartmouth, N.H., 20 April 1963.
[99] G. D. Trotter to PER, Exeter, 6 & 13 Nov. 1964.

the poet Francisco Brines (1963–5), the poet, playwright, novelist and film director Vicente Molina Foix (1976–9), the poet and novelist Félix de Azúa (1979–81) and the poet and novelist José Luis Giménez-Frontín (1981–3); the prevalence of poets reflects the extent to which *lectores* had a hand in recommending their successor. These appointments, practically all of them of Russell's making, had by 1981 turned Oxford into one of the leading centres of Spanish studies in the United Kingdom. Nor in making that assertion should his role as Director of Portuguese Studies in the university (until succeeded by Tom Earle in 1976) or the contributions of the medieval historians Evelyn Procter (Fellow and later Principal of St Hugh's from 1926 and 1946 respectively) and Roger Highfield (Fellow of Merton from 1951) and the noted scholar of modern Spain Raymond Carr (Fellow and subsequently Warden of St Antony's from 1964 and 1968 respectively) go unrecorded. It was the community fictionalised in *Todas las Almas* (1989) and described in *Negra espalda del tiempo* (1998) by one of those *lectores*, Javier Marías (1983–5), and memorialised by another in light of the acclaim of Marías' work, José Luis Giménez-Frontín in *Woodstock Road en julio* (1996). [100]

Many of these major advances were made possible by the body Russell had alluded to in his letter of June 1961, the influential University Grants Committee on whose Latin American Studies sub-committee he sat under the chairmanship of the historian J. H. Parry from 1962 to 1965. [101] The sub-committee was established on the initiative of the Foreign Office which was concerned to develop Latin America as an area of strategic interest for British diplomacy, trade and cultural exchange not only concerning Hispanic America but also the United States. The Parry Report which resulted led to a major expansion of Latin American studies in Britain in general and Oxford in particular, including the establishment of the Latin American Centre as an adjunct of St Antony's in 1965 and the aforementioned Lectureship in Latin American Literature held at that college in 1968; an Iberian Studies Centre followed in 1970 though it never secured adequate funding. [102] There can be little doubt that Russell was in no

---

[100] *Todas las Almas* (Barcelona: Anagrama, 1989), and *Negra espalda del tiempo* (Madrid: Alfaguara, 1998); translated as *All Souls* (London: Harvill, 1989) and *Dark Back of Time* (London: Chatto & Windus, 2003) respectively. Giménez-Frontín's *Woodstock Road en julio: Notas y diario* (Pamplona: Pamiela, 1996) was influenced by the acclaim received by *Todas las Almas*.

[101] Gabriel Paquette, 'The "Parry Report" and the Establishment of Latin American Studies in the United Kingdom', *The Historical Journal* 62 (2018), 1–22.

[102] *Report of the Committee on Latin American Studies* (London: HMSO, 1965). For St

small degree responsible for the successful outcome of the committee whose affairs were handled with some despatch, a point one of its members, Rodney Needham, felt moved to record after its work was done:

Russell participates in a live radio hook-up with the University of Salamanca on the BBC's Spanish Service in March 1973. With him (left to right) are two long-serving members of the Spanish Sub-Faculty, Robert Pring-Mill and Cyril Jones. BBC

> I found that the business of the Committee was remarkably efficiently conducted. [...] This happy result is not, I am sure, the product simply of the splendid virtues of the ordinary members alone, and I should like to offer you my personal appreciation of the deft and good-humoured way in which you directed the committee's discussions. I much admired your performance and should like to hope that I might succeed partly in emulating it if I were ever forced to take on such a prickly burden! [103]

The means by which Russell managed to finesse what was often a hostile, self-satisfied, inward-looking and intellectually immobile system both in Oxford and

---

Antony's see María Jesús González Hernández, *Raymond Carr: The Curiosity of the Fox* (Brighton: Sussex Academic Press, 2013), 236–66.
[103] Rodney Needham to PER, Oxford, 15 June 1965.

elsewhere are lost to us, but Needham's remarks give some insight into his method. [104] Russell followed this up with appointment to the General Board of the Faculties as the nominee of the Board of the Faculty of Medieval and Modern Languages in May 1966, the position to be held until the start of Michaelmas 1967. It was his last senior academic appointment.

Although Russell found the protocol attaching to the King Alfonso XIII chair somewhat irksome and played no part in the formation of the Association of Hispanists of Great Britain and Ireland in 1955 (his mental health was then at a nadir), he did host the inaugural congress of the International Association of Hispanists in its foundational year in 1962, taking the opportunity with two others to curate a large exhibition of Hispanic manuscripts and books drawn from Oxford libraries for the 300 attendees among whom were Menéndez Pidal, Marcel Bataillon and Russell's former tutor Dámaso Alonso. [105] The local organisation of the congress was to a large extent the work of Cyril Jones of Trinity but to Russell and others fell the mustering of attendees and the diplomatic problems with the Franco regime and political frictions with Latin American embassies in London it brought in its wake. [106] This was therefore the first and the last conference in which Russell served in an organising capacity, but many other luminaries from the world of Hispanic letters were received in Oxford during his tenure, notably the novelist Camilo José Cela in November 1954 and the poet Pablo Neruda, who was awarded an honorary doctorate in 1965; Salvador de Madariaga was similarly honoured in 1966 and Jorge Luis Borges in 1971, returning for a final visit in 1985. [107] One who might have visited in 1970 but did not was Octavio Paz, who declared himself annoyed at the length of time Russell had let him spend in Cambridge before extending an invitation by phone; his turn came later, as did that of the poet and novelist Juan Goytisolo in 1977 and the novelists Julio Cortázar, Mario Benedetti and Mario Vargas Llosa. Indifferent as he was to ceremony, for himself or for others, Russell

---

[104] I am grateful to Jeremy Lawrance for his assistance with this section.
[105] P. E. Russell, D. M. Rogers & O. N. V. Glendinning, *A Catalogue of Hispanic Manuscripts and Books before 1700 from the Bodleian Library and Oxford College Libraries Exhibited at the Taylor Institution, 6–11 September* (Oxford: Dolphin Book Co., 1962).
[106] Ian Michael, 'Sir Peter Russell (1913–2006)', *Bulletin of Spanish Studies* 83 (2006), 1133–44; at 1140. The others involved in the international organisation were Edward Wilson of Cambridge, Alec Parker of King's College London and Frank Pierce of Sheffield.
[107] Borges' 1971 visit is recalled by David Gallagher in 'Meetings with the Master: Mario Vargas Llosa's Encounters with Jorge Luis Borges', *Times Literary Supplement*, 29 Jan. 2021.

acknowledged his successor Ian Michael as having accomplished far more than he in this realm.

As noted, the heightened profile of Hispanic studies at Oxford since the war together with an expansion of higher education in the United Kingdom as a whole contributed to an influx of students, with 110 undergraduates reading Spanish by 1961. For the first time those involved in Hispanic studies at Oxford found themselves part of a large and varied community with an expanding curriculum and attendant social and intellectual life, the beneficiaries of the organisation assembled by Russell and his colleagues over fifteen years which culminated in the establishment of the Sub-Faculty of Spanish and Portuguese in 1969. One of those beneficiaries was Colin Thompson and this is what he found:

> I came up to Trinity College, Oxford in 1964 from a provincial grammar school. I didn't even know where it was. To say that I experienced mild terror would be an understatement. My tutor was Cyril Jones, recently appointed to a Fellowship at Trinity, and I and my tutorial partner were the first undergraduates he had selected. Cyril's untimely death at the age of 49 [in 1974] cast a long shadow over the early years of the Sub-Faculty. I was also taught two of my Finals papers by Fred Hodcroft, in a garret in Wellington Square, as Fred had yet to acquire a Fellowship. […] The first lectures I attended, in Room 16 [in the Taylor Institution], a soulless room for so long the soul of our academic endeavours, were given by Ron Truman, still happily with us, and Peter Russell […]. One early memory that stays with me is of having been taken by Cyril at the end of my first year to a room in New College, where selected undergraduates were introduced to Pablo Neruda, recipient of an honorary degree masterminded by Robert Pring-Mill. As I hadn't read a word of Neruda at that point I was less overawed than I should have been, and what I remember best is a conversation there with Iris Murdoch, whose reaction to the fact that I was shortly to spend my year abroad in Spain was to let me know in no uncertain terms that no decent person ought ever to go there. [108]

Other gatherings were open to the public. The Spanish Society (successor to the Spanish Club with which Russell was involved in the early 1930s) announced

---

[108] Colin Thompson, unpublished presentation, 28 Feb. 2020.

talks by Kenneth Tynan on bullfighting (1955), Stephen Spender on 'My very little Spanish' (1956) and J. M. Cohen on 'The translator's problems' (1957), a guitar recital by John Williams (1960), and Penelope Betjeman on 'A riding tour in Andalucía' (1965), among many others. [109] Colin Wight came up a decade after Thompson:

> I arrived at Queen's in October 1973 to read Modern Languages. I needed a second language to go with my Spanish and I was under the mistaken impression that it would be easier to start Portuguese from scratch than to revive my O-level French. My tutor, John Rutherford, was a reassuringly normal person in his early 30s with a sense of humour: an encouraging first impression. [...] My first recollection of seeing Peter Russell is at his undergraduate lectures on the *romancero* [anthology of Spanish ballads edited by Menéndez Pidal]. As it was not compulsory to attend lectures in the Taylorian, and no-one seemed to care if you went to all, a few or none at all, it was very unusual to find oneself in a packed room, with everyone scribbling away furiously. Although only 60, he had already led the sub-faculty for 20 years. He was a tall, vigorous-looking man with a mop of white hair that made him look both young and old at the same time. He never lost that imposing presence, especially when wearing his gown. [...] Russell was a very good lecturer, aiming his erudition, I felt at the time, at exactly the right level for his audience. It is no coincidence that the best essay I wrote in my Prelims was on the *romancero*. [110]

Fifty years on the impact of these lectures in the coffin-shaped precincts of Room 16 was recalled for this biography by a group of Russell's students and colleagues:

> Room 16 in the Taylorian, the room then used for most lectures delivered under the auspices of the Sub-Faculty, is smallish by modern standards, seating maybe 30–40. But plenty big enough for most of what went on there. The only occasions on which I can remember it being packed and there being a queue waiting to get in, Prelim courses apart, were for Peter's

---

[109] Bodleian Library, Oxford University Societies 16, Spanish Society and Portuguese Club (Modern JJ Coll). The fact that many of these events were held at Queen's suggests that Gordon Chapman was a moving force in its organisation until his early death in 1968.
[110] Colin Wight, unpublished memoir, 6 June 2020.

Thought and Taste in the Spanish Golden Age. We are, of course, back in a world where both lecturer and disciples wore gowns. Peter's, as I recall, had that incipient moss-green patina that was the long-service badge of the day. The gown could also be used as theatrical prop, and was, with one lapel, sometimes both, gripped for emphasis. Peter brought in his papers/lecture in a briefcase, which I seem to remember his opening with deliberation and in silence. As also his spectacle case. [Nigel Griffin]

My first sight of him was when he lectured to us first-year students on the *Flor nueva de romances viejos* [ballads ed. Menéndez Pidal]. For him they must have been bread-and-butter stuff, but for us they were — I hope I'm not exaggerating in retrospect — an occasion. Later, when lecturing in the eyrie of Room 16, I would stand chatting with slightly embarrassed students on those precarious stairs while we waited for the previous lecturer to finish, or I would walk into a wall of young sound and have to get myself sorted and then raise my voice to create some calm. Not so with Peter: he would appear from the cubby-hole where he kept his gown and silence would fall as he came through the door and processed up to the lectern. There was a natural authority in his physical presence and then in what he said. Rumours went round about the scar; we were in awe; this, clearly, was The Professor. [Clive Griffin]

He had genuine charisma, and it wasn't just the scar. I recall his *Romancero viejo* lectures fairly well: clear, articulate, critically nuanced, in the sense that he was never afraid to question received opinion or revered names. [Colin Thompson]

Peter used the bookstand provided in Room 16 and that enabled him to avoid too much of the up-and-down nodding and also to stand tall and straight. I do not think I had at the time an impression that he was reading from a script (and perhaps he wasn't; maybe those annotations and emendations indicate a long evening of re-reading, rethinking, and memorizing). There was never much ingratiating himself with the *hoi polloi* and both his posture and the delivery in the Queen's drawl were olympian rather than demotic. But companionable for all that, never condescending, not untouched by irony, not without humour. It seemed to me as though one were in the presence of someone who had read widely, had experience of the world beyond the schoolroom, and who was talking to others supposedly in the process of doing the same. An indication of this might be that, in my experience, he talked in exactly the same way when he was giving an academic paper at a conference or a talk directed at colleagues and/or postgraduates. (He was also quick to acknowledge any help or supposed help he received, irrespective of the standing of the helper.) [Nigel Griffin] [111]

Russell also oversaw the development of a flourishing graduate community at Oxford with a distinct *esprit de corps*, one that numbered sixteen members by 1977. Identifying a deficiency in the college system, in Hilary 1964 he instituted the seminar for graduate students here recalled by Colin Thompson:

> Social and intellectual interactions went hand in hand. There were Sub-Faculty parties, at which Joan Hodcroft would try with great good humour to drag Fred home before everyone else had left. Every Tuesday lunchtime in term the graduates gathered in Cyril Jones's set [at Trinity]. We brought our own food and Cyril and Fred, who was the co-host, provided the wine, which was becoming the drink of choice of those of us who had assumed that alcohol meant beer. Then, on Tuesday evenings we gathered for the weekly graduate seminar, presided over by Peter, at which a paper would be read and a first respondent, chosen by Peter, would kick off the discussion. I was terrified the first time he asked me to do that. You might know next to nothing about the subject of the paper but you did learn how to follow the structure of an argument, ask questions and find connections. Those gatherings took place in the Sub-Faculty's own library, a room in [65, St Giles'] presided over by Archie Seldon, the kind of librarian who appeared at first to be distinctly prickly, but once he'd got your measure could hardly have been kinder or more helpful. [112]

Colin Wight first attended the seminar in the late 1970s:

> These seminars, which I believe were instigated by Peter Russell himself, were an opportunity to air your ideas in what was intended to be a safe and informal context. In reality it was a bit like washing your dirty linen

---

[111] Nigel Griffin, Clive Griffin and Colin Thompson, 'Russell as Lecturer', 26 June 2020. Russell's 'Thought and Taste' lectures echo the title and broad-ranging content of one of his two surviving undergraduate essays, 'Taste versus thought in Calderón', *c.* 1934.

[112] Thompson, unpublished presentation, 28 Feb. 2020.

in public, as you never knew who would be present and before whom you were about to make a complete ass of yourself. The wide range of research subjects meant that you could be hearing about St John Chrysostom one week and Chilean clandestine publishing the next. Often there was little one could usefully contribute. Was there any point in being there? They were invariably polite affairs but you had to keep your wits about you. [...] Robert Pring-Mill was ever-present at the seminars. I found him something of an enigma in his jacket and tie. He clearly had immense erudition, but it had to be coaxed out of him by Russell. He wasn't one for the cut-and-thrust of academic argument. Sometimes we had visiting speakers, and it was extraordinary to see eminent figures such as J. H. Elliott joining a small group of people, some just starting out on post-graduate studies, all sitting around a table. It was even more extraordinary if a woman were present. Our discussions were followed by a drink or two in the bar of the Randolph, with Peter Russell usually being the first to buy a round.

Voluble neither in public nor in private, the graduate seminar was one of the ways in which Russell's presence, subtlety of mind and power of mental control asserted itself, the gathering awaiting a pithy intervention which often never came.[113] This power could, however, be wielded vicariously. As Nigel Griffin recalls, Robert Pring-Mill was among those who unexpectedly found themselves in the crosshairs, albeit at the hands of others:

> Essentially it was an in-house affair with both graduates and Sub-Faculty. But every now and again (perhaps once a term?) Peter would haul someone in to play the game with us. Two such occasions stand out in my memory. The first was a paper given by Robert Pring-Mill on a Calderón play of the 1650s entitled *La fiera, el rayo y la piedra*. It stuck in my mind because I assumed, not having read it, that it must have something to do with madness, a notion which seemed to baffle the speaker. But it was the occasion itself that was memorable. Fred [Hodcroft], who read voraciously but did not like anyone to know the fact, had, as ever, done his homework. Usually, when a paper was on a literary topic, he would gaze benevolently at the speaker and keep

---

[113] Giménez-Frontín, *Woodstock Road en julio*, 69.

schtum. Just this once, goaded by theological nitpicking and Thomistic triads without number, he picked up on a couple of lines of the text that Robert had seemingly misremembered. Peter chortled about it afterwards, not only because he had doubtless had enough himself of such quibbling but also because Fred had so definitively blown his cover. [114]

Russell's message that received views should be questioned and challenged occasionally produced the results to be expected of a vigorous intellectual community:

> The second occasion involved A. A. Parker [Chair of Spanish at Edinburgh University]. Peter had quietly trained us all as attack dogs and the format was that the speaker would be asked to talk for 35–40 minutes after which we would all be let off the leash. Parker, despite the briefing he would have had beforehand, generously elected to give us a full 70 minutes from the pulpit, by which time the dogs were hungry. It was clear, even to me, that Parker was discomfited, not by the substance of the subsequent interventions, which might be discounted as they did not accord with revealed truth, but rather by the perceived insolence of these young shavers who dared to question him. On the Wednesday morning I called by appointment at *palacio* to take Peter to lunch at the *Luna Caprese* [restaurant in North Oxford]; he affected to be exhausted and proceeded to give a lengthy account of the several hours he had to spend the previous evening wining, dining, and calming the speaker down. [115]

Sometimes Russell delivered the paper himself. Eric Southworth:

> What I recall vividly are the papers he occasionally gave to the Tuesday seminar. Part of the fun there — an example being his paper on Vegetius

---

[114] Nigel Griffin, email to the author, 27 May 2020.
[115] *Ibid.* The following anecdote shared by Alan Forey is in a similar vein: 'On one occasion Peter told me that a professor of Spanish in a Scottish university [possibly W. C. Atkinson of the University of Glasgow] had recently come down to Oxford and happened to see on Peter's table a lecture list for the term. He noticed that Peter and someone else were both offering lectures on the same subject. In a shocked voice he said: "But he might disagree with you", to which Peter replied: "I was rather hoping that he would".' Email to the author, 18 Sept. 2020.

— was to hear him start with what might in other hands have seemed and remained abstruse material and then draw out the sheer historical fascination of that text: the range of ways in which it was interesting and important. You might have thought you were starting in an obscure corner, and then gradually — and with perfect timing — the lights came up and the mental windows opened. There was drama in that, but theatricals of only the most understated kind. [116]

The table set amidst book stacks wreathed in cigarette and pipe smoke around which these intellectual duels were contested and minds expanded at 65 St Giles' has long gone but Russell's weekly graduate research seminar, since removed to the Taylor Institution, continues to meet on Tuesdays at 5 p.m. when the University is in session. Of his many legacies to Spanish at Oxford it may prove the most enduring.

Lecture series were delivered at the Taylorian but with no office provided by college or university Russell's tutorials were in the first instance dispensed from Belsyre Court. Clive Griffin was among the chosen few to be tutored as an undergraduate at No. 23 after Russell assumed the professorship:

> For me at first, as an undergraduate, it was formidable: somewhat old fashioned, redolent of past travels and mystery, and I was relieved to get out after tutorials without an intellectual drubbing. Later it became a place of welcome but still of a certain formality. [117]

Trepidation there might be, but where academic output was concerned everything and everyone was fair game: '[H]e encouraged me, probably prematurely, to attack orthodoxies or any critic who enjoyed a high reputation and particularly celebrated my challenging what he'd said or written himself.' [118] Graduate students were treated as colleagues who knew their own minds by a scholar who wore his learning very lightly and never talked shop more than was necessary. Griffin provides a flavour of his unobtrusive style:

> I had undergraduate tutorials and early graduate supervisions in the living room at Belsyre Court, though at some stage I remember being

---

[116] 'Russell as Lecturer', 26 June 2020.
[117] Clive Griffin, email to the author, 19 May 2020.
[118] Clive Griffin, email to the author, 15 March 2020.

introduced to the study. When I was busy teaching in the early years and doing precious little work of my own except in the summers, I think we met once a term for lunch in the *Luna Caprese*, always followed by a ritualistic tussle over the bill. I would bring up any issues I wanted to air about my thesis but, if I didn't, a passing allusion would be made to it over coffee, and this was clearly more than enough for Peter to fashion the termly supervisor's reports. That said, we did have some long and enormously helpful sessions in his living room. [...] He was always willing to set aside his own work and read with care and perceptiveness draft chapters of my thesis. Criticisms were unfailingly on target; suggestions, on the other hand, were often made so indirectly that one had to learn to listen out for them. In my case, at least, the penny sometimes dropped only a few days after our conversation. When I eventually finished my thesis Peter was very helpful in seeing it published.

To my mind one of the great virtues of Peter as a supervisor was that he didn't claim any expertise (often deceptively, of course) in your area of research. So he gave you the benefit of his wide erudition and his razor-sharp mind's application to an area in which he wasn't 'bogged down'. There was never any attempt to impose a point of view or an ideology; quite the opposite. He treated the graduate student from day one as the 'expert'. Nevertheless, his example exerted a strong influence, in particular in encouraging a historical approach to literature, challenging orthodoxies and telling us comic, but surely cautionary, tales about sloppy scholarship in others. So, years after his death I still occasionally imagine his quizzical look suggesting that I'll never get away with X without a more convincing argument or stronger evidence, and it's back to the drawing board. [119]

Some graduates had to be brought hesitatingly to the light. Alastair Saunders was one:

[Russell] suggested that I have a look at slavery in Portugal, after I had destroyed two possible thesis topics on the Spanish Frontier and Southwest Andalusia on the eve of Columbus's first voyage because of the lack of accessible archives and in the second case, no major local

---

[119] Clive Griffin, email and comments to the author, 23 June & 9 July 2020.

archives from the period at all: one was ruined by the earthquake of 1755 (which did not just affect Lisbon), another burnt down in 1920, and the third was blown up in the Civil War in 1936. I said, 'But I don't know Portuguese', to which he replied with that wonderful Oxonian serenity, 'You'll learn.' Which I did. [120]

Another who benefited from Russell's lidless eye and long antennae was Colin Thompson:

> I began my doctoral studies under the supervision of Peter Russell in the autumn of 1970, having recently completed a second BA, in Theology. In those days there was no transfer or confirmation of status. Peter simply said 'Come to see me when you've got something you'd like me to look at'. So I did, and bit by bit the thesis developed before being bashed out on an old typewriter in the days when cutting and pasting involved real scissors and glue. Peter also made sure that I received the help I needed when he didn't think he could provide it. So one term he sent me off to Anthony Kenny at Balliol, to brush up my non-existent scholastic theology, and another to the wonderfully named Vigo Demant, who had been Regius Professor of Moral and Pastoral Theology at Christ Church. He remains the only person I have ever met who was a chain-snuffer. [121]

As Thompson recalled, this understated but intellectually honed style was also deployed as head of the Sub-Faculty of Spanish:

> I first became a member of the Sub-Faculty in 1974, when I was appointed to what is now called a Junior Research Fellowship at Christ Church. As I recall, meetings were held at 8.30 pm under the chairmanship of Peter Russell, with wine and other refreshments to hand, and were usually over by 10. Peter was a masterly Chairman. His characteristic *modus operandi*, in response to some paper or other from the Faculty Board, was to say that he'd prepared a few thoughts he'd like

---

[120] Comments to the author, 4 Oct. 2020. The resulting thesis was published as *A Social History of Black Slaves and Freedmen in Portugal, 1441–1555* (Cambridge: Cambridge University Press, 1982).

[121] Colin P. Thompson, unpublished presentation, 28 Feb. 2020.

colleagues to discuss, which he duly handed out. Colleagues would find his paper fully formed, elegantly constructed and judicious in its conclusions, and adopt it without further ado. When I left Oxford four years later for pastures new on the south coast I took with me expectations based on what I had learnt, though they were not always welcome in an increasingly managerial campus university.

Another student and colleague, John Rutherford, has left this summary of his powers of leadership:

> I never heard him raise his voice or even tell anybody to do anything, he never needed to: after a brief, quiet indication that it would perhaps be as well if such-and-such an action were undertaken, and that maybe one of his younger colleagues (for example) might care to think about it, the job, however onerous, would soon be done. [122]

For Russell the business of learning was a wheel which came full circle in the person of his students. A decade after first hearing Russell's lectures on the Spanish medieval ballads in 1964 Thompson found himself given the same handwritten notes, somewhat amended, for delivery on his behalf while he was on convalescent leave in Michaelmas 1975. [123]

Beginning in the 1950s these same students began to fill an increasing number of university positions in Hispanic studies and history in Britain and abroad so that by the 1970s it was anecdotally reckoned that Russell and Professor J. W. Rees of Manchester would divide the allocation of chairs north and south of a line running between the Midlands and the Humber. Whatever the truth of the assertion, Russell's contribution as a scholar was matched by his stature as one of the preeminent teachers of Hispanic studies in the United Kingdom. He was in addition a member of the editorial board of the *Bulletin of Hispanic Studies* from 1959 to 1996 and until resigning in the mid-1970s an advisor to the increasingly moribund Oxford University Press Modern Languages Monographs series. In 1977 he instead became the founding editor of

---

[122] John Rutherford, 'Peter Edward Lionel Russell', *The Queen's College Record* (2006), 91–4; at 94; also in his unpublished address delivered in Exeter College Chapel, 28 Oct. 2006.
[123] Colin P. Thompson, 'Address Given at the Service of Thanksgiving for the Life of Professor Sir Peter Russell (24 October 1913–22 June 2006)', *Bulletin of Hispanic Studies* 84 (2007), 263–5; at 264.

the Cambridge Iberian and Latin American Studies series which became under his editorship a leading forum for new research in the field in both literature and history, extending to thirty-two volumes in print by the time he gave up his duties in 1992. [124] By then any who worked with Russell, who were taught by him in Oxford or abroad or who could appreciate the depth and influence of his writings across the many fields in which he laboured could with justice look on him as the head of their profession. This status was marked by the four *Festschriften* he had received from friends and former students on both sides of the Atlantic by the end of his life. [125] He knew, as his students knew or came to know, that he had lived in a golden age for Hispanic studies as for academic life generally in the English-speaking world. That he was one of its chief representatives had long been acknowledged.

Though they existed, there were few regrets from a great career which was recognised with election to the Portuguese Academy of History (1956), the Real Academia de Buenas Letras of Barcelona (1972) and the British Academy (1977). He received a D.Litt. from the University on his retirement in 1981 and became an honorary fellow of Queen's in 1990. Recognition was slow in coming from Madrid but partial amends were made in 1989 when he became the inaugural recipient of the Nebrija Prize conferred by the University of Salamanca, the Spanish state's highest accolade. In the same year he was made a Commander of the Spanish Order of Isabel la Católica, receiving (with no lack of irony given the controversy of earlier years) the same dignity in the Portuguese Order of the Infante Dom Henrique in 1993 which Russell was amused to learn conferred the right to use a portable altar. He was knighted in the 1995 New Year Honours 'for services to Hispanic and Portuguese History and Literature Studies', it was rumoured with the approval of Gillian Shepherd, then Secretary of Education, who had read Modern Languages at St Hilda's in the early 1960s. Who had

---

[124] Russell was joined in the capacity of associate editor by Enrique Pupo-Walker and Anthony Pagden in 1985.

[125] The *Festschriften* were (i) *Medieval and Renaissance Studies on Spain and Portugal in Honour of P.E. Russell*, ed. F. W. Hodcroft, D. G. Pattison, R. D. F. Pring-Mill & R. W. Truman (Oxford: The Society for the Study of Mediæval Languages and Literature, 1981); (ii) *Letters and Society in Fifteenth-Century Spain: Studies Presented to P.E. Russell on His Eightieth Birthday*, ed. Alan Deyermond & Jeremy Lawrance (Llangrannog, Ceredigion: The Dolphin Book Co., 1993); (iii) *Studies in Honour of Peter E. Russell on His 80th Birthday*, ed. Julian Weiss [= *Celestinesca* 17, no. 2] (Fall 1993); and (iv) *'Mio Cid' Studies. 'Some Problems of Diplomatic' Fifty Years On*, ed. Alan Deyermond, David G. Pattison & Eric Southworth (London: Queen Mary and Westfield College, 2002).

nominated him was never entirely clear. Russell speculated, correctly as it turned out, that it had been his protégé Anthony Pagden, someone who 'seems to be listened to in unexpected places', though there was at least one other well-placed nominator. [126] 'Where do you mostly do it?' asked the Queen at Buckingham Palace. 'At Oxford, Ma'am' came the reply after a moment's hesitation. Russell's one expressed professional regret was never having been awarded an honorary doctorate from a university other than his own; his failure to be elected a corresponding member of the Real Academia Española he will have put down to collateral damage from various assertions concerning Castile and Aragon in *The English Intervention*, together with the explicit and implicit criticisms contained in his articles on the *Cantar del Cid* and *Don Quixote* of 1952 and 1969 respectively which long delayed the reception of his work in that quarter. [127]

*

This, however, does not fully encompass Russell's activities in Oxford and elsewhere. More than once he declined invitations to apply for the headship of colleges both in Oxford and Cambridge. As he noted at the time of Oliver Franks's departure from Queen's in 1948, '[b]eing Provost of an Oxford College is a much less important thing than it used to be', a conviction from which he never strayed. [128] Russell in any case had no great interest in institutions or titles, any more than his concern to promote himself extended beyond being accorded the respect he reckoned was his due; it was intellectual ascendancy he prized, not formal status or position. Elsewhere, severance from MI5 in 1946 turned out to be no more total than it had been with his father in the early '20s or with Cheltenham College a decade later. By the mid-1950s he had joined two other distinguished ex-MI5 officers as a talent spotter for the intelligence services: Sir John Masterman, Provost of Worcester, Vice-Chancellor of the University and wartime chairman of the Twenty Committee whose double-cross techniques Russell had employed with CARBUNCLE in the Far East, and Professor H. L. A. Hart of University College, the legal philosopher and colleague of Alan Turing at Bletchley Park. In this capacity he was responsible for identifying and forwarding

---

[126] PER to Alastair Saunders, Oxford, 22 Jan. 1997.
[127] *The English Intervention in Spain and Portugal in the Time of Edward III and Richard II* (Oxford: Clarendon Press, 1955); 'Some Problems of Diplomatic in the *Cantar de Mio Cid* and Their Implications', *Modern Language Review* 47 (1952), 340–9; '*Don Quixote* as a Funny Book', *Modern Language Review* 64 (1969), 312–26.
[128] Journal, 13 Jan. 1948.

the names of likely candidates to London for consideration and met periodically with senior recruitment staff. One of his earliest pre-war students at St John's was Charles Elwell who ended the war as an inmate of Colditz but entered MI5 in 1949. The following year Elwell married Ann Glass, a society beauty who had joined MI5 in 1940 and probably encountered Russell in Oxford where the Security Service had its wartime headquarters, initially in Blenheim Palace. After the defection of Guy Burgess and Donald Maclean to the Soviet Union in 1951 Ann Elwell used the resources of the MI5 Registry to collate a dossier on KGB penetration of that organisation which places her among the first of its members to identify, or misidentify, Roger Hollis as the 'Fifth Man', the beginning of a witchhunt which tore the Security Service apart. [129] In 1961 Charles Elwell was responsible for breaking the Portland Spy Ring operated by the KGB agent Konon Molody (alias Gordon Lonsdale) and the following year uncovered John Vassall, the KGB spy at the Admiralty. Ann remained part of the intelligence community until 1970 and Russell was kept abreast of Service gossip until her husband took early retirement in 1979. He also continued work as an occasional broadcaster, joining Oxford colleagues as part of a live radio hook-up with the University of Salamanca on the BBC's Spanish Service in March 1973, delivering a talk on 'Spanish Fiction from the Romance to the Novel' in March 1977 as part of a series on Spanish culture on Radio 3, and being interviewed at Belsyre Court for a Radio 4 documentary on Henry the Navigator broadcast in May 1999.

As the 1970s wore on Russell began to contemplate retirement at the statutory age limit of sixty-seven. Aside from any adjustment of his own this presented complications where the appointment of his successor was concerned of a kind he spelt out in a letter to the University Registrar:

> Arising out of my impending retirement and arrangements to replace me, it is apparent that I am likely to be faced with a problem on which I would welcome your advice. Inevitably, as a result of the long time I have been en poste here, it seems that a number of probable candidates, not only internal ones but external ones too, are likely to approach me to act as a referee for them. Two potential external candidates have in fact already done so. It had been my intention to decline to act as a referee

---

[129] Peter Wright & Paul Greengrass, *Spycatcher: The Candid Autobiography of a Senior Intelligence Officer* (New York: Viking Penguin, 1987), 188–9 & 281. Ann Glass/Elwell is erroneously referred to as 'Ann Last'. Subsequent investigation identified John Cairncross as the 'Fifth Man'.

for anyone, but it has been represented to me that this would be unfair in the case of former pupils, graduate students and colleagues past and present. The reason of course is that this would deprive them of the opportunity of securing the opinion of someone who knows them and their work better than most.

I am sure there are some established precedents about this kind of problem but it has not, as far as I can recall, arisen in the case of elections to other chairs with which I have been concerned. If it were to be thought proper for me to act as a referee this, as far as I can judge, might involve four or perhaps more candidates. I would of course write solely in respect of each individual candidate, making no attempt to place them in any kind of order against each other, but it may be that the precedents make it improper to act at all. [130]

The upshot was that he wrote references for at least four of the shortlisted candidates, and as at the Galle Face Hotel in Colombo thirty-five years earlier Russell was given a prolonged exposure to human mores as candidates pressed their claims:

> [M]y time has been fully occupied writing references for applicants for my job — a task which turned out to be, when I got down to it, vastly more time-consuming than I expected. It wasn't helped in one case [Alan Deyermond] by the inability of the candidate concerned to restrain his desire, in writing and by telephone, to offer 'suggestions' about some of the things that might be said about him. These included a list of fourteen universities (named) that, he declared, had offered him chairs that he had refused and about which he thought the electors should be told. Another candidate [R. B. Tate], alluding to an article on an early printed book I had sent him as my contribution to a book he is editing, wrote to say that I had obviously inadvertently left in numbered asterisks instead of folio numbers after some quotations and that he had replaced these by the word 'fol.' and hoped that was all right! This came while a piece about him was actually on the typewriter. I gather that the electors don't meet until 6 December so there will be a vacation, with luck, for chagrin to work itself out a bit in whatever directions it is distributed. [...] I gather from an indiscreet little bird that Alan [Deyermond]'s letter

---

[130] Oxford, 24 June 1980.

of application stresses the importance of frequent publication by the members of arts departments. Another letter of application (which I have seen in the course of duty) explains that the applicant [Robert Pring-Mill], if successful, would seek to have lecturing and teaching carried out according to the norms the applicant set out in evidence to the Franks Commission [of 1964–5]. It's odd how some ambitious people cannot resist tying a hangman's rope round their own necks. [131]

As the end of his tenure approached Russell's correspondence shows a lifting of the reserve of former years and with it a release of the devastating humour and occasional execration at others' expense he had earlier confined to his journals. An opportunity for this would come at Russell's termly meetings to review lists of prospective acquisitions with John Wainwright, librarian of the Hispanic collections at the Taylorian: 'These consultations sometimes lasted up to two hours but Peter always undertook them with great enthusiasm and spiced our meetings with fascinating and sometimes racy anecdotes about the authors we were discussing, many of whom he knew.' [132] Meanwhile, all the formalities attending his retirement from the chair had to be gone through, though they evidently gave him more pleasure than he let on:

> Edinburgh seemed to go all right — unless people are even more hypocritical than usual. The professor of history [Denys Hay] gave a dinner party for 30 people in his private house, which is something I haven't seen anywhere for a long time. As in Cambridge I found the 'requiem-type' orations rather hard to take but I suppose one has to expect that sort of thing. [133]

Never one for self-promotion but in no doubt as to his status, Russell reluctantly took steps on his retirement to secure the award of a D.Litt. by the university: 'I am involved in what I regard as the rather rash business of getting (or rather seeking) a D.Litt. here — talked into it by well-meaning historian friends. […] One has to pay heavily for one's vanity — £100 with the application for judges.' [134] It was duly granted in 1981, the year he vacated the chair after twenty-eight years.

[131] PER to Nigel Griffin, Oxford, 12 Nov. 1980.
[132] John Wainwright, email to the author, 27 Oct. 2020.
[133] PER to Nigel Griffin, Oxford, 12 Dec. 1980.
[134] PER to Nigel Griffin, Oxford, 12 Nov. 1980.

MASTER OF STUDIES (1946–1987)

Russell knighted at Buckingham Palace on 7 March 1995. 'Where do you mostly do it?' asked the Queen. He crowned the day by dining his guests at Le Gavroche on Upper Brook Street.

There followed an extraordinarily active retirement both in scholarly output and teaching, a reminder of how much Russell enjoyed travel and the revivifying company of bright young people. Already in 1980 he had accepted the first in a succession of visiting professorships at the University of Virginia, to begin in 1982:

> Did I tell you I have accepted an invitation to take myself off to the University of Virginia (Charlottesville) shortly after retirement? I preferred its 2 hours per week and $22,000 for five months to the University of Sydney's 8 for ten months for scarcely more money. [135]

Russell's time in Charlottesville was a success and he was invited to extend his five-month stay there to two years against a salary of $50,000 per annum but declined the offer. Not only was he concerned at the claims liable to be made on his earnings by both the Internal Revenue Service and the Inland Revenue but rather to his surprise found himself missing Oxford. [136] This was followed by spells at Texas (1983 & 1987), Johns Hopkins (1986 & 1998) and Vanderbilt (1987) by which the Russell style was brought to a generation of students in America. 'The undergraduates I have are nice (only one is male) but incredibly ignorant' he wrote during his second stint at Texas in 1987 (later he amended the aspersion where those at Vanderbilt were concerned); 'The graduate students, as usual in American universities, are a different story altogether.' [137] One of these was Ted Parks, subsequently of Pepperdine and Lipscomb Universities and almost certainly the only student Russell ever taught with a mastery of Greek and Hebrew:

> Having grown up in a small southern city and having attended a little-known liberal arts college in Tennessee, I entered Peter Russell's course wondering how successful I would be and what Dr. Russell would think of me. I quickly felt at home in Dr. Russell's class. He was gentle and unassuming, unquestionably learned but never putting his erudition on display or assuming a position of superiority that would threaten the dignity or discourage the potential of his students. Composed of male and female graduate students largely in their twenties and thirties from

---

[135] *Ibid.*
[136] PER to Charles Kennedy, Charlottesville, Va., 21 Feb. 1982.
[137] PER to Nigel Griffin, Austin, Tx., 18 Feb. 1987; PER to Charles Kennedy, Oxford, 18 Sept. 1987.

various places in the United States, and now taught by a respected professor in his seventies from one of the most prestigious universities in the English-speaking world, the class could have been an uncomfortable oddity at the University of Texas, an awkward attempt to bridge gaps in age, academic cultures, and expectations. It was, in fact, the opposite. I valued Dr. Russell's close reading of the text, his refusal to rush past the literary and historical context of *La Celestina* in pursuit of trendier but ultimately shallower critical approaches. Intellectually he affirmed for me the ways of reading I had practiced and longed to perfect, and, personally, he accepted me for the person I was — a graduate student just beginning to learn — and nurtured me as an academic newcomer still trying to figure out the world of scholarship and teaching. [138]

The faculty of Texas, where Alec Parker had been professor from 1970–8, he found particularly convivial, affording him the opportunity to renew his friendship with the émigré Juan López Morillas, a historian of the German philosopher Christian Friedrich Krause whose writings were so influential in nineteenth-century Spain. Another was Madeline Sutherland, then assistant professor in the Department of Spanish and Portuguese:

> When Peter was in Austin he was working on *Celestina*, finishing up his edition of Fernando de Rojas's masterpiece, which as all Hispanists know, is also one of the most-debated works in the Spanish canon. As it happened, I was working on an article on *Celestina*, an interpretation using René Girard's models of mimetic desire, violence, and sacrifice. Peter generously read what I had written and commented on it, noting that 'we part company' with regard to my conclusion, which, of course, was true as I tied Girard's ideas to what was happening in Spain at the time Rojas was writing. In fact, we talked about my article one day over lunch at a Mexican restaurant near campus and our conversation about *Celestina* ran the gamut from courtly love to finer points of Spanish grammar he had become aware of writing the footnotes to his edition. (I should add that I learned those finer points as well from our conversation.) [139]

---

[138] Ted Parks, 'Reflections on Peter Russell', 18 March 2023.
[139] Madeline Sutherland-Meier, 'Sir Peter Russell in Texas', 5 Jan. 2021.

Not the least of these experiences was the social dimension. Also on the faculty was Lee Fontanella, the historian of photography in Spain:

> Residing at less than a five-minute walk from his office — a veritable accomplishment in Austin! — he made of his stay in Austin a thorough devotion to his own research and the advancement of the graduate students in the Department, who, understandably, adored him. They thrived on being in his presence, and from what I observed the feeling was mutual. He seemed to derive much from being in their company, both for the ideas shared and just for the 'society' that the students' presence provided. [...] The first time that I joined Peter Russell and a handful of students for a casual gathering, he himself had asked me to join the group. We were to meet at a place that was not on my beaten path, yet which rang a bell with me ... an outdoor hang-out where they served snacks at picnic tables, which happened to be along the walk between his office and his residence: come to think of it, a perfectly obvious place to meet up. For certain, I was the only one at the 'table' who found it anomalous to see the graduate students chatting so off-the-cuff at a raw-wood, grease-stained picnic table, at which Peter Russell seemed to be the one who felt most at home. When the *tertulia* broke up (I don't recall the topic), he expressed to me how much he thrived on such gatherings, how habitually he participated in them, how much he took to the impromptu nature of them, how very comfortable he felt just getting to know his graduate students in this manner. Peter Russell was at home nearly everywhere, maybe because in considerable measure Everywhere had been his place for his entire life. What difference, what meaningful interruption, did gatherings at some low-down Texan joint amount to in the whole course of things? [140]

Here was a tutor-student experience in the relaxed informality of American society unlike any other in his career and a fitting capstone to it, a sense that some mantle had been lifted under semi-official auspices. There were of course other dimensions to this prolonged exposure to the United States, not least the unusual experience of being mugged and then kissed by the perpetrator in a Nashville park. Taken all round, the Indian summer of his visiting professorships was 'an

---

[140] Lee Fontanella, email to the author, 8 Jan. 2021.

activity which I enjoy since it both removes one from the limbo of retirement and also rewards one financially at the same time'. [141] A second spell at Johns Hopkins in 1998 aside, the last of these missions at Vanderbilt was brought to a premature end by illness in 1987, Russell being rushed home by Concorde to face his doctors. Though it turned out to be much longer and more fruitful than he anticipated, Peter Russell had entered the concluding phase in his life.

[141] PER to W. G. L. Randles, Oxford, 15 March 1987.

CHAPTER SIX
Iconoclast: Academic Writings (1934–2006)

Among Russell's first acts on returning to Queen's in the spring of 1946 was to recover his books, many of them showing the effects of five and a half years in the college beer cellar. This was followed by a reorganisation of his papers in the manner of his MI5 registry and a concerted book-buying campaign, 'realizing how many I should buy by rights'.[1] Thus prepared, he resumed his long-postponed historical research which properly takes this narrative back to the mid-1930s.

In 1935 Russell had begun work on the rolls and other documentary holdings of the Public Record Office in search of material on the Plantagenet diplomatic and military interventions in Spain and Portugal in the late fourteenth century. The dynastic strategy pursued through these endeavours made John of Gaunt (a younger son of Edward III) titular king of Castile (1372–88), led to the marriage of his daughter Philippa of Lancaster to John I of Portugal in 1387 and to the birth from that union of Prince Henry the Navigator (1394–1460). This swathe of history encompassing half a dozen medieval kingdoms and the Iberian seaborne expansion that accompanied it over a century and a half provided the context of much of Russell's subsequent historical output. Deprived by the outbreak of the Civil War of any opportunity to carry out prolonged research in the great archives of Spain, Russell instead concentrated on the Arquivo da Torre do Tombo in Lisbon which he visited in the summer of 1936 and 1938. Much as Russell's first impressions of the Torre do Tombo were generally favourable ('The place is apparently quite without either formality or efficient catalogues [...] but it seems a good deal better than I had been led to believe') he eventually formed a low opinion of it:

> I continue to go regularly to the Torre do Tombo, the despair of anyone unfortunate enough to have to look for historical documents lost in its ill-kept and untidy maw. I have got a little out of it but the waste of time

---

[1] Journal, 12 March & 28 Jan. 1946. The MI5 Registry system was devised by Harold Potter and consisted of files arranged to read chronologically with papers and attachments secured to the right side of a folder and the index placed on the left.

required is very distressing. Baião, the old Director, is said to keep any interesting documents he finds locked up until he can look at them himself. [2]

Nonetheless, the material gathered both there and in London allowed Russell to produce his first scholarly work in Iberian studies, an article on João Fernandes Andeiro, an emissary between the Portuguese and English courts in the 1370s. [3] This was followed by a collaboration with Professor Entwistle on the court of Philippa of Lancaster as Queen of Portugal published in connection with the centenary congress which opened in Lisbon in July 1940. [4] His early research also resulted in *As Fontes de Fernão Lopes*, a study of the fifteenth-century chronicler which appeared in Portuguese translation in 1941 and on whom Entwistle had also worked, although Russell later told how he had reacted against Entwistle's monolithically philological approach to history, one that influenced him in a negative sense. [5] Russell did not learn of its publication until a small volume on the subject caught his eye in a bookshop in wartime Lisbon — his own, as it turned out, published (albeit in Russell's name) by a former teacher to whom he had supplied a pre-war typescript: António Gonçalves Rodrigues who had in 1933 become the first instructor in Portuguese studies at Oxford, with Russell as his original student. The book was a first exercise in what came to be recognised

---

[2] Journal, 26 July & 19 Aug. 1936.
[3] 'João Fernandes Andeiro at the Court of John of Lancaster', *Revista da Universidade de Coimbra* 14 (1938), 20–30.
[4] 'A Rainha D. Felipa e Sua Côrte' in *Congresso do Mundo Português: Publicações* (Lisbon: Comissão Executiva dos Centenários, 1940), II, 319–46. A byproduct of his research in the Public Record Office was the important contribution to the naval history of medieval England he eventually published in Portuguese in 1953 and translated as 'Portuguese Galleys in the Service of Richard II, 1385–89' in *Portugal, Spain and the African Atlantic, 1343–1490* (Aldershot, Hants.: Variorum, 1995), 11 pp. The congress celebrated the 800th anniversary of the foundation of the Kingdom of Portugal and the 300th anniversary of the restoration of sovereignty from Spain.
[5] Trans. António Gonçalves Rodrigues (Coimbra: Coimbra Editora, 1941); revised with a foreword as 'On the Sources of Fernão Lopes' in *Portugal, Spain and the African Atlantic*, 30 pp. It traces its origins to a paper delivered at King's College, London on 16 Feb. 1939. Entwistle had completed an edition of the second part of Lopes' *Crónica del Rei dom Joham I da boa memoria e dos Reis de Portugal o décimo* in the early 1930s but war and political change in Portugal kept it from publication until long after his death (2 vols., Lisbon: Imprensa Nacional-Casa da Moeda, 1968–73). Russell's remarks on Entwistle from RSSR.

as the Russell style, opening as it did with a demolition of the received view of Lopes as 'the father of Portuguese historiography' before moving on to a reconstruction of his sources based on wide research and skilful deduction. During the course of this exposition he dropped the bombshell that Lopes had relied heavily (and without attribution) on the Castilian chronicler Pero López de Ayala whose hostile account of the Castilian-Portuguese War of 1381 was coloured by three years' incarceration at Leiria after he was captured at the Battle of Aljubarrota in 1385. This discovery and his demonstration that Lopes was no creative chronicler in the traditional sense but made extensive use of the original sources of which he had charge in the Torre do Tombo opened up new lines of enquiry and methodology in the field as a whole. Here was history interpreted as a multidisciplinary exercise in textual criticism, philology and the handling of data, all delivered in Russell's controlled and layered prose:

> These examples of Lopes's recourse to documents [...] only serve *à titre d'exemple* of a method of writing history which the chronicler adopts generally whenever he thought archival material would serve his declared aim to write truthful, complete and fully explicated accounts of the reigns and personalities with which he was concerned. [...] While it always needs to be kept in mind that chronicle sources, however much criticized by Lopes, provided a large part of the material that appears in the three chronicles with which I have been mainly concerned in this paper, it is no less important to remember that he took it as axiomatic that, in case of conflict, a document possessed an evidential value that overrode the assertions of his chronicler predecessors. There are indeed some signs that, in the later stages of the composition of Part Two of the *Crónica de Dom João I*, Lopes may have come to see that a different kind of history could perhaps be written relying entirely on documents. [...] Fernão Lopes's obsession with the problem of historical truth is what seems to have led him to see that, in the archives for which he was responsible, lay an important and largely untapped source of that truth. [6]

Much as Russell applauded Lopes for having recourse to documentation over anecdote or invention, he was equally ready to castigate him for his unquestioning faith in the veracity of those records, a judgment implicitly extended to many of

---

[6] 'On the Sources of Fernão Lopes', 29–30.

his teachers and colleagues and exactly the type of carefully wrapped criticism he would offer up in the ensuing decades. While acknowledging the grounding Maurice Powicke, Vivian Galbraith and others had given him in diplomatic, Russell never shared the prevailing confidence of the traditional historian in the implicit reliability of original documentation, what he later described as a tendency to rely on 'exact contemporary facts whose validity cannot be challenged', the notion that the survival of a document was in some way a guarantee of its historicity. [7] In this he showed himself an early follower of the philosopher of history R. G. Collingwood whose inaugural lecture as Waynflete Professor of Metaphysical Philosophy ('The Historical Imagination') he may well have attended in 1935. Drawing on Kant and Hegel, Collingwood made the following assertion on the historian's approach to the sources which *mutatis mutandis* could be regarded as doing service for a literary critic as well:

> The web of imaginative construction is something far more solid and powerful than we have hitherto realized. So far from relying for its validity upon the support of given facts, it actually serves as the touchstone by which we decide whether alleged facts are genuine. [...] It is thus the historian's picture of the past, the product of his own *a priori* imagination, that has to justify the sources used in its construction. These sources are sources, that is to say, credence is given to them, only because they are in this way justified. For any source may be tainted [...]. The critical historian has to discover and correct all these and many other kinds of falsification. He does it, and can only do it, by considering whether the picture of the past to which the evidence leads him is a coherent and continuous picture, one which makes sense. The *a priori* imagination which does the work of historical construction supplies the means of historical criticism as well. [8]

Russell's approach also prefigured the dismantling in E. H. Carr's famous treatise *What Is History?* (1961) of the notion that history derived from original

---

[7] 'The *Celestina* Then and Now' in *Context, Meaning and Reception of 'Celestina': A Fifth Centenary Symposium*, ed. Ian Michael & David G. Pattison [= *Bulletin of Hispanic Studies* (Glasgow) 78.1] (2001), 1–11; at 8.

[8] Collected in *The Idea of History*, ed. Jan van der Dussen (Oxford: Oxford University Press, 1993), 231–49; at 244–5. Ronald Truman, who came up to Oxford in 1954, recalls Russell citing Collingwood in his lectures; email to the author, 11 Aug. 2020.

documents was necessarily scientific. But this went beyond historical practice, and if there was one dominating theme in Russell's work as it unfolded over the next seventy years it was the debunking not only of spurious claims by contemporaneous figures and their apologists but of the efforts by subsequent scholarship and vested interests to recast history and literature in the service of a regime or ideology. In adopting this approach he joined a critical vanguard destined to reap the fullest advantage of interpreting history first and foremost through the lens of a critic and philologist, and conversely by approaching literature chiefly as an expression of its historical context and that of its commentators, annotators, editors and explicators, ever mindful of the connecting discipline between the two textual forms: rhetoric. The result was an *œuvre* which, lying at the interstices of history and literature, was always broad-ranging, often sceptical and frequently iconoclastic. In 1973 Russell wrote of Cervantes that '[t]he fact that his intellect was not disciplined according to the rigid university patterns of the day must probably be accounted an important factor that contributed to his originality as a writer and his empirical and experimental intellectual attitudes.' [9] It is a description which as he was no doubt aware could with justice be applied to himself, albeit in reduced compass, a projection onto Cervantes of his own selfhood.

Russell pressed on with what was intended to be a doctoral thesis on John of Gaunt and in due course discovered that the key to his research on the English intervention in the Peninsula in fact lay in the immensely rich and largely unexamined privy seal registers of the Archive of the Crown of Aragon in Barcelona with their transcription of both incoming and outgoing correspondence. These were beyond reach while the Civil War lasted but help was at hand in the shape of Jeanne Vieilliard, subsequently General Secretary of the Institut de Recherche et d'Histoire des Textes in Paris who furnished Russell with the extensive collection of fiches and transcriptions she had amassed during her years of research in Barcelona, a debt he never forgot. [10] In September 1938 Russell reported having completed a first draft of the Gaunt manuscript which extended to 200,000 words. [11] He continued revising it as time and teaching allowed but had to set the project aside on joining the Army in the summer of

---

[9] 'Spanish Literature (1474–1681)' in *Spain: A Companion to Spanish Studies* (London: Methuen, 1973), 305. The autodidact soldier-scholar Charles Boxer, of whom Russell had a high opinion, was another who fell into this category.

[10] *The English Intervention in Spain and Portugal in the Time of Edward III and Richard II* (Oxford: Clarendon Press, 1955), xiii.

[11] Journal, 15 Sept. 1938.

1940, the beginning of a six-year hiatus. The doctorate was never completed as such but research resumed after demobilisation in the archives of Murcia, Pamplona, Burgos, Santiago and Simancas as well as in Madrid and Barcelona itself over four successive summer vacations from 1946–9. Although he worked steadily between other commitments the extent of Russell's mental collapse in early 1948 can be gauged from the fact that in late January he declared himself to have lost interest in the project:

> Wasted morning ineffectively writing about preliminaries to [the Battle of] Nájera. I find it very difficult to write that book because I'm not really in the least interested in the subject. Footnote on whether there was a 'général parlement' in Bordeaux in August before the one in Bayonne in the same month. Deduction. But the knowledge is entirely without significance. Why do it? Setting out to photograph the past — file everything — isn't worthwhile unless the photograph is going to be worth looking at. [...] Struggled with book for few pages today but alas! I do not have a trace of interest in writing it. I have, I think, worked out most of the problems and the subject is finished for me. I have no desire to <u>communicate</u> it or them. [12]

This, however, proved transitory and in 1955 he published *The English Intervention in Spain and Portugal in the Time of Edward III and Richard II*, a finely wrought account of the political and dynastic upheavals which beset the Peninsula in the late fourteenth century. As his reviewers immediately recognised, what had previously been regarded as a byproduct of the great Anglo-French struggle known as the Hundred Years' War became in Russell's hands one of the key episodes in that long conflict. With its occasional vistas, wealth of information, searching analysis and command of the sources, seventy years on it holds the field, the definitive account of a formative passage of years in the history of the Iberian Peninsula. Writing in 2013, Luís Adão da Fonseca describes its legacy from a Portuguese standpoint:

> Peter Russell laid the foundation for a more accurate understanding of this key moment in Portuguese history, designated the Crisis of 1383–

---

[12] Journal, 24 & 25 Jan. 1948. The thesis was by now titled *The English Intervention in Spain and Portugal between 1362 and 1390* and under Entwistle's supervision.

1385: the internal consequences of that civil war were pointed out, the channels of communication and influence between Portugal, the other Iberian kingdoms, and European countries were defined; the major problems and interests involved were identified; important information was provided about the war at sea. I believe that I am not exaggerating if I say that with this book, Peter Russell placed the Portuguese crisis of the late fourteenth century at the heart of the great political, diplomatic, and military debate about Europe at that time. [13]

Detailed and magisterial though it was, *Intervention* extended beyond the confines of diplomatic history and as in his work on Fernão Lopes Russell took the opportunity to engage in a certain amount of textual revisionism. In this case his research served not to rehabilitate the notorious reputation for inaccuracy of the chronicler Jean Froissart (*c.* 1337–*c.* 1405) so much as to underline those sections and aspects of his work which could be reckoned trustworthy or instructive in themselves or were based on reliable sources. [14] In light of all this Russell must have read his former supervisor Powicke's letter of congratulation with feelings of pleasure and irony:

> I can see, from what I have already read, that it will give me pleasure and broaden my understanding during the next few weeks or probably months. It seems to me a very masterly and level-headed as well as a very learned and comprehensive piece of history — good history. [15]

For himself Russell only ever admitted when pressed that the book had been 'very carefully put together' but there was more to it than that. Aside from its factual and interpretive contribution, *Intervention* is beautifully written, a rich and measured exposition of English prose of a type now largely extinct. Asked later in life about the major influence on his style the answer was the English eighteenth-century novel to which he turned after putting aside the Romantic

---

[13] Luís Adão da Fonseca, 'A Key Book about the Portuguese Fourteenth Century: *The English Intervention in Spain and Portugal in the Time of Edward II and Richard II* by Peter E. Russell', *e-JPH* 11/1 (Summer 2013), 1–14; at 9; <www.brown.edu/Departments/Portuguese_Brazilian_Studies/ejph/html/issue21/pdf/v11n1a05.pdf>.

[14] 'The War in Spain and Portugal' in *Froissart: Historian*, ed. J. J. N. Palmer (Woodbridge, Suffolk: Boydell, 1981), 82–100.

[15] Maurice Powicke to PER, Oxford, 21 Aug. 1955.

prose and enthusiasms of his youth. On 22 January 1948, days before the mental collapse described above, he noted in his journal that '[t]his evening I wrote a few pages on Nájera. It comes quite easily.' The following excerpt describes the climactic moment of that engagement ten miles west of Logroño in northern Spain when the forces of the usurper Henry of Trastámara crumpled before those of Peter I of Castile and the Black Prince after battle was joined on the morning of 3 April 1367.

> Mounted and unmounted Castilians broke ranks under the weight of the attack and, in spite of the usurper's last efforts to rally them, joined in the flight of the rest of the army westwards on horse and on foot towards the bridge at Nájera. It was now that the prince ordered up a small force of mounted men-at-arms under Jaume III of Mallorca which had been kept back to act as a mobile reserve protecting the horses and baggage. This he instructed to pursue the exhausted and completely disordered enemy — a task which En Jaume's men performed with great ferocity and daring. It is evident from all accounts that an outstanding characteristic of this engagement was its confusion. No doubt medieval battles generally lack the parade-ground precision which the chroniclers are likely to give them, but at Nájera even the normal tactical relationship between van, wings, and main body of the Trastamaran army never became effective. In the hours which followed, Enrique paid dearly for his decision to fight with his back to the Najerilla. That river had been running high since the previous day and now its swift-flowing broad stream forced the refugees — men-at-arms and footmen — to try to make their way across the narrow bridge. Once across, they packed the few narrow streets of the town without hope of escape and were an easy mark for the Mallorcan pretender's mounted men-at-arms. Many distinguished prisoners were taken in humiliating circumstances inside Nájera. [...] By afternoon the bulk of the enemy army had been either killed or captured in the most spectacular victory of English arms for many years. [16]

Aside from revealing his unheralded facility as a military historian, this account shows how closely Russell had studied the engagement both through archival

---

[16] *The English Intervention*, 103–4.

research and topographical exploration of the terrain, which he did with his student Ted Riley in the autumn of 1947. But *Intervention* also describes a second and even more consequential battle, that of Aljubarrota seventy miles north of Lisbon on 14 August 1385. Fought between John I of Portugal and John I of Castile, the encounter not only ended in the defeat of the latter by a much smaller army but snuffed out any Castilian designs on the Portuguese throne for two hundred years. By 1958 the battlefield had become the focus of a series of archaeological digs led by a Portuguese Army officer, Lieutenant-Colonel Afonso do Paço. In April 1959 Russell was flown to Lisbon as the guest of the Portuguese government to give his expert opinion on the findings at Aljubarrota. 'World-renowned historian Prof. Peter Russel landed in Lisbon yesterday' trumpeted the *Diário da Manhã* on 3 April with the orthographic creativity to which he became accustomed in the Peninsula. The trip not only yielded a splendid series of official photos of him being received in Lisbon with every formality and then touring the battlefield but the detailed reassessment of the battle in light of the excavations Russell sent to Paço in June. [17] As the Portuguese historian João Gouveia Monteiro later put it, this document was crucial in preserving the site and turning it thanks to Paço's diggings into one of the most extensively researched medieval battlefields in Europe. [18] However, *Intervention* fell on stonier ground in Spain where no translation of the work could be published during the Franco era in view of Russell's deduction that Castile had been no more than a French military protectorate during the reign of Henry of Trastámara together with what was regarded as excessive emphasis on the Aragonese influence in the political affairs of the Peninsula, backed by ample citation in Catalan. [19] Russell later discovered that a clandestine translation had circulated among scholars but when the time came to commission his own in the late '70s he had the misfortune of selecting as translator a Barcelona historian who took payment upfront before demanding a similar amount for submission of the manuscript once it had been completed. To that Russell could only ever give one answer. A second attempt yielded a translation so bad that Russell found himself induced in the process of rewriting it to update the text in such a way as to produce what would have been a second

---

[17] Nigel Griffin Archive, Pech, Lot-et-Garonne: draft typescript letter to Lt.-Col. Afonso do Paço, c. 1959; final report dated 15 June 1959.

[18] João Gouveia Monteiro, 'Sir Peter E. Russell: The 20th Century in the Palm of His Hand', <www.brown.edu/Departments/Portuguese_Brazilian_Studies/ejph/html/issue9/html/jmonteiro_main.html>.

[19] *Ibid.* and JMA, PER to Javier Marías, Oxford, 15 May 1997.

edition.[20] For reasons unclear this endeavour proved abortive so *Intervention* has yet to be published in Spanish though a Portuguese translation appeared in 2000.[21]

Russell inspecting the archaeological excavation of the battlefield at Aljubarrota accompanied by Lt-Col Afonso do Paço, April 1959.

[20] PER to Miguel Ángel Ladero Quesada, Oxford, 16 Aug. 1979.
[21] *A Intervenção Inglesa na Península Ibérica durante a Guerra dos Cem Anos* (Lisbon: Imprensa Nacional/Casa da Moeda, 2000).

From a professional standpoint *Intervention* is the key work in Russell's *œuvre*, the one which in a single bound marked him out as a significant scholar in the history of six medieval kingdoms. It also marks the end of a particular phase in his writing, and though redolent of the scepticism that characterises much of his work Russell would never again produce narrative history in the grand manner of his Oxford mentors. There were, outwardly at least, practical as well as intellectual reasons for this. Already in February 1953, with *Intervention* before the Clarendon Press and his work essentially complete, Russell had made this statement to the electors of the King Alfonso XIII Chair as part of his application:

> I should perhaps add that it is not my intention to carry on with research on Spanish medieval history. While I do not regret having undertaken this work it has certainly not been entirely convenient to find oneself committed to researches in a field different from that in which one's teaching and lecturing lies; reading and research for lectures have had to be conducted independently, though it is also true that my historical work has thrown up some results which aid the interpretation of Spanish and Portuguese literary texts. [22]

What followed from his hand in that discipline would instead be crafted in the interlaced, multifaceted style he made his own over the ensuing decades and upon which much of his reputation as a scholar stands. That road took him through the great literary texts of medieval, Renaissance and Golden Age Spain as it did the torments of his inner life.

*

As discussed in a previous chapter, Russell had in 1952 published the first of his groundbreaking articles in Spanish literature, 'Some Problems of Diplomatic in the *Cantar de Mio Cid* and Their Implications' concerning one of the great epic poems of medieval Europe. [23] Russell was a scholar who always went back to first principles in analysing a text or source material and in doing so drew on the uncommon range and depth of his learning in other realms. In this case his long formation in diplomatic under Powicke and Galbraith was never put to better

---

[22] OUA/UR 6/SPC/1B, file 2, PER to Maurice Bowra, Oxford, 8 Feb. 1953.
[23] *Modern Language Review* 47 (1952), 340–9. Russell had shown an early draft to George Kolkhorst; Kolkhorst to PER, Yarnton, 25 Oct. 1950. It was delivered as a lecture in the autumn of 1951.

advantage than in his analysis of the dating of this work which also offered fresh insights on the authorship of the poem. As his former student Alan Deyermond wrote decades later,

> The reasoning behind this was cogent, the evidence massive. How could anyone have missed the point? [...] That article was a turning-point in epic studies, and although details have been modified the main structure stands, towering over the academic landscape. [24]

The article immediately recalls the detached formalist analysis Russell had first exhibited in his earliest known academic contribution, a short piece on Pirandello published at the age of twenty in 1934 but which he scarcely ever mentioned again:

> For all its violence and stridency and noise his work is austerely intellectual. He seeks to show emotions rather than to arouse them and these emotions belong to the mind and not to the senses. Nor in this rather depressing metaphysical void, is there any place for sentimentalism. The old drama with its interminable triangles and its constant subjection of character to plot is one where, according to Pirandello's conception of the drama, fiction and sentiment are constantly overcoming reality. As far as the nineteenth century bourgeois comedies are concerned this is obviously true. In the new drama reality is to overcome the fiction of the plot and reality knows no such thing as sentiment. [25]

'Some Problems of Diplomatic' was followed by a series of articles on the *Cantar* which, without entering into literary criticism *per se*, focused on challenging the rigid categorisations of geography, historicity, audience and authorship in which the work had previously been interpreted. Where was Alcocer, a fortified place mentioned frequently in the poem but which somehow resisted identification? Russell had himself sought it in vain in the 1950s. The answer on reflection was patently obvious: 'Given all the indications that the Alcocer episode as described in the *Cantar de Mio Cid* is fictitious, it seems certain that one cannot have

---

[24] *The Independent,* 5 July 2006.
[25] 'Pirandello' in *Miscellany* (Oxford: The Queen's College, 1934), 10–14; at 13.

recourse to geography to assert the contrary.' [26] There was as Gertrude Stein put it in another context 'no there there'. Similarly, in view of the obvious and documented connections of the Cid with the Benedictine monastery of San Pedro de Cardeña, how plausible was it to construe the *Cantar* as purely lay in inspiration when there was constant interchange between both cultures? [27] And where the lengthy prayer uttered by his wife Doña Jimena before her husband's exile is concerned, why should it not be an invented form governed by artistic necessity rather than the recitation of some lost liturgy no amount of searching could uncover? [28] And so on. Here was a velvet-clad wrecking ball demolishing many of the received views on the *Cantar* and implicitly some of the mental strictures in which they had been formulated and fostered with official and quasi-official sanction. At the centre of this cultural orthodoxy stood the person of Ramón Menéndez Pidal himself in respect of whom Russell had conceived a private obsession and whose continued influence delayed the reception of his insights for decades.

In the early 1950s Russell turned to the *Comedia de Calisto y Melibea*, the prose dialogue work by Fernando de Rojas usually known as *Celestina* and sometimes reckoned (though not by Russell) the earliest novel in European literature. Apparently printed in Burgos in *c.* 1499 and then in an expanded edition a few years later, *Celestina* was a curious hybrid whose ambiguity lent itself in Rojas' hands to an exploration of human psychology which broke new ground in Western literature. Russell had first come to it as an undergraduate, of which records survive not only in his wistful memoir on the subject published in 2001 but in diary entries for 24 March 1933 and particularly 22 September 1934: '3 a.m. Have been working late doing Celestina which is a great piece of early Renaissance narrative-drama or rather dramatic novel.' [29] This work, which Russell later identified as a play in the Terentian style intended for recitation in a university setting, may have formed part of his pre-war teaching syllabus but by 1948 had become the focus of independent research: 'Spent some time later proving Celestina to be a local university legend at Salamanca' reads a journal entry for 17 January. It was a text he would return to time and again in his

---

[26] 'Nuevas reflexiones sobre el Alcocer del "Poema de Mio Cid"' in his *Temas de* La Celestina *y otros estudios del* Cid *al* Quijote (Barcelona: Ariel, 1978), 45–69; at 66. My translation.

[27] 'San Pedro de Cardeña y la historia heroica del Cid' in *Temas de* La Celestina, 73–112.

[28] 'La Oración de Doña Jimena ("Poema de Mio Cid", vv. 325–367)' in *Temas de* La Celestina, 115–58; at 153.

[29] 'The *Celestina* Then and Now', 1–11.

academic writings, a source not only of intellectual fascination but of emotional consolation in the trials that beset him, a reservoir from which he could draw as he strove to reconcile the image of himself he gave to the world with the inner life that shaped it, the ambiguity and duality he identified at the heart of his personality first given aesthetic endorsement through his undergraduate readings of Proust. Aside from the wealth of information fashioned into the essays and ultimately the critical edition he devoted to it, Russell's output on *Celestina* stands as the main vehicle by which he set himself to challenge the efforts of past and above all contemporary scholarship before presenting his own interpretive vision of the work and its context. [30] The impact of this criticism on his audience was enhanced by his preference for the life of a solitary scholar whose usual practice it was to work quietly and send his manuscripts to press with little or no input from his colleagues before settling back to enjoy the fluttering in the dovecots generated by his findings. [31] Occasionally his work suffered from his reluctance to place it before a second pair of eyes but few critics were spared in the intervening period. [32]

The first sally came in 1957 in a review article prompted by the publication of *The Art of 'La Celestina'* by the American scholar Stephen Gilman, a student and follower of Américo Castro whom Russell had first encountered in 1933 and whose highly influential theories on Spanish race, religion and national identity he came to regard as untenable. [33] In his review Russell castigated Gilman among many other things for his recourse to a 'private language' for which no key was supplied and for his habit of inserting himself too readily between the author and

---

[30] For a summary of the early criticism of *Celestina*, and of Russell's criticism of the critics, see 'The *Celestina* Then and Now', 4–11.

[31] His former teacher and ultimately colleague George Kolkhorst seems to have been the first and the last scholar to whom he showed first drafts of his work, though in the latter case not after 1952. Another scholar with whom he shared his work in the infancy of word processing and for his formation in the Classics was his graduate student Jeremy Lawrance.

[32] For examples of these errors see Ian Michael, 'Sir Peter Russell (1913–2006)', *Bulletin of Spanish Studies* 83 (2006), 1133–44; at 1141.

[33] Stephen Gilman, *The Art of 'La Celestina'* (Madison, Wis.: University of Wisconsin Press, 1957). Castro's major work in this field was *España en su historia* (Madrid: Losada, 1948; subsequently revised); it was later challenged by Claudio Sánchez-Albornoz whose *España: un enigma histórico*, 2 vols. (Buenos Aires: Editorial Sudamericana, 1956) Russell flattened in a review article three years later: 'The Nessus-Shirt of Spanish History', *Bulletin of Hispanic Studies* 36 (1959), 219–25.

his immediate audience, a theme underlying all Russell's critical writings. [34] This was followed in 1961 by an influential piece on magic in *Celestina*, a dimension Russell found to have been overlooked by all the leading critics of that work, including the pioneering figure of Marcelino Menéndez y Pelayo, Russell's friend Marcel Bataillon, the Argentine scholar María Rosa Lida de Malkiel (also a student of Castro's) and inevitably Gilman. [35] Another review article of what Russell regarded as Bataillon's idiosyncratic interpretation in *La Célestine selon Fernando de Rojas* allowed him to develop his sense of the ambiguity with which moral themes were handled in the work. [36] Before long the publication of Lida de Malkiel's weighty volume on *La originalidad artística de 'La Celestina'* generated a further review article in which Russell pointed out deficiencies in interpretation together with a failure to grasp the wider social and literary context of the time. [37] When Russell concluded by noting that the recently deceased 'Mrs Malkiel's *magnum opus* shows that even the most devoted admirers of *Celestina* have failed, in the past, to grasp the full scope of its originality' the ungenerous implication is that she was included in that judgement, a view not supported by subsequent scholarship, including his own. [38] Probably his feathers had been ruffled by the footnote in that work, signposted by an index entry, in which she dismissed a point he had made in his review of Gilman's 1957 volume, nor did their meeting in Oxford in November 1959 form the basis of any discernible friendship. [39] Russell did not come back to *Celestina* until 1971 when he published a paper on Fernando de Rojas' legal training which recalls an approach used by him in his assault on Ménendez Pidal's dating of the *Cantar de Mio Cid*

---

[34] 'The Art of Fernando de Rojas', *Bulletin of Hispanic Studies* 34 (1957), 160–7; at 161.
[35] 'La magia como tema integral en la *Tragicomedia de Calisto y Melibea*' in *Studia philologica: Homenaje a Dámaso Alonso por sus amigos y discípulos con ocasión de su 60 aniversario*, ed. Alonso Zamora Vicente, 3 vols (Madrid: Editorial Gredos, 1963); III, 337–54. Revised and amplified c. 1965 and retitled 'La magia, tema integral de *La Celestina*' in *Temas de* La Celestina, 243–76.
[36] Marcel Bataillon, *La Célestine selon Fernando de Rojas* (Paris: Librairie de Marcel Didier, 1963); 'Ambiguity in *La Celestina*', *Bulletin of Hispanic Studies* 40 (1963), 35–40.
[37] María Rosa Lida de Malkiel, *La Originalidad artística de 'La Celestina'* (Buenos Aires: Editorial Universidad de Buenos Aires, 1962).
[38] 'Literary Tradition and Social Reality in *La Celestina*', *Bulletin of Hispanic Studies* 41 (1964), 230–7; at 237.
[39] Malkiel, *La Originalidad artística de 'La Celestina'*, 340. In 2001 Russell was still highlighting the shortcomings of Malkiel's and Bataillon's approach; see 'The *Celestina* Then and Now', 6.

twenty years earlier, the argument in this instance being supported by evidence contained in a largely ignored sixteenth-century manuscript commentary of *Celestina*. [40]

However, Russell reserved his most trenchant statement in the field of *Celestina* for Gilman whose second volume on the subject, *The Spain of Fernando de Rojas*, appeared in 1972. [41] This took the form of a lengthy review article published in *Comparative Literature* in 1975 in which Russell for the first time set forth the full breadth of his erudition on the subject. In it he argued that Gilman had overreached himself technically and methodologically by writing what was effectively a biography of Fernando de Rojas in which intuition too often served as the inadequate replacement for hard fact: 'In the end what we are asked to accept are the author's intuitions — as he freely admits. There is no arguing with a man's intuitions and I wonder if Professor Gilman himself has fully realized the authoritarian posture that his approach involves.' [42] Not only that but the text was as Rojas had admitted from the outset the work of two authors, not one, 'a point that much modern criticism, anxious to avoid having to maintain a tiresome distinction that makes critical generalization difficult, is perhaps still [...] all too prone to gloss over'. [43] Russell particularly takes Gilman to task for the way in which he enlists his sources to further his Princeton mentor Américo Castro's overarching thesis on the racial overtones collectively shared in Spanish culture, Rojas having been born into a family of converted Jews. It was representative of what he elsewhere described as a fashionable but facile tendency to treat literature as a sociological document. [44] The result, he said, too often bordered on historical fiction. Observing the courtesies of those days, Gilman sent Russell a pre-publication reply to these criticisms which served only to accentuate their divergence of approach, but this was not the extent of the matter.

---

[40] '*La Celestina* y los estudios jurídicos de Fernando de Rojas' in *Temas de* La Celestina, 325–40, and 'The *Celestina comentada*' in *Medieval Hispanic Studies Presented to Rita Hamilton*, ed. A. D. Deyermond (London: Tamesis, 1976), 175–93.

[41] Stephen Gilman, *The Spain of Fernando de Rojas: The Intellectual and Social Landscape of* La Celestina (Princeton, N.J.: Princeton University Press, 1972).

[42] Review of Stephen Gilman, *The Spain of Fernando de Rojas: The Intellectual and Social Landscape of 'La Celestina'* (Princeton, N.J.: Princeton University Press, 1972) in *Comparative Literature* 27 (1975), 59–74; at 72.

[43] *Ibid.*, 64.

[44] PER to Registrary, University of Cambridge, Oxford, 25 April 1972. This statement was made in connection with a request from the university for an opinion in connection with Prof. R. O. Jones' application for the recently vacated chair in Spanish.

As Gilman made clear in his covering letter, his displeasure was heightened by a belief that Russell was behind a move to prevent him using the trove of documents concerning Rojas in the care of his descendant Fernando del Valle Lersundi, after they were offered for sale at Rosenthal's Antiquarian Books on Broad Street in Oxford in 1962. [45] In this, however, Gilman exhibits the same tendency to creative deduction as that pointed out by Russell in his review and by other commentators on his work including Bataillon and the Venezuelan scholar Miguel Marciales. [46] To these allegations Russell sent a detailed response in September 1975 which presumably disabused Gilman of his suspicions if not his conviction that Russell had a personal animus against him; the documents had in any case been returned to Lersundi, no buyer having been found (their correspondence on the subject is reproduced with commentary in Appendix I). Unable to publish his reply in the same journal, Gilman was left to do so elsewhere in what is an expanded version of the typescript he had sent to Oxford in August 1975. [47] In it he again acknowledged Russell's criticism of him as untrained in the practice of history but countered by describing him as 'a historian with little skill in the area of literary comprehension'. [48] Be all that as it may, Russell's devastating review of *The Spain of Fernando de Rojas* remains a major contribution in its own right, the work in which he planted his standard in the field, not only in *Celestina* studies but where his own approach as literary critic was concerned:

> A prime business of the [...] critic is, obviously, to try [...] to show genius at work — why and how genius rather than mere superior talent is involved. If, however, the critic is tempted to go further than this and to inquire exactly what it was that triggered the operations of genius or,

---

[45] 'The *Celestina* Then and Now', 2–4. See also Appendix I.

[46] See in particular Keith Whinnom's review in *Bulletin of Hispanic Studies* 52 (1975), 158–61.

[47] 'Sobre la identidad histórica de Fernando de Rojas: (Contestación al Profesor Peter Russell)', *Nueva Revista de Filología Hispánica* 26 (1977), no. 1, 154–8.

[48] *Ibid.*, 158. My translation. The expanded version of his review article he published in 1978 aside, Russell's only known response comes in a letter to Miguel Marciales, Oxford, 9 March 1978: 'I am sorry to say that instead of taking up the many individual points of criticism I try to make in this review article, Gilman has chosen to attribute my criticisms to personal animosity, though I have no grounds for feeling any animosity towards him as a person since I have never met him.' For the expanded review, see 'Un crítico en busca de un autor: reflexiones en torno a un reciente libro sobre Fernando de Rojas', *Temas de* La Celestina *y otros estudios del* Cid *al* Quijote (Barcelona: Ariel, 1978), 343–75.

more ambitiously still, how genius itself came to be, he is venturing into deeper waters. In the switch that is then necessarily involved from work to author, from literature to biography, the literary critic has, perforce, to set himself up as historian and that switch is a good deal less easy to make than professional critics of literature often suppose — partly because of the different kinds of evidence literary critics and historians respectively are accustomed to handling and partly because of fundamental differences in the appropriate methods of appraising it. [49]

Nonetheless, for all the innovative approaches he was destined to bring to his work Russell by no means emerged fully formed as a literary critic. His review of Gilman's *The Art of 'La Celestina'* of 1957 begins with a number of no doubt much-regretted solecisms of which Gilman was all too ready to remind him in their correspondence in 1975:

> There are a good many signs nowadays that readers of Spanish literature — at any rate outside Spain — are beginning to feel that, among Spanish prose classics, *La Celestina* may have a more pointed communication to make to our contemporary world than has *Don Quijote*. Certainly, on its most obvious level, the lesson which Cervantes seems to want to teach seems rather bathetic to the modern reader. We scarcely need, these days, to be warned against Quixotism. At the same time we have become more aware of the serious defects which exist in *Don Quijote* as a work of art — defects which seem, in the main, due to its author's uncertainty as to what he was about, and to his hypersensitivity to the possibility of adverse criticism. [50]

That Russell took the cultured order he saw in *Celestina* against the apparent chaos of *Don Quixote* as a measure of the worth of the two works no doubt in part reflects his own state of mind at the time. In any case, the distance he travelled on the subject of *Celestina* and indeed as a critic can be measured in his 1957 and 1975 reviews of Gilman's studies.

The culmination of his long meditation on *Celestina* came in the edition of that work he published in 1991, mindful always of the 'textual problems this

---

[49] Review of Gilman, *The Spain of Fernando de Rojas*, 59.
[50] 'The Art of Fernando de Rojas', 160.

famous work may present young readers today, and perhaps sometimes even their elders'. [51] Here are the closing lines of his introduction:

> It may be concluded that *Celestina* critics must resign themselves to the fact that, from an ideological standpoint, there can be no definitive solutions, only possibilities. Is it possible that the great discovery of the authors of *La Celestina*, heirs to a dogmatic culture, was that scepticism was not only a feasible intellectual posture but also capable of revealing new and fruitful literary forms and perspectives? In an age when it can be asserted, with Roland Barthes, that literature is, by definition, ambiguous, one will of course find in the complex ambiguity of *La Celestina* at least a partial explanation of the genius of the text, and not a sign of artistic failure or a series of puzzles it is the duty of critics to resolve definitively. [52]

The farthest expression of this scepticism in Spanish letters was that of the Jesuit *conceptista* Baltasar Gracián, on whom Russell published little but much admired for a prose style which always succeeded in expressing more than was at first suggested. Needless to say, what Julian Weiss refers to as Russell's 'sceptical empiricism' and his 'creative power of doubt' as part of what was always an outsider's approach have not enjoyed universal acceptance. [53] As Enrique Baltanás noted, 'My view is that Russell confuses ambiguity with depth. As far as I am concerned, *La Celestina*, like any other masterpiece is inexhaustible due to its depth, not its ambiguity.' [54] The distinction may in fact be a very fine one, but there was one work in respect of which Russell drew the clearest possible line between critical interpretations and that was *Don Quixote*, on which he wrote the most influential article of his career.

---

[51] *Comedia o Tragicomedia de Calisto y Melibea* (Madrid: Castalia, 1991), revised as *La Celestina: Comedia o Tragicomedia de Calisto y Melibea* (Madrid: Castalia, 1992); 1st ed., 178. My translation.
[52] *Ibid.*, 158.
[53] 'Presentation' in *Studies in Honour of Peter E. Russell on His 80th Birthday*, ed. Julian Weiss [= *Celestinesca* 17.2] (Fall 1993), 1–8; at 2 & 3.
[54] Enrique Jesús Rodríguez Baltanás, 'El matrimonio imposible de Calisto y Melibea: notas a un enigma' in *Dejar hablar a los textos: Homenaje a Francisco Márquez Villanueva*, ed. Pedro M. Piñero Ramírez (Seville: Universidad de Sevilla, 2005), 281–308; at 282. My translation.

*

Delivered as a paper in Liverpool in April 1968 and published in 1969, '*Don Quixote* as a Funny Book' is a landmark in the field of Spanish literary criticism. [55] In it Russell took on practically the entire received corpus of Cervantine scholarship both in substance and in critical approach in a brilliant and incisive piece of erudition which left the subject transformed. The article consisted in a demolition of the Romantic view of Don Quixote as a tragic figure which had come to dominate the interpretation of that work, what late in life he described as 'rescuing *Don Quixote* from the predicament in which nineteenth-century Romanticism's dedication to myth, symbols and high seriousness had left it.' [56] More even than with *Celestina* no one escaped censure:

> I suppose one ought not to be too surprised that Spanish critics almost invariably follow this line; they have allowed themselves to be persuaded that the book somehow synthesises important aspects of the national character and that, of course, makes it rather difficult to entertain the possibility that Cervantes simply wanted to give his readers something to laugh at. However, the same view is generally taken by non-Spanish critics too. [57]

Starting with a rebuttal of the view that 'it is not adult to laugh at Don Quixote', Russell asserts that 'in electing to consider *Don Quixote* as a funny book, I do not

---

[55] *Modern Language Review* 64 (1969), 312–26; revised as '*Don Quijote* y la risa a carcajadas' in *Temas de* La Celestina, 409–40. Russell had in fact held this interpretation of the work since at least 1951: 'Russell will tell you that, in spite of Dr. [A. A.] Parker, Don Quixote was laughed at; & that a world is a healthy world that can laugh at Don Quixote'; G. A. Kolkhorst to Charles Kennedy, Yarnton, 27 March 1951, at the Taylor Institution Library, Oxford, MS.Fol.E.20, in I. D. L. Michael's unpublished edition of that correspondence [GKCK], 73. However, the writing of this article was also prefigured in the closing lines of Russell's review of Anthony N. Zahareas, *The Art of Juan Ruiz, Archpriest of Hita* (Madrid: Estudios de Literatura Española, 1965) in *Times Literary Supplement*, 13 Oct. 1966, 941: 'Perhaps, some day, a critic will remember, with similar profitable consequences, that Cervantes repeatedly tells us that he intended *Don Quixote* to provoke the laughter of his readers.' I owe this reference to Nigel Griffin. Russell met Zahareas in Oxford in March 1968, a month before he delivered the paper upon which '*Don Quixote* as a Funny Book' was based.
[56] 'Edward Calverley Riley', *The Queen's College Record* 7 (2001), 93–5; at 94.
[57] '*Don Quixote* as a Funny Book', 312–3.

think that I am denying it either profundity as a work of art, or its own kind of seriousness'. [58] He goes on to discuss the literary notions of comedy and of madness on which Cervantes drew and the reception of his multifarious creation until changing views on insanity from the late eighteenth century brought on the critical interpretation based on sympathy to which scholarship had fallen heir. [59] Although the effect had become generalised, this recasting had been perpetuated for an English readership by successive translations, not least those produced by J. M. Cohen (1950) and Walter Starkie (1954). [60] Russell also took aim at the state of criticism where comic literature was concerned, noting the traditional complication that it was hard to write seriously about comic material. He therefore issued the chastening view that '[m]odern criticism may well, by its over-literal understanding of allusions to the knight's lucid intervals, miss a disturbing seam of ambivalence which Cervantes exploited comically: that madness speaks at times with a voice which is indistinguishable from the voice of sanity', an author who 'also knows, and exploits in artistic terms, the principle that the mentality of the psychotic includes the essential qualities of normal thinking'. [61] As he concluded later, 'Cervantes demonstrated in his most famous book how ambiguity and uncertainty could lie at the centre of great art. He was only able to do so by showing that great art could be comic art.' [62]

That Russell should treat the psychology of mental illness in the course of exploring the madness of Don Quixote comes as no surprise in such a deeply researched and considered article, but the twenty years of psychoanalysis of which he had been in receipt by the late 1960s suggests that his remarks in this vein are no mere byproduct of that research. Indeed, no one familiar with Russell's most intimate writings could read some of his comments on the knight's mental state without a degree of recognition. Psychiatry, he explains, interprets Don

---

[58] *Ibid.*, 313.

[59] In revising the article for translation Russell pointed out that the first critical edition of *Don Quixote* had in fact been published not in Spain but in England: that of the Rev. John Bowle of 1781; '*Don Quijote* y la risa a carcajadas', 410. This labour of love, printed in six volumes and extending to 300 pages of apparatus in Spanish, is accepted as a starting point for all subsequent editions; see R. W. Truman, 'The Revd John Bowle's Quixotic Woes Further Explored', *Cervantes. Bulletin of the Cervantes Society of America* 23.2 (2003), 9–43; at 9.

[60] '*Don Quixote* as a Funny Book', 313. Russell met Cohen in Oxford in October 1957 and February 1958; he first met Starkie in 1940 and flattened his translation of *Don Quixote* in a review in *Bulletin of Hispanic Studies* 32 (1955), 53–4.

[61] '*Don Quixote* as a Funny Book', 316 & 313.

[62] *Cervantes* (Oxford: Oxford University Press, 1985), 109.

Quixote's fantasies as 'regressive in character and regression is a main characteristic of psychosis'. [63] When discussing the 'topsy-turvy logic with which [Don Quixote] can always defend his hallucinatory world against the challenge of reality' Russell describes it (in a neat reversal of the patient–analyst role) as 'the kind of defence familiar to those who try to treat cases of hallucination'. [64] Later he points out Cervantes' 'compulsion to remind his readers how quite opposing qualities often coexist in the same person or situation'. [65] Similarly, in recounting Samuel Johnson's analysis of *Don Quixote* in 1750 Russell explains how

> [i]t was Johnson, too, who declared that, when Cervantes described the fantasies of his hero, he was admitting to literature the species of imaginings (though usually of a different sort) which most readers, if they were honest, would admit privately to having. The inner imagination thus enters the world of realistic prose fiction described as madness. Johnson here gets near to inviting readers of *Don Quixote* to identify themselves with the mad knight on the grounds that this madness was no more than the workings of ordinary human imagination writ large. This represented a radical change in traditional attitudes to the book. It heralded the coming of the root-and-branch reappraisal by Romanticism. [66]

That of course was the same Romanticism to which Russell had cleaved in his own writings and convictions in his younger days, and one may speculate how much consolation Russell *qua* reader *qua* critic *qua* patient found in formulating his evolved interpretation of the universality and timeless quality of Cervantes' creation. The origin of this formulation can be traced to his reading of Jung's *Psychology of the Unconscious* (1912) which he absorbed 'over breakfast' one day in 1948:

> Notion that subconscious images and dreams represent thinking in a medium easier and more malleable than language is interesting; the application of this to literature is worth thinking about. I begin to suspect one wastes much time looking for aesthetic and intellectual reasons to

---

[63] '*Don Quixote* as a Funny Book', 313.
[64] *Cervantes*, 76.
[65] *Ibid.*, 91.
[66] *Ibid.*, 93.

explain the interest of many works and it would be more appropriate to look at their appeal to the subconscious mind directly — I imagine 'the great classics' may be so because they are all capable of understanding <u>this</u> way. [67]

Russell also took the opportunity presented by this article to commit the ultimate and, for him, overdue act of scholarly patricide by citing his former teacher W. J. Entwistle as an exemplar of the critical tradition here exploded. [68] In a later exposition of his thesis he singled out the eminent figures of Unamuno and Ortega y Gasset for the same reason. [69] There was no room for tin gods in Russell's critical approach. Out of the wreckage grew a new stream of Cervantine criticism which, fifty years on, is still with us, *mutatis mutandis*. For Russell, meanwhile, one cannot avoid the impression that something had been settled, even expiated deep in the heart of him.

How, then, might Russell's approach as a literary critic be summarised as it unfolded over more than half a century? An early adherent of the New Criticism with its stress on a formalist instead of a purely philological approach to literature that took shape in the work of I. A. Richards, C. K. Ogden and F. R. Leavis at Cambridge from the 1920s and an undergraduate pupil of the leading Spanish critic Dámaso Alonso with his concern (via Menéndez Pidal) for historical grounding, Russell's first recorded statement on the discipline is contained in the fragment of a commonplace book he kept in the early 1940s, and from it he never deviated:

> In literary criticism there can be no question of finite truth. Criticism depends on taste, taste is always changing, so in a way the work too is always changing to succeeding generations and succeeding readers. Questions of fact when discovered remain static but the work itself never can. (Same is true for interpretation of history.)

If Russell had abandoned the Modern Languages School for history in 1935 over its addiction to philology and impermeability to the New Criticism, he was quite

---

[67] Journal, 14 Feb. 1948.
[68] W. J. Entwistle, *Cervantes* (Oxford: Clarendon Press, 1940).
[69] Russell, *Cervantes*, 100–1. The works alluded to were Miguel de Unamuno's *Vida de don Quijote y Sancho* (Madrid: Librería de Fernando Fé, 1905) and José Ortega y Gasset's *Meditaciones del Quijote* (Madrid: Publicaciones de la Residencia de Estudiantes, 1914).

ready to pick up the reins after the war and apply the discipline to the Spanish literary canon via his historicist approach, part of the articulated duality of method that became his hallmark. As Russell was citing the philosopher Collingwood in his lectures in the 1950s, so also was he offering up the name of another leading Cambridge critic in the context of the poet Luis de Góngora, that of William Empson, whose *Seven Types of Ambiguity* (1930) gave schematic endorsement to his critical style. [70] Interestingly enough, the first formulation of this critical approach comes in 1937 in the context not of his writing but of his teaching, a reminder of the interconnectedness of Russell's scholarly outlook:

> In the intervals of hard reading for the essays on the Spanish theatre I shall have to listen to next term I have been thinking of the necessary basis for academic teaching. In a foreign literature I am convinced it is essential to make the pupil keep an eye on English literature, make him consider aesthetic, psychological and historical aspects, interest him in these and show him how to find them. Otherwise his critical sense and cultural knowledge will remain undeveloped and he will be wallowing bestially in a morass of half-understood second-hand thoughts. At same time close-thinking and sound basis for broader conclusions must be emphasised too. For [the] tutor the essential would seem to be always to have a few suggestive remarks to make. [71]

In 1977 Russell set down in the foreword to a collection of his most important articles what may be taken as his testament as a literary critic:

> In not a few of these [articles on the *Cantar de Mio Cid* and the *Celestina*], as well as in those that treat other literary topics [including *Don Quixote*], the reader will notice a generalised concern: that of establishing what happens when we look to history in search of clarification of a literary text. Sometimes, as occurs in some of the studies on the Cid, this simply concerns adducing historical data to explain textual problems or to question the validity of traditional theories. More frequently, however, it is a question of having recourse to the information provided us by history to establish how a literary work was

---

[70] London: Chatto and Windus, 1930. As with Collingwood, I owe this memory to Ronald Truman who attended Russell's lectures on Góngora in 1956.
[71] Journal, 25 Sept. 1937.

conceived by its author or understood by its readers, bearing in mind both its historico-social and ideological context and the literary traditions of the age in which it was written. However, it should not be understood that in frequently opting here for an 'historicist' critique I disregard the vital contributions that can be made by formalist criticism whose methodology, theoretically at least, rejects any use of material extrinsic to the text itself. This is because we are often dealing here with themes and problems that, in my judgment, require recourse to extratextual data to make an effective clarification.

Nonetheless, I am acutely aware that establishing appropriate relations between literature and history is an extremely delicate task and one full of pitfalls. In the study on the *poesía negra* ['black poetry'] of Rodrigo de Reinosa, as well as in all of the studies on the *Celestina*, I attempt to point out some of the errors that can occur when the historian, forgetting all the ahistorical pressures that are brought to bear on the formation of any literary work to modify or distort the representation of daily realities, approaches the latter as if it were a historical document like any other. No less dangerous is the situation of the literary critic in attempting to make use of history if he or she fails to bear in mind that interpretive literary criticism is based on intuitions of a type the historian could never allow. In the present volume I draw attention to the confusions that can result from a failure to appreciate this methodological difference between both disciplines as well as those that can arise from 'intuitional' history and any other attempt to force history to yield results that it is, by its nature, incapable of providing. [72]

In this Russell reveals himself to be an early exponent of what was later formalised as *Rezeptionsästhetik* (reception theory) by the Constance school of Hans Robert Jauss though he would no doubt have shied away from the association or anything else that could be interpreted as an overarching scheme. [73] He therefore refrained from direct engagement in print with the new and highly influential currents of literary criticism and theory that began emerging from Paris in the 1960s and were represented in Oxford in subsequent decades by Terry Eagleton and, latterly, Toril Moi, preferring to confine himself to the occasional reminder,

---

[72] Introduction to *Temas de* La Celestina, 9–10. My translation.
[73] I am grateful to Jeremy Lawrance and Julian Weiss for their assistance with these paragraphs.

historicising in itself, that the conviction with which a particular school pursues its interpretations is no guarantee of their survival. One such occasion was the symposium held to celebrate the fiftieth anniversary of his own seminal article on the *Cantar de Mio Cid*:

> I have to admit, though, that the link that has been made between the 1952 article and Cidian scholarship today is for me not without its ironical side since I have always taken what some have thought the unnecessarily pessimistic view that most literary criticism of whatever kind is by its nature a fruit destined to fall ripe from the bough. Or, to recall a Persian proverb of which Paco Rico recently reminded me, the caravan always moves on leaving behind it dogs that go on barking at the site where it previously stood because change has passed them by. [74]

Discussing *neotradicionalismo* and *individualismo*, the two opposing strands of literary criticism officially identified by Spanish scholarship under Franco with Menéndez Pidal at the head of the former, Russell went on to issue these comments which as far as he was concerned did service for the gamut of postmodernist theory as it unfolded from the 1960s:

> My objection to them is that they both suggest subservience to an ideological stance that lays out in advance the general lines the users' critical conclusions need to take. They are therefore anti-pragmatic in theory even if not always in practice. [75]

As he added, '[t]he caravan may have moved on but no one yet knows definitely where it is going.' That said, Russell in no wise took the approach common in British academia of rejecting structuralism and its various applications to critical theory out of hand and unread, and it is a measure of his strength as a scholar that he continued to develop his interpretive spectrum even if he resisted any in-depth conceptualisation. He was an early if unpersuaded reader of Foucault and the reference to Barthes cited above indicates that he had familiarised himself with

---

[74] 'Reinventing an Epic Poet: 1952 in Context' in *'Mio Cid' Studies. 'Some Problems of Diplomatic' Fifty Years On*, ed. Alan Deyermond, David G. Pattison & Eric Southworth (London: University of London, 2002), 63. Francisco Rico, then Professor of Medieval Literature at the Universitat Autònoma de Barcelona.
[75] *Ibid.*, 70.

these theoretical approaches, no doubt in part because his sojourns as a visiting professor in the United States in the 1980s required him to be on his mettle with schools of thought that found a much readier audience in that country than his own.[76] This is not to say that some of what he took to be the more arcane expressions were not regarded with distaste, particularly when they were interpreted as tendentious, untethered from historical reality or as lending themselves to the sort of critical abdication or uneuphonious dogmatism that was anathema to him. Among the earliest applications of contemporary critical theory to Hispanic literature in Britain came in the work of Paul Julian Smith and Malcolm K. Read, the former in the guise of gender studies and the latter via a Marxist reading, both often couched in terms highly critical of the manner in which domestic scholarship had shaped and interpreted the canon since the Great War.[77] These works, none of which referenced Russell, left him unmoved in print, and it was for others to issue public response, including his former student Nicholas Round and as here in Colin Thompson's homily at his memorial service in October 2006:

> Coming to literary studies from an intellectual formation as a historian, Peter had little time for the subjective and the impressionistic as a substitute for hard evidence and proper methodology. He taught us first to be quite sure that we understood what the words meant when they were written. He taught us to argue from evidence, not from prior, untested assumptions, and to distinguish the persuasive but specious ('bogus', he would call it) from the accurate and demonstrable. If you want to know why Spanish at Oxford is as it is, and why it believes more in the search for what is true rather than what is fashionable at any given moment, you will find the answer in Peter's legacy, which his spiritual children are committed to preserving, both within our own discipline and the life of this University itself.[78]

---

[76] The first published evidence of this comes in 1983 with a reference to Barthes' *Mythologies* (1957) in *Prince Henry the Navigator: The Rise and Fall of a Culture Hero, Taylorian Special Lecture, 10 November 1983* (Oxford: Clarendon Press, 1984), 6.

[77] Paul Julian Smith, *Writing in the Margin: Spanish Literature of the Golden Age* (Oxford: Clarendon Press, 1988) and Malcolm K. Read, *Language, Text, Subject: A Critique of Hispanism* (West Lafayette, Ind.: Purdue University Press, 1992).

[78] Thompson, 'Address', 264; Nicholas G. Round, 'The Politics of Hispanism Reconstrued', *Journal of Hispanic Research* 1 (1992), 134–47.

The charge has been levelled against Russell as literary critic that his historicist approach does not perhaps offer much in the way of detailed analysis in the strictest sense of the discipline, that he was first and foremost a critic of critics with a tendency to positivism, an exemplar indeed of 'British empiricism'. There is surely much in this but after Russell no one could approach the major Spanish texts or their critical treatment without grounding them firmly in their social, cultural and historical context while accepting the artistic licence inherent in literature. As a literary scholar that is his main legacy.

*

That Russell found solace in his research during a long period of mental anguish is demonstrated by his output which he sustained throughout. Indeed, when the known course of his psychoanalysis is set alongside the roster of his published and as yet unpublished work (1951–77) it can be seen to correspond with the most creative phase in his career. This is borne out by such of his private writings as have survived for the period in question during which with the exception of episodes in 1958 and 1959 the restless acuity of his mind can be seen to have survived in all its vigour. In fact, as during the war his powers otherwise give every impression of being heightened by the experience, attributable in part to an enhanced awareness arising from his therapy and readings in psychoanalysis, fulfilment of a dictum repeated in Gracián: know thyself. This is not, however, the whole story. When Russell had looked back on his boyhood and adolescence from the vantage point of the mid-1930s he acknowledged his steadfast refusal to engage in any activity in which he could not excel, in which he could not master those who might stand against him since defeat was unendurable. Now as a scholar he wanted not only to produce work that was of itself groundbreaking in substance, innovative in style and brilliant in execution, but also to expose obvious deficiencies in approach, interpretation and sometimes even of application and common sense among his academic peers. In some cases, such as that of Edgar Allison Peers, Menéndez Pidal, Gilman and others, there was a clear desire to vanquish intellectually, despite claims to the contrary.[79] The root of these antagonisms was of course personal distaste, linked in Peers's case to his religious outlook, to his limitations as a scholar, to his penchant for anonymous review (pseudonymous in the case of his own work) and latterly recourse to aliases to

---

[79] In 1950 Kolkhorst persuaded Russell to withhold what the former labelled an 'arrogant' review of a recent publication by Peers, possibly *A Critical Anthology of Spanish Verse* (Liverpool: Liverpool University Press, 1948); Yarnton, 25 Oct. 1950.

keep the *Bulletin of Spanish Studies* founded by him supplied with wartime content. Probably it had also to do with the discernible vacillation in his posture vis-à-vis the various parties before, during and after the Civil War, one quietly experienced by Russell himself as the years passed. Then there was Entwistle, the only person to whom he was ever directly' answerable academically, the earnest and highly strung philologist in the German mould whose appearance and physique as Russell chose to record them in print as late as 2004 recall his description of another scarred veteran of the Great War: his father. [80] With some of these he repaired the aspersion but with others the repine endured to the end. This is hardly unusual in the psychology and practice of scholarly discourse but by 1960 Russell had enlarged the focus of his attention from his colleagues in the Academy to the national myths of an entire state: those surrounding the person of the Infante Dom Henrique, Prince Henry the Navigator (1394–1460) whom the Portuguese had elevated to the status of a culture hero, the latest iteration of which was that crafted during the dictatorship of António de Oliveira Salazar (1932–68).

The task Russell set himself in writing a biography of Henry the Navigator was the most challenging of his career. In it he not only faced an almost complete dearth of material verifiably from the Infante's own hand or chancery, but an extraordinary tissue of contemporaneous and posthumous embellishment which served first to conceal the man behind the myth and then as a vehicle for successive appropriation and reshaping of his legacy. This situation was due not only to the fact that Henry was an assiduous curator of his own reputation but also to a near-total loss of documentation to various causes, not least that of the Casa da Índia in the Great Lisbon Earthquake of 1755. Except for a number of telling lapses, the chronicles the Prince commissioned from Gomes Eanes de Zurara and Diogo Gomes create the impression of himself Henry wished to leave for posterity and for which countervailing data has long been hard to come by. Such machinations were of course hardly unprecedented: 'History, one needs to remember, was still universally acknowledged to be a branch of Rhetoric [in which] the exclusive function of historical writing is to stimulate those who read it to try to imitate the moral perfection and memorable deeds of those who have gone before.' [81] Nor by the same token was the challenge of rebutting such sources an altogether unfamiliar one:

---

[80] See 'Entwistle, William James (1895–1952)', *Oxford Dictionary of National Biography*, <doi.org/10.1093/ref:odnb/33024> (revised version, 25 May 2006).

[81] *Prince Henry the Navigator: The Rise and Fall of a Culture Hero*, 9–10.

History is always liable to come off second-best when it tries to vanquish heroic myth and all the more so in this case when the myth seems to have historical authority and offers a simple, coherent, and unproblematic explanation of things, together with romantic appeal. When we turn to look at things as they were, less romantic questions immediately tend to pose themselves. [82]

Henry's reconnaissance of the coast of West Africa is therefore presented by his biographers as an exercise in crusade, conversion and proselytisation whereas it was effectively governed by commercial interests ultimately focused on gold but trading largely in slaves and other commodities. To these Russell identified the Prince as having affixed an ideal of chivalry in pursuit of which he was ready to drop all other concerns whenever the opportunity for knightly endeavour presented itself, such as his ill-conceived and disastrous attack on Tangier in 1437 which resulted in the capture and eventual death of his brother Fernando in a Barbary dungeon. Another example was the Prince's perpetual, misguided and eventually fruitless obsession with the conquest of the Canaries, the crusading, proselytising, economic and territorial motives of which Russell addressed in a long overdue reassessment in 1979. [83]

In the course of his research Russell therefore demolished a succession of pervasive myths surrounding the Prince. The 'Navigator' sobriquet, a German coinage of the nineteenth century, he dismissed by establishing that the Infante's seafaring credentials were confined by circumstance and protocol to coastal waters and a few trips between the Algarve and North Africa. The hoary myth of Henry having set up a 'school of navigation' at Sagres was put to rest once and for all for want of evidence he ever set foot in the place and in light of the fact that data on the discoveries had to be sent away to Venice for cartographic elaboration in 1458. A good deal of this mythologising was of British origin, the Prince having from the eighteenth century been enlisted by dint of his Plantagenet lineage as the earliest exemplar of the English seaborne expansion. In fact, rather than the enlightened Renaissance humanist and pioneer scientist of later historiography, Russell paints the picture of a rapacious and pious late medieval magnate with a taste for chivalric adventure and theology, one given dimension by the lively and urbane character that emerges from his only surviving item of private

---

[82] *Ibid.*, 10.
[83] *O Infante D. Henrique e as Ilhas Canárias: Uma Dimensão Mal Compreendida da Biografia Henriquina* (Lisbon: Academia das Ciências, 1979).

correspondence. Making use of the Prince's horoscope, he shows how astrological imperatives guided him in a relentless effort to fulfil his twin destiny of crusade and exploration. Moreover, in an impressive feat of deduction, Russell posited that Henry's early expeditions up to 1443 were not in fact peaceful trading missions but raids against the Moroccan coast with an eye to booty over commerce and discovery. [84] When he learnt in the 1990s that what had traditionally been taken as Henry's likeness on the famous *Saint Vincent Panels* by the artist Nuno Gonçalves was more probably the Burgundian ambassador to the Aviz court his sense of a fallacious image was complete. Ethical considerations apart, Henry's accomplishment was real enough for all that. Quite aside from its seafaring dimension, the administration, financing and organisation implied by the Henrican discoveries was a remarkable achievement involving the formation of a geographic and economic complex extending from Portugal to the Barbary Coast, West Africa and the Atlantic islands. It also bore witness to the tenacity of its sponsor in the face of intense scepticism over many decades. The crusading and chivalric zeal underpinned by commerce which from approximately 1422 drove Henry to send his caravels to and then beyond the mental barrier of Cape Bojador (eventually rounded in 1434) so that they were operating off Sierra Leone by the time of his death in 1460 laid the foundation of the Portuguese expansion in the Indian Ocean and the great trading empire which followed it. As Russell concluded, 'the Henrican discoveries surely represent the only occasion when the ideology of chivalry can be said to have served a scientific end and directly furthered European man's knowledge about the kind of world in which he lived'. [85]

Many of these theses were first laid before an unsuspecting audience in a lecture at Canning House in London in May 1960 which put the efforts of five centuries of historical manipulation and invention at a discount. [86] The lecture so incensed the Portuguese Embassy that strenuous efforts were made to buy up all copies for destruction, particular exception being taken to the remarks linking the Prince with slavery and astrology. In fact, Russell found himself driven to warn the

---

[84] *Prince Henry the Navigator: The Rise and Fall of a Culture Hero*, 19.
[85] *Ibid.*, 26. Russell's favoured title for the Henry biography, *Useful Glory*, was rejected by Yale University Press on commercial grounds. He was forestalled as to the original title, *The Greatest Man Uncrowned*, by his former student Nicholas Round who took it for his biography of Don Álvaro de Luna (London: Tamesis, 1986).
[86] *Prince Henry the Navigator, Canning House Seventh Annual Lecture, 4 May 1960*, Diamante 11 (London: The Hispanic and Luso-Brazilian Councils, 1960).

ambassador Adolfo do Amaral Abranches Pinto that any continuation of this effort would result in him writing a letter to *The Times* whose editor William Haley he knew personally. [87] So it was that the same government which had invited Russell to give his expert opinion at the battlefield of Aljubarrota the previous year now unavailingly attempted to suppress his work. The assault on the personality cult carefully propagated by the Infante himself and remodelled by successive interest groups was completed in a valedictory lecture delivered at Oxford in November 1983 and published under the apt title of 'Prince Henry the Navigator: The Rise and Fall of a Culture Hero'. Among other things it contained a wholly unwelcome reminder that the French had in fact beaten the Portuguese in rounding the cherished goal of Cape Bojador (or what was taken to be that promontory) by a matter of over thirty years. Russell had in the meantime started a full-length biography of the Prince in the late 1950s. In doing so he had taken on the most exacting assignment that can fall to any practising the historian's craft in the absence of documentation, that of constructing an armature through intuition and lengthy research on the peripheries of the subject to which such scraps of information are attached as might build a picture which, if never complete, is nonetheless plausible. A case in point is the extensive research done on the Genoese and particularly the Catalan slave trade in the late Middle Ages, the only part of the Iberian Peninsula then reckoned to be adequately documented in the field. In the course of this process Russell had also to deploy a literary critic's skill in analysing the coded language or deafening silence used by Henry's first chronicler Zurara:

> Of course history so presented is still invaluable for, once we recognize what the chronicler is up to, it is often possible, as in the case of Zurara, to decode his panegyrical statements and discover the realities that he can only allow himself to hint at, or that he over-carefully avoids discussing at all. [88]

The endeavour, however, bit back and Russell completed the book in the early 1970s to find himself dissatisfied with the result. The reasons for this are not altogether clear and indeed were wondered at by Russell himself in later years. In a letter to a colleague written in 1986 he explained himself to be lacking information from Italian sources on the supply of knowledge and perhaps finance

---

[87] I am grateful to Ronald Truman for this information.
[88] *Prince Henry the Navigator: The Rise and Fall of a Culture Hero*, 10.

for the Henrican voyages from that quarter, and surviving memories of the typescript as originally completed are of a more contextual and less biographical work than eventually appeared. [89] More probably Russell recognised the difficulty not only of finding adequate factual support for many of his interpretations — what he later referred to as 'the fog of ambiguity that surrounds the reality of that legendary personage' — but of overcoming the biographer's dilemma of striking the requisite balance between the subject and his time, problems he never fully resolved and which to some degree made him the prisoner of his approach in an evolving field. [90] Whatever the reason, the project was burdensome to him in the extreme and he would mordantly refer to it as 'the Alligator', the pun no doubt given added force by the Ceylonese crocodiles that long filled his nightmares and hallucinations. [91] It was twenty-five years before Russell, now well into his eighties, turned once more to the Infante and in 2000 produced the long-awaited *Prince Henry 'the Navigator': A Life* into which he poured his historical, literary and psychological intuition together with the fruit of his many travels. [92] Though it remains in some degree tied in conception and coverage to the years in which it was first drafted and occasionally exhibits the mental and physical exertion required to bring it to completion, *Prince Henry* was nonetheless the crowning achievement of a brilliant career, a work of immense subtlety and authority half a century in the making. [93] Its publication, wrote João Gouveia Monteiro, confirmed Russell as 'undoubtedly one of the men who did most for the improvement of Portuguese Studies in Europe during the 20th century'. [94] The

---

[89] PER to Marco Spallanzani, Oxford, 14 July 1986. On the original typescript, see the review article by Felipe Fernández-Armesto, 'His Was a World of Shabby Swagger: Henry the Navigator', *Literary Review* (June 2000), 17–18. Although containing much new material, the published volume was a considerable abbreviation of the typescript as first completed. At least some of the text Russell ended up cutting concerned slavery, a field subject to extensive reappraisal over the forty-five year gestation of the work.

[90] PER to Ted Parks, Oxford, 6 Nov. 1995. I am grateful to Alastair Saunders and the late Professor Sir John Elliott for their comments on this section. Russell's failure to give full coverage to the domestic context of Henry's policy and his legacy after 1460 have also been cited in criticism.

[91] The project was in fact christened thus by C. R. Boxer; I am grateful to Alastair Saunders for this memory.

[92] New Haven, Conn.: Yale University Press, 2000.

[93] See the review by Isabel Morgado S. E. Silva in *Journal of World History* 14 (Sept. 2003), 411–14.

[94] Monteiro, 'Sir Peter E. Russell'.

acclaim, however, was not universal. The indignant official response of 1960 was echoed by Duarte, Duke of Bragança, who condemned the publication of a book 'so unjust and insulting to Portugal' in its depiction of the slave trade, a judgment greeted with guffaws at Belsyre Court. [95]

*

Russell's scholarly writings of the 1970s, '80s and '90s offered a refinement of many of his earlier themes. An article on the Council of Trent and lay literature in Spain and Portugal published in 1978 took another swipe at Américo Castro while revisiting some of his earlier work on English seventeenth-century readings of Spanish literature and James Mabbe, the Anglican priest and Oxford don who in 1622 published the translation of Mateo Alemán's *Guzmán de Alfarache* which introduced that work to a wide readership in England, clerical and lay. [96] In doing so he was not only able to dismantle A. A. Parker's contention that the *Guzmán* of 1599 was an avowedly Counter-Reformation work and one of the great literary expressions of the mind of the Council of Trent but also make a wider point on the reception of Spanish literature generally. [97] Having disposed of the simplistic frame of reference which had characterised Parker's writings since the 1930s on Spanish Catholic civilisation, Russell served up this reminder to his own readership:

> In concluding I should like to draw attention to a fact relating to the problem we have been discussing [lay literature in the Spanish Golden Age] and which may be more apparent to a foreign Hispanist than to a Spanish one. This is the fact that in speaking of the literature of the Spanish Golden Age excessive emphasis may be placed on the Council of Trent and the Counter-Reformation as if these created a form of closed cultural frontier in Europe. [...] The dogmatic differences between the Catholic and Protestant worlds were sharp, well known, but

---

[95] D. Duarte de Bragança, '"Discoveries Did Most for Human Progress": D. Duarte Defends D. Henrique', *Anglo-Portuguese News*, 17 Aug. 2000, 10.

[96] 'El Concilio de Trento y la literatura profana: reconsideración de una teoría' in *Temas de La Celestina*, 443–78; 'English Seventeenth-Century Interpretations of Spanish Literature', *Atlante* 1 (1953), 65–77; 'A Stuart Hispanist: James Mabbe', *Bulletin of Hispanic Studies* 30 (1953), 78–84. Russell benefitted from perceptive comments on the proofs of the *Atlante* article by G. A. Kolkhorst, Yarnton, 8 Jan. 1953.

[97] A. A. Parker, *Literature and the Delinquent* (Edinburgh: Edinburgh University Press, 1967), 21–2 & 83. I am grateful to Ronald Truman for drawing this point to my attention.

also of limited application outside of the field of theology. They did not succeed, at least in the case of profane literature, in hiding everything that Catholic and Protestant culture and comprehension still had in common. If it is worth translating Spanish works it is because of their universality. [98]

If these comments echo Russell's earlier observations on the Cid and San Pedro de Cardeña in which he questioned the imposition of barriers and distinctions by critics either unfamiliar with social and historical realities or unwilling to accept them, they also reflect Russell's awareness of the reluctance of Spanish criticism in particular to absorb many of his groundbreaking interpretations, whether on the *Cantar de Mio Cid*, the Quixote ('I am afraid that article still infuriates many American and some Spanish Hispanists') or *Celestina* on which he recognised the work of Gilman and his mentor Castro as 'still set[ting] the agenda'. [99] Frustration turned to irritation when he found that his interpretations were being appropriated without acknowledgment:

> I read in *El País* of 9 December [2000] both Lázaro Carreter's surprisingly sycophantic comments on Paco Rico's recent *Celestina* as well as those of Juan Goytisolo. I suppose one has no right to complain on finding that some views on that masterpiece that one has been peddling from abroad for years are now presented in Spain as the critic's new and original personal insights. The last sentence of Lázaro's review confirmed my impression that he is one of the happily very small group of academic critics around nowadays in Spain who have not realized that there is an inescapable price to pay for owning a world literature. That is that you cannot prohibit world readers from reading the works concerned in the way they choose, which may well not be (and perhaps can never be) the way a Spanish reader would read them. [100]

In 1985 he produced a volume on translation and translators in Spain and Portugal which developed the ideas set forth in another seminal article, 'Arms

---

[98] 'El Concilio de Trento', 473–4. My translation.
[99] PER to T. R. A. Mason, Oxford, 1 Aug. 1996; 'The *Celestina* Then and Now', 9.
[100] JMA, PER to Javier Marías, Oxford, 28 Feb. 2001. Fernando Lázaro Carreter (1923–2004) was Director of the Real Academia Española; Professor Francisco Rico (b. 1942; see n. 75) is a member of the RAE, and Juan Goytisolo (1931–2017) was a major novelist.

versus Letters: Towards a Definition of Spanish Humanism' of 1967. In it a cultural explanation was provided for the failure of classical Italian humanism to take root in Spain, England and France, which not only lacked the socio-economic milieu in which the Renaissance was cradled but whose lay audiences retained a strong preference for domestic and vernacular forms well into the sixteenth century. [101] As so often, the problem where Spain was concerned rested less in the subject matter itself than with the agenda of its latter-day students and would-be explicators:

> By contrast, historians of Spanish culture, with respect to Spain, find it difficult to accept this patent truth. Accordingly, it is frequently averred that the mere fact of Spain having had, as I stated above, close political and military ties with Italy, made Spaniards particularly open to the influence of the phenomenon of Italian humanism. Perhaps lying behind this assertion, which tends not to enjoy documentary support, is a fear that yet another chapter will be written in the Black Legend [of Spanish cruelty and backwardness] unless a solid foundation can be demonstrated. [102]

Not only that but such approaches served to occlude accomplishments in other areas, namely that of the poet Garcilaso de la Vega in introducing the conventions of Italian humanism to Spain in the 1530s. It was a typical example of Russell attempting to clear cultural detritus and refocus attention based on a dispassionate assessment of the field as a whole.

Then came a series of articles on the documentary, ethnological and socio-linguistic dimensions of the European reconnaissance of West Africa and the Canaries with its attendant culture and permutations. [103] The first, published in 1971 and based on Spanish chancery sources, shed new light on the doomed efforts of the Crown of Castile to break into the Portuguese commercial

---

[101] *Traducciones y traductores en la Península Ibérica, 1400–1550* (Barcelona: Universidad Autónoma de Barcelona, 1985); 'Arms versus Letters: Towards a Definition of Spanish Humanism' in *Aspects of the Renaissance: A Symposium*, ed. Archibald R. Lewis (Austin, Tx.: University of Texas, 1967), 45–58; revised as 'Las armas contra las letras: para una definición del humanismo español del siglo' in *Temas de* La Celestina, 209–39.

[102] 'Las armas contra las letras', 234. My translation.

[103] Several of these are collected in *Portugal, Spain and the African Atlantic, 1343–1490* (Aldershot, Hants.: Variorum, 1995); see Appendix V.

monopoly of the Guinea Coast and the Atlantic islands in the late 1470s. [104] Two years later came a multidisciplinary study on Rodrigo de Reinosa's 'black poetry' drawing on his research into the history of slavery and freedmen in the Peninsula, Spanish, Portuguese and Wolof linguistics and the faintly discernible culture of black people in dance, song and music as it entered the sixteenth century. [105] In 1978 he produced a textual analysis of an important source both for that Castilian initiative and the Portuguese expansion in Guinea itself, Eustache de la Fosse's *Voyage à la Guinée* (1479–80). [106] The Portuguese navigation of the African Atlantic and the ensuing contact with the populations both of Guinea and the Canaries raised a series of complex issues on which Russell was able to bring his insight to bear from the late 1970s. He began in 1978 with an article on the discovery of the Canaries and the medieval debate on the rights of indigenous peoples, one that prefigured similar ethical concerns in the context of Spanish conquest in the sixteenth century. [107] Not the least of the challenges facing the Portuguese was that of language, among the clearest expressions of the newness of this 'new world' they were encountering and on which Russell dedicated an article in 1980, followed by another in 1986 under the title of 'White Kings on Black Kings' in which he used the case of the Wolof chief Bemoim to explore Portuguese attitudes on the status of African dignitaries in the late fifteenth century. [108] As the quincentenary of the discovery of America approached Russell turned his attention to the legacy of the Portuguese seaborne reconnaissance on the Castilian-led discovery and colonisation of America to which it owed so much from a legal, navigational, organisational, cultural, economic, linguistic and

---

[104] 'Fontes documentais castelhanas para a história da expansão portuguesa na Guiné nos últimos anos de D. Afonso V', *Do tempo e da história* 4 (1971), 5–33.

[105] '"Towards an Interpretation of Rodrigo de Reinosa's "poesía negra"' in *Studies in Spanish Literature of the Golden Age Presented to Edward M. Wilson*, ed. Royston O. Jones (London: Tamesis Books, 1973), 225–45.

[106] 'Novos apontamentos sobre os problemas textuais do *Voiaige à la Guinée* de Eustáquio de la Fosse (1479–1480)', *Revista Portuguesa de História* 16 (1978) (*Homenagem ao Doutor Torquato da Sousa Soares*), 209–21.

[107] 'El descubrimiento de Canarias y el debate medieval acerca de los derechos de los príncipes y pueblos paganos', *Revista de Historia Canaria* 36/171 (1978), 9–32.

[108] 'Problemas Sócio-Linguísticos relacionados com os Descobrimentos Portugueses no Atlântico Africano', *Anais da Acadêmia Portuguesa da História* (2nd series) 26 (1980), 227–50; 'White Kings on Black Kings: Rui de Pina and the Problem of Black African Sovereignty' in *Mediæval and Renaissance Studies in Honour of Robert Brian Tate*, ed. Ian Michael & Richard Cardwell (Oxford: Dolphin Book Co., 1986), 151–63.

juridical perspective. In 1992 he took the opportunity to administer one of his characteristic rebukes, noting that 'despite the fact that Portuguese discovery and expansion in the Atlantic had been under way for some sixty years before Columbus' first voyage, for most Americanists the early modern history of America seems to begin, without more than a glancing backward look, in 1492', chastising those who 'usually do not see any need to concern themselves in any depth with the extent to which Portuguese models dictated, influenced or ran parallel to the early processes of discovery and conquest in the New World of America'. [109] The following year Russell memorably evoked the image formed of the Atlantic world by the Portuguese and those they brought with them (Columbus included) on the eve of the first voyage to America, fruit of decades of patient research and cogitation. [110] Aptly titled '*Veni, vidi, vici*', Russell used it to explain how these travellers' narratives 'were able to present European readers with something more than just Africa observed through European eyes [...] However dimly, we can also hear in these writings distant echoes of the voice of Black Africa describing itself.'

Towards the end of his life Russell renewed his interest in the Peninsular translations of Vegetius' influential treatise on military organisation, the *Epitoma rei militaris*, a reminder of the expertise in that branch of history first brought to bear in *Intervention* half a century earlier. [111] And always there was *Celestina* in its infinite variety and ambiguity, not least 'Why did Celestina Move House?' which expanded on the urban setting of the work. [112] His last original contribution to

---

[109] 'Some Portuguese Paradigms for the Discovery and Conquest of Spanish America', *Renaissance Studies* 6 (1992), 377–90; at 377.
[110] '*Veni, vidi, vici*: Fifteenth-Century Eyewitness Accounts of Travel in the African Atlantic before 1492', *Historical Research* 66/160 (1993), 115–28.
[111] 'The Medieval Castilian Translation of Vegetius' *Epitoma de rei militaris*: An Introduction' in *Spain and Its Literature: Essays in Memory of E. Allison Peers*, ed. Ann L. Mackenzie (special issue of *Bulletin of Hispanic Studies*) (Liverpool: Liverpool University Press, 1997), 49–63, 'De nuevo sobre la traducción castellana medieval de Vegecio, *Epitoma de rei militaris*' in *Essays on Medieval Translation in the Iberian Peninsula*, ed. Tomàs Martínez Romero & Roxana Recio Castelló (Castelló de la Plana: Universitat Jaume I, 2001), 325–40, and 'Terá havido uma tradução medieval portuguesa do *Epitome rei militaris* de Vegécio?', *Euphrosyne* 29 (2001), 247–56. A critical edition of one of the Spanish translations of the work remained incomplete at the time of his death.
[112] 'Why did Celestina Move House?' in *The Age of the Catholic Monarchs, 1474–1516: Literary Studies in Memory of Keith Whinnom*, ed. Alan Deyermond & Ian Macpherson (special issue of *Bulletin of Hispanic Studies*) (Liverpool: Liverpool University Press, 1989),

scholarship other than memoirs or biographical material was published in his eighty-eighth year in 2001. [113]

This scholarly output was complemented by Russell's main collecting interest, that in early printed books of which he gathered a fine private library. His first recorded purchase was an early edition of the *Quixote* for 4/- from an Oxford bookshop in 1934 but within a few years he was browsing the catalogues of the major London dealers. [114] The prize among many rare volumes was his copy of Petrarch's *Omnia Opera* printed by Amerbach of Basel in 1496, much consulted by Fernando de Rojas in writing *Celestina* and bought from the London firm of Bernard Quaritch for £1000 in the 1960s. Another volume he purchased from Quaritch's was the last chivalric romance published in Golden Age Spain, Juan de Silva's *Don Policisne de Boecia* of 1602. This work, of a type wistfully lampooned by Cervantes in the Quixote, had languished unsold in Quaritch's catalogues for many years before Russell resolved to buy it for £200 in 1975. Quaritch's next catalogue disclosing its absence provoked an anguished phone call from his friend Joan Gili in nearby Cumnor, descendant of a family of Catalan book publishers, dealers and collectors who had watched without buying for too long. It formed the subject of an article in 1982 and Russell eventually left his copy to the Bodleian Library. [115] Between whiles he found time to gather the leading lights in the field to produce what together with his many entries in the *Encyclopaedia Britannica* must be reckoned the most widely read of any work in which he had a hand, in this case as general editor: *Spain: A Companion to Spanish Studies*, a matchless primer in its day for a generation of students in both the English- and Spanish-speaking worlds and a testament to the contribution made to the field by post-war British scholarship. [116]

155–61.
[113] 'Terá havido uma tradução medieval portuguesa do *Epitome rei militaris* de Vegécio?', *Euphrosyne* 29 (2001), 247–56.
[114] Diary, 26 Sept. 1934; JMA, PER to Javier Marías, Oxford, 8 April 1999.
[115] 'The Last of the Spanish Chivalric Romances: *Don Policisne de Boecia*' in *Essays on Narrative Fiction in the Iberian Peninsula in Honour of Frank Pierce*, ed. R. B. Tate (Oxford: The Dolphin Book Co., 1982), 141–52.
[116] *Spain: A Companion to Spanish Studies* (London: Methuen, 1973; revised 1977); Spanish transl. *Introducción a la cultura hispánica*, 2 vols (Barcelona: Crítica, 1982). Russell anchored much of the coverage on medieval Spain for the 1964 and 1967 revisions of the 14th edition of *Encyclopaedia Britannica* with a total of thirty-five entries. Only one was retained (with revisions) in the 15th edition, *The New Encyclopaedia Britannica* (1974), that on 'Cid, El' (IV, 615–16), though it has remained available (with amendments) in subsequent

Scholars seldom attract the undivided attention of biographers. Obituary frequently, prosopography eventually one may suppose, but biography only rarely. A scholar's life and legacy is largely that of their work and teaching, and when not revealed in their own words the factors dictating their choice of field, subject, approach and interpretation can usually be inferred by circumstance, association or personal choice. Although this was and is as true of Russell as of any other scholar, no disclosure was ever made to identify the underlying motivations that lent such depth to his work from the 1950s. The attraction and challenge of working on *Celestina*, the *Quixote* and Prince Henry rested not only in the controversy to be elicited by his interpretations and deductions but in the scope they provided him for exploring the varied themes of ambiguity he discerned in them and in their legacy at the hands of others, complemented by and complementing in their turn the duality he continued to explore in his own mind and trajectory, subjects which in their way offered paradigms for his ongoing emotional predicament. In the final reckoning Russell's power of logical deduction as a literary critic and in historical analysis matched that of which he was capable as the observer of his own afflictions. The melding of the three in the context of his erudition and the rich seams of experience from which he could draw in the ideation of his work places him in rarefied company as a scholar.

editions and media to date (2024), the last of Russell's works to be in print.

CHAPTER SEVEN
Awaiting the Reaper

If the span of Peter Russell's life be divided into the conventional stages of childhood, adulthood and old age there can be no doubt from a personal standpoint that the latter began with the final illness and death of his mother Rita. In 1956 she had brought an end to the semi-itinerant existence which had characterised her life since 1914 by settling at Lee Cottage in Charlbury fifteen miles northwest of Oxford. Here she could indulge her love of gardening between extended visits to New Zealand as Russell began the ritual of driving over each Saturday evening for dinner before returning to Belsyre Court the following afternoon. 'It's a nice break for him and me' she wrote in the early 1960s, a judgement with which he could never entirely concur however much he wished to. [1] Within ten years Rita had begun losing her mobility and in the summer of 1973 moved at her own request to St Luke's nursing home on Linton Road in Oxford where Russell remained her frequent visitor. In the 1950s he had taken an allotment behind nearby Norham Road on which he began by cultivating fruit and vegetables but later took the uncommon step of growing flowers instead, the result of over-frequent watering by passing dogs and a desire to keep his mother supplied with fresh-cut blooms. After a steady deterioration in her health Russell received a phone call at Belsyre Court in the early hours of 12 December 1976 informing him of her death. 'Mother died at 3 a.m.' was the entry in his pocket diary that day, an event unfailingly marked there with a cross in the ensuing years. Her remains were cremated four days later and the ashes buried at Charlbury by Russell himself on the 22nd in a committal at which he was the only attendee. If her death at the age of eighty-nine brought an end to years of declining health and devoted care, it was also an unmitigated defeat that left him physically and mentally prostrate, the extinguishing of any prospect that he would receive from his mother the thing he craved most in his life: her praise. In later years Russell would put a gloss on his grief, telling a former student in 1997 that '[t]hough at 83 I am, as you may imagine, fairly accustomed to losing relatives and friends I still

---

[1] RMR, 44.

miss my own mother after twenty years, much though she used to irritate me when she was around!'[2] This as so often with Russell was only part of the story. Though the sense is that he eventually made peace with his demons, the overwhelming traumas of his childhood and his midlife crisis and the attendant sadnesses and frustrations of which she was the focus were of a kind not to be surmounted so much as kept at bay. Closer to the mark in the context of December 1976 are the eleven lines of untitled verse he composed during the war and which one cannot help associating with the irreconcilable yearnings that never left him, a man fated not for union but an eternity of shadowing:

>Now,
>Tired inheritors of time,
>Side by side
>We drift
>Like listless swans on songless lakes of memory,
>Exiles of the hours
>Searching the deepening waters
>Where they lie
>Who sleep on after sunset,
>Half-hidden in the twilight shadows
>Of the time-freed years.

*

On his retirement in 1981 Russell began to entertain the possibility of buying a property in southern Spain to escape the long winters and year-round damp of Oxford but decided against it after a reconnaissance of the Costa de la Luz and the Costa del Sol. The reason was never entirely clear but he may have wondered whether congenial company could be found among the ex-pats kitted out for tennis who would become his neighbours, or perhaps he quailed at the prospect of maintaining his own property after fifty years in college-owned accommodation of one type or another.[3] A plan to buy a house with a garden in North Oxford also came to nothing though in this case the decision may have been due to his being domiciled for tax purposes in the Channel Islands, Russell having since the 1960s entrusted his complex affairs to his friend Charles

---

[2] PER to Alastair Saunders, Oxford, 22 Jan. 1997.
[3] I am grateful to Clive Griffin for this information.

Kennedy, the noted economist and financial advisor to the University of Kent. As it was, lengthy spells as a visiting professor in the United States and trips to the Antipodes and elsewhere evidently satisfied his need for radical changes of scene. This phase ended abruptly in 1987 when he rushed home from Nashville after developing what seems to have been a recurrence of the prostate problems first diagnosed and operated on in early 1975. Despite his impressive physique not since adolescence had Russell led what could in current parlance be regarded as a healthy lifestyle. In November 1959, then at the nadir of his psychological afflictions and under heavy prescription of barbiturates, he resolved from the Hotel Borges in Lisbon to ring the changes on returning to Oxford: 'When I get back a regime must start. Come what may, 2 hours' exercise in open air a day, no more than 30 cigarettes a day and fewer pills.' [4] What Russell's current intake was and whether he abided by the regime is not on record but the prescriptions went on into the 1960s and he continued to smoke (though apparently not inhale) his ubiquitous Kent cigarettes until Charles Kennedy's death of lung cancer in 1997 caused him to kick the habit for good, literally overnight. In a letter sent to the former *lector* and novelist José Luis Giménez-Frontín in 1996, Russell — then eighty-two — declared that 'I tend to think of myself as being no more than forty, totally rejecting the possibility that the face I see in the mirror can be other than an evil caricature'. [5] But change was afoot and he had already developed essential tremor which was treated with beta blockers though not before a consultant had misdiagnosed him with Parkinson's Disease. [6] 'Terrible decline' he'd mutter at some dispiriting moment between the heaves and exhalations characteristic of his last years. If the tremor brought with it the curse of spilt beverages and fumbling fingers, the latter was the cause of much needless anxiety and pharmaceutical prescription, and for many years the most thumbed volume in Belsyre Court was not his modern edition of Sebastián de Covarrubias' *Tesoro de la lengua castellana* of 1611 but the medical desk reference he would turn to whenever symptoms real or imagined appeared. When Russell described his friend and successor in the Oxford chair Ian Michael as a '*malade imaginaire*' in the contribution he wrote to the latter's *Festschrift* in 2004 he did so with an intimate knowledge of the condition. [7]

---

[4] Journal, 9 Nov. 1959.
[5] PER to José Luis Giménez-Frontín, Oxford, 18 June 1996.
[6] I am grateful to Barbara Russell and Eric Southworth for this information.
[7] 'Ian Michael: A Personal Appreciation', *The Iberian Book and its Readers: Essays for Ian Michael*, ed. Nigel Griffin, Clive Griffin & Eric Southworth [= *Bulletin of Spanish Studies* 81]

As the years advanced the subject would occasionally arise of Russell writing his autobiography. So far as he was concerned the idea had no merit whatsoever. Besides entailing the sort of overt self-promotion he loathed he would declare his career to be of scant interest to any outside academia and that it was in any case on public record. As for those episodes reckoned to be of wider interest, namely his involvement in secret intelligence, not only was he bound till death by the Official Secrets Act but a visit to Belsyre Court by an MI5 oral history team in around 2000 revealed to him how little he in fact knew of the context of his wartime activities. What he of course left unsaid was that there was too much about his personal and family life, his frustrated literary ambitions, his pre-war political stance and his post-war mental collapse he could never make public, nor for that matter wished to dredge up even privately. To do so would be to bring down on himself exactly the sort of attention he had so carefully avoided for so long, whereas to exclude such information would result in a distortion concealing more than it disclosed. Both scenarios were anathema to him. Moreover, as any review of his life could hardly fail to show, Russell's outlook and personality had changed greatly under pressure of time and events. Although the war disposed of most of his antebellum political views and some of his snobbery, Russell retained many of the proprieties and affectations of his class and his generation, though not without a measure of wistful humour as attitudes changed and informality became the norm. By the 1990s, for instance, he had begun to weary of sending out every single item of clothing or linen for laundering, the war years having provided positively his first and last experience of dhobeying in any form. When however it was suggested to him that a washer-dryer unit could easily be installed in the spare bedroom at Belsyre Court he protested between chortles that to do so would make him 'the sort of person who does laundry in his bedroom'. To that extent Belsyre Court was the much attenuated continuation of Knowlescourt with its complement of servants.

More consequentially his views on women experienced a significant alteration both personally and professionally in the decades following his arrival in Oxford in 1931. Leaving aside the patriarchal society in which he was nurtured, Russell's journals from the late 1930s and particularly the '40s show him to have had a vein of misogyny no stated desire for a heterosexual relationship was likely to overcome. His general attitude to women in those years, all too frequently one of distaste bordering on dislike or worse, is already apparent in an untitled and

(2004), no. 7–8, vii–x; at x.

apparently unpublished short story he completed in around 1934, but by 1948 had evidently spilled over into his correspondence. [8] As discussed earlier, this response was among other things a direct result of the crushing impotence which originated in the Oedipus complex with its many ramifications. The chaste bachelor status remained unaltered in all its sadness and frustration but the long course of psychotherapy centring on his relationship with his mother evidently cured him of the bitter misogyny of former years, a process which began with a male analyst in around 1951 and was completed under a woman practitioner as late as 1977. The arc of his relationship with women can in some degree be traced through Russell's association with the eccentric and flamboyant Enid Starkie, sister of Walter, Fellow of Somerville College, University Lecturer and eventually Reader in French who became his undergraduate tutor in the early 1930s. [9] The first surviving mention of Starkie in Russell's papers comes in a diary entry in September 1934:

> In middle of book by Enid Starkie on Baudelaire — I have felt compelled to walk out on her lectures in the past and will do so a lot more in the future. Never was the mind of the female don revealed to greater disadvantage — a mass of incoherent facts, prejudices and curiosities on 'every' subject under the sun not I think any of them very worth while. And why does she find it necessary to correct the spelling of Shakespeare? Nevertheless, it is often interesting rather in the way of a gossip writer. [10]

It may for the sake of context be added that for all her distinction Starkie was as she herself recognised known neither for her lecturing nor her prose style nor for her strength as a literary critic. [11] Now a college lecturer himself, Russell was seeing Starkie socially by the autumn of 1938 though he was still skewering her output in his journal for March 1948, this time her acclaimed biography of Rimbaud: 'Find Enid Starkie on Rimbaud really rather dull so far — which is no great distance.' [12] Further progress with this volume did not alter his view much

---

[8] Kolkhorst to PER, Yarnton, 31 Dec. 1948.
[9] Joanna Richardson, *Enid Starkie: A Biography* (London: Macmillan, 1973); Russell is mentioned in the acknowledgments.
[10] Enid Starkie, *Baudelaire* (London: Victor Gollancz, 1933). Diary, 3 Sept. 1934.
[11] Richardson, *Enid Starkie*, 1–2 & 102–3.
[12] Enid Starkie, *Arthur Rimbaud* (rev. ed., London: Hamish Hamilton, 1947). Journal, 2 Jan. 1939 & 7 March 1948.

though Russell's capricious state of mind in Hilary 1948 has also been alluded to elsewhere. In the same vein comes this telling entry in his journal:

Enid Starkie in her rooms at Somerville College, photographed by Norman Parkinson in 1951. National Portrait Gallery

> Went to Congregation this afternoon where a motion to increase the number of women allowed in University by 120 was to be proposed. Scenting scandal a quite exceptionally large number of people turned up and a very remarkable sight it was to see them. Hordes of women dons

of quite incredibly ugly countenance or just nothing at all; elderly battle-axes in boots and self-knitted sweaters, bewhiskered beldams, pallid and soapy-faced blue-stockings their faces vacant of experience all turned up in enormous numbers. The men mostly consisted of people I had never seen before — many looked as they had not been out of doors since before the War. There were also a large proportion of the younger sort — complacent, well-fed and untidily dressed. In the event the whole thing was a damp squib of the most tame variety. Four speeches were made in which incoherence, contradiction, and faulty logic seemed to be the chief features. It was alleged — and admitted — that few women got firsts and many got thirds but otherwise the reasons given for opposing the motion were merely founded on prejudice — especially as its immediate effect will be to reduce the numbers of women here at present. The Principal of St. Hilda's [Julia de Lacy Mann] said she hoped it would soon be possible to see that all the women who could not live in College were settled in 'authorised houses'. [13]

At least Russell voted in favour of the motion, ethics prevailing over narcissism on this occasion. Yet Starkie is the same irrepressibly gregarious figure with whom he was now dining frequently as 'Colonel' Kolkhorst's guest at Yarnton Manor and at Somerville and elsewhere and continued to do so for twenty years. Though his private papers offer no detail on the matter, there can be little doubt that a close tie of friendship developed between them ('Enid', Kolkhorst told him, 'has a warm spot for you') to which his psychotherapy was no doubt a contributory factor. [14] Indeed, there are no more poignant letters in Russell's archive than those she sent him after her terminal cancer diagnosis in 1965. 'You are' she wrote 'one of the people who goes furthest back in my life, since the days when I was a young don, and you were my pupil.' [15] No doubt they bonded over their mutual love of Spain (through which Starkie had rambled solo in the summer of 1934) and André Gide, the writer who influenced Russell as much as any outside of Spanish letters, whose honorary doctorate Starkie had sponsored in 1947 and whose biography she published in 1953. [16] But there was more to it than that. Like the female friends outside of academia to whom he

---

[13] Journal, 27 Jan. 1948.
[14] Yarnton, 28 June 1948.
[15] Oxford, 28 March 1965. Starkie died in April 1970.
[16] Richardson, *Enid Starkie*, 105–7.

turned at his lowest ebb in the late '50s — the aristocratic Carmen Roca de Togores of the Instituto de España in London, the civil servant Pauline Parry-Jones and possibly his fiancée Piedad Márquez — Starkie, heir to an intricate sexuality of her own, was presumably among the many who gave Russell the benefit of her wisdom and support at this time. Although he is unlikely to have revealed his own predicament to Starkie, this may conceivably have extended to her perspective on the mother fixation complex he shared with Baudelaire whose biography Starkie was revising in the middle years of the decade. [17] In short, Russell will like so many others have been drawn to Starkie by the most compelling aspects of her personality as they emerge from her writings and biography: her individuality, brilliance, honesty, zest for life and humanity.

One of Russell's five woman graduate students was Maria da Graça de Almeida Rodrigues. A *lisboeta*, Rodrigues reached Oxford from King's College London in 1968 where Russell in due time advised her to extend her research on the chronicler Damião de Góis from the intended B.Litt. to a doctorate, a decision that led to a chair at the Universidade Nova de Lisboa and eventually a second career as Cultural Counsellor in the Portuguese diplomatic service:

> He was a sophisticated man and I was a Portuguese woman coming from nowhere. However, I do not feel he treated me differently from any of the men students mentioned in your biography (in my time at Oxford there were seven men for every woman). Although our relationship was strictly professional, I felt recognised, supported and encouraged both as a person and in my work. [...] But what defined Peter Russell for me, besides following my work consistently and in great detail, was my last meeting with him at Oxford. The grant I had received for three years was about to end and [...] [w]hen I suggested my intention [to submit for a B.Litt.] he told me 'No!' and in his words (which I haven't forgotten!) 'What you have done is doctoral material.' This advice changed the course of my life. Had I gone for a B.Litt., a degree that no one in Portugal had heard of, my career would not have been the same. [18]

Others benefited from the informal mentorship in which he excelled and which led to lasting friendships, particularly Xon de Ros, eventually Professor of Modern

---

[17] *Baudelaire* (2nd ed., London: Faber and Faber, 1957).
[18] Graça de Almeida Rodrigues, emails to the author, 21 & 12 Oct. 2020, respectively.

Spanish Studies at Oxford, and Kirstin Kennedy, now curator of Renaissance and Baroque silver at the Victoria and Albert Museum. In the memoir she prepared for this volume Ros, a native of Barcelona who was appointed to the Sub-Faculty of Spanish as a *lectora* in 1989, captures the quiet encouragement Russell extended his younger colleagues and the emotional intelligence and sensitivity that underpinned it:

> I remember feeling subdued during a dinner at High Table [in Exeter College], surrounded by scholars — my shaky English usually going into meltdown on such occasions. Sitting across the table Peter addressed me in a commanding tone: 'Well, Xon, what do you have to tell me?' Heads turned. It was his way of teasing me for feeling intimidated. […] Once Peter apologized to me for having included a quote from the *Libro de buen amor* in the inscription to the copy he gave me of his edition of *Celestina*: 'al torpe faze bueno e omne de prestar' [makes a proper and influential man of any who is awkward or inept]. Ian Michael had told him that however unintended it was an inappropriate thing to say to a woman. I reassured Peter that no offence had been found or taken. I could see the relief on his face as he reached to stub out his cigarette on an ashtray with the image of Pope John Paul II. In my experience he was never in the least patronizing. After my viva he gave me the two volumes of the María Moliner dictionary he had ordered from Casa del Libro in Madrid. On that occasion he switched to English, circumventing the question of gender — 'I believe you may be the first Spaniard to be awarded a D.Phil. by the Faculty'. He had a way of leaving all kinds of questions open. [19]

Just as his conscience no doubt pricked him in later years to pay tribute in public to a figure he had earlier excoriated in private and exposed at least once in print — his teacher, mentor and predecessor Professor W. J. Entwistle — Russell would take pains to acknowledge the intellectual debt he owed to women scholars of the past, whether it was Jeanne Vieilliard for sharing her copious pre-war notes from the Archive of the Crown of Aragon, the Portuguese medieval historian Virgínia Rau, or Evelyn Procter of St Hugh's whose research laid the

---

[19] Xon de Ros, notes to the author, 16 Sept. 2020. The *Libro de buen amor* citation comes in *copla* 490; María Moliner, *Diccionario de uso del español*, 2 vols (Madrid: Editorial Gredos, 1966–7; subsequently revised).

ground for his attack on Menéndez Pidal's dating of the *Cantar de Mio Cid* in 1952. Fifty years on he put the latter debt on record:

> I want to begin by recalling the name of a much-respected Oxford historian and hispanist of those days. I refer to Evelyn Procter — even now I hardly dare to omit the formal 'Miss' —, the Principal of St Hugh's. Miss Procter had a unique archivally-acquired knowledge of documents of all kinds associated with Alfonso X of Castile and other monarchs. As a result she became one of the earliest medievalists in this country to express in print doubts about the historicity of [the] Spanish epic according to orthodox Pidalian theory. [20]

Procter, whose final work Russell published in his Cambridge Iberian and Latin American Studies series in 1980, had in all probability joined Starkie in voting for the same motion of Congregation of which his journal painted such an unflattering picture. [21] Not that Russell experienced any sort of Road to Damascus where women were concerned and many would find themselves brushed off in his middle years just as they had in his youth. Others would find that he no more than tolerated them whereas he perhaps felt the beam of their curiosity a little too keenly. Encounters with strong and assertive women he would in later years refer to as 'being put in my place' while generally avoiding the experience or much repetition. One such was Emily Hahn, the feminist, noted writer and journalist and wife of Charles Boxer with whom he shared an unhappy visit to Ireland *à deux* in the late 1960s. Perhaps Hahn, a native of Missouri and quite innocent of any form of reserve, subjected him to the inquisition about his private life few dared venture. However, as time went on he took a more detached approach to such encounters. A case in point was the challenging personality of Cynthia Macdonald, widow of Russell's erstwhile colleague and adversary Iain at Queen's, who latched herself onto him and for whom he showed endless forbearance before she succumbed to emphysema in 2000. Another was his taciturn and none-too-diligent cleaner of two decades, Mrs Drennan ('the Drennan'), a devout Irish Catholic from County Mayo to whom he nonetheless bade farewell in hospital during her final illness in the mid-'90s. For many years he also enjoyed supportive friendships with Margaret Wind, widow of the art

---

[20] 'Reinventing an Epic Poet: 1952 in Context', 64.
[21] Evelyn S. Procter, *Curia and Cortes in León and Castile, 1072–1295* (Cambridge: Cambridge University Press, 1980).

historian Edgar whose flat in Belsyre Court outdid his own for opulence, and also Joan Hodcroft, the wife of one of his first appointees who together with her Fred for many years hosted congenial roast dinners in Kidlington every other Sunday. [22] All of these women satisfied an intellectual and emotional curiosity in later life he had not previously entertained — not at any rate before the death of his mother. Half a century on he even had chortling memories of Ruth Lee Kennedy, she of the incessant prattle and drenched pate, remembered now as 'the oldest of us all'. [23] Still, Russell's relations with women were never, in his mind at least, free of complication.

As it was, Russell had by now savoured discrimination himself, albeit of quite a different kind: ageism. In 1987 the University passed a statute barring those reaching seventy-five from membership of the Faculty of Medieval and Modern Languages or use of its facilities including the lending library of the Taylor Institution. Sure enough, two weeks before his seventy-fifth birthday in October 1988 Russell, emeritus professor, was sent a curt letter to that effect by the Modern Languages Board. [24] The closing lines ran as follows: 'I would very much like to take this opportunity, if I may, to thank you most sincerely for your help and advice over the years. We do wish you well.' So ended nearly sixty years' formal membership of the University and Russell's indignation is to be imagined. Eleven years later in 1999 the Modern Languages Board, 'well aware of the not insignificant contribution made to the life of the faculty by many retired colleagues', was back offering to restore his status in the context of the latest government Research Assessment Exercise which made funding partially dependent on the published output of faculty members. [25] Russell obliged with much of the scholarly fruit of his retirement but it was one of the episodes that taught him how much academia had altered both culturally and from an organisational perspective. A foretaste of this had been provided in 1985 when Congregation had handily voted down a motion to award Somerville graduate Margaret Thatcher an honorary degree, a decision his pragmatic side regarded as 'absolutely stupid'. This same evolution prompted him in his last years to assess the institutional structure of British Hispanic Studies to which he had fallen heir and helped build in his turn. Looking back, Russell could even give the pioneering figure of Edgar Allison Peers due recognition, recognising him

---

[22] Xon de Ros, notes to the author, 16 Sept. 2020.
[23] Kennedy, born in Texas in 1895, died in 1988 at the age of ninety-two.
[24] G. P. V. Collyer to PER, Oxford, 7 Oct. 1988.
[25] P. D. Gambles to PER, Oxford, 4 Nov. 1999.

as 'not my kind of man at all' but nonetheless 'responsible for getting Spanish going as an academic subject', an entrepreneur who not only knew how to importune university vice chancellors to set up departments but also understood that teaching had to be promoted in schools to generate a flow of students. [26] 'Quite a good scholar', he ventured, 'a comic figure but also a serious figure', one whose legacy Russell unexpectedly found himself able to defend in words if not in print.

This brings us in connection with the autobiography he never thought to write to Russell's characteristically ambivalent view of his own scholarly achievement. The accomplishment both professional and intellectual was and is real enough but as time passed and academic life changed his innate scepticism turned into a form of encompassing pessimism admitting little consolation, one given expression by the Golden Age writer with whom he most identified in old age, Baltasar Gracián:

> One's mature years are destined for contemplation, which thereby imparts that strength to the soul as is lost by the body, tipping the scales in the upper part with what is depleted in the lower. Quite a different complexion on things results as old age adds interest to discourse and relationships. [...] This philosophy is nothing other than meditation on death, one needing to be meditated on many times beforehand in order for it to be employed correctly just once thereafter. [27]

The dimensions of this pessimism where literary criticism was concerned have already been touched on, and as there the origins lay in the distant past. In July 1937 he offered this psychoanalysis of his chosen path as a scholar:

> The unfortunate consequences of the academic existence are that one ceases to have any firm convictions but adopts a series of varying and opposed points of view to experiment intellectually and emotionally with them. Thus I feel sometimes that I suffer from a hopeless intellectual and spiritual sickness, the source of which seems to be this. [28]

---

[26] RSSR.
[27] *El Discreto, Realce* 25. My translation.
[28] Journal, 26 July 1937.

'I wonder' he mused in February 1948 'if all this intellectual business is not really taking time off from living [...] but the irrational is vastly more exciting than intellectualism which has no purpose.' [29] These sentiments were as he suspected consistent with the depression to which he was prone and which later brought him to his knees, but towards the end of his life they assumed a more generalised form. In 1993 an invitation by Professor Dorothy Severin of the University of Liverpool to contribute to a volume in memory of Peers himself received this facetious response:

> I was also tempted for a moment to offer an article asking why not just non-Spanish Hispanists but all non-national university specialists in foreign languages and literatures never ask themselves in public how or why they justify their existence but, on reflection, I decided I did not want to let that particular cat loose from the safety of retirement! [30]

In support of this proposition and others like it Russell would privately reel off some dispiriting statistic he had picked up concerning how infrequently scholarly articles in the humanities were read, the implication being that such an outcome hardly warranted the effort or the clamour. Although this may have reflected his impression that academic life had become more self-justifying and self-involved than was good for it along with his inveterate tendency to question the accepted state of things, as usual it drew on something far deeper as he contemplated his personal legacy: an abiding regret at the early demise of his literary aspirations, the sense of himself as having fallen on the nether side of the Shavian dictum that 'those who can, do; those who can't, teach'. In this, however, Russell received solace from an unexpected quarter. During his tenure as a *lector* in Spanish at Oxford from 1983 to 1985 the novelist Javier Marías had come under Russell's spell and proceeded to write him into a succession of novels set in or partly in Oxford, beginning with *Todas las almas* (1989) and then *Negra*

---

[29] Journal, 4 Feb. 1948.
[30] Oxford, 5 June 1993. Russell eventually contributed an article on Vegetius's *Epitoma rei militaris*. He elaborated on his reservations on scholarly output in a letter to Javier Marías: 'I, too, have long realized that Rylands's [the character Marías based on him in two of his novels] view that the work of scholars and critics is, not always but usually, condemned to end up *inservible* [unusable] and *a ser olvidado* [be forgotten] is entirely correct and inevitable'; JMA, Oxford, 28 Feb. 2001.

espalda del tiempo (1998). [31] In 1999 Russell accepted the title of 'Duke of Plazatoro' in Marías's inherited imaginary Kingdom of Redonda and thereafter entered into the spirit of its formalities as and when his flagging energy allowed. The following year he agreed to appear in the *Tu rostro mañana* (2002–7) trilogy (of which he became a dedicatee) as Sir Peter Wheeler, the name he had borne until it was changed by deed poll in 1929. [32] Interestingly enough, the suggestion upon Marías's original enquiry was Russell's own, confessing that 'the Peter Russell you know already holds a fictitious card of identity'. [33] Not only that but this circumstance allowed Russell to take an unexpected and on the whole beneficial conspectus of his life in the context of his painful family relationships, on what might have been had no such change been necessary: 'Now I'll find out what happened to that fellow Peter Wheeler, with whom I parted company so very long ago.' [34]

From a purely *biographical* standpoint and leaving aside any artistic embellishment, the information drawn on by Marías in developing the character of Toby Rylands [35] in his first two Oxford novels follows in broad

---

[31] *Todas las almas* (Barcelona: Anagrama, 1989); translated as *All Souls* (London: Harvill, 1989). *Negra espalda del tiempo* (Madrid: Alfaguara, 1998); translated as *Dark Back of Time* (London: Chatto & Windus, 2003).

[32] *Tu rostro mañana* (Madrid: Alfaguara, 2002–7); translated as *Your Face Tomorrow* (London: Chatto & Windus, 2005–9).

[33] JMA, PER to Javier Marías, Oxford, 4 Sept. 2000. Marías had in fact included Russell's biographical information in *Negra espalda del tiempo*, 38–9, gleaned from his entry in *Who's Who* (London: A. & C. Black, 1997), 1707.

[34] Javier Marías, 'Como un caballero bueno', *El País*, 23 July 2006. Russell made this reflection in correspondence with Marías: 'As is the norm in old age my childhood and early adolescent memories of the time when my acoustic label was "Wheeler" have become more accessible than they were so, in a way, there may in the end be three of me competing for recognition. Bring on Wittgenstein!'; JMA, Oxford, 1 May 2001. Peter Wheeler reappears in *Berta Isla* (Madrid: Alfaguara, 2017) and in his last work *Tomás Nevinson* (Madrid: Alfaguara, 2021). Friendship aside, Marías drew a connection between Russell and his father the philosopher Julián Marías (1914–2005) whom Russell had received in Oxford to give a lecture at the Taylor Institution in March 1962.

[35] Marías took the name from the avuncular figure of Toby in Laurence Sterne's *Tristram Shandy* for which he had produced the first translation into Spanish in 1978. Russell later explained to him the wider and less fortunate cultural connotations of the name to Marías: 'As on a previous occasion [i.e. in *Todas las almas*] I felt sorry for the poor devil who had to spend his novelistic existence linked to the name "Toby", a word that always makes me think of the mistreated dog in *Punch and Judy* or the disagreeable knight in *Twelfth Night*, one that is also

outline those allusions to his life, career and involvement in secret intelligence Russell began sharing with his friends late in life and as subsequently exchanged between them, supported by his entry in *Who's Who*. [36] For *Tu rostro mañana*, however, Russell supplied additional information on his wartime activities at Marías's request, albeit explicitly within the strictures of the Official Secrets Act. [37] This was augmented from 2006 by obituary information on which Marías drew heavily in the concluding volume in the trilogy, *Veneno y sombra y adiós* (2007). [38] That Russell disclosed little of his family history and nothing of his private life as set down in his most intimate writings can be inferred from an exchange of letters with Marías in September 2002. In it he declared without further elaboration that his mother Rita had divorced his father in the early 1920s for 'John Galsworthy sort of reasons'. [39] Russell was referring to John

---

linked to those little Toby jugs used by English tavern drinkers in the 18th century' (my translation); JMA, Oxford, 3 June 1998.

[36] The main factually based descriptions of Russell as Rylands in the English translations of Marías's books are in *All Souls*, 127–44, and *Dark Back of Time*, 31–46.

[37] JMA, PER to Marías, Oxford, 4 June 2002. The information Russell provided Marías, which was mainly of a geographical rather than an operational nature, equates to that he included in the four-page account of his life up to 1953 'for necrological use' he deposited with the British Academy in November 1992 (cited herein as PELR). Marías explained the context of the trilogy in an interview given in October 2007: 'Although novels do not embrace everything that reality embraces, reality *does* embrace everything, including the strangest and most absurd coincidences of a kind one would not credit in a novel. It is a fact that Sir Peter Russell was a British spy during the Second World War, and I obtained information about how those secret services operated from him and from other colleagues. It was a useful dimension for the novel. They lent me part of their biographies which I converted into fiction, and now they too are fiction. The strange thing is that many people regard as true much that is not. I remain silent as it's not necessary for the scaffolding to be revealed'; <javiermarias.es/main.html> 'Entrevistas 1' (my translation).

[38] News of Russell's death in June 2006 reached Marías when he had completed approximately 120 of the 700 pages of *Veneno y sombra y adiós* (Madrid: Alfaguara, 2007); translated as *Poison, Shadow and Farewell* (London: Chatto & Windus, 2009); see particularly 496–8. The obituaries published immediately were: Alan Deyermond, 'Professor Sir Peter Russell', *The Independent*, 5 July 2006; Jeremy Lawrance, 'Professor Sir Peter Russell', *The Daily Telegraph*, 10 July 2006; Bruce Taylor, 'Professor Sir Peter Russell' (abridged) in *The Times*, 14 July 2006; Nigel Griffin, 'Sir Peter Russell', *The Guardian*, 22 Aug. 2006; Ian Michael, 'Sir Peter Russell (1913–2006)', *Bulletin of Spanish Studies* 83 (2006), 1133–44; and John Rutherford, 'Peter Edward Lionel Russell', *The Queen's College Record* (2006), 91–4.

[39] JMA, PER to Marías, Oxford, 6 Sept. 2002.

Gawsworthy [*sic*], the character Marías depicts in *Todas las almas* and *Negra espalda del tiempo* as a thrice-married alcoholic poet, itself derived from a fixture of the London Bohemian scene, Terence Ian Fytton Armstrong, alias John Gawsworth (1912–70). [40] The fact that Bernard Wheeler — the feckless shellshocked abuser of his progeny — not only bore no relation to the fictitious Gawsworthy but was a far more destructive individual explains the evasion, a revisiting of the past of a kind Russell avoided except on very rare occasions at Belsyre Court. Even so, Russell came to recognise his characterisation as the literary immortality to which in a different guise he had first aspired seventy years earlier. Unable to make a career of fiction he had become fiction himself and in doing so had the uncovenanted benefit of slipping some of the bonds of his carefully guarded privacy in the context of another's art, 'an unexpected kind of Resurrection'. [41]

*

From the 1980s Russell gave the impression of a scholar enjoying a physically and intellectually active retirement, a wealthy *bon vivant* observing the world and its doings with a measure of detachment and amusement from the comfortable surroundings of Belsyre Court. Although he remained preternaturally incapable of anything resembling handiness, losing his motor skills the moment he was confronted by any task of dexterity and giving up immediately, he was an effective cook with a repertoire of dishes produced with high proportions of first-class ingredients: salmon kedgeree, a beef and vegetable 'soup' more nearly a stew, grilled turbot, an old-style English curry, all meat, and very occasionally *canard à l'orange*. The staples in his kitchen, which preserved its 1950s décor and fittings quite intact, were smoked salmon and pâté bought on standing order from a delicatessen in Summertown and taken on malted bread. Breakfast unfailingly consisted of coffee prepared in a Bialetti percolator cut with warmed milk and drunk over *The Times*, though with less enthusiasm after the latter moved to a tabloid format in 2004. In the evening he took a gin or vermouth and tonic and much enjoyed champagne, particularly Lindauer from New Zealand, assisted always by a range of expensive nibbles. A bar of chocolate was kept near the front door, nagged at in private. The day closed with what he asserted to be one of his favourite exercises: washing up.

---

[40] See <www.javiermarias.es/REDONDIANA/JohnGawsworth.html>.
[41] JMA, PER to Marías, Oxford, 4 Sept. 2000.

Russell engaged in therapeutic painting in the Canaries, c. 1955.

This opulent yet measured existence was interspersed by the foreign travel which was his chief recreation. He remained a frequent visitor to Spain and Portugal, but beginning in the 1960s the cruises in European waters and to the Atlantic islands gave way to visits by sea to Jamaica while Charles Kennedy held the Chair of Economics at the University of the West Indies, venues for him to pursue a therapeutic interest in painting and cine film. Then with the advent of the jetliner came a series of round-the-world journeys with New Zealand always on the itinerary. Leisure aside, these lengthy excursions capture the extent to which Russell remained a traveller in his mind and in his writings as much as in his person, always seeking new experiences, always observing, comparing, analysing and absorbing the development of the culture in which he had been allotted to live. The constant mental renewal and depth it afforded him as an individual and as a scholar in light of his own experiences and convictions is a defining quality of his work as of his life since his earliest years. Nor in the same context were opportunities lost to deliver a lecture, a paper on *Don Quixote* at La Trobe University in Melbourne being intercalated with a personal trip to Australia and New Zealand in April 1985. As always, and even for a man who had long since ceased to be under any great misapprehension as to himself or those about him, the benefit of these solitary journeyings was that they allowed the focus of his relentless observation to be trained anew on himself. The emotions ranged from amusement to self-deprecation. Reaching Kingston during one of his many trips to Jamaica in the 1960s Russell found himself received on the quay with guard and band, the local authorities expecting King Alfonso XIII rather than the holder of his namesake chair. [42] In Gran Canaria in the '90s a scholarly paper on *Celestina* was as the result of a misconnected cable boomed out to the good people of Las Palmas on a public address system. At other times he felt burdened by his reputation and the synthetic responses it occasionally induced in others. 'I really don't like it when they are so fulsome about my work when it hasn't been good' he noted after lecturing as a guest of the Portuguese government in November 1959, and well-intentioned efforts at praise would always be received with polite forbearance. [43] Equally, although always ready to venture scholarly criticism in print, Russell was much too retiring to stir up administrative trouble in the manner of a Trevor-Roper or a Raymond Carr even if he appreciated their capacity to give themselves the indulgence and the skill with which they did so. [44] Nor by extension did he relish competition, and much as he admired the gifts of his academic peers and the many distinguished people who crossed the threshold of Belsyre Court or with whom he otherwise came into contact, his carefully chosen circle of friends contained no figures of his own stature.

By the 1980s the décor of that residence, fruit of his post-war acquisitions and inheritance from his mother, had assumed its final form, the past affirmed by a repainting in the same light shade of duck egg green. Many of these furnishings were not only fixtures at Belsyre Court but in their way part of the experience of being with him there. Hanging over the sitting room mantlepiece was no painting but a convex mirror which, as in Van Eyck's *Arnolfini Wedding*, lent dual focus to the room and its occupants whom it always reflected. Beneath it on the mantle sat a torsion pendulum clock under a cloche flanked by items of jade purchased in Singapore in 1945 along with a slow rotation of postcards from his friends. To the side was a large Hispano-Moresque dish decorated with fish in a reddish lustre, a gift from his mother, along with one or two items of fine Chinese porcelain, a taste acquired from Kolkhorst. Most arresting in the home of a confirmed atheist was the large Flemish fifteenth-century polychrome statue of St Barbara with her tower

---

[42] I am grateful to Jeremy Lawrance for this memory, and to Ronald Truman for that which follows it.

[43] Journal, 7 Nov. 1959.

[44] The only notable administrative intervention is the resolution proposed for submission to Congregation concerning the lack of secretarial assistance of which Russell was a signatory in 1969.

which stood ward on a low book-lined partition between the sitting and dining rooms. Facing Russell under the main window looking towards Oxford lay one of the two deep sofas with which the room was furnished and where his guests invariably sat, Persian rugs underfoot. Behind his winged chair stood the glass cabinet filled with the rare book collection which framed any conversation with him at Belsyre Court. At his right hand was a campaign table with his ever-present university pocket diary, lighter, cigarettes and the phone. The ashtray rested on a side table and between you and he lay, electronics apart, the only concession to modern design in the entire property, a spare coffee table in chrome and plate glass. Ranged upon it were items carefully selected to be of interest to the visitor. This was the unwavering *mise en scène* for any engagement with Peter Russell, an indication of the physical and mental preparation of which one would be the beneficiary, so much so that overeager guests would sometimes be asked to walk around the block if they presented themselves much before the appointed hour.

'*I really don't like it when they are so fulsome about my work when it hasn't been good.*' Russell and the archaeologist Lt-Col Afonso do Paço at a conference in Portugal, November 1959.

Where Russell's appearance is concerned, one can do no better than cite the descriptions by which Javier Marías introduces the character of Professor Toby Rylands in *Todas las almas*, albeit with a degree of artistic licence:

He was a very big man, truly enormous, who had kept all his hair, wavy and white — a sort of bavaroise — on his statue-like head, and was always well dressed [...] The most impressive feature was his fissured eyes, each a different colour: his right eye of an oily hue and his left that of pale ashes, so that if you looked at him from the right he wore a keen expression not lacking in cruelty — the eye of an eagle or perhaps of a cat — while if you looked at him from the left the expression was grave, meditative and honest as only that of the northern peoples can be — the eye of a dog or perhaps a horse, which of all animals seem the most honest; and if you looked at him from the front then you encountered two gazes, though not with two colours so much as a single gaze which was simultaneously cruel and honest, meditative and keen. From a distance the oil-coloured eye predominated (assimilating the other) and when on Sunday mornings the sun shone into his eyes so as to illuminate them the density of the iris dissolved and the tone lightened to that of the sherry in the glass he sometimes had in his hands. As for his laugh, that was the most diabolical thing about Toby Rylands: his mouth scarcely moved, only just enough — horizontally — so that beneath the purplish and fleshy upper lip a row of small slightly pointed but very straight teeth appeared, perhaps a good imitation by a well-paid dentist of the set of which age had deprived him. But what was most demonic about that short, dry laugh was not its aspect but its sound which bore no relationship to the standard written onomatopoeia [...] but was in his case undeniably plosive, a very clear alveolar *t*, as the English *t* is. *Ta-ta-ta*: that was Professor Toby Rylands' spine-chilling laugh. *Ta-ta-ta. Ta-ta-ta.* [45]

It was one of the passages Russell selected for reading at his memorial service. Direct observation yielded a similar picture. Here is José Luis Giménez-Frontín's memory of Russell in 1994, a decade or so after seeing him at the end of his professorial tenure and removed on this occasion from the sanctuary of Belsyre Court:

> Though he must now be around eighty, Peter Russell has not aged particularly as he already had that leonine and stolid aspect at the time

---

[45] *Todas las almas* (Barcelona: Anagrama, 1989); 2nd ed. (1998), 184–7; my translation. Russell's passports, some of which date from a time when bearers could fill in their own personal information, always describe his eyes as grey and his height as 6 ft 1 in. The earlier ones record his hair as brown or dark brown, the later ones grey.

of his retirement, the same opaque gaze, sometimes scarcely bearable, the same rictus as if restraining himself from issuing a judgment. But he now looks more serious or weary and not once that evening does he issue any of those inimitable guffaws of his in which he seems not so much to inhale as aspirate gusts of air. [...] I now notice the conversational silences with Russell to be longer than they used to be, and have the impression that the ex-chair, now emeritus professor, seems not so much bemused as disgruntled at the changes to his immediate environment, which he takes personally like the ravages of age. Or perhaps it's the opposite. He floats over the occasion like the palpable veil of a certain apathy that impregnates this gathering of whispered voices. [46]

This brings us to what for anyone who knew him was Peter Russell's greatest gift, his command of the art of communication in its fullest sense, and to spend time in his company was to witness a subtle concert of gestures and motions which conveyed more than words ever could. His usual attitude was to sit with his legs crossed, and in his right hand was (until he gave up smoking in the late '90s) the essential prop of any conversation, a lighted cigarette. His presence was never more immense at such times, the imposing figure unbent by age, the huge lion-like head and inscrutable eyes, the person from whom not a word or thought was wasted when things really mattered. The usual coded response in ordinary discourse was 'I see', which under certain circumstances would become a refrain that unerringly directed his guest's words back onto them in a sort of devastating counterpoint. Conversation with him was in this way an appeal to one's better and more intelligent self — or to the dictates of the patently obvious — invariably delivered in the form not of any lengthy statement but of a brief utterance or perfect silence. When being told something of consequence his left hand would come up to his mouth in rapt attention, a sign that every faculty was engaged. Information of a regrettable nature would be greeted with a prolonged sympathetic grimace or a commiserating grunt issued through the set of his jaw, all punctuated by long draws on his cigarette or disposal of the ashes. If the moment came to make a really telling point he would slowly uncross his legs, bring his knees together, rest his hands on his thighs and deliver, the nearest he ever came to imploring anyone.

---

[46] *Woodstock Road en julio*, 60 & 63–4; my translation. Russell was also the inspiration for the character of an Oxford tutor in Giménez-Frontín's novel *Señorear la tierra* (Barcelona: Seix Barral, 1991), 151–2.

When peeved for whatever reason he would bring his left arm up to rest against the wing of his chair, but he had long since learnt to master his impatience with those who failed to draw the obvious conclusion or proved stubborn in the face of reasonable persuasion. His remained the way of suggestion not instruction, and this was as true in his friendships as it had been in his teaching and his management style. Russell took it all in his stride, always master of the situation, always a model of self-control, never losing his composure, never putting himself in a position in which that composure could be lost.

En palacio. *Peter Russell at Belsyre Court,* c. *1995.*

There was of course much more to this than the application of a honed technique with its mastery of silence and stillness. It drew on his intellect, humanity and experience sure enough, but was foregrounded by the indefeasible integrity of the man, something rock-like in his personality around which all else flowed. He had a deep-seated loathing of coarseness and abuse in all its forms and a memory to match, a visit to Belfast in 1969 marred by the sight of some Ulster dockers ramming a tin can over a kitten's head and enjoying the spectacle of it thrash itself into the harbour. Then there was the case of extortion at the hands of a Gibraltar taxidriver in 1959. Both incidents were sufficient to decide him as to the merit of their respective territorial interests. As in his research he had no time for humbug of any sort — 'bogus' was a word that fell often from his lips — but there was no more humane way of being disabused of error or having one's mind expanded than at his hands. He also knew exactly when to apply the balm of humour if one's crest had fallen or threatened to, either the gentle half-interrogative, half-exclamatory 'w'hot, w'hot?' chortle now falling out of usage, or a conspiratorial 'nyah-nyah-nyah' or else Marías's full-blown 'ta-ta-ta'. The scholar who had written '*Don Quixote* as a Funny Book' was also an extremely amusing man with a rich fund of memories and a capacity to laugh in the face of adversity and the parade of human folly and frailty which came before him, including his own. Exposure to his penetrating wit was in its way to be paid his highest compliment, the sense that you had both shared a facet in the absurdity of life he came to regard as its ruling characteristic. 'Fantastic' he'd say, using the term in its descriptive rather than exclamatory sense, slouched somewhat now with legs extended and crossed at the ankles, left hand clutching the wing of his chair, cigarette at high port on the right or, latterly, fingering the rim of his glass or resting on his stomach. Nor were any who crossed him likely to forget it, cut down with a smart rebuke or a few words of feigned encouragement. One might josh him slightly, even tease him, but anything that showed the least sign of disrespect would be snuffed out immediately, head set and body stiffened. Steady, constant and solicitous friendship there might be on both sides but matiness was no part of the arrangement, any more than he was one for easy conviviality in Giménez-Frontín's large groups. When it was time for one to go Russell would wait for you to look his way and then shoot a glance at the clock with a flicker of a smile, the cigarette stubbed out with finality or glass pushed away. The ability of his guests to read these cues was essential to the progression of the relationship beyond what would otherwise be one of politeness or sufferance, the kind of situation in which someone was found 'impervious to the reluctance with which his company was kept'. [47] Those on the other hand who had come far to visit might look up from the courtyard of Belsyre Court on taking their leave to see him standing massive at the window of No. 23 and exchange a wave. More than any detail or aggregation of his career or accomplishments, it was from this physical and intellectual solidity, product of a lifetime's observation and introspection, that Marías and so many others drew inspiration. Had they but known the inner torment out of which it was fashioned.

---

[47] Journal, 28 Sept. 1948.

Much as he had a circle of friends and helpers, it is also true that Russell's native reserve bordering on shyness, his formidable presence and reputation and the image he cultivated and allowed to be cultivated of himself resulted in an increasingly lonely retirement. The reason was that it was difficult even for his closest friends to square the solidity and achievement with the extremely fragile personality that lay behind it, so closely had he kept his privacy. This outcome as Colin Thompson recalled had like so much else in his life been prefigured: 'Shortly before he retired [in 1981], Peter confessed to me that he was worried that people would begin to forget him when he was no longer in post, worried that people respected him for the office he held rather than admired and loved him for the man he was.' [48] The respect, admiration and love never waned but it became harder and harder for him to ask for the assistance he increasingly needed which despite his physical decline was less of a practical than of an emotional kind. With Peter Russell there was always another layer, another dimension, suspected, detectable even, but never disclosed. Encounters with friends at Belsyre Court in this way not only provided blessed relief from the loneliness and depression that flooded back in his final years but also satisfaction of a deep-seated need of his own always to be in control, to be the focus of attention and recognition on *his* terms and in *his* setting, generous and beneficent though they were, and not anyone else's. In 1958 Russell, King Alfonso XIII Professor of Spanish Studies at the University of Oxford, found himself yearning for the untrammelled recognition he had last received at Dane Court, the preparatory school at Parkstone in Dorsetshire he attended for a term at the age of twelve before the desolation of Sedbergh and the frustrations of Cheltenham, the last summer before the onset of those complications destined to govern his emotional life, the place where he was happiest 'because I was accepted there as top-dog' with none to set rolling the kaleidoscope of his agonies. [49] Naturally enough, not everyone accepted the unspoken premise and became a votary of what some then and later identified as a cult of admirers with its formalities, any more than he always welcomed the attention on that ground.

Though his was by choice a solitary calling, Russell's immediate interest outside of his scholarly and literary pursuits was therefore people, their qualities and talents as individuals, what they had to teach him about life and the opportunity they offered him not only to be himself and to curate his image, but to elaborate the ambiguity he prized in his research and wove about his person. In

---

[48] Thompson, 'Address', 265.
[49] Freudian journal, 18 June 1958, 26.

this endeavour Russell, who was never in any doubt as to his powers, had the benefit of a natural charisma and the gift, when in the mood, of being able to hit it off with anyone. Not only that but those found worthy of his interest were apt to reveal themselves anywhere and in any guise. In Lisbon in 1936 he made the sobering acquaintance of the wife of a York doctor 'whose loyalty and affection for a man who has been a chronic gas invalid since the war is wholly admirable'. [50] Returning from the Far East in the troopship *Antenor* in 1946 with a thousand souls embarked, Russell had no hesitation in pronouncing a fourteen-year-old Dutch boy newly released from an internment camp in Sumatra as '[t]he most pleasing character on the ship [...] who has more guts and intelligence than most of the officers'. [51] During a visit to Spain two years later he took the opportunity to drive into the mountains above Valencia, a journey which brought him to the outskirts of a village not far from Segorbe. Here is what he found:

> Young peasant in cart came up road where I was trying to take photograph of village and took me in his cart to what he said was much better view. It was. Wore straw hat and really had dignity and poise. He said a lot of people did not like the *pueblo* and wanted bigger things but he thought it made one happier to stay where one belonged. I almost reduced to tears by this. [52]

This appreciation of honesty and informality and the common touch that went with it was mirrored in facets of his own behaviour, such as the habit recalled by his student and colleague John Rutherford of bringing Spanish scholarly eminences along to Norham Road as he tended his allotment. [53] It would also find its way into his writing, most arrestingly in his rich use of idiom and the colloquial 'got', a *conceptista* reminder of the levelling human experience that underlay everything, whatever the formal lineaments of the context. With this came an extraordinary level of personal generosity. Awarded the inaugural Nebrija Prize by the University of Salamanca in 1989, he responded by endowing a £3000 travelling scholarship for a Spanish postgraduate in the humanities to research in Britain, just one example of decades of munificence to institutions of one kind or another. Then there was his discreet kindness to those of scarcer financial means

---

[50] Journal, 3 Aug. 1936.
[51] Journal, 17 Jan. 1946.
[52] Journal, 18 Sept. 1948.
[53] John D. Rutherford, unpublished address delivered at St Mary's, 28 Oct. 2006.

and there can have been few people he cared for who were not favoured with his largesse in one form or another, often on the least pretext: a carefully chosen gift, a cheque pressed into one's hand, a subsidy to keep the wolf from the door, a new suit to improve one's interview prospects, all in enhancement of the existing relationship. This continued to the end of his life so that his last cleaner, Jayne, scarcely a quarter of his age, received support and encouragement to secure the professional qualification which would take her out of his service and on to better things. Sixty years separated his efforts on her behalf and those for his Tamil servant Sockalingam in wartime Ceylon. The culmination of this side of his personality were the detailed provisions in his will.

In his last years, though much preoccupied with his own mortality, he never lost his sense of humour or boyish glee at the absurdities of life. Asked how he was, he would sometimes reply 'Awaiting a visit from the Reaper', or just 'Surviving', his voice lowered an octave before issuing a guffaw. However, neither his mental faculties nor his flexibility of mind were much impaired by the passage of time. He had the unusual ability to cast aside the tastes and convictions of a lifetime if a better alternative recommended itself. The IT revolution was early and enthusiastically embraced and his home was always filled with the latest gadgets and contrivances which he delighted in showing off, sometimes with alarming results. 'My latest toy is the Internet and email' he wrote in 1997. [54] 'The Internet clearly is a champion new way of wasting time if one lets it loose.' He was addicted to the Antipodean soap operas that began appearing on British television in the 1980s and at the time of his death was plotting the purchase of high-definition TV to watch the World Cup in Germany. To that extent Peter Russell was much the youngest of his circle.

The end when it came on Thursday, 22 June 2006 was merciful and dignified for a man who had harboured the twin fears of disabling illness or lying undiscovered in Belsyre Court, a fate that had overtaken too many of his friends and neighbours over the years. It was possible to trace his final steps that last summer morning. He had collected the paper, made and served himself his breakfast which he had taken to his bedroom on a tray, and it was here, at the venue of many of his most agonising hallucinations, that he died propped up in bed against his pillows. His body was found within a few hours by the caretaker having been alerted by Russell's GP when his phone call went unanswered. As his appointee and friend Eric Southworth later wrote in allusion to Don Quixote, 'like a good knight, Peter died in his bed'. He was ninety-two.

---

[54] PER to Charles Kennedy, Oxford, 23 April 1997.

Russell, who made much of being an atheist while not lacking in Christian virtue, had long wanted to be laid to rest without any formality. Having cited them in a review article in 1975 he no doubt had Garcilaso de la Vega's instructions on the disposal of his remains in mind where this was concerned: [55]

> Entiérrenme en San Pedro Mártil, en la capilla de mis agüelas, y si muriere pasado la mar, déxenme donde me enterraron. No conbiden a nadie para mis honrras ni aya sermón en ellas.
> Bury me in St Peter Martyr's church [in Toledo], in my grandparents' chapel, and should I die oversea leave me where they bury me. Invite none to my exequies and let no sermon be preached at them.

However, the funeral of the Spanish Sub-Faculty librarian Archie Seldon in 1985, a joyless secular affair held at Oxford Crematorium to an unshepherded band of mourners, persuaded him of the comfort offered by the familiar Anglican funeral service. [56] He therefore left clear instructions for a memorial service which after a private ceremony in Exeter College chapel on 4 July was held at St Mary's in Oxford on 28 October 2006, arrangements that were nearer the death preparations of Prince Henry on which Russell had published in 1992 than those of Garcilaso the soldier. [57] By the time of the autumn memorial service his ashes had been scattered on his mother's grave in the churchyard of St Mary's, Charlbury where he had interred hers thirty years earlier. In 1933 Russell had added these lines from Swinburne as an epigraph to his unfinished novel *The Woven Raiment* and no more appropriate committal can be found for him:

> I will go back to the great sweet mother,
> Mother and lover of men, the sea.
> I will go down to her, I and none other,
> Close with her, kiss her, and mix her with me.
> Cling to her, strive with her, hold her fast:

---

[55] Review of Stephen Gilman, *The Spain of Fernando de Rojas: The Intellectual and Social Landscape of 'La Celestina'* (Princeton, N.J.: Princeton University Press, 1972) in *Comparative Literature* 27 (1975), 63. My translation.
[56] I am grateful to another attendee at Seldon's funeral, Nigel Griffin, for his memories of the occasion.
[57] 'Prince Henry and the Necessary End' in *Studies in the Portuguese Discoveries*, ed. T. F. Earle & Stephen Parkinson (Warminster, Wilts.: Aris and Phillips, 1992), I, 1–15.

> O fair white mother, in days long past
> Born without sister, born without brother,
> Set free my soul as thy soul is free. [58]

So it was that Russell, dying, went not to his fathers but to his mother.

To know Peter Russell, to sit with him at Belsyre Court as he gazed southward to Carfax musing on the events and emotions of a lifetime, was to be admitted to a world — many worlds — to which one could otherwise never have gained access. Whether they were of his uncovering such as the Portuguese Atlantic or of his own experience such as wartime counterespionage, those who shared them always understood that something special was being vouchsafed, just as they appreciated the innate depth and elegance in which they were lived and revealed. To those who knew him in Oxford and elsewhere his passing marked the close of an era richer and more refined than their own.

---

[58] 'The Triumph of Time', ll. 257–64.

APPENDIX I
Stephen Gilman and the Valle Lersundi Archive

Aside from his fraught though evidently one-sided relationship with Ramón Menéndez Pidal, the only scholarly dispute of note in Russell's career was that carried on (albeit separated by an interval of eighteen years) with Stephen Gilman of Harvard University in connection with that author's two volumes on the *Celestina*: *The Art of 'La Celestina'* (1957) and *The Spain of Fernando de Rojas* (1972). [a] The exchange, which reached a climax in September 1975, is interesting not only as an expression of the divergent approaches to the work by two of the leading *Celestina* scholars of the time but also for the light it sheds on the collection of thirteen manuscripts concerning Fernando de Rojas (including his will) long held at Deva (Guipúzcoa) in the archives of his descendants, the Valle Lersundi family.

The opening salvo in the exchange was fired by Russell in the hostile review article of Gilman's 1957 volume he published in the *Bulletin of Hispanic Studies* that same year. [b] Although Gilman left this unanswered, note was taken of a number of Russell's aspersions and solecisms for use at the appropriate moment. That opportunity came in 1975 after Russell published another and even more damning review of Gilman's 1972 volume on the subject in *Comparative Literature*. [c] In the intervening period Gilman had had the mortifying experience of being given access to and then restricted in his use of the trove of Rojas documents in the care of Fernando del Valle Lersundi (1881–1970) which he ultimately employed in his work but could not cite. The context for this turn of events rested on Lersundi's decision in 1962 to sell the archive in Britain using the Oxford branch of the prominent book and manuscript dealer A. Rosenthal as his

---

[a] Stephen Gilman, *The Art of 'La Celestina'* (Madison, Wis.: University of Wisconsin Press, 1957) and *The Spain of Fernando de Rojas: The Intellectual and Social Landscape of* La Celestina (Princeton, N.J.: Princeton University Press, 1972).
[b] 'The Art of Fernando de Rojas', *Bulletin of Hispanic Studies* 34 (1957), 160–7.
[c] Untitled review article in *Comparative Literature* 27 (1975), 59–74. Russell's assessment was, however, restrained by comparison with that published by Keith Whinnom in *Bulletin of Hispanic Studies* 52 (1975), 158–61.

agent, the business then operated by Maurice Ettinghausen from premises on Broad Street. [d] The rationale asserted by Lersundi and Ettinghausen for barring Gilman from making his citations — that this would reduce the likelihood of the collection being acquired by a public library — more nearly equates to the improved prospect of its being bought by a private collector. It has also been suggested that Lersundi, whose sympathies were to the Right, may have been influenced in his decision by the fact that Gilman had married into the family of the poet Jorge Guillén, who had been a *lector* at Oxford from 1929–31 but was then living in exile in the United States. [e] Whatever the case, this inept and quite probably illegal effort to dispose of a segment of Spain's national heritage abroad was also part of a desperate attempt by Lersundi to shore up the family finances, and it was under these circumstances that Russell found himself handling the documents in Oxford in 1962. [f] As revealed in the covering letter he enclosed with his typescript reply to Russell's 1975 review, Gilman had long since formed the impression that the latter was behind an attempt to deny him unfettered use of these documents by purchasing them for what in 1962 was the hefty sum of £10,000 (£175,000 in 2024). Gilman reports having reached this conclusion on the basis of information given to him by unnamed British scholars attending a congress in Mexico City, while himself admitting to an unsuccessful approach to the Houghton Library at Harvard with a view to purchase. [g] It is not known whether the letter Russell sent Gilman by way of response in September 1975 (see below) disabused him of that belief, but he nonetheless published a reply to Russell's review in *Nueva Revista de Filología Española* in 1977 which expands considerably on the 'Reply' printed below while making no explicit mention of

---

[d] The information contained in this appendix corrects the chronology of events offered in Ian Michael's 'Sir Peter Russell (1913–2006)', *Bulletin of Spanish Studies* 83 (2006), 1133–44; at 1139–40.

[e] I am grateful to Prof. Gilman's son Antonio for the suggestion.

[f] Russell recounted this incident in one of his final articles, 'The *Celestina* Then and Now', *Context, Meaning and Reception of 'Celestina': A Fifth Centenary Symposium*, ed. Ian Michael & David G. Pattison [= *Bulletin of Hispanic Studies* (Glasgow) 78.1] (2001), 1–11; at 2–3.

[g] Although Gilman gives a date of 1967, the occasion was presumably the third congress of the International Association of Hispanists held in Mexico City in August 1968 at which he gave a plenary paper. The only British scholars mentioned in the *acta* at least are Alan Deyermond, Peter Dunn (then at SUNY Rochester), Robert Pring-Mill, Donald Shaw and Brian Tate; *Actas del Tercer Congreso Internacional de Hispanistas, celebrado en México, D. F., del 26 al 31 de agosto de 1968*, ed. Carlos H. Magis (Mexico City: Colegio de México, 1970).

the Oxford affair. [h]

In closing, one may speculate whether Russell might not have taken more trouble to alert Gilman of the appearance of the Lersundi documents in Oxford in 1962 had a greater degree of scholarly sympathy existed between them. As it was, Russell went on to include an expanded version of the 1975 review article in the collection of essays he published in Barcelona three years later, and it must be supposed that the amplified critique to be found there, beginning with the title, to some considerable degree reflects his indignation at the claim that he had played what he describes in his correspondence as 'both an active and despicable role in this affair'. [i] Whatever the case, the Rojas documents were still in the possession of the Lersundi family in 1992 and were last on display in Talavera de la Reina in 1999, the town in La Mancha where Rojas spent the second half of his life and of which he was several times *alcalde mayor* before his death in 1541. [j] At the time of writing they apparently remain unavailable for consultation by scholars in any form. Stephen Gilman died in 1986.

*

Note on the sources

The documents reproduced below were found among Russell's papers following his death in 2006. Beyond silent correction of a few spelling errors, the omission of some minor erasures and the resolving of two journal titles, they are printed in their entirety as they appear in the original typescripts, including the numbered notes to Gilman's reply; this editor's footnotes are included alphabetically.

[typescript, 6 pp.]
A Reply to P. E. Russell
Two fundamental misconceptions in Professor Russell's "review-article" of <u>The Spain of Fernando de Rojas</u> [1] should be corrected. The first (and by far the more important) has to do with the way he understands the relationship of <u>La Celestina</u> to its author. Russell begins by stating that, after the introduction of printing as

---

[h] 'Sobre la identidad histórica de Fernando de Rojas: (Contestación al Profesor Peter Russell)', *Nueva Revista de Filología Hispánica* 26 (1977), no. 1, 154–8.

[i] 'Un crítico en busca de un autor: reflexiones en torno a un reciente libro sobre Fernando de Rojas', *Temas de* La Celestina *y otros estudios del* Cid *al* Quijote (Barcelona: Ariel, 1978), 343–75.

[j] Inés Valverde Azula, 'Documentos referentes a Fernando de Rojas en el Archivo Municipal de Talavera de la Reina', *Celestinesca* 16.2 (1992), 81–104.

well as before, "authors who wrote literature of entertainment could ... proceed on the assumption that the generality of their readers would not start looking for the mind behind the work." [2] And he closes by hoping that the bad example of my book will bring "to a conclusion the excessive concern of critics to pursue the elusive authors of La Celestina and will cause them instead to get on with the task of solving the many literary and linguistic problems which the text they wrote still presents." [3] Now, granting that there are many kinds of works of literature — for example, printed romances and oral ballads or folktales — which do not "need" an author (whether real or imaginary) and which may not even have an author, I still would ask: can such authorial evanescence be applied to Rojas, reading in person to "diez personas [que] se juntaren a oir esta comedia" and explicitly concerning himself with their varied reactions?

In other words, to read La Celestina as generically authorless and to dismiss communication with Rojas as Romantic eccentricity amounts to a denial of the work's built-in irony. Which is to say, Rojas' irony, the irony of an ironist searching for our complicity. We must look for him, simply because he is looking for us. In another "review article" attacking an earlier book of mine (the reader can be grateful that we're not immortal!), Professor Russell criticized my failure to perceive the "humor of La Celestina".[4] The objection puzzled me at the time, but, now, his use of the phrase, "literature of entertainment" leads to the suspicion that he reads the 21 acts as a kind of authorless mock tragedy, perhaps comparable to such an authorless mock epic as Renard the Fox.

I would certainly not frown on the laughter of Celestina-readers — whether those of the past or those in my classes — for I should have to begin by silencing my own. The real question is: does Professor Russell get the point of the joke? Does he realize — to offer a comparable example — that, though there is much to laugh at in the first part of the Divine Comedy, the comedians are all in Hell? We shall have "to wait sitting down" (as they say in Spanish) for him to publish a book giving a definitive answer. But, on the basis of available evidence, it would seem that he has not noticed the pitch-blackness of Rojas' humor. Cervantes' famous stricture, " ... si encubriera mas lo humano," indicates that he knew what Rojas was saying, but then Professor Russell is one of those Hispanists who demonstrate their originality by patronizing the Quijote. [5]

In the meantime — and putting to one side the special autobiographical implications of Rojas' irony — it would be interesting to know how far Professor Russell would be willing to go with his virtual denial of meaningful lives to early authors. If he should discover something new about Juan Ruiz, Juan del Encina,

Sem Tob, or Jean de Meung (all of them writers whose works indicate they would be fascinating to meet), would he discard it as insignificant by definition? An even more elementary query might be: why make such a fuss about examining the Valle Lersundi documents [6] (transcriptions of which I am quite willing to make available, if asked politely),[7] if the life they attest to is not worth investigation?

The second misconception has to do with my intention. Professor Russell evidently thinks that I have dared to try to write a conventional biography of Rojas on the basis of half a dozen half-facts, half-guesses which he spends most of his efforts demolishing or trying to demolish. I refer to such speculative excursions as the interpretation of the acrostic, the Mollejas coincidence, the description of Talaveran domesticity, etc. Indeed the review only really succeeds in offending me when it assumes that I am inane enough as to use such admittedly vulnerable conjectures [8] as the foundation for a pointlessly enormous biographical edifice. It would seem that, if it had occurred to Professor Russell to go to Deva, to examine the archives, and to try to see what he could make of them, he would have proceeded in some such fashion. And he probably — and rightly — would have abandoned the project as either impossible or perilous. The biographies of a Rojas or a Shakespeare can at best be surmised.

The point is that Professor Russell — as he would be the first to proclaim — is not and never has been a disciple of Américo Castro. That is to say, he has not been trained to contemplate human life in terms of its dimension of collective consciousness: its "morada vital" or, using Castro's final formulation, its "nosotros." Stated as plainly as possible in our common language, I have tried to envisage Rojas not so much as a <u>self</u> [9] but rather as a <u>member</u>, a member of a region, of a caste, of a class, of a profession, of a family, and of several communities. This is at best the possibility of a biography: how could such a man as the author of <u>La Celestina</u> must have been come to be? It did not, therefore, seem to me unsound or unscholarly to play imaginatively with those secondary possibilities which emerge from hints of selfhood both in the texts and in the documents and which Professor Russell spends so much time quibbling about. In fact I conceived of those sections as a kind of relaxation or reward designed to compensate the reader for the patience I demanded of him.

It is easy to guess that Professor Russell would dismiss contemplation of membership as even more perverse than speculating with potential facts. But at least let him understand what I was trying to do and then face squarely the undeniable actual facts I wanted to have him (and those who share his incredulity) face: there were Castilians who were "conversos" and students and residents of places like the Puebla, Toledo, and Talavera, and some of them became lawyers, money-handlers, and municipal officials, and they lived their lives in characteristic ways under a kind of pressure that was very extreme and very special. All one has to do is go to the archives, learn to decipher the atrocious script, and there they are waiting to be found, all together, side by side.

Professor Russell opens by suggesting that the failure of my book may be in part due [to] the fact that I am a literary scholar unprepared for the role of historian. He is, of course, right, but I am sorry I cannot reverse the order of the stricture in his case. Instead, I fear that an historian capable of reading La Celestina as an anonymous burlesque show ("hilariously funny" sexual scenes) perhaps interspersed with episodes from the Grand Guignol must be an anachronistic historian. Which is to say the kind of historian who fails to recognize that the only importance of the fossil facts he collects and exhibits in his professional museum is their mute testimony to living consciousness in the past: consciousness that is at once like ours and at the same time historically unique.

Stephen Gilman
Harvard University

---

[1] C[omparative] L[iterature], XXVII, 1975, pp. 59–74.
[2] [*Ibid.,*] p. 59.
[3] [*Ibid.,*] p. 74.
[4] "The Art of Fernando de Rojas," B[ulletin of] H[ispanic] S[tudies], XXXIV, 1957, pp. 160–167.
[5] Op. cit., "... the lesson which Cervantes seems to want to teach seems rather Bathetic to the modern reader"; p. 160.
[6] It is ironical that Professor Russell who is so irritated by my showing off (Renaissance "admiratio"?) should characterize as "absurd" and — at least by inference — deceitful my sincerely modest confession of incompetence as a paleographer.
[7] The offer is explicit on page xi of the book under review.
[8] I really do not think that the "condemnation" of Rojas' father by the Inquisition is a conjecture. Most of what we consider to be historically true is based on evidence that is more conjectural.
[9] If I did, I certainly would not confuse him with Alvaro de Montalban as Russell seems to do: "a traumatized, insecure, hypocritical individual." (p. 73) To try to sketch the character of an unknown genius is the height of absurdity, but, judging from many of Rojas' fellows, I would be inclined to keep the last of Russell's three adjectives and to substitute "sardonic" and "prudently self-confident" for the other two.

[typescript, 2 pp.]
[Nerja,] August 12, 1975
Dear Professor Russell:

The enclosed speaks for itself. What remains to be settled privately between us, are the clear implications in your review of some sort of malfeasance on my part in connection with the Valle Lersundi documents. I was tempted to put the whole story in print — perhaps you even intended to provoke me into so doing — but since that would involve the reputation of Valle Lersundi whom I respect and admire in spite of everything, I decided once again to refrain.

To begin with the account given in the Preface — the agreement, the payments, the years of work — is true. What I did not say is that on a later visit to Deva the old gentleman in a state of great embarrassment asked me to abandon the projected article because he hoped to be able to sell parts of the archive to an English collector for a million pesetas. I replied that, if he would retain photocopies from which he could scrutinize, and correct my transcriptions, there was no reason not to go ahead and sell. He agreed.

Then upon my return to this country, Valle Lersundi wrote me saying that the prospective purchaser had heard that I was working on the documents and that he would only be interested in acquiring them if I would abandon the project.

At that point I realized it was not a collector but a colleague attempting to muscle in, as we describe such intervention where I come from, and I refused. I was sorry to deprive the family of much needed capital, but agreements are agreements; two years are a long time professionally; and my prior claim as a scholar first on the ground was clear. Then to make sure that the anonymous and wealthy colleague got the point, I sent Xeroxed copies of what had been done to appropriate Celestinistas. Bear in mind that I had not promised to keep the contents of the documents secret and that Valle Lersundi was well aware that a resumé of my work in progress would be published by the American Council of Learned Societies in its annual report — as in fact it was later. In any case the result was that the sale was not made.

Subsequently I tried to have Houghton Library purchase the documents, but I'm sorry to say that we were unable to come to a satisfactory agreement.

Why am I writing you this elaborate explanation? Because I was informed by British Hispanists in 1967 at the Mexico City meeting that you were the prospective purchaser and that furthermore you accused me "of breaking the spirit of the agreement" with Valle Lersundi by sending out copies and not surrendering to your superior financial resources. Obviously this is hearsay; it may even be malicious gossip; but if there is anything to it, you will understand why I would like to see how you can justify your published remarks.

I might add that this is a private letter which will not be circulated for the reasons given above.
Sincerely
[signed:] *Stephen Gilman*

[photocopy of typescript, 4 pp.]
PERSONAL AND CONFIDENTIAL
23 Belsyre Court,
Woodstock Road,
Oxford.
2 September 1975
Dear Professor Gilman,

Your letter and enclosure posted in Nerja were awaiting me on my return. There has been no sign yet of the original letter and enclosures referred to in the letter you sent me shortly before your departure from America.

Thank you for sending me a copy of your 'Reply'. I naturally expected you would wish to say something about what I had written and I do not think any useful purpose would be served by further argument about a number of questions of principle and method about which, unhappily, we hold such divergent views.

The contents of your letter are quite another matter and will require detailed attention to an extent which will make this answer inordinately long but that cannot be helped. What a pity you did not see fit to write to me personally in 1967 to tell me of your suspicions of my professional and personal integrity as at that time the totally unfounded nature of these could have been nailed by reference both to Valle Lersundi himself and to the agent in England whom he employed, in his attempt to dispose of the Rojas documents to foreign libraries. Now both Lersundi and the agent are dead and I am left with the task of refuting the totally false version of events set out in your letter without the chance of referring you to those who would have confirmed the truth. Let me begin, nevertheless, by stating (i) I had no part whatever in bringing or causing the Lersundi Rojas manuscripts to be brought to Oxford; (ii) I never had either the wish or the opportunity to work on them; (iii) I am not wealthy and depend on my stipend and sundry earnings like most people; (iv) Valle Lersundi and his agent here failed to sell the

MSS in this country partly, at least, because I compelled disclosure of the fact that you had been working on this material for some time and thereby caused the price asked by Valle Lersundi to appear even more ridiculously out-of-line than it was anyway.

Now for details. As I said in my review-article, I received out of the blue in 1962 the descriptive catalogue of thirteen MSS from the Valle Lersundi archives mentioned there with the heading as given. The catalogue (typewritten) was sent to me by Dr. Maurice Ettinghausen, the well-known dealer in Spanish and Portuguese antiquarian material who ran the Oxford branch of A. Rosenthal Ltd., 9 Broad Street, Oxford, until his death early this year. [k] Ettinghausen asked me to call in at his establishment as he wanted my help in connection with the disposal of the MSS. When I went to see him he, to my great astonishment, produced all the manuscripts listed in the catalogue. It was, of course, an odd experience to have all this material in front of one in a bookshop in Oxford. I did not enquire about the legality, from the point of view of the Spanish authorities, of the removal of the documents from Spain but since Ettinghausen was so anxious that nothing should be said about them until they were sold I suspected that the 'subject to an export licence being issued' restriction was probably a cover.

It turned out that what Ettinghausen wanted me to do was to provide independent confirmation, for use in his negotiations with libraries, that the documents were indeed what the catalogue said they were. I looked through them while he sat on the other side of the table to see that I took no notes. I asked him how he expected any library to buy them without seeing them. He said that of course potential library buyers could see them at leisure but that was a different thing from allowing notes to be taken by specialists. Though I was none too pleased at being treated in this way, my curiosity, of course, was greater than my pride. I spent, I suppose, about an hour and a half confirming that the documents were what they purported to be. That was the only occasion I ever saw them.

Ettinghausen told me he was offering them to British and American libraries for £10,000. I told him that no one would pay that kind of money for historical documents of this type unless it was a Spanish library but he was sure they would. Naturally there was no question of me as a possible purchaser. Ettinghausen knew quite well that if I paid him £50 for an antiquarian book I regarded that as pushing the boat out rather far. [l]

---

[k] No list was found in Russell's papers.
[l] Russell may never have spent over £50 at Rosenthal's but there was no lack of expenditure on antiquarian books, not least the £1000 he paid Quaritch's in London for the incunable of

Before I left, Ettinghausen showed me the covering letter he was going to send to libraries together with the catalogue. It contained a categorical statement that, apart from the items published by Valle Lersundi, the documents had never been seen by scholars. ᵐ I told him that I thought this statement was probably untrue since I had heard that you had been working on this material for some time. Ettinghausen said this could not be the case as Valle Lersundi had assured him they were unknown to scholars. I gave him your address and suggested that he should write to you to check directly before circulating his letter to libraries. In fact he telephoned Valle Lersundi since he called me the next day to thank me for having given him a timely warning. ⁿ Valle Lersundi agreed that you had had access to the material. I <u>think</u>, but I am not quite sure of this, that it was at that time that Ettinghausen told me that this fact should not affect the sale value of the material since, according to Valle Lersundi, you had agreed not to publish the documents.

The only other hand I had in any of this was when the documents were offered by Ettinghausen to the Bodleian. I had some brief correspondence with the then Keeper of Western Manuscripts, Dr. R.W. Hunt, to whom I confirmed that, given their nature, they were not the sort of thing that the Bodleian should spend its money on unless it could get them for a tiny fraction of the asking price. I also mentioned that you had been working on their contents so that, presumably, they would very soon be reduced to the status of published material.

That was the end of the matter as far as I was concerned except that, a long time later, I met Ettinghausen in the street and asked him if he had sold these documents. He said he had not and that they had gone back to Spain. °

As for the anonymous English collector who was supposedly willing to give a million pesetas for this material if you agreed not to use the results of your work, I

Petrarch's *Omnia Opera* in the 1960s.
ᵐ Fernando del Valle Lersundi, 'Documentos referentes a Fernando de Rojas', *Revista de Filología Española* 12 (1925), 385–96, and *id.*, 'Testamento de Fernando de Rojas, autor de La Celestina', *Revista de Filología Española* 16 (1929), 365–88.
ⁿ In a letter he sent to Dr. Víctor Infantes from Oxford on 7 April 2000 Russell declares this telephone conversation to have occurred in his presence, with Valle Lersundi 'grudgingly' confirming Russell's information and resulting in Ettinghausen reducing the offer price.
° Russell does not share with Gilman what he reported in his letter to Infantes twenty-five years later, namely that Ettinghausen reported during their chance encounter having learnt from Valle Lersundi that a number of books from Rojas' library had been discovered in a cellar at Deva, although badly damaged by damp. Russell promptly contacted Valle Lersundi who extended an invitation to visit him and discuss the matter, one he was unable to take up due to a prolonged bout of ill health.

trust that you will now be persuaded that the well-heeled personage was, at least, not me. I am bound to say that I think that, if any such individual existed at all, either myself or one of the other people here interested in Celestina studies would have been approached! Certainly Ettinghausen never, when talking to me, mentioned any individual as a possible purchaser — only libraries. I do however have some vague recollection that Dr. Martin Bodmer, the Swiss collector, with whom I had some dealings about his 1500 Comedia, said something that suggested he may have been offered the documents and even seen them. But it may be that I thought he was the only private collector in Europe with the resources and the interest to make him a possible buyer. There is, I see, nothing about it in my correspondence with Bodmer so, if he did mention it, it could only have been when I visited the Bodmer Library and I have no notes of any conversation.

I would guess, from the way your letter is worded and the fact that eight years have passed since you were fed with totally mendacious information in Mexico by some British Hispanists who, one supposes, must have had too much tequila, that you may find the true facts of this matter difficult to accept. You could write to A. Rosenthal to see if there is anything on file which they would be willing to disclose though, since Dr. Maurice Ettinghausen was a much respected figure in his world, I would not be too hopeful of securing results there. Besides Ettinghausen may, on this occasion, have been free-lancing. I don't suppose that, after such a long period, the Bodleian Library has kept their correspondence on the subject since it involves material they did not buy. But you could try. I presume that you yourself will have used your contacts with the Lersundi family to try to get at the truth. If you want to see the typewritten descriptive catalogue of the manuscripts which were offered for sale I am quite willing to send you a xerox of that.

There was, of course, no suggestion in my article as regards this particular matter that you had indulged in any sort of 'malfeasance'. What I wrote is carefully worded to exclude that possibility. What I do imply, I think with justification, is that the scruples you express in your book are unjustified because the other party concerned had let you down quite badly; I did not realize how badly until I read your letter and I certainly had no idea that I was allotted both an active and despicable role in this affair.

As for the supposed accusation that you were breaking the spirit of any agreement with Valle Lersundi by circulating details of your discoveries I categorically deny this. In the first place my sympathies were entirely with you as

I knew what had been going on behind your back and, if I had been included among the <u>celestinistas</u> who received information about what you had been doing, I should probably have felt it incumbent on me to give you a hint. In the second place, being a fairly reasonable person, I never believed for a moment that you would have made any agreement with Valle Lersundi that precluded you using the results of your own work. I supposed that this notion came into existence only when Ettinghausen pointed out to Valle Lersundi that the chances of getting a good price for his manuscripts was greatly jeopardized by the fact that you had worked on them extensively. I suppose I must have said something that could be twisted to give it a malicious significance though I have no recollection of this. It was most likely a comment that Valle Lersundi would be unhappy about the publication of your account of your work since he was claiming that you had taken vows of silence. But that is another matter.

I can only end by repeating again that I am very sorry that you did not immediately communicate to me years ago the suspicions you had developed concerning me. I would much have preferred to have referred you to Dr. Ettinghausen and to Valle Lersundi for the facts rather than to have to produce them myself.

I have marked this letter confidential and rely on you not to give currency to the information in it about Dr. Ettinghausen in the same way as I shall, as you request, treat your letter as private between us. Inevitably what I have had to put on paper casts a somewhat ambiguous light on Dr. Ettinghausen's part in the attempt to dispose outside Spain of papers which clearly properly belong in a Spanish library. He is not here to defend himself and I would be very sad if what I have had to say upset his family. One of his sons, Dr. Walter Eytan, is an old friend of mine whom you may have heard of as a distinguished Israeli diplomat and civil servant. One of his grandsons is a former pupil of mine and now works in this country as an academic in the Hispanic field.

As I think I mentioned to you in the note sent to Nerja I shall be <u>incomunicado</u> for (D.v.) about six weeks from the 11th of September. If you want to pursue any of this further perhaps you would defer doing so until I am around again here. I hope, though, that these three-and-a-half pages will suffice to supply you with the information you have asked for.

Yours sincerely,

[signed:] *Peter Russell*

APPENDIX II
Oxford University Spanish Syllabus (1931–1932)

Michaelmas 1931
(Pass School)

Azorín: *Las confesiones de un pequeño filósofo*	G. A. Kolkhorst
Oxford Book of Spanish Verse, ed. James Fitzmaurice-Kelly (1913 etc.)	Kolkhorst
Composition	Kolkhorst
La novela realista y naturalista desde 1875	Dr. Dámaso Alonso
Prescribed Books	Alonso

(Honour School)

Romance Philology: General Principles	Prof. Alfred Ewert
Spanish Phonology	Ewert
Early Prescribed Texts	Kolkhorst
Aspects of the Lopean Drama	Kolkhorst
Fonética moderna	Alonso
Neoclasicismo y tradicionalismo (siglo XVIII)	Alonso
Composition (for second-year/third-year students)	Alonso

Hilary 1932
(Pass School)

Benavente: *Los intereses creados*	Kolkhorst
Oxford Book of Spanish Verse	Kolkhorst
Composition (Class A/Class B)	Kolkhorst
El teatro desde 1875 hasta 1925	Alonso
La Prosa (1898–1925)	Alonso
Ortega y Gasset: *Meditaciones del Quijote*	Alonso

(Honour School)

Romance Philology: Vocabulary	Ewert
Historical Spanish Syntax	Ewert
Juan Ruiz: *Libro de Buen Amor*	Kolkhorst

APPENDIX II: OXFORD UNIVERSITY SPANISH SYLLABUS (1931–1932)

Calderón	Kolkhorst
La Lírica en el siglo XVI	Alonso
El Romanticismo	Alonso
Composition (for second-year/third-year students)	Alonso
La prosa didáctica en el Siglo de Oro	Miss María Victoria de Lara (for Madariaga)

Trinity 1932
(Pass School)

Azorín: *Las confesiones de un pequeño filósofo*	Kolkhorst
Oxford Book of Spanish Verse	Kolkhorst
Composition	Kolkhorst
Principales tendencias literarias (1875–1925)	Alonso
Ortega y Gasset: *Meditaciones del Quijote*	Alonso

(Honour School)

Introduction to Romance Philology	Ewert
Cantar de Mio Cid	Ewert
Primera Crónica General de España, ed. Ramón Menéndez Pidal	Prof. W. J. Entwistle
Fray Luis de León	Entwistle
The Formation of the Spanish Language	Entwistle
Juan Ruiz: *Libro de Buen Amor*	Kolkhorst
Calderón	Kolkhorst
Cervantes	Alonso
Poesía y teatro	Alonso
Composition (for second-year/third-year students)	Alonso

Note: All lectures and classes given in the Taylor Institution.

Source

Oxford University Gazette 62 (Oxford: Clarendon Press, 1931–2), 56, 58, 254, 256, 460 & 462; see also *University of Oxford Examination Statutes* (Oxford: Clarendon Press), published annually.

APPENDIX III
Graduate Students Supervised (1951–1984)
Compiled by Nigel Griffin, Jeremy Lawrance and the author

Following is a list of the graduate students whose D.Phil., B.Litt. and B.Phil. theses and dissertations Russell formally supervised either wholly or in part; it does not include those theses in which he served in a purely advisory capacity or those he examined, nor the many students on whose research he had a significant influence including Keith Whinnom (Queen's, 1945–8, Laming Travelling Fellow, 1950–1), Douglas J. Gifford (Queen's, 1946–9), Edward C. Riley (Laming Scholar, Queen's, 1946–9), Robert D. F. Pring-Mill (New College, Magdalen, St Catherine's, 1947–88) and Anthony R. D. Pagden (Oriel, Merton, 1973–80). The assistance of Ronald Truman in the preparation of this list is gratefully acknowledged.

Key: * Professor; † Deceased; ° Fellow of the British Academy; ‡ Did not complete degree

D.Phil.

Student	Dates	Title	College	Permanent Positions/Remarks
Gareth A. Davies†	1951–5	The life and works of Don Antonio Hurtado de Mendoza, 1586–1644	Queen's	Leeds* Started with W. J. Entwistle, finished with PER
Alan D. Deyermond°†	1953–7	Petrarchan borrowings and reminiscences in *La Celestina*	Pembroke	Westfield, thence QMW*
E. Bryan Strong	1955–64	A critical assessment of the	Trinity	Bath University of Technology, thence

Appendix III: Graduate Students Supervised (1951–1984)

		poetry of Pero López de Ayala based on investigation into his sources and his treatment of them		University of Bath
Alan J. Forey	1956–63	The expansion and provincial organisation of the Temple in the Crown of Aragon	Wadham	St Andrews, Durham
Ronald W. Truman	1957–63	The idea of the prince in the Latin and vernacular writings of sixteenth-century Spanish theorists	St Edmund Hall	Birkbeck, Christ Church Started with PER, finished with T. M. Parker from 1959
Nicholas G. Round°†	1959–67	Pero Díaz de Toledo: A study of a fifteenth-century *converso* translator in his background	Pembroke	QUB, Glasgow, Sheffield*
Henry M. Ettinghausen	1961–9	Quevedo and Neo-stoicism	Queen's	Hull, Southampton*
A. J. R. Russell-Wood†	1963–7	The Santa Casa da Misericórdia of Bahia: A social study, 1550–1750	St Antony's	Johns Hopkins* Started with PER, finished with H. R. Trevor-Roper
John D. Rutherford	1963–70	Literature and revolution: A study of prose fiction and autobiography relating to the	Wadham	St Antony's, Queen's Started with PER, finished with A. R. M. Carr

		Mexican Revolution, 1910–1917		
Michael J. Woods†	1963–70	The rhetorical treatment of nature in Spanish baroque poetry in the age of Góngora	Keble	KCL Started with PER, finished with R. O. Jones at KCL 1965–6
John A. Crosbie	1967–76	A study of lyric poetry *A lo divino* in Spain, with particular reference to the second half of the sixteenth century	Queen's	Southampton Started with PER, finished with C. A. Jones
David P. Gallagher	1968–75	A critical study of the prose works of Jorge Luis Borges	St Antony's	‡; St Antony's; investment banking; public policy; latterly Chilean ambassador to the United Kingdom Started with PER, then J. F. Wordsworth, then supervised jointly with C. A. Jones
Maria da Graça de Almeida Rodrigues	1968–75	A critical edition of the *Chronica do Principe dom Ioan* by Damião de Góis	St Anne's	Universidade Nova de Lisboa*; subsequently cultural counsellor, Portuguese diplomatic service Started with C. R. Boxer at KCL, finished with PER and F. W. Hodcroft
Philip A. Lloyd-Bostock†	1968–79	A comparative study of the influence of emblematic	Lincoln	Wadham Started with PER, finished with R. D. F. Pring-Mill

Appendix III: Graduate Students Supervised (1951–1984)

		theory and practice on poetry in Spain, Italy and France between 1580 and 1680		
Thomas F. Earle	1968–75	Image and theme in the works of Sá de Miranda	Wadham	Linacre, St Peter's* Started with PER (B.Phil.), completed D.Phil. with Luís de Sousa Rebelo at KCL
John C. Kinnear	1969–73	The irony of Machado de Assis	Wadham	Liverpool Started with PER, finished with Luís de Sousa Rebelo at KCL
Max W. Wheeler	1969–74	Some rules in a generative phonology of modern Catalan	Corpus Christi	Sussex Started with PER (B.Litt.), completed D.Phil. with D. R. Harris
Nigel H. Griffin	1969–76	Some aspects of Jesuit School drama 1550–1600 with special reference to Spain and Portugal	Keble, New College	Manchester, Christ Church Supervised jointly with R. D. F. Pring-Mill
Maurice J. Hemingway†	1969–76	Pardo Bazán: The novelist, and spiritual naturalism. Theory and practice	Worcester	Exeter Started with PER (B.Litt.), completed D.Phil. with C. A. Jones
Colin P. Thompson	1970–4	The background, interpretation and evaluation of the *Cántico espiritual* of San Juan de la Cruz	Trinity, Christ Church	Sussex, St Catherine's Supervised jointly with A. J. P. Kenny

Daniel V. Waissbein	1970–4	Some aspects of poetic creation in Spain 1550–1650. Innovation, tradition, poet's conception of his task	St Catherine's	‡; interpreter Started with R. D. F. Pring-Mill, then PER
David Hook	1971–7	A critical edition of *La estoria del noble Vaspasiano Emperador de Rroma* with a literary and historical study including an account of the transmission of the text	St Catherine's	KCL*, Bristol*
Alastair C. de C. M. Saunders	1971–9	A social history of black slaves and freedmen in Portugal, 1441–1555	Exeter (Rhodes Scholar)	Cornell; subsequently civil servant, Government of Nova Scotia Started with PER, finished with J. R. L. Highfield
Felipe F. R. Fernández-Armesto	1972–7	The government and society of the Canary Islands after the conquest, 1497–c. 1525	Magdalen, St John's	QMW*, Tufts*, Notre Dame* Started with PER, finished with J. R. L. Highfield
Martin G. Cunningham	1974–6	The relationship between poetry and music as seen in polyphonic settings of Spanish poems	Worcester	‡; Trinity College Dublin, University College Dublin

APPENDIX III: GRADUATE STUDENTS SUPERVISED (1951–1984)

		between 1530 and about 1600		
Clive H. Griffin	1974–84	The Crombergers: A study of a sixteenth-century Seville printing house, with descriptive bibliography	Keble	Trinity
Jeremy N. H. Lawrance°	1975–83	Nuño de Guzmán: Life and works	Balliol, Wolfson, Magdalen	Manchester*, Nottingham*
Julian M. Weiss	1979–84	The poet's concept of his art: Castilian vernacular verse, c. 1400–60	Magdalen, Queen's	Liverpool, Virginia, Oregon, KCL* Started with PER, then I. D. L. Michael, finished with A. D. Deyermond at Westfield

B.Litt.

Student	Dates	Title	College	Permanent Positions/Remarks
Sylvia F. Gibson	1953–4	Letters of Pere el Ceremoniòs	Lady Margaret Hall	
Janet A. Chapman	1955–60	The *Libro de Buen Amor*	St Anne's	Westfield
Terence Wilson	1956–9	(Probationer)	Queen's	‡
William Greve Cardwell	1961–9	A descriptive catalogue (with introduction) of the books formerly	Worcester	

Scholar-Spy

		belonging to Sir William Godolphin (1634?–1696) and now in the libraries of Wadham College and Worcester College, Oxford		
José Luz Morales	1963–6	(Probationer)	Linacre	‡
Charles Kelly	1968–72	(Probationer)	Trinity	‡; started with PER, then with Luís de Sousa Rebelo at KCL
Christopher John Buttery	1969–72	(Probationer)	Queen's	‡; started with PER, then with Luís de Sousa Rebelo at KCL
Colin M. O'Halloran	1970–2	Spanish Golden Age thought and education	Trinity	
Lia Noêmia Rodrigues Correia Raitt	1972–9	Garrett's debt to England	St Anne's	Started with PER, then with Luís de Sousa Rebelo at KCL

B.Phil.

Student	Dates	Title	College	Permanent Positions/Remarks
John Bernard Hall	1964–7	Arthurian literature in Spain: an examination of its popularity and influence, 1170–1535	St John's	University College of Swansea, thence University of Wales, Swansea Started with PER, then with R. A. Sayce 1965–6
Anthony F. Lambert	1965–8	The satire of Silverio Lanza (Juan Bautista	St John's	Southampton

APPENDIX III: GRADUATE STUDENTS SUPERVISED (1951–1984)

		Amorós), 1856–1912		
Ian Gowans	1968–73	Imagery in Leopoldo Alas's *La Regenta*, with reference to Flaubert's *Madame Bovary*	St John's	Started with PER, then with John D. Rutherford and C. A. Jones
Dorothy M. Burgoyne	1970–2	Thematic development in Veiga Tagarro's *Laura de Anfriso*	Linacre	Started with PER, then with C. A. Jones

Sources

Oxford University Calendar (Oxford: Clarendon Press, 1946–81)
Oxford University Gazette 77–112 (Oxford: Clarendon Press, 1946–81)
C. A. Jones, *Theses in Hispanic Studies Approved for Higher Degrees by British Universities to 1971* in *Bulletin of Hispanic Studies* 49 (1972), 325–54
F. Hodcroft, *Theses in Hispanic Studies Approved for Higher Degrees by British and Irish Universities (1972–1974) (with some Additional Earlier Titles)* in *Bulletin of Hispanic Studies* 52 (1975), 325–44
D. Mackenzie, *Theses in Hispanic Studies Approved for Higher Degrees by British and Irish Universities (1975–1978) (with some Additional Earlier Titles)* in *Bulletin of Hispanic Studies* 56 (1979), 283–304
M. Johnson, *Theses in Hispanic Studies Approved for Higher Degrees by British and Irish Universities (1979–1982) (with some Additional Earlier Titles)* in *Bulletin of Hispanic Studies* 61 (1984), 233–61
———, *Theses in Hispanic Studies Approved for Higher Degrees by British and Irish Universities (1983–1987) (with some Additional Earlier Titles)* in *Bulletin of Hispanic Studies* 66 (1989), 417–44
Bodleian Library catalogue (SOLO): <solo.bodleian.ox.ac.uk/>.
British Library thesis catalogue (EThOS): <ethos.bl.uk/Home.do>.

APPENDIX IV
University Lectures and Classes Imparted (1938–1981)
Compiled by Nigel Griffin and the author

Sets of 8 lectures (unless otherwise indicated); M — Michaelmas; H — Hilary; T — Trinity.
Translation classes: H47 T47 H48 H49 T49
Composition classes/Composition: Problems of Syntax: H48 H56 H57 H60
Technique and Practice of Literary Commentary/Practical Textual Commentary: H54 M59 M61 (6)
Non-Romance Elements/Etymologies in Spanish/Spanish Place Names: M48 T51 H55 M57
Paper V Prescribed Texts (Philological/Linguistic): M60 H61 (4) M61 M62 M64 H64 (4) M68
Latin American/Spanish American Spanish: H62 H64
Alfonso the Wise: T58
Primera Crónica General: T47 H49 M50 T51 H52 T52 (cont.) T54
Problems of Medieval Spanish Literature: T39
Poema/Cantar de Mio Cid/Some Cidian Problems: H47 M48 T50 M51 M54 T56 H58 H61 H63 H64 M66 M68 H74 T74 H79
Spanish Ballads/*Flor nueva de romances viejos*: M63 M64 (4) M66 M67 M68 M69 M70 M71 M73 M74 M76 M78 M79 M80
Galician-Portuguese *Cancioneiros*: T55 T56 T57 H60 H61 T62 T63 T64 T65
Libro de buen amor: M46 T49 H51 M52 H53
Portuguese Fifteenth-Century Chronicles/Fernão Lopes and the Portuguese Historiographical Tradition: T54 H67 T68 T70 (4) M70 (4)
Celestina: M47 (4) H48 (4) M49 T51 T53 T55 T57 M59 M60 M61 T61 H64 T64 (1 to conclude) H67 T67 (2 to conclude) M71 H76 T76 T79 M80
Intellectual Movements in the Golden Age/Thought and Taste in the Golden Age (from M46):[1] M38 H40 M46 H49 M51 H52 M55 H56 M57 H58 T60 M60 T62 M62 T64 M64 T67 M67 M69 H70 M73 (i) H74 (ii) M76 (i)

---

[1] The sets delivered in 1951–2, 1953–6 and 1957–8 were of sixteen lectures each.

Appendix IV: University Lectures and Classes Imparted (1938–1981)

H77 (ii) M79 (i) H80 (ii) T80 (4 to conclude)
The Spanish Renaissance (seminar with C. A. Jones): H54
Chivalric and Pastoral Romance/Romances of Chivalry: M49 M56 H63 H76
Sixteenth-Century Literary Theory/Literary Criticism from Herrera to Castillo y Sotomayor: T48 M52 H53
Sixteenth-Century Lyric Poetry/Garcilaso/Garcilaso and Herrera: H48 ~~H50~~ T50 T51 M52 M53 H56 T56 T57 T58 M59 H62 M63 H68 M74 H81
Textual Study of Sixteenth-Century Poetry from *Oxford Book of Spanish Verse*: T46
Pastoralism, Petrarchism and Classicism in Sixteenth-Century Spanish Poetry/Literature: T70 H77 T77
Golden Age Balladry: H69 (4)
Sixteenth-Century Novel: M39 T47 T51 T52
The Role of the Prose Romance in Spanish Golden Age Literature: H79
Cervantes: M78
Don Quixote: ~~H50~~ M50 H51 T53 H55 T55 H57 T57 (cont.) T61 M63 T67 (6) H68 T68 (cont.) H72 (4) H73 T80
Cervantes without *Don Quixote*: H75 T75
Seventeenth-Century Spanish Verse: M46
Góngora: T46 T48 T51 M54 M56 H60 H63 T69 H72 (4) T79
Bécquer: M51 M52 H53 M53 M54 M55 M56
Ganivet and Unamuno: H51 H52
Generation of 1898: H38 H39 H47 M47 M48 M49
Galdós: T38 T46 T48 T49 T50
Una hora de España (Azorín): T52
Tigre Juan (Ramón Pérez de Ayala): H60
Informal Instruction (third-year class): M47
Advanced Class for Research Students/Post-Graduate Seminar[2]/Problems of Research in Spanish Literature/Approaches to Literature: M57 H64 H69 T69 (4) H72 H73 H74 H75 H76 H77 H79 H80

Notes
Russell was on sabbatical leave in M58 H59 T59 M65 H66 T66 H71 T71 T72 M72 T73 T77 M77 H78 T78 and T81.
He was on sick leave in H50 resulting in the postponement of his lecture

---

[2] The Post-Graduate Seminar is believed to have been held every term since Hilary 1964.

series on Sixteenth-Century Lyric Poetry and *Don Quixote*, and on convalescent leave in M75 following prostate surgery, the lecture series on *Flor nueva de romances viejos* being delivered by Colin Thompson in his stead.

Source
Oxford University Gazette 68–112 (Oxford: Clarendon Press, 1937–81). The assistance of Joanne Ferrari of the Taylor Institution Library and Anne Mouron of the Bodleian Library in facilitating access to the lecture inserts in many of the later volumes is gratefully acknowledged.

APPENDIX V
Publications
Compiled by Nigel Griffin and the author

1933

1. 'The Pool', *Isis* no. 867, 1 March, 13 [short story].
2. [anon.] 'Professor Castro in Oxford', *The Oxford Magazine*, 9 March, 528–9.
3. 'Spanish Club Dinner: Argentine Ambassador's Oxford Tribute to the Prince', *Oxford Mail*, 4 March.
4. 'Red Earth', *Isis* no. 871, 10 May, x–xi (insert between 10 & 11) [short story].
5. 'The Witch', *Isis* no. 879, 25 October, 10–11 [short story].

1934

6. ['P.E.R.'] 'Pilgrimage', *Isis* no. 886, 24 January, 19–20 [short story].
7. 'Nocturne', *Isis* no. 895, 9 May, 5–6 [short story].
8. 'Pirandello', *Miscellany*, ed. Robert Daubney & Harold Cooper, Oxford: The Queen's College, 10–14.
9. 'Mrs. Midgett's Immortality', *Miscellany*, ed. Robert Daubney & Harold Cooper, Oxford: The Queen's College, 47–50 [short story].

1938

10. 'João Fernandes Andeiro at the Court of John of Lancaster, 1371–1381', *Revista da Universidade de Coimbra*, 14: 20–30. Repr. with original pagination in *Portugal, Spain, and the African Atlantic* (1995).
11. [anon.] 'Spain, 1938–I' and 'Spain, 1938–II', *The Oxford Magazine*, 10 November 1938, 146–9, & 17 November 1938, 179–81.

1939

12. [Short notice on E. Allison Peers, *A Handbook to the Study and Teaching of Spanish*, London: Methuen, 1938], *Modern Language Review*, 34: 480.

1940

13. [with W. J. Entwistle] 'A Rainha D. Felipa e a sua Côrte', *Congresso do mundo português: Publicacões*, II: *Memórias e Comunicações Apresentadas ao Congresso de História Medieval*, Lisbon: Comissão Executiva dos Centenários, 317–46.

14. [Review of *Chancelarias Medievais Portuguesas*, I: *Documentos da Chancelaria de Afonso Henriques*, ed. Abiah Elisabeth Reuter, Coimbra: Publicações do Instituto Alemão da Universidade de Coimbra, 1938], *Medium Ævum*, 9: 177–81.

15. [Review of Karl Brandi, *The Emperor Charles V*, trans. C. V. Wedgwood, London: Jonathan Cape, 1939], *The Oxford Magazine*, 25 January: 161–2.

1941

16. *As Fontes de Fernão Lopes*. Transl. A. Gonçalves Rodrigues, Coimbra: Coimbra Editora, iv + 51 pp. [rev. version of a 1939 lecture delivered at King's College London]. Rev. & transl. Kirstin Kennedy as 'On the Sources of Fernão Lopes', *Portugal, Spain, and the African Atlantic* (1995), 30 pp.

1947

17. [Review of *Spanish Golden Age Poetry and Drama*, ed. E. Allison Peers, Liverpool: Institute of Hispanic Studies, 1946], *Modern Language Review*, 42: 522–3.

18. [Review of José M. Millás Villacrosa, *Las traducciones orientales en los manuscritos de la Biblioteca Catedral de Toledo*, Madrid: Instituto Arias Montano, 1942], *Modern Language Review*, 42: 392–5.

1948

19. [Short notice on Remigio U. Pane, *English Translations from the Spanish*, New Brunswick, N.J.: Rutgers University Press, 1944], *Modern Language Review*, 43: 132–3.

1949

20. [Review of Harold V. Livermore, *A History of Portugal*, Cambridge: Cambridge University Press, 1947], *History*, n.s. 34: 132–3.

21. [Short notice on Malcolm J. Gray, *An Index to Guzmán de Alfarache*, New Brunswick, N.J.: Rutgers University Press, 1948], *Modern Language Review*, 44: 597.

1950

22. 'Bédier, Joseph', II, 190 [repaginated in 1966 rev.: II, 191–2]; 'Bopp, Franz', II, 438–9 [rev. by Douglas Gifford and repaginated in 1966 rev.: II, 434]; 'Grimm, Jakob Ludwig Karl and Wilhelm Karl', VI, 597–8 [in part; rev. by W. J. Entwistle & Douglas Gifford and repaginated in 1966 rev.: VI, 605]; 'Humboldt, Karl Wilhelm von', VII, 286 [repaginated in 1966 rev.: VII, 288], *Chambers's Encyclopedia*, rev. 8th edn, Oxford: George Newnes.

1951

23. 'Fernão Lopes e o Tratado de Santarém', *Revista Portugesa de História*, 5 (= *Homenagem a Gama Barros*): 455–73. Rev. & transl. Kirstin Kennedy as 'Fernão Lopes and the Text of the Treaty of Santarém', *Portugal, Spain, and the African Atlantic* (1995), 19 pp.

24. [Review of Homero Serís, *Manual de bibliografía de la literatura española*, Syracuse, N.Y.: Centro de Estudios Hispánicos, 1948], *Modern Language Review*, 46: 283–4.

25. [Review of Inez I. Macdonald, *Don Fernando de Antequera*, Oxford: Dolphin Book Co., 1948], *History*, n.s. 36: 121–2.

1952

26. 'Some Problems of Diplomatic in the *Cantar de Mio Cid* and their Implications', *Modern Language Review*, 47: 340–49. Repr. as an Appendix with original pagination in *'Mio Cid' Studies: 'Some Problems of Diplomatic' Fifty Years On*, ed. Alan Deyermond, David G. Pattison, & Eric Southworth, Papers of the Medieval Hispanic Research Seminar, London: Department of Hispanic Studies, Queen Mary University of London. Transl. Alejandro Pérez as 'Algunos problemas de diplomática en el *Poema de Mio Cid* y su significación', *Temas de la Celestina* (1978): 13–33.

27. ['P.E.R.'] 'William James Entwistle (1896–1952)', *The Oxford Magazine*, 16 October, 6–8.

28. [Review of *El Fuero de Teruel*, ed. Max Gorosch, Stockholm, 1950], *Medium Ævum*, 21: 93–7.

29. [Review of Jules Horrent, *La Chanson de Roland dans les littératures française et espagnole au Moyen Âge*, Paris: Les Belles Lettres, 1951, and Horrent, *Étude sur le fragment de cantar de gesta conservé à l'Archivo de Navarra (Pampelune)*, Paris: Les Belles Lettres, 1951], *Modern Language*

Review, 47: 586–7.

1953

30. 'A Stuart Hispanist: James Mabbe', *Bulletin of Hispanic Studies,* 30: 75–84.

31. 'English Seventeenth-Century Interpretations of Spanish Literature', *Atlante,* 1: 65–77.

32. 'Galés portuguesas ao serviço de Ricardo II de Inglaterra (1385–89)', *Revista da Faculdade de Letras de Lisboa,* 2nd s. 18/i: 61–73. Transl. Kirstin Kennedy as 'Portuguese Galleys in the Service of Richard II, 1385–89', *Portugal, Spain and the African Atlantic* (1995), 11 pp.

33. [Review of Evelyn S. Procter, *Alfonso X of Castile: Patron of Literature and Learning,* Oxford: Clarendon Press, 1951], *Modern Language Review,* 48: 88–90.

34. [Review of *Estudios dedicados a Menéndez Pidal,* IV, Madrid: CSIC, 1953], *Bulletin of Hispanic Studies,* 30: 116.

1954

35. [Review of José María Mohedano Hernández, *El espéculo de los legos,* Madrid: CSIC, 1951], *Modern Language Review,* 49: 94.

36. [Review of *Studies in Romance Philology and French Literature Presented to John Orr,* Manchester: Manchester University Press, 1953], *Bulletin of Hispanic Studies,* 31: 240–1.

37. [Short notice on Baltasar Gracián, *The Oracle,* transl. L. B. Walton, London: J. M. Dent, 1953], *Modern Language Review,* 49: 117–18.

1955

38. *The English Intervention in Spain and Portugal in the Time of Edward III and Richard II,* Oxford: Clarendon Press, xxiv + 611 pp. + 11 maps. Portuguese translation published 2000.

39. '"King of Castile and Leon, Duke of Lancaster": John of Gaunt's Spanish Court.' First published in *The English Intervention in Spain and Portugal:* 173–85, repr. in *Portugal, Spain and the African Atlantic* (1995).

40. [Review of: Miguel de Cervantes Saavedra, *Don Quixote of La Mancha,* ed. & transl. Walter Starkie, London: Macmillan, 1954], *Bulletin of Hispanic Studies,* 32: 53–4.

41. [Review of *Estudios dedicados a Menéndez Pidal*, V, Madrid: CSIC, 1954], *Bulletin of Hispanic Studies*, 32: 121–2.

42. [Review of *Portugal and Brazil: An Introduction*, ed. Harold V. Livermore & William J. Entwistle, Oxford: Clarendon Press, 1953, and Charles E. Nowell, *A History of Portugal*, London: Macmillan, 1952], *History*, n.s. 40: 126–7.

43. [Review of Gerald de Gaury, *The Grand Captain, Gonzalo de Cordoba*, London: Longmans, 1955], *History*, n.s. 42: 219.

44. [Review of J. de Vallata, *Poliodorus: Comedia humanística desconocida*, ed. José María Casas Homs, Madrid: CSIC, 1953], *Modern Language Review*, 50: 348–9.

45. [Review of *Two Old Portuguese Versions of the Life of Saint Alexis*, ed. Joseph H. D. Allen Jr., Urbana-Champaign, Ill.: University of Illinois Press, 1953], *Medium Ævum*, 24: 117–18.

46. [Review of María Rosa Lida de Malkiel, *La idea de la Fama en la Edad Media castellana*, Mexico City & Buenos Aires: Fondo de Cultura Económica, 1952], *Medium Ævum*, 24: 118–20.

1956

47. 'Where was Alcocer? (*Cantar de Mio Cid*, ll.553–861)', *Homenaje a J. A. Van Praag, catedrático de la Universidad de Amsterdam, 1930–1955*, ed. G. F. Pijper *et al.*, Amsterdam, L. J. Veen: 101–7. Transl. Alejandro Pérez as '¿Dónde estaba Alcocer? (*Poema de Mio Cid*, vv. 553–861)', *Temas de la Celestina* (1978): 37–44.

48. [Review of Sacheverell Sitwell, *Portugal and Madeira*, London: Batsford, 1954, and H. V. Morton, *A Stranger in Spain*, London: Methuen, 1955], *Bulletin of Hispanic Studies*, 33: 104–5.

1957

49. 'The Art of Fernando de Rojas' [review of Stephen Gilman, *The Art of 'La Celestina'*, Madison, Wis.: University of Wisconsin Press, 1956], *Bulletin of Hispanic Studies*, 34: 160–7.

50. [Review of Daniel Bodmer, *Die granadinischen Romanzen in der europäischen Literatur*, Zürich: Juris, 1955], *French Studies*, 11: 187–8.

51. [Review of Don Juan Manuel, *Obras*, ed. José María Castro y Calvo & Martín de Riquer, Barcelona: CSIC, 1955], *Modern Language Review*, 52: 126.

52. [Review of Tomás Navarro, *Métrica española: Reseña histórica y descriptiva*, Syracuse, N.Y.: Syracuse University Press, 1956], *Modern Language Review*, 52: 614–16.

53. [Review of *Estudios dedicados a Menéndez Pidal*, VI, Madrid: CSIC, 1956], *Bulletin of Hispanic Studies*, 34: 50–1.

54. [Review of Edmund de Chasca, *Estructura y forma en el 'Poema de mio Cid'*, Iowa City, Iowa: University of Iowa Press & Mexico City: Patria, 1956], *Bulletin of Hispanic Studies*, 34: 174–5.

55. [Short notice on *The Book of the Wiles of Women*, ed. & transl. John Esten Keller, Chapel Hill, N.C.: University of North Carolina Press, 1957], *Bulletin of Hispanic Studies*, 34: 235.

1958

56. 'San Pedro de Cardeña and the Heroic History of the Cid', *Medium Ævum*, 27: 57–79. Amplified version transl. Alejandro Pérez as 'San Pedro de Cardeña y la historia heroica del Cid', *Temas de la Celestina* (1978): 71–112.

57. 'Mr. G. A. Kolkhorst, Gifted Teacher of Spanish', *The Times*, 16 September 1958.

58. [Review of *Cancionero de Juan Fernández de Ixar*, ed. José María Azaceta, Madrid: CSIC, 1956, and *Segunda parte del Cancionero General*, ed. Antonio Rodríguez-Moñino, Oxford: Dolphin Book Co., 1956], *Modern Language Review* 53: 443–5.

59. [Review of Mário Martins, *Estudos de literatura medieval*, Braga: Livraria Cruz, 1956], *Medium Ævum*, 27: 209–11.

1959

60. 'The *Memorias* of Fernán Álvarez de Albornoz, Archbishop of Seville, 1371–80', *Hispanic Studies in Honour of I. González Llubera*, ed. Frank Pierce, Oxford: Dolphin Book Co.: 319–30.

61. 'The Nessus-Shirt of Spanish History' [review of Claudio Sánchez-Albornoz, *España: un enigma histórico*, 2 vols, Buenos Aires: Sudamericana, 1956], *Bulletin of Hispanic Studies*, 36: 219–25. Repr. with original pagination in *Portugal, Spain, and the African Atlantic* (1995). Transl. Alejandro Pérez as 'La historia de España: Túnica de Neso', *Temas de la Celestina* (1978): 479–91.

62. 'George Alfred Kolkhorst, 1897–1958', *Bulletin of Hispanic Studies*, 36: 51–2.

63. [Short notice on *The Poem of the Cid*, transl. Lesley Byrd Simpson, Berkeley & Los Angeles, Calif.: University of California Press, 1959], *Bulletin of Hispanic Studies*, 36: 114.

1960

64. *Prince Henry the Navigator, Canning House Seventh Annual Lecture, 4 May 1960*, Diamante 11, London: The Hispanic and Luso-Brazilian Councils: 30 pp. + plate + map. Repr. with original pagination in *Portugal, Spain, and the African Atlantic* (1995).

65. 'Medieval Portuguese Students at Oxford University', *Portugiesische Forschungen der Görresgesellschaft*, 1: *Aufsätze zur portugiesischen Kulturgeschichte*, I: 183–91. Repr. with original pagination in *Portugal, Spain, and the African Atlantic* (1995).

66. [Review of A. H. de Oliveira Marques, *Hansa e Portugal na Idade Media*, Lisbon: Albano Tomás dos Anjos, 1959], *Economic History Review*, 14: 388–90.

67. [Short notice on Herbert Ramsden, *An Essential Course in Modern Spanish*, London: Harrap, 1959], *Modern Language Review*, 55: 145.

68. [Short notice on Richard H. Trame, *Rodrigo Sánchez de Arévalo, 1404–1470: Spanish Diplomat and Champion of the Papacy*, Washington, D.C.: Catholic University of America, 1959], *English Historical Review*, 75: 339–40.

1961

69. 'Robert Payn and Juan de Cuenca, Translators of Gower's *Confessio Amantis*', *Medium Ævum*, 30: 26–32.

70. 'Flexible Stipends', *The Oxford Magazine*, 8 June, 401.

71. [Review of Domingo Ricart, *Juan de Valdés y el pensamiento religioso europeo en los siglos XVI e XVII*, Mexico City: Colegio de México & Lawrence, Kan.: University of Kansas Press, 1959], *Modern Language Review*, 56: 129–30.

72. [Review of Julio Casares, *Diccionario histórico de la lengua española*, Madrid: RAE, 1960], *Modern Language Review*, 56: 441–2.

73. [Review of *Amadís de Gaula*, ed. Edwin B. Place, I, Madrid: CSIC, 1959], *Modern Language Review*, 56: 443–5.

74. [Review of Manuel Milá y Fontanals, *De la poesía heroico-popular castellana*, ed. Martín de Riquer & Joaquín Molas, Barcelona: Iona, 1959], *Bulletin of Hispanic Studies*, 38: 163–4.

75. [Review of Jaime Vicens Vives, *Aproximación a la historia de España*, 2nd edn, Barcelona: Teide, 1960], *Bulletin of Hispanic Studies*, 38: 309–11.

76. [Short notice on Bartolomé de Torres Villarroel, *The Remarkable Life of Don Diego*, transl. William C. Atkinson, London, 1958], *Bulletin of Hispanic Studies*, 38: 181.

1962

77. 'Os ingleses em Albujarrota: um problema resolvido através de documentos do "Public Record Office" de Londres', *Revista Portuguesa de História*, 10 (= *Homenagem ao Prof. Doutor Damião Peres*): 419–33.

78. [with David Rogers & Nigel Glendinning] *A Catalogue of Hispanic Manuscripts and Books before 1700 from the Bodleian Library and Oxford College Libraries Exhibited at the meeting 6–11 September*, Oxford: Primer Congreso Internacional de Hispanistas: viii + 56 pp.

79. [Review of Eunice Joiner Gates, *Documentos gongorinos: Los discursos apologéticos de Pedro Díaz de Rivas, El Antídoto de Juan de Jáuregui*, Mexico City: El Colegio de México, 1960], *Modern Language Review*, 57: 116–17.

80. [Review of Lope de Vega, *La Dorotea*, ed. Edwin S. Morby, London: Cambridge University Press, 1958, and George Haley, *Vicente Espinel and Marcos de Obregón: A Life and its Literary Representation*, Providence, R.I.: Brown University Press, 1959], *Modern Language Review*, 57: 119–21.

81. [Review of Karl-Ludwig Selig, *The Library of Vicencio Juan de Lastanosa, Patron of Gracián*, Geneva: Droz, 1960], *Modern Language Review*, 57: 121.

82. [Short notice on Archpriest of Talavera, *Corbacho (Little Sermons on Sin)*, transl. Lesley Byrd Simpson, Berkeley & Los Angeles, Calif.: University of California Press, 1959], *Bulletin of Hispanic Studies*, 39: 65–6.

83. [Short notice on Julius A. Molinaro, *A Bibliography of Comedias sueltas in the University of Toronto Library*, Toronto: University of Toronto Press, 1959], *Modern Language Review*, 57: 150–1.

APPENDIX V: PUBLICATIONS

1963

84. 'La magia como tema integral en la *Tragicomedia de Calisto y Melibea*', *Studia philologica: Homenaje a Dámaso Alonso por sus amigos y discípulos con ocasión de su 60 aniversario*, ed. Alonso Zamora Vicente, 3 vols, Madrid: Gredos, 1963, III, 337–54. Rev. & amplified *c.* 1965 as 'La magia, tema integral de *La Celestina*', *Temas de la Celestina* (1978): 241–76. Partial repr. in *Historia y crítica de la literatura* española, I: *Edad Media*, ed. Alan Deyermond & Francisco Rico, Barcelona: Crítica, 1980: 508–12.

85. 'Ambiguity in *La Celestina*' [Review of: Marcel Bataillon, *La Célestine selon Fernando de Rojas*, Études de Littérature Étrangère et Comparée 42, Paris: Marcel Didier, 1961], *Bulletin of Hispanic Studies*, 40: 35–40.

1964

86. 'Alfonso (kings of Aragon)', I, 592; 'Alfonso (kings of Asturias, León and Castile)', I, 592–4; 'Aragon', II, 204–5; 'Asturias', II, 658–9; 'Behetría', III, 404; 'Castile', V, 35–6; 'Celestina, La', V, 137; 'Cid, The', V, 763–4 [rev. as 'Cid, El', *The New Encyclopaedia Britannica*, 15th edn (1974), IV, 615–16, and in subsequent editions and media (with amendments) to date (2024)]; 'Cortes', VI, 556–7; 'Extremadura', IX, 3; 'Ferdinand I (king of Aragon)', IX, 178; 'Ferdinand (kings of Castile and León)', IX, 179–80; 'Fuero', IX, 988; 'Galicia', IX, 1086; 'García (kings of Pamplona)', IX, 1137; 'Gelmírez, Diego', X, 56; 'Henry (kings of Castile)', XI, 358; 'Hermandad', XI, 431; 'John (kings of Aragon)', XIII, 88 [repaginated in 1967 rev.: XIII, 22]; 'John (kings of Castile)', XIII, 89 [repaginated in 1967 rev.: XIII, 23], 'Spain: History: D. The Visigoths', XXI, 115–16 [repaginated in 1967 rev.: XX, 1084–5]; 'Spain: History: F. Christian Spain to 1479', XXI, 117–21 [repaginated in 1967 rev.: XX, 1085–90], *Encyclopaedia Britannica*, rev. 14th edn, Chicago: Encyclopaedia Britannica.

87. 'Don Alberto Jiménez', *Bulletin of Hispanic Studies*, 41: 247–8.

88. 'Literary Tradition and Social Reality in *La Celestina*' [Review of: Rosa María Lida de Malkiel, *Two Spanish Masterpieces: The Book of Good Love and The Celestina*, Illinois Studies in Language and Literature 49, Urbana-Champaign, Ill.: University of Illinois Press, 1961, and Rosa María Lida de Malkiel, *La originalidad artística de 'La Celestina'*, Buenos Aires: EUDEBA, 1962], *Bulletin of Hispanic Studies*, 41: 230–37. Transl. Alejandro Pérez as 'Tradición literaria y realidad social en *La Celestina*', *Temas de la Celestina* (1978): 277–91.

89. [Review of Virgínia Rau & Jorge de Macedo, *O Açúcar de Madeira nos Fins do Século XV: Problemas de Produção e Comércio*, Funchal: Junta-Geral do Distrito Autónomo do Funchal, 1962], *Economic History Review*, 17: 415–16.

90. [Review of Helga Thomae, *Französische Reisebeschreibungen über Spanien im 17. Jahrhudert*, Bonn: Romanisches Seminar an der Universität Bonn, 1961, and Léon-François Hoffmann, *L'Image de l'Espagne en France entre 1800 et 1850*, Princeton, N.J., University of Princeton & Paris: PUF, 1961], *French Studies*, 18: 159–61.

1965

91. 'Una alianza frustrada: Las bodas de Pedro I de Castilla y Juana Plantagenet', *Anuario de Estudios Medievales*, 2: 301–32. Repr. with original pagination in *Portugal, Spain, and the African Atlantic* (1995).

92. [Review of Francis M. Rogers, *The Travels of the Infante Dom Pedro de Portugal*, Cambridge, Mass.: Harvard University Press, 1961], *Modern Language Review*, 60: 132–3.

93. [Review of Frank Pierce, *La poesía épica del Siglo de Oro*, Madrid: Gredos, 1961], *Modern Language Review*, 60: 289–90.

94. [Review of Otis H. Green, *Spain and the Western Tradition: The Castilian Mind from 'El Cid' to Calderón*, I, Madison, Wis.: University of Madison Press, 1963], *Romance Philology*, 19: 360–3.

1966

95. 'The Archpriest's Jokes' [review of Anthony N. Zahareas, *The Art of Juan Ruiz, Archpriest of Hita*, Madrid: Estudios de Literatura Española, 1965], *Times Literary Supplement*, 13 October: 941.

96. [Review of José Antonio Maravall, *El mundo social de la Celestina*, Madrid: Gredos, 1964], *Bulletin of Hispanic Studies* 43: 125–8.

97. [Review of Otis H. Green, *Spain and the Western Tradition: The Castilian Mind from 'El Cid' to Calderón*, II, Madison, Wis.: University of Madison Press, 1964], *Romance Philology*, 19: 646.

1967

98. 'Arms Versus Letters: Towards a Definition of Spanish Fifteenth-Century Humanism', *Aspects of the Renaissance: A Symposium*, ed. Archibald R. Lewis, Austin, Tex. & London: University of Texas Press: 45–58. Amplified

version transl. Alejandro Pérez as 'Las armas contra las letras: Para una definición del humanismo español del siglo XV', *Temas de la Celestina* (1978): 207–39. Partial repr. in *Historia y crítica de la literatura* española, I: *Edad Media*, ed. Alan Deyermond & Francisco Rico, Barcelona: Crítica, 1980: 442–46.

99. 'León, Kingdom of', XIII, 963; 'Lopes, Fernão', XIV, 306; 'Mendoza, Pedro González de', XV, 153; 'Navarre, Kingdom of', XVI, 137–8; 'Pedro the Cruel (king of Castile)', XVII, 517; 'Pelayo', XVII, 535; 'Peter (kings of Aragon)', XVII, 740; 'Raimundo', XVIII, 1129; 'Ramiro (kings of Aragon)', XVIII, 1148; 'Sancho (kings of León and Castile)', XIX, 993–4; 'Sancho (kings of Pamplona and Aragon)', XIX, 994–5; 'Urraca', XXII, 805; 'Viana, Charles of Aragon', XXII, 1028, *Encyclopaedia Britannica*, rev. 14th edn, Chicago: Encyclopaedia Britannica.

100. [Review of Francis M. Rogers, *The Travels of the Infante Dom Pedro de Portugal*, Cambridge, Mass.: Harvard University Press, 1961], *Modern Language Review*, 60: 132–3.

1968

101. 'Obituary' [of W. Gordon Chapman], *The Oxford Magazine*, 8 March, 239.

102. 'Spanish Manuscripts' [review of Antonio Rodríguez-Moñino & María Brey, *Catálogo de los manuscritos poéticos castellanos (siglos xv, xvi, xvii) de The Hispanic Society of America*, 3 vols, New York: Hispanic Society of America, 1965–6], *Times Literary Supplement*, 27 June: 688.

103. [Review of Derek W. Lomax, *La Orden de Santiago (1170–1275)*, Madrid: CSIC, Escuela de Estudios Medievales, 1965], *Bulletin of Hispanic Studies*, 45: 46–9.

1969

104. '*Don Quixote* as a Funny Book', *Modern Language Review*, 64: 312–26. Amplified version transl. Alejandro Pérez as '*Don Quijote* y la risa a carcajadas', *Temas de la Celestina* (1978): 407–40.

1970

105. [Review of *Actas del segundo congreso internacional de hispanistas celebrado en Nijmegen del 20 al 25 de agosto de 1965*, ed. Jaime Sánchez Romerolo & Norbert Poulussen, Nimegen: Instituto Español de la Universidad, 1967], *Bulletin of Hispanic Studies*, 47: 60–2.

1971

106. 'Fontes documentais castelhanas para a história da expansão portuguesa na Guiné nos últimos anos de D. Afonso V', *Do Tempo e da História*, 4: 5–33. Transl. Kirstin Kennedy as 'Castilian Documentary Sources for the History of the Portuguese Expansion in Guinea in the Last Years of the Reign of Dom Alfonso V', *Portugal, Spain and the African Atlantic* (1995).

107. [Review of Pero da Ponte, *Poesie*, ed. Saverio Panunzio, Biblioteca di Filologia Romanza 10, Bari: Adriatica, 1967], *Medium Ævum*, 40: 195–7.

1972

108. [Review of Vitorino Magalhães-Godinho, *L'Économie de l'empire portugais aux XV et XVI siècles*, Paris: SEVPEN, 1969], *English Historical Review*, 87: 577–80.

1973

109. (ed.) *Spain: A Companion to Spanish Studies*, London: Methuen, xv + 592 pp. + map. Paperback edn 1976; 2nd edn 1977, repr. 1989.

110. 'Fifteenth-Century Lay Humanism', *Spain: A Companion*: 237–42, 245.

111. 'Spanish Literature (1474–1681)', *Spain: A Companion*: 265–380.

112. 'Towards an Interpretation of Rodrigo de Reinosa's "poesía negra"', *Studies in Spanish Literature of the Golden Age Presented to Edward M. Wilson*, ed. Royston O. Jones, Colección Támesis A30, London, Tamesis Books: 225–45. Transl. Alejandro Pérez as 'La poesía negra de Rodrigo de Reinosa', *Temas de la Celestina* (1978): 377–406.

113. [Review of A. H. de Oliveira Marques & S. S. Wyatt, *Daily Life in Portugal in the Late Middle Ages*, Madison, Wis. & London: University of Madison Press, 1963], *Romance Philology*, 29: 362–3.

1974

114. [with Anthony R. D. Pagden] 'Nueva luz sobre una versión española cuatrocentista de la *Ética a Nicomaco*: Bodleian Library, MS.SPAN.d.1', *Homenaje a Guillermo Guastavino: Miscelánea de estudios en el año de su jubilación como Director de la Biblioteca Nacional*, Madrid: Asociación Nacional de Bibliotecarios, Archiveros y Arqueólogos: 125–46.

115. [Review of Adrienne Schizzano Mandel, *'La Celestina' Studies: A Thematic Survey and Bibliography (1824–1970)*, Metuchen, N.J.: Scarecrow, 1971],

Bulletin of Hispanic Studies, 51: 170–2.

116. [Review of Eduardo Sarmiento, *Concordancias de las obras poéticas en castellano de Garcilaso de la Vega*, Madrid: Castalia, 1970], *Modern Language Review*, 69: 435–7.

117. [Review of Alban K. Forcione, *Cervantes, Aristotle, and the 'Persiles'*, Princeton, N.J.: Princeton University Press & London: Oxford University Press, 1970], *Modern Language Review*, 69: 438–40.

118. [Review of Bernard Rekers, *Benito Arias Montano (1527–1598)*, London: Warburg & Leiden: E. J. Brill, 1972], *Modern Language Review*, 89: 631–3.

1975

119. [Review of Stephen Gilman, *The Spain of Fernando de Rojas: The Intellectual and Social Landscape of 'La Celestina'*, Princeton, N.J.: Princeton University Press, 1972], *Comparative Literature*, 27: 59–74. Rev. version transl. Alejandro Pérez as 'Un crítico en busca de un autor: Reflexiones en torno a un reciente libro sobre Fernando de Rojas', *Temas de la Celestina* (1978): 341–75.

1976

120. 'The *Celestina comentada*', *Medieval Hispanic Studies Presented to Rita Hamilton*, ed. Alan D. Deyermond, Colección Támesis A42, London: Tamesis Books: 175–93. Transl. Alejandro Pérez as 'El primer comentario crítico de *La Celestina*: Cómo un legista del siglo XVI interpretaba la Tragicomedia', *Temas de la Celestina* (1978): 293–321.

121. 'Novos apontamentos sobre os problemas textuais do *Voiaige à la Guineé* de Eustáquio de la Fosse (1479–1480)', *Revista Portuguesa de História*, 16 (= *Homenagem ao Doutor Torquato da Sousa Soares*): 209–21. Transl. Kirstin Kennedy as 'New Light on the Text of Eustache de la Fosse's *Voiaige à la Guineé* (1479–1480)', *Portugal, Spain, and the African Atlantic* (1995), 13 pp.

1977

122. [Review of A. D. Deyermond, *Apollonius of Tyre: Two Fifteenth-Century Spanish Prose Romances — 'Hystoria de Apolonia' and 'Confisyón del amante: Apolonyo de Tiro'*, Exeter: Exeter University, 1973], *Medium Ævum*, 46: 157–8.

123. [Review of Kathleen V. Kish, *An Edition of the First Italian Translation of the 'Celestina',* Chapel Hill, N.C.: University of North Carolina Press, 1973, and Fernando de Rojas, *Celestine or the Tragick-Comedie of Calisto and Melibea,* transl. James Mabbe, ed. Guadalupe Martínez Lacalle, London: Támesis, 1972], *Bulletin of Hispanic Studies,* 54: 49–52.

1978

124. *Temas de 'La Celestina' y otros estudios: Del 'Cid' al 'Quijote',* transl. Alejandro Pérez, Letras e Ideas, Maior 14, Barcelona: Ariel, 508 pp.

125. 'Nuevas reflexiones sobre el Alcocer del *Poema de Mio Cid*, *Temas de 'La Celestina'* (1978): 45–69.

126. 'La oración de doña Jimena ('Poema de Mio Cid', vv. 325–367)', *Temas de 'La Celestina'* (1978): 111–58.

127. '*La Celestina* y los estudios jurídicos de Fernando de Rojas', *Temas de 'La Celestina'* (1978): 323–40. Originally delivered as a paper in 1971; repr. in *Actas del IV congreso de la Asociación Internacional de Hispanistas celebrado en Salamanca, agosto de 1971*, ed. Eugenio de Bustos Tovar, 2 vols, Salamanca: Asociación Internacional de Hispanistas [1982], II, 533–42.

128. 'El "Poema de Mio Cid" como documento de información caminera', *Temas de 'La Celestina'* (1978): 159–205.

129. 'El Concilio de Trento y la literatura profana: Reconsideración de una teoría', *Temas de 'La Celestina'* (1978): 441–78.

130. 'El descubrimiento de Canarias y el debate medieval acerca de los derechos de los príncipes y pueblos paganos', *Revista de Historia Canaria,* 36/clxxi: 9–32.

131. 'Un libro indebidamente olvidado: La *Retórica en lengua castellana* (1541) de fray Miguel de Salinas', *Libro-homenaje a Antonio Pérez Gómez,* ed. J. Pérez Gómez, 2 vols, Cieza: La Fonte que Mana e Corre: II, 133–41.

132. [Review of J. N. Hillgarth, *The Spanish Kingdoms, 1250–1516,* I: *Precarious Balance,* Oxford: Clarendon Press, 1976], *Medium Ævum,* 47: 369–71.

133. [Short notice on John Ure, *Prince Henry the Navigator,* London: Constable, 1977], *Bulletin of Hispanic Studies,* 55: 355–56.

1979

134. *Infante D. Henrique e as Ilhas Canárias: Uma Dimensão Mal Compreendida da Biografia Henriquina*, Instituto de Altos Estudios, n.s. 5, Lisbon, Academia das Ciências, 55 pp.

135. 'Francisco de Madrid y su traducción del *De remediis* de Petrarca', *Estudios sobre literatura y arte dedicados al profesor Emilio Orozco Díaz*, ed. Antonio Gallego Morell, Andrés Soria, & Nicolás Marín, 3 vols, Granada: Universidad de Granada: III, 203–20.

136. [Review of: Angus Mackay, *Spain in the Middle Ages: From Frontier to Empire*, London: Macmillan, 1977], *International History Review*, 1: 273–77.

1980

137. 'Problemas Sócio-Linguísticos relacionados com os Descobrimentos Portugueses no Atlântico Africano', *Anais da Academia Portuguesa da História*, 2nd s. 26/ii: 227–50. Transl. Kirstin Kennedy as 'Some Socio-Linguistic Problems Concerning the Fifteenth-Century Portuguese Discoveries in the African Atlantic', *Portugal, Spain, and the African Atlantic* (1995), 15 pp.

138. [Review of Charles R. Boxer, *The Church Militant and Iberian Expansion 1440–1770*, Baltimore, Md. & London: Johns Hopkins University Press, 1978], *Journal of Ecclesiastical History*, 31: 113–15.

1981

139. 'The Infante Dom Henrique and the *Libro del conosçimiento del mundo*', *In Memoriam Ruben Andresen Leitão*, ed. José Sommer Ribeiro, 3 vols, Lisbon, Imprensa Nacional: II, 259–67.

140. 'The War in Spain and Portugal', *Froissart: Historian*, ed. J. J. N. Palmer, Woodbridge: The Boydell Press: 83–100, 172–4. Repr. with original pagination in *Portugal, Spain, and the African Atlantic* (1995).

1982

141. (ed.) *Introducción a la cultura hispánica*, I: *Historia*, transl. Josep Maria Portella, Barcelona: Crítica, 376 pp. Part translation of *Spain: A Companion* (1973).

142. (ed.) *Introducción a la cultura hispánica*, II: *Literatura*, transl. Alberto

Magnet, Barcelona: Crítica, 368 pp. Part translation of *Spain: A Companion* (1973).

143. 'The Last of the Spanish Chivalric Romances: *Don Policisne de Boecia*', *Essays in Narrative Fiction in the Iberian Peninsula in Honour of Frank Pierce*, ed. Brian Tate, Oxford: Dolphin Book Co.: 141–52.

144. 'Secular Literature and the Censors: A Sixteenth-Century Document Re-examined', *Bulletin of Hispanic Studies*, 59: 219–25.

145. [Review of Pere III of Catalonia (Pedro IV of Aragon), *Chronicle*, transl. Mary Hillgarth with intro. & notes by J. N. Hillgarth, 2 vols, Toronto: Pontifical Institute of Medieval Studies, 1980], *Medium Ævum*, 51: 265.

146. [Review of: E. Llamas Martínez, *Bartolomé de Torres: teólogo y obispo de Canarias*, Madrid: CSIC, 1979], *Journal of Ecclesiastical History*, 33: 140–1.

1984

147. *Prince Henry the Navigator: The Rise and Fall of a Culture Hero*, Taylorian Special Lecture, 10 November 1983, Oxford: Clarendon Press, 1984, 30 pp. Repr. with original pagination in *Portugal, Spain, and the African Atlantic* (1995).

1985

148. *Cervantes*, Past Masters, Oxford: Oxford University Press, 1985, viii + 117 pp. Chinese translation published 1988. Czech and Japanese translations published 1996.

149. *Traducciones y traductores en la Península Ibérica (1400–1550)*, Monografies de Quaderns de Traducció i Interpretació 2, Bellaterra: Escuela Universitaria de Traductores e Intérpretes, Universidad Autónoma de Barcelona, 63 pp.

1986

150. 'White Kings on Black Kings: Rui de Pina and the Problem of Black African Sovereignty', *Mediæval and Renaissance Studies in Honour of Robert Brian Tate*, ed. Ian Michael & Richard Cardwell, Oxford: Dolphin Book Co.: 151–63. Repr. with original pagination in *Portugal, Spain, and the African Atlantic* (1995).

1987

151. 'Harry Wilfred House (1895–1987)', *The Queen's College Record*, 6: 4–6.

152. 'La heráldica en el *Libro del conosçimiento*', *Studia in honorem prof. M. de Riquer*, ed. Carlos Alvar *et al.*, 2 vols, Barcelona: Quaderns Crema: II, 687–97.

1988

153. *Cervantes*, transl. Te-Hsing Shan, Taipei: Linking Publishing Co., 127 pp. Chinese translation of 1985 English original.

154. 'Discordia universal: *La Celestina* como "Floresta de philosophos"', *Ínsula*, 43/cdxcvii: 1, 3. Partial repr. in *Historia y crítica de la literatura* española, I: *Edad Media; primer suplemento*, ed. Alan Deyermond & Francisco Rico, Barcelona: Crítica, 1991: 400–5.

1989

155. 'Why did Celestina Move House?', *The Age of the Catholic Monarchs, 1474–1516: Literary Studies in Memory of Keith Whinnom*, ed. Alan Deyermond & Ian Macpherson, *Bulletin of Hispanic Studies*, special issue: 155–61.

1990

156. [Review of Fernando de Rojas, *La Celestina*, ed. Dorothy S. Severin, Madrid: Cátedra, 1987, and Fernando de Rojas, *Celestina*, ed. & transl. Dorothy S. Severin, Warminster: Aris & Phillips, 1987]. *Bulletin of Hispanic Studies*, 67: 294–6.

1991

157. (ed.), Fernando de Rojas, *Comedia o Tragicomedia de Calisto y Melibea*, Clásicos Castalia 191, Madrid: Castalia, 634 pp. Rev. edn 1993.

1992

158. 'Prince Henry and the Necessary End', *Studies in the Portuguese Discoveries*, I: *Proceedings of the First Colloquium of the Centre for the Study of the Portuguese Discoveries*, ed. Thomas F. Earle & Stephen Parkinson, Warminster: Aris & Phillips with Commisão Nacional para as Comemorações dos Descobrimentos Portugueses: 1–15. Repr. with original pagination in *Portugal, Spain, and the African Atlantic* (1995).

159. 'Some Portuguese Paradigms for the Discovery and Conquest of Spanish America', *Renaissance Studies*, 6 (= *The Encounter of Two Worlds in the Renaissance*, ed. John Larner): 377–90.

1993

160. (ed.), Fernando de Rojas, *La Celestina: Comedia o Tragicomedia de Calisto y Melibea*, 2nd edn of 1991 original, Clásicos Castalia 191, Madrid: Castalia, 634 pp. Rev. edn 2001.

161. '*Veni, vidi, vici*: Some Fifteenth-Century Eyewitness Accounts of Travel in the African Atlantic before 1492', *Historical Research*, 66/clx: 115–28. Repr. in *Medieval Ethnographies: European Perceptions of the World Beyond*, ed. Joan-Pau Rubiés, Ashgate Variorum, Farnham: Ashgate, 2009: 315–28. Transl. Xon de Ros as '*Veni, vidi, vici:* La lucha para captar lo desconocido: Cómo algunos viajeros extranjeros percibieron antes de 1492 el nuevo mundo atlántico de los portugueses', *Actas del primer congreso anglo-hispano*, 3 vols, Madrid: Castalia for AHGBI, 1993, II: *Literatura*, ed. Alan Deyermond & Ralph Penny: 3–23.

1995

162. *Portugal, Spain, and the African Atlantic, 1343–1490: Chivalry and Crusade from John of Gaunt to Henry the Navigator*, Variorum CS496, Aldershot: Variorum, xiv + 327 pp.

163. 'Archivists as Historians: The Case of the Portuguese Fifteenth-Century Chroniclers', *Historical Literature in Medieval Iberia*, ed. Alan Deyermond, Papers of the Medieval Hispanic Research Seminar 2, London: Department of Hispanic Studies, Centre for Medieval Studies, Queen Mary & Westfield College: 67–83. Repr. in *Portugal, Spain, and the African Atlantic* (1995), 16 pp.

164. 'El problema de lo inconsecuente textual en *La Celestina*', *La Célestine, comedia o tragicomedia de Calisto y Melibea: Actes du Colloque International du 29–30 janvier 1993*, ed. Françoise Maurizi, Caen: Université de Caen: 9–18.

1996

165. *Cervantes*, transl. Jiří Kasl, with epilogue by Josef Polišenský, Prague: Argo, 127 pp. Czech translation of 1985 English original.

166. *Cervantes*, transl. Tajima Shingo, Tokyo: Kyobunkan, 220 pp. Japanese translation of 1985 English original.

1997

167. 'The Medieval Castilian Translation of Vegetius, *Epitome de rei militaris*: An Introduction', *Spain and its Literature: Essays in Memory of E. Allison Peers*, ed. Anne L. Mackenzie, *Bulletin of Hispanic Studies*, special issue, Hispanic Studies TRAC 15, Liverpool: Liverpool University Press for the MHRA: 49–64.

168. 'A Quest Too Far: Henry the Navigator and Prester John', *The Medieval Mind: Hispanic Studies in Honour of Alan Deyermond*, ed. Ian Macpherson & Ralph Penny, London: Tamesis Books: 401–16.

169. 'Professor Charles Kennedy', *The Independent*, 27 November 1997, <www.independent.co.uk/news/obituaries/obituary-professor-charles-kennedy-1296535.html>.

2000

170. *A Intervenção Inglesa na Península Ibérica durante a Guerra dos Cem Anos*, transl. Maria Ramos, Lisbon: Imprensa Nacional & Casa da Moeda, 649 pp. Translation of 1955 English original.

171. *Prince Henry 'the Navigator': A Life*, New Haven, Conn. & London: Yale University Press, xvi + 448 pp. + map. Portuguese translation published 2004.

2001

172. (ed.), Fernando de Rojas, *La Celestina: Comedia o Tragicomedia de Calisto y Melibea*, 3rd edn of 1991 original, Clásicos Castalia 191, Madrid: Castalia, 648 pp.

173. 'The *Celestina* Then and Now', *Context, Meaning, and Reception of 'Celestina': A Fifth Centenary Symposium*, ed. Ian Michael & David G. Pattison (= *Bulletin of Hispanic Studies* (Glasgow), 78/i): 1–11.

174. 'Terá Havido uma Tradução Medieval Portuguesa do *Epitome rei militaris* de Vegécio?', *Euphrosyne*, 29: 247–56.

175. 'De nuevo sobre la traducción castellana medieval de Vegecio, *Epitoma de rei militaris*', *Essays on Medieval Translation in the Iberian Peninsula*, ed. Tomàs Martínez Romero & Roxana Recio Castelló, Castelló de la Plana: Universitat Jaume I, 325–40.

176. 'Edward Calverley Riley', *The Queen's College Record*, 7: 93–5.

2002

177. 'Reinventing an Epic Poet: 1952 in Context', *'Mio Cid' Studies: 'Some Problems of Diplomatic' Fifty Years On*, ed. Alan Deyermond, David G. Pattison, & Eric Southworth, Papers of the Medieval Hispanic Research Seminar, London: Department of Hispanic Studies, Queen Mary University of London: 63–72.

2004

178. *Henrique O Navegador*, transl. Ana Carvalho, Lisbon: Livros Horizonte, 390 pp. Translation of 2000 English original.

179. 'Ian Michael: A Personal Appreciation', *The Iberian Book and its Readers: Essays for Ian Michael*, ed. Nigel Griffin, Clive Griffin, & Eric Southworth (= *Bulletin of Spanish Studies*, 81.7–8): vii–x.

180. 'Entwistle, William James (1895–1952)', *Oxford Dictionary of National Biography*, <doi.org/10.1093/ref:odnb/33024>; revised 25 May 2006.

Sources

I. UNPUBLISHED SOURCES

The remains of Russell's archive, occupying approximately three yards of shelf space, is in the care of the author. Listed below in sections a. and b. are the main private records in that collection together with significant bodies of correspondence with others. Sections c. and d. list a surviving unpublished paper and three recordings, two of them produced for the BBC. Section e. lists such memoirs etc. of those who knew him as have been gathered in the preparation of this biography, and section f. lists documents available in public archives. Other scattered items from the archive and the author's email exchanges with the many contributors to this volume are referenced in the footnotes.

a. Journals, Diaries, Memoirs etc.
Pocket diary, 1 Jan.–15 May 1926.
Pocket diary, 1 Jan.–31 Dec. 1932.
Fair copy of expurgated pocket diary, 1 Jan.–9 Aug. 1933.
Pocket diary, 9 Aug.–29 Dec. 1933.
Partially expurgated pocket diary, 4 Jan.–31 Dec. 1934.
Notes on a trip to Germany, Summer 1934.
'Beauty', Summer 1934.
Drafts of short stories and unfinished novel, typescript and manuscript, 1932–4.
'Notes made in Kunst-Historisches Museum in Vienna', Summer 1935.
'À la recherche du temps perdu' [ALRTP], memories of boyhood in Christchurch, New Zealand and Southsea, England, 1913–1926, manuscript, Aug.–Dec. 1935, 40 pp.
Commonplace book, 1930s.
Journal, 27 June–12 Sept. 1936.
Journal and memoir kept in Oxford, 25 Sept. 1937–March 1942.
Memoir of 23 Aug.–20 Dec. 1940.
Commonplace book, 1940s.
Address book, 1940s–1960s.

Official MI5 reports and correspondence, West Indies, West Africa and Ceylon, 1942–5.
Notes of travels in West, Central and East Africa, 1944–5.
Journal kept in Ceylon, India, the Andaman Islands, Singapore, in SS *Antenor* and Oxford, 20 Sept. 1945–22 March 1946.
Journal of trip to Spain, 8 Aug.–22 Sept. 1946.
Journal of trip to France and Spain, 1 Sept.–5 Oct. 1947.
Journal kept in Oxford and of trip to Ireland, 9 Jan.–6 April 1948.
Journal of trip to Spain and France, 5–28 Sept. 1948.
Freudian journal, 1955–62.
Journal of trips to Caribbean, Mexico and the United States (Summer 1959), to Portugal and Spain (Autumn 1959), and to New Zealand via Nandi, Queensland (Autumn 1961).
Oxford University pocket diaries (1938–9, 1946–8, 1949–51, 1952–61, 1962–71, 1975–7, 1980–2006).
Desk diary, 1967.

b. Private Correspondence
Nigel Griffin Archive, Pech, Lot-et-Garonne: correspondence with PER, 1971–87.
Jo Heigham correspondence with PER, 1945.
Charles Kennedy correspondence to PER, 1950–64.
George Kolkhorst correspondence to PER, 1945–57.
Javier Marías Archive, Madrid [JMA]: correspondence with PER, 1998–2002.
Ted Parks Archive, Nashville, Tenn.: correspondence with PER, 1991–6.
E. C. Riley correspondence to PER, 1947–86.
Rita Russell correspondence with PER, 1949–65.

c. Academic Paper
'Some Thoughts After Editing *La Celestina*', undated printout, c. 1992.

d. Recordings
'Spanish Fiction from the Romance to the Novel', BBC Radio 3, 27 March 1977.
'Recollections of the Second Spanish Republic: Sir Peter Russell, FBA (King Alfonso XIII Professor of Spanish Studies 1953–81) in conversation with Dr Xon de Ros (King's College, London)', Taylor Institution, Spanish Graduate Seminar, 26 May 1998 [RSSR]; Taylor Institution Library, TAPES.137.
'The Prince of Navigators', BBC Radio 4, 1 May 1999.

e. Memoirs and Reminiscences

Lee Fontanella, memoir, 8 Jan. 2021.

Nigel Griffin, Clive Griffin, Eric Southworth and Colin Thompson, 'Russell as Lecturer', 26 June 2020.

Ronald Hilton, *Spain, 1931–36: From Monarchy to Civil War. An Eye Witness Account*, word-processed copy, 71 pp.

David Hook, memoir, 22 Sept. 2020.

Kirstin Kennedy, memoir, 10 Nov. 2023.

Ted Parks, 'Reflections on Peter Russell', 18 March 2023.

Xon de Ros, notes to the author, 16 Sept. 2020.

Rita Muriel Russell, *Life Story* [RMR], 1964, word-processed copy edited by Hugh Russell, 67 pp.

John Rutherford, address delivered at memorial service in Exeter College Chapel, 28 Oct. 2006.

Madeline Sutherland-Meier, 'Sir Peter Russell in Texas', 5 Jan. 2021.

Colin P. Thompson, presentation, 28 Feb. 2020.

Colin Wight, memoir, 6 June 2020.

f. Documents in Public Archives

Archives New Zealand [ANZ], Wellington:

Service record of Hugh Bernard Wheeler in the New Zealand Staff Corps, Item Code: R23514060, Series Code: 18805, 405 pp; at <ndhadeliver.natlib.govt.nz/delivery/DeliveryManagerServlet?dps_pid=IE19153613>.

British Academy Archive, London:

'Peter Edward Lionel Russell' [PELR], account of his life up to 1953 prepared 'for possible necrological use', word-processed, deposited Nov. 1992, 4 pp.

Canterbury Museum, Christchurch:

Macdonald Dictionary Record of the early settlers of the Canterbury region, at <collection.canterburymuseum.com/objects?query=Macdonald+Dictionary+Record>.

Cheltenham College Archive, Cheltenham:

Peter Edward Lionel Russell Wheeler documents, application, academic reports etc.

Exeter College Archive, Oxford:

Russell Letters LIV 6, 16 pp.

The National Archives [TNA], Kew:

KV [Security Service] 4/18, Report on the work of Defence Security Officers in British colonies and liaison with the Dominions, 1945.

KV 4/185–196, 4/466–467, Liddell Diaries, 20 vols., at <discovery.nationalarchives.gov.uk/browse/r/h/C11090133> (etc.)

KV 4/447, Organisation of and liaison with British Security Coordination, USA, at <discovery.nationalarchives.gov.uk/details/r/C11541089>.

WO [War Office] 339-43150, Service record of Hugh Bernard Wheeler in the British Army, 43 pp.

Oxford University Archive [OUA], Oxford:

Election to the Alfonso XIII Chair of Spanish Studies, 1952–3:

OUA/UR 6/SPC/1B, file 2.

Staff academic personnel files for P. E. L. Russell:

OUA/FA 9/1/265 PEL Russell, 1945–53.

OUA/FA 9/2/765 PEL Russell, 1957–81.

The Queen's College Archive, Oxford:

Provost E. M. Walker's interview notes on PER, 1931.

The Taylor Institution Library, Oxford:

ALMA 990209434290107026, MS of speech delivered at the Spanish Club by George Kolkhorst on 24 Feb. 1932, when the guest of honour was Ramón Pérez de Ayala (Spanish Ambassador).

MS.Fol.E.20, George Kolkhorst correspondence to Charles Kennedy, 1949–57 [GKCK], with word-processed transcript ed. I. D. L. Michael (2006), 99 pp.

II. PUBLISHED SOURCES

anon., 'Modern Language Scholarships at Oxford', *The Oxford Magazine*, 4 Feb. 1926, 249–50.

Alden, Dauril, *Charles R. Boxer. An Uncommon Life. Soldier, Historian, Teacher, Collector, Traveller* (Lisbon: Fundação Oriente, 2001).

Annan, Noel, *The Dons: Mentors, Eccentrics and Geniuses* (London: Harper Collins, 1999).

Anstee, Margaret Joan, *JB: An Unlikely Spanish Don. The Life and Times of Professor John Brande Trend* (Brighton, E. Sussex: Sussex Academic Press, 2013).

Atkin, Malcolm, *Pioneers of Irregular Warfare: Secrets of the Military Intelligence Research Department in the Second World War* (Barnsley, S. Yorks.: Pen & Sword, 2021).

Baird, Liz, *One Hundred Years of Spanish at Oxford 1905–2005* (Oxford: Taylor Institution, 2005); available as 'A History of Spanish at Oxford' at

<www.mod-langs.ox.ac.uk/spanish/history-spanish-oxford>.

Balsdon, Dacre, *Oxford Now and Then* (London: Macmillan, 1970).

Barthes, Roland, *Mythologies* (Paris: Editions du Seuil, 1957).

Bataillon, Claude, *Marcel Bataillon: Hispanisme et engagement. Lettres, carnets, textes retrouvés (1914–1967)* (Toulouse: Presses Universitaires du Mirail, 2009).

Bataillon, Marcel, *Erasme et l'Espagne: Recherches sur l'histoire spirituelle du XVIe siècle* (Paris: Droz, 1937).

——, *La Célestine selon Fernando de Rojas* (Paris: Librairie de Marcel Didier, 1963).

Betjeman, John, *Summoned by Bells* (London: John Murray, 1960).

——, *Letters*, ed. Candida Lycett Green, 2 vols. (London: Methuen, 1994–5).

Bloch, Michael, *The Duke of Windsor's War* (London: Weidenfeld & Nicolson, 1982).

——, *Operation Willi: The Nazi Plot to Kidnap the Duke of Windsor, July 1940* (London: Weidenfeld & Nicolson, 1984).

Bowra, Maurice, *Memories 1898–1939* (London: Weidenfeld & Nicolson, 1966).

Bragança, D. Duarte de, '"Discoveries Did Most for Human Progress": D. Duarte Defends D. Henrique', *Anglo-Portuguese News*, 17 Aug. 2000, 10.

Brooks, J. L., 'Walter Fitzwilliam Starkie (1894–1976)', *Bulletin of Hispanic Studies* 54 (1977), no. 4, 327.

Burns, Jimmy, *Papa Spy: Love, Faith, and Betrayal in Wartime Spain* (New York: Walker & Company, 2009).

Carr, E. H., *What Is History?*, ed. R. W. Davies (Harmondsworth, Middx.: Penguin, 1961).

Castro, Américo, *España en su historia* (Madrid: Losada, 1948; subsequently revised).

Coleman, E. C., *The Royal Navy and Polar Exploration*, vol. II: *From Franklin to Scott* (Stroud, Glos.: Tempus, 2007).

Collingwood, R. G., *The Idea of History*, ed. Jan van der Dussen (Oxford: Oxford University Press, 1993).

Conroy, Bill, 'The Final Tragedy: Remembering Hilda Evans', *Antarctic* [New Zealand Antarctic Society] 33.3 (2015), no. 233, 26–8, at <antarcticsociety.org.nz/wp-content/uploads/2018/05/Antarctic.V33.3.2015.pdf>.

Crispin, John, *Oxford y Cambridge en Madrid. La Residencia de Estudiantes (1910–1936) y su entorno cultural* (Santander: La Isla de los Ratones,

1981).

Curry, John, *The Security Service, 1908–1945: The Official History* (Kew: Public Record Office, 1999).

Cuthbertson, Ken, *Nobody Said Not to Go: The Life, Loves, and Adventures of Emily Hahn* (London: Faber and Faber, 1998).

Danchev, Alex, *Oliver Franks: Founding Father* (Oxford: Oxford University Press, 1993).

Debicki, Andrew P., *Dámaso Alonso* (New York: Twayne Publishers, 1970).

Deyermond, Alan, 'Professor Sir Peter Russell', *The Independent*, 5 July 2006.

―――, ed., *A Century of British Medieval Studies* (Oxford: Oxford University Press & British Academy, 2007).

―――, 'Introduction' in *id.*, Pattison & Southworth, eds., *'Mio Cid' Studies: 'Some Problems of Diplomatic' Fifty Years On*, 7–14.

―――, 'Introducción' in Axayácatl Campos García Rojas & Daniel Gutiérrez Trápaga, eds., *Estudios de Alan Deyermond sobre la 'Celestina': in memoriam* [= *Medievalia*, 40] (2008), 9–16.

―――, 'Rereading Stephen Gilman's *The Art of "La Celestina"*, *Bulletin of Hispanic Studies*, 86 (2009), 121–32.

Deyermond, Alan, & Jeremy Lawrance, eds., *Letters and Society in Fifteenth-Century Spain: Studies Presented to P.E. Russell on His Eightieth Birthday* (Llangrannog, Ceredigion: The Dolphin Book Co., 1993).

Deyermond, Alan, David G. Pattison & Eric Southworth, eds., *'Mio Cid' Studies. 'Some Problems of Diplomatic' Fifty Years On* (London: University of London, 2002).

Disney, A. R., *A History of Portugal and the Portuguese Empire*, 2 vols. (Cambridge: Cambridge University Press, 2009).

Donaldson, Frances, *The British Council: The First Fifty Years* (London: Jonathan Cape, 1984).

Dunham, Laura, 'The Domestic Architecture of Collins and Harman in Canterbury, 1883–1927', Ph.D. thesis, University of Canterbury, 2013, at <core.ac.uk/download/pdf/35471212.pdf>.

Eccles, Sybil & David, *By Safe Hand: Letters of Sybil and David Eccles, 1939–42* (London: Bodley Head, 1983).

Elwell, Charles, *Ann Catherine Elwell: A Memoir* (Guildford, Surrey: privately, 1997).

Empson, William, *Seven Types of Ambiguity* (London: Chatto and Windus, 1930).

Entwistle, William J., *The Scope of Spanish Studies. An Inaugural Lecture Delivered before the University of Oxford on 3 November 1932* (Oxford: Clarendon Press, 1932).

―――, 'Modern Language Studies in Oxford', *The Oxford Magazine*, 16 Feb. 1933, 427–9.

――― ['W. J. E.'], 'Don Miguel de Unamuno', *The Oxford Magazine*, 10 Nov. 1938, 369–70.

―――, *Cervantes* (Oxford: Clarendon Press, 1940).

―――, 'British Hispanism during the War', *Bulletin Hispanique* 48 (1946), no. 1, 44–9.

Evans, Edward R. G. R., *South with Scott* (London: Collins, 1921); *see also under* Mountevans.

Evans, Julian, 'Lt. "Teddy" Evans and Hilda Russell, 1902–1913: Biographical Research' (2011), at <pdfs.semanticscholar.org/ee0e/d769fc03fbf19562da14446e908de46411b2.pdf>.

Ewert, Alfred, 'William James Entwistle', *Proceedings of the British Academy* 38 (1952), 333–43.

Faber, Sebastiaan, *Anglo-American Hispanists and the Spanish Civil War: Hispanophilia, Commitment and Discipline* (New York: Palgrave Macmillan, 2008).

Fernández-Armesto, Felipe, 'His Was a World of Shabby Swagger: Henry the Navigator', *Literary Review* (June 2000), 17–18.

Fiennes, Ranulph, *Captain Scott* (London: Hodder & Stoughton, 2003).

Firth, Sir Charles, *Modern Languages at Oxford, 1724–1929* (London: Oxford University Press, 1929).

Fisher, G. F., reply to 'Modern Language Scholarships at Oxford', *The Oxford Magazine*, 11 Feb. 1926, 290.

Foligno, Cesare, 'The School of Modern Languages', *The Oxford Magazine*, 15 May 1930, 705–8.

Fonseca, Luís Adão da, 'A Key Book about the Portuguese Fourteenth Century: *The English Intervention in Spain and Portugal in the Time of Edward II and Richard II* by Peter E. Russell', *e-JPH* 11, no. 1 (Summer 2013), 1–14; <www.brown.edu/Departments/Portuguese_Brazilian_Studies/ejph/html/issue21/pdf/v11n1a05.pdf>.

Frost, Ann, *The Emergence and Growth of Hispanic Studies in British and Irish Universities* (n.p.: Association of Hispanists of Great Britain and Ireland, 2019).

Gallagher David, 'Meetings with the Master: Mario Vargas Llosa's Encounters with Jorge Luis Borges', *Times Literary Supplement*, 29 Jan. 2021.

Gathorne-Hardy, Jonathan, *The Interior Castle: A Life of Gerald Brenan* (London: Sinclair-Stevenson, 1992).

Gilman, Stephen, *The Art of 'La Celestina'* (Madison, Wis.: University of Wisconsin Press, 1957).

_____, *The Spain of Fernando de Rojas: The Intellectual and Social Landscape of* La Celestina (Princeton, N.J.: Princeton University Press, 1972).

_____, 'Sobre la identidad histórica de Fernando de Rojas (Contestación al Profesor Peter Russell)', *Nueva Revista de Filología Hispánica* 26 (1977), no. 1, 154–8.

Giménez-Frontín, José Luis, *Señorear la tierra* (Barcelona: Seix Barral, 1991).

_____, *Woodstock Road en julio: Notas y diario* (Pamplona: Pamiela, 1996).

González Hernández, María Jesús, *Raymond Carr: The Curiosity of the Fox* (Brighton, E. Sussex: Sussex Academic Press, 2013).

Greene, Graham, *The Heart of the Matter* (London: Heinemann, 1948).

Griffin, Nigel, 'Sir Peter Russell', *The Guardian*, 22 Aug. 2006.

Griswold-Morley, Sylvanus, & Albert E. Sloman, 'William James Entwistle: Two Memoirs', *Bulletin of Hispanic Studies* 29 (1952), 183–92.

Harrison, Brian, ed., *The History of the University of Oxford*, vol. VIII: *The Twentieth Century* (Oxford: Clarendon Press, 1994).

Hillier, Bevis, *John Betjeman: New Fame, New Love* (London: John Murray, 2002).

_____, *Young Betjeman* (London: John Murray, 2003).

Hinsley, F. H., & C. A. G. Simkins, *British Intelligence in the Second World War*, vol. IV: *Security and Counter-Intelligence* (Cambridge: Cambridge University Press, 1990).

Hilton, Ronald, *Spain, 1931–36, From Monarchy to Civil War, An Eyewitness Account* (2000), at <historicaltextarchive.org/books.php?action =nextpre& bid=11>.

Hodcroft, F., *Theses in Hispanic Studies Approved for Higher Degrees by British and Irish Universities (1972–1974) (with some Additional Earlier Titles)*, *Bulletin of Hispanic Studies* 52 (1975), 325–44.

Hodcroft, F. W., D. G. Pattison, R. D. F. Pring-Mill & R. W. Truman, eds., *Medieval and Renaissance Studies on Spain and Portugal in Honour of P.E. Russell* (Oxford: The Society for the Study of Mediæval Languages and Literature, 1981).

Hurtley, Jacqueline, *Walter Starkie: An Odyssey* (Dublin: Four Courts Press, 2013).

Huxley, Elspeth, *Scott of the Antarctic* (London: Weidenfeld & Nicolson, 1977).

Hyde, H. Montgomery, *The Quiet Canadian: The Secret Service Story of Sir William Stephenson* (London: Hamish Hamilton, 1962).

Jiménez Fraud, Alberto, *Epistolario, 1905–1964*, ed. James Valender, José García-Velasco, Tatiana Aguilar-Álvarez Bay & Trilce Arroyo, 3 vols. (Madrid: Publicaciones de la Residencia de Estudiantes, 2018).

Johnson, M., *Theses in Hispanic Studies Approved for Higher Degrees by British and Irish Universities (1979–1982) (with some Additional Earlier Titles)*, Bulletin of Hispanic Studies 61 (1984), 233–61.

———, *Theses in Hispanic Studies Approved for Higher Degrees by British and Irish Universities (1983–1987) (with some Additional Earlier Titles)*, Bulletin of Hispanic Studies 66 (1989), 417–44.

Jones, C. A., *Theses in Hispanic Studies Approved for Higher Degrees by British Universities to 1971*, Bulletin of Hispanic Studies 49 (1972), 325–54.

Kelshall, Gaylord T. M., *The U-Boat War in the Caribbean* (Port of Spain: Paria Publishing, 1988).

Lancaster, Osbert, *With an Eye to the Future* (London: Century Hutchinson, 1986; first published 1967).

Lawrance, Jeremy, 'Professor Sir Peter Russell', *The Daily Telegraph*, 10 July 2006.

Lopes, Fernão, *Crónica del Rei dom Joham I da boa memoria e dos Reis de Portugal o decimo*, ed. William J. Entwistle, 2 vols. (Lisbon: Imprensa Nacional, 1968–73).

Lowe, John, *The Warden: a Portrait of John Sparrow* (London: HarperCollins, 1998).

Lownie, Andrew, *Traitor King: The Scandalous Exile of the Duke and Duchess of Windsor* (London: Blink Publishing, 2021).

Lyth, Oliver, 'Wilfrid Ruprecht Bion', *The International Journal of Psycho-Analysis* 61 (1980), 269–73.

Macdonald, Bill, *The True 'Intrepid': Sir William Stephenson and the Unknown Agents* (Surrey, B.C.: Timberholme Books, 1998).

Macedo, Jorge Borges de, 'A propósito do centenário da Aliança Luso-Britânica: A historiografia britânica em Portugal', *Palestra: Revista de Pedagogia e Cultura* 42 (1973), 7–43.

Mackenzie, D., *Theses in Hispanic Studies Approved for Higher Degrees by*

British and Irish Universities (1975–1978) (with some Additional Earlier Titles)', *Bulletin of Hispanic Studies* 56 (1979), 283–304.

Madariaga, Salvador de, *Morning Without Noon: Memoirs* (Farnborough, Hants.: Saxon House, 1974).

Malkiel, María Rosa Lida de, *La Originalidad artística de 'La Celestina'* (Buenos Aires: Editorial Universidad de Buenos Aires, 1962).

Marías, Javier, *Todas las Almas* (Barcelona: Anagrama, 1989).

―――, *Negra espalda del tiempo* (Madrid: Alfaguara, 1998).

―――, *Tu rostro mañana*, 3 vols. (Madrid: Alfaguara, 2002–7).

―――, 'Como un caballero bueno', *El País*, 23 July 2006.

―――, *Berta Isla* (Madrid: Alfaguara, 2017).

―――, *Tomás Nevinson* (Madrid: Alfaguara, 2021).

McCallum, R. B., 'The Advance of the Advanced Students', *The Oxford Magazine*, 30 April 1936, 512–4.

Michael, Ian, 'Afterword: Spanish at Oxford, 1595–1998', *Bulletin of Hispanic Studies* (Glasgow) 76 (1999), 173–93.

―――, 'Sir Peter Russell (1913–2006)', *Bulletin of Spanish Studies* 83 (2006), 1133–44.

―――, 'Russell, Sir Peter Edward Lionel (1913–2006), Spanish and Portuguese scholar', *Oxford Dictionary of National Biography*, <doi.org/10.1093/ref:odnb/97323>; revised 10 Jan. 2013.

Mitchell, Leslie, *Maurice Bowra: A Life* (Oxford: Oxford University Press, 2009).

Monteiro, João Gouveia, 'Sir Peter E. Russell: The 20th Century in the Palm of His Hand'; <www.brown.edu/Departments/Portuguese_Brazilian_Studies/ejph/html/issue9/html/jmonteiro_main.html>.

Mountevans, Admiral Lord [E. R. G. R. Evans], *Adventurous Life* (London: Hutchinson & Co., 1946).

Nares, Gordon, 'Yarnton Manor, Oxfordshire', *Country Life* no. 110, 21 Dec. 1951, 2096–9, & no. 111, 28 Dec. 1951, 2162–5.

Oxford University Calendar (Oxford: Clarendon Press, 1931–81).

Oxford University Examination Papers. Second Public Examination. Honour School of Modern Languages (Oxford: Clarendon Press, 1932–5).

Oxford University Gazette 62–112 (Oxford: Clarendon Press, 1931–81).

Paquette, Gabriel, 'The "Parry Report" and the Establishment of Latin American Studies in the United Kingdom', *The Historical Journal* 62 (2018), 1–22.

Parker, A. A., *Literature and the Delinquent* (Edinburgh: Edinburgh University Press, 1967).

Pérez de Arcos, Marina, 'Individual, Institution, and Impact: The Untold History of the de Osma Studentship in Spanish Studies at Oxford', *Hispanic Research Journal: Iberian and Latin American Studies* 21 (2020), no. 3, 276–320, at <tandfonline.com/doi/full/10.1080/14682737.2020.1874721>.

———, 'Education, Intelligence and Cultural Diplomacy at the British Council in Madrid, 1940–1941' in two parts: 'Part 1: Founding a School in Troubled Times' & 'Part 2: Shock Troops in the War of Ideas', *Bulletin of Spanish Studies* 98 (2021), no. 4, 527–55, & no. 5, 707–38, at <doi.org/10.1080/14753820.2021.1896232> and <doi.org/10.1080/14753820.2021.1896233> respectively.

Pound, Reginald, *Evans of the Broke: A Biography of Admiral Lord Mountevans K.C.B., D.S.O., LL.D.* (London: Oxford University Press, 1963).

———, *Gillies: Surgeon Extraordinary. A Biography* (London: Michael Joseph, 1964).

Powys, E. L. G., P. G. Smith & L. de Oriol, eds., *El Imán: Revista del Oxford University Spanish Club* (Oxford: Holywell, 1928).

Prieto, Gregorio, *Students: Oxford-Cambridge, 20 Drawings* (London: Dolphin Bookshop Editions, 1938).

Pring-Mill, R. D. F., 'William James Entwistle', *Romanistisches Jahrbuch* 5 (1952), 43–7.

Pryce, Mike, 'Centenary of Scott of Antarctic', at <nzshipmarine.com/nodes/view/1077>.

Richardson, Joanna, *Enid Starkie: A Biography* (London: Macmillan, 1973).

Riley, E. C., *Cervantes's Theory of the Novel* (Oxford: Clarendon Press, 1962).

Riley, Judy, 'E. C. Riley (1923–2001)', *Cervantes: Bulletin of the Cervantes Society of America* 22.1 (2002), 5–7.

Rodríguez Baltanás, Enrique Jesús, 'El matrimonio imposible de Calisto y Melibea: notas a un enigma' in Pedro M. Piñero Ramírez, ed., *Dejar hablar a los textos: Homenaje a Francisco Márquez Villanueva* (Seville: Universidad de Sevilla, 2005), 281–308.

Round, Nicholas G., 'The Politics of Hispanism Reconstrued', *Journal of Hispanic Research* 1 (1992), 134–47.

———, 'Alan David Deyermond, 1932–2009', *Biographical Memoirs of Fellows of the British Academy* 12 (2013), 79–122.

Russell, G. W., *A New Heaven* (London: Methuen, 1919).

———, *New Zealand Today: "A Priceless Gem in the Imperial Crown"* (Christchurch: G. W. Russell, 1919).

Russell, Hugh Bernard Langford, *One Man's Journey through Life* (Edinburgh: privately, 2008).

Rutherford, John, 'Peter Edward Lionel Russell', *The Queen's College Record* (2006), 91–4.

Sánchez-Albornoz, Claudio, *España: un enigma histórico*, 2 vols. (Buenos Aires: Editorial Sudamericana, 1956).

Saunders, A. C. de C. M., *A Social History of Black Slaves and Freedmen in Portugal, 1441–1555* (Cambridge: Cambridge University Press, 1982).

Savours, Ann, *The Voyages of the* Discovery*: The Illustrated History of Scott's Ship* (London: Virgin Books, 1992).

Silva, Isabel Morgado S. E., review of Peter Russell *Prince Henry the Navigator*, *Journal of World History* 14 (Sept. 2003), 411–14.

Sisman, Adam, *An Honourable Englishmen: The Life of Hugh Trevor-Roper* (London: Weidenfeld & Nicolson, 2010).

Smith, Colin, *Ramón Menéndez Pidal, 1869–1968* (London: The Hispanic & Luso Brazilian Councils, 1970).

Taylor, Bruce, 'Professor Sir Peter Russell' [abridged], *The Times*, 14 July 2006.

———, 'Peter Edward Lionel Russell, 1913–2006', *Proceedings of the British Academy* 172 (2011), 275–89.

Thirlwall, A. P., *Charles Kennedy 1923–1997: An Appreciation*, Studies in Economics No. 98/15 (Canterbury: University of Kent, Department of Economics, 1998).

Thompson, Colin P., 'Address Given at the Service of Thanksgiving for the Life of Professor Sir Peter Russell (24 October 1913–22 June 2006)', *Bulletin of Hispanic Studies* 84 (2007), 263–5.

Trevor-Roper, Hugh, *Letters from Oxford: Hugh Trevor-Roper to Bernard Berenson*, ed. Richard Davenport-Hines (London: Weidenfeld & Nicolson, 2006).

———, *The Secret World: Behind the Curtain of British Intelligence in World War II and the Cold War*, ed. Edward Harrison (London: I.B. Tauris, 2014).

Truman, R. W., 'The Revd John Bowle's Quixotic Woes Further Explored', *Cervantes. Bulletin of the Cervantes Society of America* 23 (2003), 9–43.

University Grants Committee, *Report of the Committee on Latin American Studies* [The 'Parry Report'] (London: HMSO, 1965).

University of Oxford Examination Statutes (Oxford: Clarendon Press, 1926–40).

Valle Lersundi, Fernando del, 'Documentos referentes a Fernando de Rojas',

Revista de Filología Española 12 (1925), 385–96.

_____, 'Testamento de Fernando de Rojas, autor de *La Celestina*', *Revista de Filología Española* 16 (1929), 365–88.

Valverde Azula, Inés, 'Documentos referentes a Fernando de Rojas en el Archivo Municipal de Talavera de la Reina', *Celestinesca* 16.2 (1992), 81–104.

Weber, Ronald, *The Lisbon Route: Entry and Escape in Nazi Europe* (Landham, Md.: Ivan R. Dee, 2011).

Weiss, Julian, ed., *Studies in Honour of Peter E. Russell on His 80th Birthday* [= *Celestinesca* 17.2] (Fall 1993).

Whinnom, Keith, review of Stephen Gilman, *The Spain of Fernando de Rojas: The Intellectual and Social Landscape of 'La Celestina'*, *Bulletin of Hispanic Studies* 52 (1975), 158–61.

Wight, Colin, 'Don Javier Marías Franco', 21 Feb. 2019: <colinwight.blog/2019/02/21/d-javier-marias/>.

Williamson, Edwin, 'E. C. Riley (1923–2001)', *Bulletin of Hispanic Studies* 78 (2001), 635–8.

Wright, Peter, & Paul Greengrass, *Spycatcher: The Candid Autobiography of a Senior Intelligence Officer* (New York: Viking Penguin, 1987).

Young, Louisa, *A Great Task of Happiness: The Life of Kathleen Scott* (London: Macmillan, 1995).

Ziegler, Philip, *King Edward VIII: The Official Biography* (London: Collins, 1990).

Index

Page numbers in bold indicate photographs.

Aberdeen, University of, 86, 109, 114, 248, 261
Abranches, Adolfo do Amaral, 317
Academia Portuguesa da História, 276
Accra, 142, 144, 145, 151, 152, 154, 186, 187, 198, 203
Achimota, 146, 147
Acton, Harold, 89
Addison, Joseph, 79
Addison Society, 79
Admiralty, 132
Æquator (coaster), 141
Aeschylus, *The Suppliants*, 103
Alba, Jacobo, 17th Duke of, 88
Alcocer, 297–8
Aldershot, 44, 131–2, 166
Aleixandre, Vicente, 92, 188, 190
Alemán, Mateo, *Guzmán de Alfarache* (1599–1604), 319
Alfonso X ('the Wise'), 232, 335
Alfonso XIII, 73, 77, 82, 343
Algarve, 315
Aljubarrota, Battle of (1385), 288, 294–5, **295**, 317
All Souls College, Oxford, 89
Allen, T. W., 224
Alonso, Dámaso, **78**, 83, 83–4, 85, 248, 265, 308, 366–7
Álvarez del Vayo, Julio, *The Last Optimist* (1950), 247
Amerbach, Basel, 324
American Council of Learned Societies, 360
Amiens, 127

Amoy (Xiamen), 37
Amundsen, Roald, 32, 33, 52
anarchists, 73
Andaman Islands, 158–9
Andeiro, João Fernandes, 287
Andersen, Hans Christian, *Fairy Tales*, 171
Anderson, A. K., 59
Andreis, Esther de, 259
Anglo-Spanish Society, 222
Anscombe, 2nd Engineer, 64, 213
Antenor, SS, 165, 222, 350
Aorangi, SS, 33
Aquinas, Thomas, 83
Arawa, SS, 45
Armson, Collins and Harman, Christchurch, 40
Arteaga y Pereira, Fernando de, 77, 81–2
Artigas y Ferrando, Miguel, 85–6
Arugum Bay, 162
Asencio y Toledo, José María de, 255–6
Ashigara, 156
Association of Hispanists of Great Britain and Ireland, 265
Asturias, 119
Asturias, HMHS, 46
Atkinson, William, 248–9, 250, 271
Atlee, Clement, 225
Auckland, 48, 50, 51, 172
Auckland, University of, 51
Auckland Infantry Regiment, 48
Auden, W. H., 90, 190
Austin, Texas, 283–4
Auvergne, 124
Avellaneda, Alonso Fernández de, *Segundo*

412

tomo del ... Quixote (1614), 256
Avignon, 123
Avon (river), New Zealand, 35
Azorín, 85, 92; *Una hora de España* (1924), 232
Azúa, Félix de, 263
Bacon, Col., 162
Baden-Baden, 101
Bahamas, 130
Baião, António Eduardo Simões, 287
Baker, Josephine, 202
Balliol College, Oxford, 73, 105, 274
Balsdon, Dacre, 87
Baltanás, Enrique, 304
Barber, Eric, 248
Barcelona, 73, 258, 259; Archive of the Crown of Aragon, 290, 334
Barcelona, Universitat Autònoma de, 311
Barne, Lt. Michael, 28–30, 31
Barnsley Hall, Bromsgrove, 132
Baroja, Pío, 85
Barranquilla, 140
Barthes, Roland, 304, 311–12; *Mythologies* (1957), 312
Bataillon, Marcel, 228, 265, 300, 302
Bathurst (Banjul), 148
Baudelaire, Charles, 186
bauxite, 137
Bayonne, 291
BBC, 98, 247–8, 258; Monitoring Service, 126; Radio 3, 232, 248, 278; Spanish Service, **264**, 278
Bécquer, Gustavo Adolfo, 232
Bedfordshire and Hertfordshire Regiment, 135, 164
Beethoven, Ludwig van, 103
Belfast, 347
Belgian Congo, 142, 151; diamond smuggling from, 148
Bell, Clive, *Art* (1914), 83
Benedetti, Mario, 265
Bennett, Arnold, 92
Berlin, 90; Air Ministry, 102; PER visits (1935), 102
Bermuda, 130
Betjeman, John, 89, 155, 217, 225
Betjeman, Penelope, 267
Bilbao, 118
Bion, Wilfred, 210
Bird, Charles Hayward, **29**
Birmingham, University of, 248
Black Forest, 71, 100, 101–2
Black Legend, 321
black market (in Spain), 258
Black Prince, Edward of Woodstock, the, 293
Black Watch, The, 261
Blenheim Palace, 278
Bletchley Park, 90, 277
Bloomsbury Group, 193
Blunt, Anthony, 278
Boabdil, 94
Bodmer, Martin, 364
Bodmer Library, Coligny, 364
Bojador, Cape, Western Sahara, 316, 317
bolshevism, 113–14
Bombay, 162
Bordeaux, 291
Borges, Jorge Luis, 265
Bose, Subhas Chandra, 158
Bournemouth, Royal Bath Hotel, 129
Bowers, Lt. Henry, 32
Bowle, Rev. John, 306
Bowra, Maurice, 71, 85, 89, 248–9, 251
Boxer, C. R., 85, 233, 318, 335
Boy Scouts, 70
Bragança, Duarte, Duke of, 319
Brazilian army, 146
Brenan, Gerald, 251; *The Face of Spain* (1950), 247; *The Literature of the Spanish People* (1951), 247
Brines, Francisco, 263
Bristol, 142, 144; Grammar School, 74
British Academy, 236
British Army, 72, 121, 132
British Cameroons, 142

British Columbia, University of, 248
British Council, Lisbon, 128; Madrid, 129, 248
British Eastern Fleet, 155
British Guiana, 137
British National Antarctic Expedition (BNAE) (1901–4), 25–8, 30
British Overseas Airways Corporation (BOAC), 129
British Security Coordination, 136–7, 140
Brittain, Lt. Norman, 164, 213
Brittany, 124
Brontë sisters, 94
Brough, Mary, 77
Brown, Winnie (great aunt by marriage), 41
Brussels, 30, 109, 144
Buick cars, 51, 53
Bulletin of Hispanic Studies, 275, 314, 354
Burford, Oxon., 133
Burgess, Guy, 278
Burgos, 291, 298
Burgoyne, Dorothy, 375
Burma, 144, 165
Butler, Charles, 166
Buttery, Christopher John, 374
Byron, George Gordon, Lord, 79
Byron, Robert, 89
Cairncross, John, 278
Cairo, 155
Calabar, 147; slavery in, 148
Calderón de la Barca, Pedro, 83, 108, 236; *La fiera, el rayo y la piedra* (1652), 270–1
Calella de Palafrugell, 188–90, **190**
California, University of, 248
Cambrai, Battle of, (1917), 85; (1918), 47
Cambridge, University of, English studies at, 308; modern languages at 80; Spanish at, 114, 248, 251, 266
Cambridge University Press, Cambridge Iberian and Latin American Studies, 275–6, 335

Cambridge Literary Agency, 93
Cameroon, Mt., 147
Canarias (cruiser), 119
Canary Islands, 118, 131–2, 140, 315, 322, **342**
cancioneiros, 232
Cantar de Mio Cid, 218–20, 232, 277, 296–8, 300–1, 309, 311, 320, 334–5
Canterbury, New Zealand, 19, 172; earthquakes (2010 & 2011), 43
Cap d'Antibes, 129
Cap de la Nao, 259
Caparica, Lisbon, 196
Cape Guardafui, Somalia, 49
Cap-Haïtien, 142
'Carbuncle', 156, 158–9, 277
Cardenal, Ernesto, 236
Cardwell, William Greve, 373–4
Carmarthen, 135
Carr, E. H., 289–90
Carr, Raymond, 251, 263, 343
Carter, A. T., 238
Carter, Maurice, 177
Cascais, 130
Castejón, Navarre, 259
Castilian-Portuguese War (1381), 288
Castro, Américo, 79, 106, 299, 301, 319, 320, 358; *España en su historia* (1948), 247, 299
Catholic Herald, The, 114
Cayman Islands, 140–1; Home Guard, 141
Cela, Camilo José, 265
Celestina, Comedia de Calisto y Melibea, 135, 232, 283, 298–304, 309, 320, 324, 325, 334, 343, 354–65
Cervantes, Miguel de, 79, 103, 193, 290, 303, 305–8, 325; *Ocho comedias*, 256; *Don Quixote* (1605–16), 230, 232, 250, 256, 303, 304–8, 320, 324, 342, 351, 357; *Persiles y Sigismunda* (1616), 256
Ceylon, 156–8, 162–4, 165–6, 318
Ceylon Police, 156

INDEX

Cézanne, Paul, 76, 77, 103, 123
Chamberlain, Neville, 113, 121, 124
Chamonix, 123
Chapman, Gordon, 261, 267
Chapman, Janet, 373
Charlbury, Oxon., 326, 352
Châteauroux, Indre, 124
Chekhov, Anton, 92, 108
Cheltenham, 50, 64, 71, 208
Cheltenham College, 64–5, 65–73, **67**, 100, 176–7, 211, 349
Cherry-Garrard, Apsley, 27
Chile, 87, 96
Chilver, G. E. F., 226, **227**
Chinese Labour Corps, 47
Christ Church, Oxford, 73, 84, 105, 156, 262, 274
Christchurch, New Zealand, 15, 19–23, 26–8, 32, 55, 170, 172–3; Canterbury College, 19; Fendalton, 21–2; Linwood Cemetery, 15, 45; McDougall Art Gallery, 40; McLean Institute, 21, 22; Merivale, 39; New Brighton, 35; Papanui, 43; St Barnabas' Church, Fendalton, 27–8, 36; Saint Mary's Convent School, 25
Cid, El, 298, 325
Cíes, Islas de, 119
Civil Guard (Guardia Civil), 116, 119, 259
Civil Service, 68
Clarín, 85
Clermont-Ferrand, 124
Cocos Islands, 49
Coghill, Neville, 225
Cohen, J. M., 267, 306
Colchester, Essex, 15
Cold War, 245
Colditz, 278
Coldstream Guards, 37
Collingwood, R. G., 289, 309
Collins, J. J., 40
Colman, Ronald, 204
Colombo, 49, 155, 161, 163, 203; Galle Face Hotel, 49, 155, 163, 198, 202, 279
Colonial Office, 138, 147
Colonial Service, 72
Columbus, Christopher, 273, 323
communism, 98, 258
Comparative Literature (journal), 301, 354
conceptismo, 232, 304, 350
Concorde, 285
Condor Legion, 119
Connolly, Cyril, 89
Conrad, Joseph, 92
Conroy, Bill, 33
Constable, John, 98
Constance, 101
Consular Service, 68
Corpus Christi College, Oxford, 73
Correia Raitt, Lia Noêmia Rodrigues, 374
Cortázar, Julio, 265
Costa de la Luz, 327
Costa del Sol, 327
Côte d'Azur, 123
Cotonou, Dahomey, 152
Cotswolds, 71
Country Life, 89
Covarrubias, Sebastián de, *Tesoro de la lengua castellana* (1611), 328
Coward, Noël, *Cavalcade* (1931), 98
Crooke, John, 164
Crosbie, John, 370
Croydon Airport, 254
Cuba, 187
Cunliffe-Lister, Philip, Viscount Swinton, 142
Cunningham, Martin, 372
Curacoa, HMS, 164
Dafundo, Portugal, 87
Dahomey (Benin), 152
Daily Express, The, 98
Daily Mail, The, 98
Dakar, 148
Dane Court School, Parkstone, Dorset, 65, 349

415

Dannevirke Advocate, The, 18
Dante, 40; *Divine Comedy,* 357
Dartmouth College, Hanover, N.H., 262
Daudet, Alphonse, 123
Davidson, Alan Eaton, 236–40
Davies, Gareth, 234, **239**, 249, 368
Dawkins, R. W., 224–5
De Osma Studentship, 82, 105, 255
de Valera, Éamon, 94
Delhi, 155, 162
Demant, Vigo, 274
Depression Riots (New Zealand) (1932), 96
Depression, The, 95
Destroyers-for-Bases deal (1940), 140
Deva, Guipúzcoa, 354, 358, 363
Deyermond, Alan, 234, 279–80, 297, 355, 368
Diário da Manhã (Lisbon), 294
Dickens, Charles, 92
Directorate of Military Intelligence, 127, 135
Discovery, RRS, 25–8
Dixon, Col. C. E., 157
Donne, John, 150
Doorly, Gerald, 27
Dostoyevsky, Fyodor, 93; *Crime and Punishment* (1866), 230
Douala, Cameroon, 147
Dravidia (Karnataka), 162
Drennan, Mrs, 335
Droitwich, Worc., 132
Duero (river), 260
Dunedin, St Hilda's Collegiate School, 24–5, 34
Dunkirk, Evacuation from (1940), 127
Dunn, Peter, 355
Durham, University of, 248
Durham Light Infantry, 132
Dutch colonial empire, 162
Eagleton, Terry, 310
Earle, Tom, 263, 371
East Grinstead, 121

Ede, Lt.-Col. Bertram, 166
Edinburgh, University of, 271
Edwards, Agustín, 82
Einstein, Albert, 106
El Greco, 95
El País, 320
Eliot, T. S., 190
Elizabeth I, 94
Elizabeth II, 277
Elliott, J. H., 270, 318
Elliott-Smith, Alan Guy, 71
Elmsett, Suffolk, 15
Elwell, Charles, 278
Emden, SMS, 49
Empson, William, *Seven Types of Ambiguity* (1930), 309
Encina, Juan del, 358
Entwistle, W. J., **78**, 79, 81, 82–3, 114, **237**, 248, 250–1; PER and, 86, 106–7, 108, 128, 165, 195–6, 227, 235, 287, 308, 314, 334
Escorial, El, 257–8
Espasa Calpe, 255
Estoril, 112, 130, 196, 201
Ettinghausen, Henry, 365
Ettinghausen, Maurice, 355, 361–5, 369
Euterpe (full-rigger), 18–19
Evans, PO Edgar, 30–1
Evans, Lt. E. R. G. R. (Teddy), Lord Mountevans, 26–35, **29**, 43, 46, 65, 96, 208
Evans, Elsa (*née* Andvord), 46
Evans, Richard, 46
Ewert, Alfred, 248, 366–7
Excalibur, SS, 130
Exeter, Miss (Major) Yarde Buller's convalescent home, 47, 54
Exeter, University of, 262
Exeter College, Oxford, 86–7, 224–5, 248, 252, 253, 334, 352
Eytan, Walter, 90, 365
Faber & Faber, 154
Fabergé, 89

INDEX

Fairbairn, William Ewart, 134
Falange, 116, 119
Farkas, Francine, 130
fascism, 96, 98, 113–14
Federal Bureau of Investigation (FBI), 136
Fernández-Armesto, Felipe, 372
Fernando, Infante, 315
Fernando Pó (Bioko), 143–4, 148
First Aid Nursing Yeomanry (FANY), 204
Fitzmaurice-Kelly, James, *Oxford Book of Spanish Verse* (1913), 83, 231–2
Flaubert, Gustave, 103
Foligno, Cesare, 80, 106
Fonseca, Luís Adão da, 291–2
Fontanella, Lee, 284
Foreign Office, 263
Foreign Service Course, 135
Forey, Alan, 271, 369
Fosse, Eustache de la, 154; *Voyage à la Guinée*, 322
Foster, Idris Ll., 248
Foucault, Michel, 311
France, Anatole, 92
Franco, Francisco, 113, 114, 116, 119, 131; regime, 254, 258–60, 265, 294, 311
Franks, Oliver, Baron, 74, 225–6, **226**, 244, 246; Commission of Inquiry (1964–5), 246, 280; Falklands Inquiry (1982), 246
Freetown, 148
French Cameroon, 147; diamond smuggling from, 148
French Morocco, 144–5
Freud, Sigmund, 103
Frilford, Berks., 178
Froissart, Jean, 292
Gabbitas and Thring, 65
Gadrat, Madeleine, 52
Gadrat, Martial, 51–2
Gadrat, Suzanne, 52
Galbraith, V. H., 108, 289
Galicia, PER in (1938), 115–120
Gallagher, David, 262, 370

Gambia, 142
Gambia (river), 148
Ganivet, Ángel, 110, 232; *Idearium español* (1897) 215
García Lorca, Federico, 105, 200
Garcilaso de la Vega, 229, 231, 232, 321, 352
Garlick, George, 177
Gauguin, Paul, 76, 77
Gaunt, John of, Duke of Lancaster, 232, 246, 290
Gautier, Théophile, *Voyage en Espagne* (1843), 73
Gawsworth, John (Terence Ian Fytton Armstrong), 340–1
Gazette Law Reports, 20
General Strike (1926), 64
Generation of 1898, 110, 215, 231
Generation of '27, 85
Geneva, 123
George Town, Grand Cayman, 141
George VI, 227
Geraldine, Sister (headmistress), 24–5
Géraldy, Paul, 205
Germany, PER visits (1933), 100–3
Gibraltar, 131, 347–8
Gibson, Sylvia F., 373
Gide, André, 93, 332; Journals, 221
Gifford, Douglas, 234, 236, **239**, 368
Gili, Joan, 75, 324
Gillies, Sir Harold, 133
Gilman, Antonio, 355
Gilman, Stephen, 299, 301–3, 313–14, 320, 354–65; *The Art of 'La Celestina'* (1957), 299, 303, 354; *The Spain of Fernando de Rojas* (1972), 301–3, 354, 356–61
Giménez-Frontín, José Luis, 263, 328, 345; *Señorear la tierra* (1991), 346; *Woodstock Road en julio* (1996), 263, 345–6
Giner de los Ríos, Francisco, 105
Girard, René, 283

Glasgow, University of, 86, 248, 271
Glass, Ann, 278
Goering, Herman, 139
Góis, Damião de, 333
Gold Coast, 142, 144, 146–7, 149, 152, 154
Gomes, Diogo, 314
Gonçalves, Nuno, Saint Vincent Panels, 316
Goncourt Journal, 233
Góngora, Luis de, 228, 231, 309
Gosport, 29
Gowans, Ian, 375
Goytisolo, Juan, 265, 320
Gracián, Baltasar, 304, 313, 337, 336
Granada, 199, 206; violence in (1936), 113; Alhambra, 100, **192**; Generalife, 100
Granada, University of, 100
Grand Cayman, 141
Grand Turk, 142
Greene, Graham, 94, 148; *The Heart of the Matter* (1948), 148
Grenoble, 123
Griffin, Clive, 148, 262, 373
Griffin, Nigel, 267–8, 268–9, 270–1, 272–3, 371
Guillén, Jorge, 355
Guy, CSM, 132
Haggerston, 18
Haguro, 156
Hahn, Emily, 335
Haiti, 139, 141
Haley, William, 317
Halifax, N.S., 36–7, 135–6
Hall, John Bernard, 374
Hamblen, Derek, 119, 121, 185–6, 201
Hanmer Springs, New Zealand, 53; Dog Creek (Stream), 189–90; Queen Mary Army Convalescent Hospital, 54–5, 171, 190
Hardy, H. H., 70
Harewood House, W. Yorks., 133

Harrison, Wilfred, 126
Hart, H. L. A., 277
Harvard University, 262; Houghton Library, 355, 360
Havelock Is., Andaman Is., 158
Hay, Denys, 280
Healey, Lt.-Cdr. J. E. B., 160
Hegel, G. W. F., 83, 289
Heigham, Maj. Jo, 144, 148–51, 152, **153**, 154, 163, 167, 186–7, 194, 196, 203–4
Hemingway, Ernest, 92
Hemingway, Maurice, 371
Hennell, John, 179–82, 203
Henry of Trastámara, 293, 294
Henry 'the Navigator', Prince, 154, 278, 286, 314–19, 325, 352
Herrera, Fernando de, *Comentario a Garcilaso* (1580), 256
Hertford, Marquess of, 30
Highfield, J. R. L., 263
Hillgarth, Alan, 118
Hilton, Ronald, **78**, 84, 105–6
Hinshelwood, Cyril, 248
Hispanic Studies in Britain, 251, 263, 312, 324, 336–7, 338
Hitler, Adolf, 100, 101, 103, 104, 121
Hitler Youth, 101
Hobart, 18, 45
Hodcroft, F. W., 261, 262, 266, 269, 270–1, 336
Hodcroft, Joan, 269, 336
Hodgkin, R. H., 125, 225
Hollis, Roger, 278
Home Security, Ministry of, 125
Hong Kong, 85
Hong Kong Volunteer Corps, 37
Hook, David, 372
Horton College, Tasmania, 18
House, Wilfred, 84–5, 88, 125
Huggins, Sir John, 138
Hundred Years' War, 291
Hunt, R. W., 363

INDEX

Huxley, Aldous, *Point Counter Point* (1928), 197–8
Huxley, Elspeth, 28
Hypocrites Club, Oxford, 89
Iberia (airline), 254
Iberia, SS, 211
Ibsen, Henrik, 79, 108
Iffley, 210
India, 162, 164
Indian Army, 72
Indian Civil Service, 72
individualismo, 311
Infantes, Víctor, 363
Influenza epidemic, 50, 51
Inland Revenue, 282
Inquisition, Spanish, 359
Institución Libre de Enseñanza, Madrid, 85
Intelligence Corps, 132, 135
Internal Revenue Service, 282
International Association of Hispanists, Inaugural Congress (Oxford, 1962), 265; 3rd Congress (Mexico City, 1968), 355, 360, 364
Invergordon Mutiny (1931), 96
Ireland, 93
Isherwood, Christopher, 90
Isis (magazine), 93
Isla de Pinos (Isla de Juventud), Cuba, 141
Jamaica, 203; Gibraltar Camp, 140; Goat Island, 140; Port Royal, 140; Vernam, 140
Jaume III of Mallorca, 293
Jauss, Hans Robert, 310
Jersey, 121, 124, 126, 201; occupation of (1940–5), 104, 127, 201
Jesus, Society of, 73
Jimena, Doña, 298
Jiménez, Juan Ramón, 124
Jiménez Fraud, Alberto, 105–6
John I of Castile, 294
John I of Portugal, 294
John Paul II, 334
Johns Hopkins University, 282, 285

Johnson, Samuel, 307
Jollies Pass Hotel, Canterbury, New Zealand, 19
Jones, C. A., 232, 260, 262, **264**, 265, 266, 269
Jones, John Walter, 245, 249
Jones, R. O., 301
Jordan, Barry, 312
Joyce, James, *Dubliners* (1914), 94; *Ulysses* (1922), 94, 190, 205; *Finnegans Wake* (1939), 190
Jung, Carl, *Psychology of the Unconscious* (1912), 210, 307–8
Kaiapoi, Canterbury, 19
Kandy, 155, 157, 162
Kant, Immanuel, 289
Karachi, 155
Karlsruhe, 100
Kashmir, 162
Keir, Sir David Lindsay, 245
Kelly, Charles, 374
Kennedy, Charles, 90, 193–4, **193**, 211, 216, 327–8, 342
Kennedy, George, 193
Kennedy, Maj. John D., 127–9
Kennedy, Kirstin, 334
Kennedy, Ruth Lee, 256–7, 336
Kenny, Anthony, 274
Kent, George, Duke of, 128
Kent, University of, 328
Kenyon, Maj. Lionel, 128
Keta, Gold Coast, 152
Keynes, J. M., 106, 193
KGB, 278
Kidlington, 336
King's College, University of London, 233, 249, 251, 265, 287, 333
Kingston, Jamaica, 137, 139, 342–3
Kinnear, John, 371
Kitchener Scholarship, 66
Klein, Melanie, 210
Knowlescourt, mansion, Christchurch, 36, **38**, 39–43, **40**, 50, 51–52, 61, 62, 72,

91, 170, 253, 329
Kojonup, WA, 56–7
Kolkhorst, George ('Colonel'), 77, **78**, 79, 177, 252, 260, 305, 366–7; PER and, 83, 86–91, 155, 191, 196, 210, 217–18, 225, 235, 239, 241, 242, 296, 299, 313–14, 319, 332, 343
Krause, Friedrich, 283
Kumasi, Gold Coast, 149
La Coruña, 119
La Trobe University, Melbourne, 342
Labour Party (of Great Britain), 258
Lady Margaret Hall, Oxford, 85
Lagos, Nigeria, 147, 152
Lahore, 162
Lake Edward (East Africa), 151–2
Lamb, Henry, 193
Lambert, André, 259
Lambert, Anthony, 374
Laming, Henry, 82, 84
Laming Scholarships, 67, 71–2, 82, 91; Travelling Fellowships, 82, 193; Resident Fellowships, 84, 261, 262
Lancaster, Osbert, 89, 107, 155
Lanka Sama Samaja Party (Ceylon), 156
Lara, María Victoria de, 83, 367
Las Palmas, 132, 343
Launceston, Tasmania, 16, 18
Launceston Emigration Aid Society, 17
Launceston Examiner, The, 16
Laval, Mayenne, 124
Lawrance, Jeremy, 299, 310, 373
Lawrence, D. H., *Lady Chatterley's Lover* (1928), 92
Lázaro Carreter, Fernando, 320–1
Leavis, F. R., 308
Lechlade, Glos., 36
Lehmann, Karl, 126
Lehmann, Rosamond, 89; *Dusty Answer* (1927), 196
Leiria, 288
León, Fray Luis de, *La perfecta casada* (1583), 256

Leopoldville, 151, 201
Leuchars, Miss, 55
Lewers, Neville, 176
Libro de buen amor, 232, 334
Lida de Malkiel, María Rosa, 300; *La originalidad artística de 'La Celestina'* (1962), 300
Liddell, Col. Guy, 156, 157–8, 165–6, 166
Lincoln College, Oxford, 107
Lipscomb University, Nashville, 282
Lisboa, Universidade Nova de, 333
Lisbon, 113, 128–30, 142, 143, 144; Earthquake (1755), 274, 314; Arquivo da Torre do Tombo, 112, 286–7, 288; Casa da Índia, 314; Centenary Congress (1940), 128, 287; Hotel Borges, 328; PER in, (1944), 287; (1959), 294
Livermore, Harold, 248
Liverpool, 49, 165, 222
Liverpool, University of, 251, 338
Lloyd, George Ambrose, Lord, 94
Lloyd-Bostock, Philip, 262, 370–1
Llull, Ramon, 236
Lobel, Edgar, 224, **226**
Loch Quoich, HMS, 160
Lochailort, Paramilitary Training School, 134
Logroño, 293
London Gazette, The, 70
London Mercury, The, 99
London, 28–9, 48, 64, 73; Lord Mayor of, 82; Buckingham Palace, 277, **280**; Canning House, 316; Criterion Bar, 179; Fitzroy Tavern, 194; Le Gavroche, 281; Instituto de España, 248, 333; Piccadilly, 203; Portuguese Embassy, 233, 316; Public Record Office, 108, 287; Spanish Embassy, 222; Tavistock Institute, 210; Victoria and Albert Museum, 334; PER and, 203
Longás, Fr. Pedro, 255

longfin eel, 189
Lope de Vega, 83, 108, 114
Lopes, Fernão, 287–8; *Crónica del Rei dom Joham I*, 287, 288, 292
López de Ayala, Adelardo, *Consuelo* (1878), 102
López de Ayala, Pero, 288
López Morillas, Juan, 283
LST-3017 (tank landing ship), 160–1
Lucena, Lorenzo, 80
Ludendorff Offensive (1918), 48
Lugo, 119
Luna, Álvaro de, 316
Luz Morales, José, 374
Lynn, Ralph, 77
Lyth, Oliver, 209–10, 213, 214, 220–1, 330
Lyttelton, 26, 27, 30, 43
Mabbe, James, 319
MacAndrews Line, 73
Macdonald, Cynthia, 335
Macdonald, George, 19
Macdonald, Iain, 224, 244, 335
Macdonald, Inez Isabel, 248
Maclean, Donald, 278
McAdam, N.B., 136
McIver, Col. Alan, 156–7
McKenzie, Elizabeth, 157
McMurdo Sound, 32
McNeile, Mike, 177
McSpadden, George E., 248
Madariaga, Salvador de, 82, 83, 86, 252, 265
Madras, 162
Madrid, 129, 201, 291; violence in (1931), 73, 114; Ateneo, 85; Biblioteca Nacional, 85–6, 256; Barajas airport, 254; Casa del Libro, 334; Instituto de Valencia de Don Juan, 88, 255; Institución Libre de Enseñanza, 85; Residencia de Estudiantes, 105–6; Universidad Central, 85; PER visits (1931), 73; (1933), 100; (1935) 105–6; (1946) 254–7; (1948) 257–8

Magallanes, SS, 258
Magdalen College, Oxford, 73, 84, 262
Magrath, J. R., 74
Majestic, HMS, 26, 28
Málaga, 100
Malaya, 160
Malbrán, Manuel, 77
Malta, 155, 166
Man, Isle of, 154–5
Manawatu Herald, The, 18
Manchester, University of, 86, 251, 261, 275
Manet, Édouard, 77
Mann, Julia de Lacy, 332
Manson, Joseph, 248
March, Ausiàs, 231
Marciales, Miguel, 302
Marías, Javier, 104–5, 220, 338–41, 348; *Todas las Almas* (1989), 201, 263, 338–9, 340, 344–5; *Negra espalda del tiempo* (1998), 263, 338–9, 340; *Tu rostro mañana* (2002–7), 148, 339, 340–1; *Berta Isla* (2017), 339; *Tomás Nevinson* (2021), 339; PER characterised by, 201, 338–41, 344–5
Marías, Julián, 339
Markham, Sir Clements, 25
Márquez, Baltasar, 205
Márquez Cano, Piedad, 205, 333
Marshall Plan (1948), 246
Massey, William, 50
Masterman, J. C., 156, 277
Maud of Norway, Queen, 27
Mayne, Mrs (schoolmistress), 59
Mende, 123, 124
Menéndez y Pelayo, Marcelino, 300
Menéndez Pidal, Ramón, 85, **219**, 247, 248, 265, 298, 308, 311, 313–14; editor of *Flor nueva de romances viejos* (1928), 267, 268; PER and, 105–6, 218–20, 298, 300–1, 334–5, 354
Menteath, Mr (schoolmaster), 61

Menzies, Isabel, 210
Mercantile Gazette of New Zealand, The, 20
Merchant Taylors' School, 26
Merimée, Prosper, 73
Merton College, Oxford, 263
Meun, Jean de, 358
Mexico City, 212
MI(R), 127–9, 131
MI5 (Security Service), 137–9, 140, 142–3, 166–7, 155–6, 156–8, 165–7, 277–8; Overseas Section, 135, 138; 'Double-Cross' system, 156; Twenty Committee, 277; Registry, 278, 286; PER joins, 135; as Defence Security Officer Jamaica, 135–42, **137**; as Security Liaison Officer West Africa, 142–54, **146, 149, 150**; as Defense Security Officer Colombo, 154–66, 228; opts to leave, 166–7; as recruiter for, 277; oral history team, 329
MI6 (Secret Intelligence Service), 143, 148
Miami, 137, 142
Michael, Ian, 201, 266, 328, 334
Milburn, Alan Ray, 248
Minho (river), 119
Miranda de Ebro, 258
Miró, Gabriel, 85, 110
Moi, Toril, 310
Molière, 83; *Les Précieuses ridicules* (1659), 91
Molina Foix, Vicente, 263
Moliner, María, *Diccionario de uso del Español* (1966–7), 334
Molody, Konon (Gordon Lonsdale), 278
Molotov–Ribbentrop Pact (1939), 123
Mombasa, 155
Monet, Claude, 77
Montalbán, Álvaro de, 359
Monteiro, João Gouveia, 294, 319
Montevideo, 213
Moore, Sir Henry Monck-Mason, 157, 165
Moreno Báez, Enrique, 114

Morning (relief ship), 26–7
Morning Post, The, 18
Morris, William, Lord Nuffield, 82
Mountbatten, Lord Louis, 155, 159–60
Mountevans, Lord; *see* Evans, Lt. E. R. G. R.
Munich Crisis (1938), 104, 122
Murcia, 291
Murdoch, Iris, 89, 266
Murillo, Bartolomé Esteban, 83, 256
Nájera, Battle of (1367), 291, 293–4
Najerilla (river), 293
Naples, 33–4
Nashville, 284, 328
NATO, 246
Nauru, 56
Nazism, 101–2; SS, 102
Nebrija Prize, 276, 350
Needham, Rodney, 264–5
neotradicionalismo, 311
Neruda, Pablo, 105, 236, 265, 266
New College, Oxford, 73, 235, 261, 266
New Criticism, 106–7, 308–9
New Statesman, The, 98
New York City, 51, 136, 142, 212–13; Rockefeller Center, 136
New York Times, The, 90
New Zealand Army Ordnance Department, 52
New Zealand Automobiles Ltd., 51
New Zealand Division, 172
New Zealand Expeditionary Force, 47
New Zealand Magistrates' Court Reports, 19–20
New Zealand Staff Corps, 37, 52
Newfoundland, 140
Newport, S. Wales, 135
Newport News, Va., 45
Niagara, SS, 50
Nicholas II, 186
Nietzsche, Friedrich, 101
Nigeria, 142, 147
Nîmes, 123

Noah, 94
Normandy landings (1944), 147
North Caicos, 141
North Mymms, Herts., 98
Nueva Revista de Filología Española, 355–6
O'Halloran, Colin, 374
Oakes, John, 90
Oates, Capt. L. E., 31
Obolensky, Dimitri, 253
O'Callaghan, Will (uncle), 35
Ochs family, 90
Office of the Coordinator of Information, U.S., 136
Officer Cadet Training Unit, 128, 131, 160
Official Secrets Act (1911), 166, 329, 340
Ogden, C. K., 308
ON79, convoy (1942), 135–6
Ordem do Infante D. Henrique, 276
Orden de Isabel la Católica, 276
Orduna, SS, 164
Organisation for European Economic Cooperation, 246
Oriel College, Oxford, 133
Ortega y Gasset, José, 308
Osma, Guillermo de, 82
Otranto, SS, 33–4
Ouagadougou, 151
Oxford, 44, 124; Air Raid Prevention control room (1940); Carfax, 353; Clarendon Hotel, 45; Crematorium, 352; George Café, 75–6, 239; Luna Caprese, 203, 271, 273; Observatory, 252; Parson's Pleasure, 196; Pheasant Inn, 75; Playhouse, 75; Radcliffe Infirmary, 124, 133; Randolph Hotel, 77, **78**, 252, 270; A. Rosenthal Antiquarian Books, 302, 354–5, 362, 364; St Luke's nursing home, 326; St Mary's Church, 352; Town Hall, 122, 126; Warneford Hospital, 90, 210
Oxford Magazine, The, 116–17, 222, 261–2

Oxford Times, The, 77
Oxford, University of, 73–4, 95; Congregation, 331–2, 336, 339; Bodleian Library, 324, 363, 364; New Bodleian Library, 227; Franks Commission of Inquiry (1964–5), 246, 280; Registry, 250; Registrar, 278; Research Assessment Exercise (2000), 336; Union, 95; *Calendar*, 178
General Board of the Faculties, 265; Faculty of Arts, 80; Faculty of English, 80; Faculty of Medieval and Modern Languages, 80, 83, 106–7, 265, 336; Faculty of Modern History, 106–7; Honour School of Modern Languages, 80–1, 83, 106–7, 227, 308; King Alfonso XIII Chair, 79, 82; Pass School at, 80, 83; research at 73–4, 107–8; women at, 80, 81, 331–2
Modern languages at, 79–84; Catalan at, 83; French at, 81, 83, 84–5; German at, 81, 83; Hispanic studies at, 266–75, 312; Italian at, 81; Latin American studies at, 236, 262, 263; Portuguese at, 79, 83, 287; Russian at, 83; Spanish at, 79–84, 85–8, 227, 260–3; Spanish syllabus at, 82–3, 85, 227, 261, 366–7; Spanish-American studies at, 83, 227; *lectores*, 262–3; Spanish Graduate Seminar, 200, 269–72; Sub-Faculty of Spanish and Portuguese, 266, 267, 274–5, 334; Sub-Faculty Library, 269, 272, 352; *see* Russell (Career)
French Club, 77; Liberal Club, 96; Spanish Club, 77–9, **78**; Spanish Democratic Defence Committee, 115; Spanish Society, 266–7
Oxford University Press, Clarendon Press, 193, 296; Modern Languages Monographs series, 275
Oxfordshire, SS, 48–50, 172, 213–14
Pabst, Georg Wilhelm, *L'Atlantide* (1932),

77
Paço, Lt.-Col. Afonso do, 294, **295**, **344**
Pagden, Anthony, 276, 277, 368
Palmerston North, New Zealand, 37
Pamplona, 291
Panama Canal, 64
Pardo Bazán, Emilia, 85
Paris, 127, 129; Casino, 202; Collège de France, 228; Comédie-Française, 91; Institut de Recherche et d'Histoire des Textes, 290; Musée de Jeu de Paume, 76; Sorbonne, 228; Théâtre du Grand-Guignol, 359; PER visits (1933), 76–7, 179
Park Prewett Hospital, Basingstoke, 133
Parker, A. A., 114, 248–9, 251, 265, 271, 283, 305, 319
Parks, Ted, 282–3
Parry, J. H., 263; Parry Report, 263
Parry-Jones, Pauline, 210–11, 333
Passchendaele, Battle of (1917), 85
Pater, Walter, 233
Pattison, David, 262
Paukenschlag, Operation (1942), 136–7, 140
Paz, Octavio, 265
Peers, Edgar Allison, 251, 313–14, 336–7
Pennsylvania, University of, 248
Pepperdine University, Malibu, Calif., 282
Pereda, José María de, *Sotileza* (1885), 73
Pérez de Ayala, Ramón, 79, 103; *Tigre Juan* (1926), 232
Persimmon, HMS, 160
Perth, WA, 56
Peter I of Castile, 293
Petrarch, 232; *Omnia Opera* (1496), 324, 362–3
Petrie, Sir David, 157, 161–2, 166
Philippa of Lancaster, 128, 287
Philpot, F. H., 66, 68, 69
Picasso, Pablo, 77
Pierce, Frank, 265
Pirandello, Luigi, 83, 108, 297

Pitt-Rivers, Julian, 251
Plantagenet, House of, 286, 315
Plato, 313
Plymouth, 46
Polícia Internacional e de Defesa do Estado (PIDE), 119
Poole, Dorset, 129, 130
Poole, Austin Lane, 249
Port Blair, Andaman Is., 158, 159
Port Chalmers, Dunedin, 26, 32
Port-Étienne, Mauritania, 146
Port Melbourne, SS, 64, 135–6, 213
Portland Spy Ring, 278
Porto, Escondidinho restaurant, 119
Portuguese colonial empire, 162, 166
Portuguese Guinea, 143–4
Portuguese Restoration War (1640), 128
Potter, Harold, 286
Powell, Anthony, 89, 94
Powicke, Maurice, 108, 289, 292, 296
Priestley, C. T., 71, 211
Prieto, Gregorio, 75
Primera Crónica General, 232
Primo de Rivera, Miguel, 77
Princeton University, 301
Pring-Mill, Robert, 234–6, 249, 261, 262, **264**, 266, 270–1, 280, 355, 368
Procter, Evelyn, 249, 263, 334–5; *Curia and Cortes in León and Castile* (1980), 335
Proust, Marcel, 15, 299
Provence, 123
Pryce, Mike, 31
Puebla, 359
Punch and Judy, 339
Pupo-Walker, Enrique, 276
Quamby, mansion, Christchurch, 21–3, **22**, 23, 27, 39
Quamby Brook, Tasmania, 18, 21
Quaritch, Bernard, Bookseller, 324, 362–3
Queen Elizabeth, RMS, 142
Queen Mary, RMS, 164
Queen's College, Oxford, 67, 71, 73, 74–5,

84, 88, 105, 122, 125, 127, 178, 179, 193, 208, 210, 241, 243, 244, 267; SCR, 208, 224, 225, **226**, 227, 244–5, 335; sports clubs, 243; *see* Laming; Russell (Career)
Queen's Own (Royal West Kent Regiment), 37, 44, 47, 48
Rabat, 144–5
Racine, Jean, 83, 108; *Britannicus* (1669), 91
Rakaia (river), 23; Is., 23
Rangiora, Canterbury, 43
Rangoon, 161, 164
Read, Malcolm K., 312
Real Academia de Buenas Letras de Barcelona, 276
Real Academia Española, Madrid, 277, 321
Rees, J. W., 251, 275
Reinosa, Rodrigo de, 310, 322
Renusakai, Col. Jochi, 159
Reventlow, Countess Benika, 201
Rezeptionsästhetik, 310
Rhodes House, Oxford, 79
Rhône (river), 123
Richards, Sir Arthur, 137, 142
Richards, I. A., 308
Richmond, Va., 45
Rico, Francisco (Paco), 311, 320
Riley, E. C. (Ted), 107, 187–93, **192**, 194, 197–8, 209, 234, 237, 249, 294, 368
Rimbaud, Arthur, 190
Ríos, Fernando de los, 106
Roberts, Phyllis, 203–4
Robertson, Gordon, 109
Robertson, Lt.-Col. T. A., 156
Roca de Togores, Carmen, 333
Rodrigues, António Gonçalves, 79, 287
Rodrigues, Maria da Graça de Almeida, 333, 370
Roedean School, 204
Rojas, Fernando de, 283, 298, 301, 324, 354, 356–9
Roman Catholicism, 97, 101, 113, 259–60, 334
Romanticism, 99, 292–3, 305, 307, 357
Ros, Xon de, 88, 333–4
Ross, Tasmania, 18
Ross Ice Shelf, 28
Rotorua Military Hospital, 54
Rotorua, SS, 45–6, 135
Round, Nicholas, 312, 316, 369
Rousseau, Jean-Jacques, 101
Royal Air Force, 164–5, 261
Royal Asiatic Society, 162
Royal Doulton, 40
Royal Geographical Society, 25
Royal Navy, 96, 118, 148
Royal Society, 25
Royal Ulster Rifles, 135
Rubió i Balaguer, Jordi, 259
Ruiz, Juan, 358
Russell, Cecil Ruffell (uncle), 21, 23, 35, 41, 58
Russell, Donald, 253
Russell, Doris (*née* Baldwin) (stepgrandmother), 51
Russell, Ethel Nellie (aunt), 20, 35, 64
Russell, George Warren (great uncle), 18, 50, 54
Russell, Gerald Warren (uncle), 18, 29, 52, 55, 58, 172; PER relations with, 41, 58, 61, 122, 133, 174; death, 173
Russell, Gertrude (Gertie) (*née* Brown) (stepgrandmother), 42, 51
Russell, Gregory Ruffell (great-grandfather), 15–16, 18
Russell, Helen (Nellie) (*née* Stringer) (grandmother), 19, **20**, 20–21, 23, 36, 45, 51
Russell, Hilda Beatrice (aunt), 21, 27–35, **29**, 43
Russell, Hugh Bernard Langford (*né* Wheeler) (brother), 29, 39, 45, 46, 47, **48**, 54–5, 55–6, 57, **60**, 64, 65, **67**, 69, 133, **170**, 173, 208; PER relationship with, 170, 179, 206, 213

Russell, Jabez (great uncle), 18
Russell, John Ruffell (great uncle), 18
Russell, Joseph (great uncle), 18
Russell, May (aunt by marriage), 43, 52
Russell, Miriam (great aunt), 18
Russell, Miriam (*née* Warren) (great-grandmother), 16, 18
Russell, Lt. Neil Ruffell (first cousin, once removed), 48
RUSSELL, Peter Edward Lionel Russell (*né* Wheeler)
   LIFE: birth, 43; childhood, **44**, 47, **48**, 170–6; education, 58–62, 65–73; oceanic journeys, 44–6, 49–50, 63, 64; name changed by deed poll, 58, 66, 67, 339; travel, 73, 100–3, 105, 112–20, 144–54, 162–3, 254–60, 342–3; love of sunbathing, 75, 112, 196; motor accident and convalescence (1941), 133–4, 225; interest in art, 76–7, 83; interest in film, 77; interest in theatre, 77; Belsyre Court, 205, 210, 212, 252–4, **253**, 329, 336, 341–9, **347**, 351, 353; décor of Belsyre Court, 341, 343–4; allotment, 215–16, 316, 350; finances, 327–8; book collector, 324, 344; painting, 342, **342**; cine film, 342; food and cooking, 341; pets, 172; and IT, 351; later life, 326–9, 341–4, 349–51; no interest in autobiography, 329, 337; death, 351; funeral arrangements, 352
   PERSONALITY AND CHARACTER: general: 72, 109–10, 119–20, 134–5, 169, 182–4, 218, 221, 233–4, 313–14, 326–7, 329, 346–51; appearance, 76, 178, 267, 268, 328, 344–6; voice, 88, 232, 268; physique, 59, 178, 328; 'heart murmur', 61, 65, 122, 133, 174, 204, 213; early aversion to sports, 60–1, 174, 213; sports, 67, 75; at Cheltenham, 66–9; at Oxford, 91; friendships, 178–86, 217, 332, 343, 348–9; aversion to coarseness, 62, 347–8; competitiveness, 59, 174, 236, 299, 313–14, 343, 354–6; confidence in his intellect, 68, 92, 93, 109, 111, 121–2, 196; ambition, 90–1, 222–3; snobbery, 99–100, 329; exercise of power, 167–8; mental control, 182, 270; no interest in intrigue, 245, 343; humour, 105, 280, 329, 348, 351; tolerance, 197–8; and praise, 326; 343; pragmatism, 336; pessimism, 337–8; generosity, 350–1; impact of war on, 167; political views, 96–8, 104–5, 113, 215, 246–7, 329; on colonialism, 146–7, 149, 151, 160; on religion, 343, 352; on Roman Catholicism, 95, 97, 101, 114, 258, 259, 260, 334; anti-Semitism of, 101; theory of beauty, 93–4, 182, 190, deism, 98, 100–1; love of nature, 98–9; and Romanticism, 99, 292–3, 305, 307; and ageism, 336
   MIND AND SEXUALITY: general: 178, 194–205; psychosexuality, 92, 174, 182, 187–91, 205–16; Oedipus complex, 209, 213, 215, 217, 330, 342; sensitivity, 174, 176, 182–4, 349; depression, 65, 109, 110, 164, 210, 337–8, 349; loneliness, 100, 109, 178, 180, 212, 221, 231, 349; introspection, 65, 95, 182, 187,

221, 348; sexually abused, 57, 214; premature sexualisation, 172; trauma, 172–6, 213–14; corporal punishment, 58–9, 61–2, 174–6; flagellation complex, 176, 177, 213; catatonia, 65, 176, 214; adolescent infatuations, 176–7; undergraduate infatuations, 178–82; adult infatuations, 185–94; homosexuality, 177, 194–5, 199–201, 216; heterosexuality, 196–7, 198–9, 203–5; *demi-monde*, 202–3; misogyny, 202, 204, 215, 329–32, 335; proposed marriage, 203–5; relations with women in later life, 332–6; *abulia*, 110, 215, 217–18; impotence, 215, 216; physical health, 109, 110, 187, 209–10, 224, 229, 328, 341; mental health, 187, 209–21, 229, 231, 243–4, 328; under psychoanalysis, 209–10, 212, 220–1, 306–7, 313; psychosis, 210–14, 254; ego, 93, 218–20; narcissism, 195–6; mental collapse, 93, 187, 210–16, 240, 242, 291, 292, 329, 338; barbiturates, 210, 212, 328; suicidal, 164, 216; 'ambiguity', 104–5, 167, 299, 325, 349; *malade imaginaire*, 328; *see* Russell, Rita; Wheeler, Bernard
ACADEMIC CAREER: becomes interested in Spanish, 72; scholar at Queen's, 74–5; as undergraduate, 81, 82, 86, 90–1, 17; and OU Spanish Club, 77–9, **78**; Spanish accent, 88; and French studies, 110; turns to history, 106–7; as historian instead of Hispanist, 110, 114–15, 247; doctoral research, 86, 107–8, 246, 290–1; graduate scholar (Taberdar) at Queen's, 108–9; college lectureships, 108–9, 111; career aspirations and ambitions, 91, 109–10, 114, 277; University lectureship, 86, 165; Laming Resident Fellow of Queen's, 71, 111, 165, 222, 225, 249; Dean of Queen's, 226–7, 241–2, 247, 249; Honorary Fellow of Queen's, 276; King Alfonso XIII Chair, 248–51, 252–3, 260, 265, 296, 349; Director of Portuguese Studies, 251, 263; on the General Board of the Faculties, 265; teaching style, 111–12, 228; teaching load, 228, 242–3; as undergraduate tutor, 125, 229–30, 234–41; as graduate tutor, 260, 272–4, 282–5, 333; as lecturer, 228, 231–3, 267–9, 271–2, 342, 376–8; lectures on *Flor nueva de romances viejos*, 267, 268, 378; lectures on Thought and Taste in the Golden Age, 81, 267–8, 269; on leave, 377–8; as administrator, 263–5, 274–5, 343; editorial board member of *Bulletin of Hispanic Studies*, 275; advisor to Oxford Modern Languages Monographs series, 275; editor of Cambridge Iberian and Latin American Studies, 275–6, 335; influence of, 275–6; *Festschriften*, 276; honours and awards, 276–7; knighted, 276–7, **281**; retirement, 278, 327; successor, 278–80; D.Litt., 280; visiting professorships, 282–5, 311–2, 328; on academic life,

336, 337–8; obituaries, 340; *see* Oxford, University of

OEUVRE: listing, 379–98; literary aspirations, 91–6, 99, 329, 338, 341; poetry, 134, 152–3, 183, 327; fiction, 93–6, 352; short stories (1933–4), 56, 93, 95, 151, 329–30; unfinished novel, 93–5, 100; anonymous article on Spanish Civil War (1938), 116–17; travelogue: *Before God's Eyes* (1944; unfinished) 154; psychological writings: *Dark Tower* (1948), 188–90, 191; *Calella Eclogue* (1948), 190; scholarship: general, 287–90, 296, 325; works: 'Pirandello' (1934), 83, 297, 313–14; 'João Fernandes Andeiro' (1938), 287; *As Fontes de Fernão Lopes* (1941), 250, 287–8; 'Some Problems of Diplomatic' (1952), 218–20, 277, 296–8, 300–1, 311, 320, 334–5; 'English Seventeenth-Century Interpretations' (1953), 248; 'Portuguese galleys' (1953), 287; *English Intervention* (1955), 246, 249, 251, 277, 290–6; 'Nessus-Shirt' (1959), 216, 299; *Cantar* articles, 297–8, 309; *Celestina* articles, papers and reviews, 216–17, 299–303, 309, 320, 323, 325, 343, 354, 356–61; '*Don Quixote* as a Funny Book' (1969), 277, 305–8, 320, 348; *Spain: A Companion to Spanish Studies* (1973), 324–5; *Traducciones y traductores* (1985), 320–1; *Celestina* edition (1991), 88, 283, 303–4; Henry the Navigator lectures (1960 & 1984), 316–17; *Henry 'the Navigator'* (2000), 317–19, 325; and Vegetius, *Epitoma rei militaris*, 323; sundry literature articles, 319–20, 324; sundry history articles, 321–3; *Encyclopaedia Britannica* articles, 324–5; writing style, 95–6, 292–3, 350; as solitary scholar, 299; as historian, 287–90, 296–7, 314–15, 325; history as a branch of rhetoric, 314–15; as military historian, 293–4; multifaceted style, 296–7, 308–9; as historicist, 313; as iconoclast, 299; as literary critic, 302–4, 308–13, 325, 337; scepticism, 303–4; and critical theory, 310–13; academically competitive, 236, 299, 313–14, 320–1; broadcasting, 232, 247–8, 278; academic distinction, 58, 59, 66–7, 71, 72, 176; evaluation, 296, 312, 325, 337

INTELLIGENCE CAREER: recruited into intelligence, 117–18; service in intelligence 117–19, 123, **131**, 205, 329, 340; military training, 131–3; MI5, 135–66, 277–8; *see* MI(5)

Russell, Rita Muriel (mother), 15, 19, 21–5, 28–30, 31, 34, 35, 46, **48**, 50, 51, 52, 57, 64, 65–6, 109, 124, 126, 133, **155**, **207**, 326–7; personality, 24–5, 206, 208–9; courtship, 35; marriage, 36, **38**; pregnancy, 43, 44–5; married life, 39, 44, 46–7, 48–9, 52–5; divorce, 53, 55–6, 171, 340; death, 326–7, 352; PER relationship with, 15, 24, 54, 90–1, 170, 172, 179, 205–9, 212–13, 214–15, 326–7, 330, 352–3

Russell, Susan Helen (great aunt), 18
Russell, Suzanne (cousin), 58
Russell, Thomas Gregory (grandfather),

INDEX

15–16, 19–24, **20**, 27, 35, 36, 39, 39–40, 41, 42, 43, 50–2, 53, 54, 55, 58; PER relationship with, 15, 42, 58, 71, 90–1, 106, 107, 171–2
Russell, William Henry (great uncle), 18
Russell-Wood, A. J. R., 369
Rutherford, John, 262, 267, 275, 350, 369–70
Ruwenzori range, 151
Sabang, 160
Sagres, 315
St Andrew's College, Christchurch, 58–62, 174, 176, 213
St Antony's College, Oxford, 262, 263; Latin American Centre, 263; Iberian Studies Centre, 263
St Catherine's College, Oxford, 262
St Cross College, Oxford, 262
St Edmund Hall, Oxford, 248
St Helier, Le Gallais depository blaze (1949), 209
St Hilda's College, Oxford, 276, 332
St Hugh's College, 249, 263, 334–5
St John's College, Oxford, 109, 111, 249, 252, 278
Saint-Malo, 123, 124
St Peter's College, Oxford, 262
St Thomas's Hospital, London, 133
Salamanca, University of, 276, 278, 298, 350
Salas, Xavier de, 248, 250
Salazar, António de Oliveira, 128, 260, 314
Salinas, Pedro, 85
Salvation Army, 57
San Pedro de Cardeña, 298, 320
San Sebastián, 102–3
Sánchez-Albornoz, Claudio, *España: un enigma histórico* (1956), 299
Sant Boi de Llobregat, 259
Santander, 73, 119
Santiago de Compostela, 116, 291
Sarmiento, Edward, 248
Saunders, Alastair, 142, 148, 273–4, 318, 372
Schiele, Mrs, 218, 330
Scott, Kathleen, **29**, 30–2, 33, 34
Scott, Robert Falcon, 25–35, **29**
Security Intelligence Far East (SIFE), 165
Sedbergh School, 65, 66, 176, 214, 349
Segorbe, 350
Segovia, 256–7
Seldon, Archie, 262, 269, 352
Senegal, 148
Serédi, Cardinal Jusztinián György, 117–18
Severin, Dorothy, 338
Severn (river), 70
Shackleton, Ernest, 26
Shakespeare, William, 83, 103, 330, 358; *Twelfth Night*, 339
Shanghai Municipal Police, 134
Shaw, Dominic, 355
Shaw, George Bernard, 338
Sheffield, University of, 265
Shem Tob, 358
Shepherd, Gillian, 276
Sickert, Walter, 76
Sierra Leone, 142, 148, 316
Sigiriya, 162–3
Sillitoe, Sir Percy, 166
Silva, Juan de, *Don Policisne de Boecia* (1602), 324
Silva, Ricardo do Espírito Santo, 130
Simancas, Archivo General de, 291
Singapore, 156, 157, 159, 159–60, 161, 165
Singapore, Battle for (1941–2), 164
Sinhalese, 162, 166
Sisley, Alfred, 77
slavery, 148, 273–4, 315, 317, 318, 319, 322
Slessor, Mary, 147
Sloman, Albert, 251
Smedley's Hydro, Derbys., 133
Smith, Paul Julian, 312
Smith College, Northampton, Mass., 256
Snow, C. P., *The Masters*, 245

socialism, 96, 98
Sockalingam, 163, 351
Somerset Maugham, W., 93
Somerville College, Oxford, 73, 251, 330, 332, 336
Sotterley Hall, Suffolk, 28
Soulbury Commission (1944), 166
South East Asia Command (SEAC), 155, 159–60
Southampton, 121, 124, 241
Southsea, 46
Southworth, Eric, 83–4, 262, 271–2, 351
Spain, Black Legend, 248; PER opinions on, 103, 109–11, 257–60
Spanish Civil War (1936–9), 108, 109, 113–20, 255–6, 274, 314; impact of on British Hispanism, 114, 314; impact of in Oxford, 114–15; PER on 104–5, 113–14, 115–16; PER in (1938), 115–20, 205
Sparrow, John, 89
Special Operations Executive (SOE), 127, 143
Spender, Stephen, 90, 267
Star of India (barque), 19
Star, The (Christchurch), 21
Starkie, Enid, 89, 93, 251, 330–3, **331**; *Baudelaire* (1933), 330, 333; *Rimbaud* (1938), 330
Starkie, Walter, 129, 248–9, 250–1, 306, 330
Start Point, 46
Stein, Gertrude, 298
Stendhal, 92
Stephenson, Sir William, 136–7
Sterne, Laurence, *The Life and Opinions of Tristram Shandy, Gentleman* (1759-67), 339
Stevens, Col. Robin ('Tin-eye'), 156
Stewart, Mr (schoolmaster), 62
Stokes Bay, 46
Strasbourg, 100, 123, 179, 201
Stretford, Manchester, 261

Stringer, Ada (great aunt), 33–4
Stringer, Harry (great uncle), 52
Strong, Bryan, 368–9
Stuttgart, 201
Sudeten Crisis (1938), 121
Suez, 49
Sumatra, Japanese surrender of (1945), 160
Supply, Ministry of, 225
Sutherland, Halliday, 258
Sutherland, Madeline, 283
Swinburne, Algernon, 91–2, 94; *Atalanta in Calydon* (1865), 92, 93, 190; 'The Woven Raiment' (1866), 352–3
Sydney, 33; Mosman, 56; North Ryde, Northern Suburbs General Cemetery, 56
Sydney, HMAS, 50
Talavera de la Reina, 356, 359
Tamale, Gold Coast, 149
Tangier, Portuguese attack on (1437), 315
Tarn, 123
Tasmania, 16–18
Tate, R. B., 279, 355
Tauranga, HMS, 27
Taylor Institution, Oxford, 79, 80, 82, 86, 262, 266, 267–9, 272, 280, 339, 367
Tenerife, 44
Tennyson, Alfred, Lord, *Ballad of the Revenge* (1878), 72
Terence, 83, 298
Terra Nova, RRS, 27–8, 31–2; Expedition (1910–13), 30–3, 35
Tewkesbury, 70
Texas, University of, 282–4
Thatcher, Margaret, 336
Thompson, Colin, 266, 268, 269, 274–5, 275, 312, 349, 371, 378
Thomson, Ian Wright, 178–9
Times, The, 98–9, 113, 317, 341
Times Literary Supplement, The, 223
Togo, 152
Toledo, 359; Priory of San Pedro Mártir, 352

Toulon, 33–4, 35
Touraine, 124
Tours, 51–2
Trans-Siberian Express, 36
Trend, J. B., 114, 248, 250, 251
Trent, Council of (1545–63), 319
Trevor-Roper, Hugh, Lord Dacre, 246, 251, 343
Trincomalee, 155, 156, 160
Trinity College Dublin, 193, 251
Trinity College, Oxford, 248, 260, 262, 266, 269
trotskyism, 156
Troubadours, 123
Truman, R. W., 110, 262, 277, 289, 309, 317, 319, 368, 369
Tucurinca, SS, 135–6
Turakina, SS, 44
Turing, Alan, 277
Turks and Caicos Islands, 141–2
Túy, 119; International Bridge, 119, **120**
Tynan, Kenneth, 267
Tyrol, 71, 76
U-509, 141
U-Boot-Waffe, 136–7
UC-17, 46
UC-66, 46
Uganda, 151
Unamuno, Miguel de, 85, 88, 232, 308
United Nations, 187
University College, Oxford, 277
University Grants Committee, 262, 263–4
Upper Volta, 151
Urquhart, F. F. ('Sligger'), 80
Utrillo, Maurice, 76
V-2 rocket, 155
Valencia, 119, 255; University of, 85
Valente, José Angel, 262
Valera, Juan, 85; *Pepita Jiménez* (1874), 103
Valéry, Paul, 106
Valle Lersundi, Fernando del, 302, 354–65
Valle Lersundi manuscripts, 354, 356, 360, 361–5
Valle-Inclán, Ramón del, 103
van den Bosch, Janie, **78**, 85
Van Druten, John, *The Voice of the Turtle* (1843), 235
van Eyck, Jan, *Arnolfini Wedding* (1434), 343
van Gogh, Vincent, 77
Vanceboro, Maine, 136
Vanderbilt University, 282, 285, 328
Vargas Llosa, Mario, 265
Vassall, John, 278
Vegetius, 271–2; *Epitoma rei militaris*, 323
Venice, 315
Verlaine, Paul, 103
Vicente, Gil, 111; *Barca do Inferno* (1517) 111
Vichy regime, 142–3
Vieillard, Jeanne, 290, 334
Vigo, 115–16; Castro, 116; Hotel Continental, **118**, 119; Ría de, 119
Villeneuve, Provence, 123
Villon, François, 243
Virginia, University of, 282
Wadham College, Oxford, 89, 262
Wagner, Richard, 103
Wainwright, John, 262, 280
Waimairi (river), 21, 58
Wainwright, John, 262, 280
Wairoa, Hawke's Bay, 53, 54
Waissbein, Daniel, 372
Walker, E. M., 74
Walmate, Canterbury, 19
War Intelligence Course, 133
War Office, 'I' Section, 128
Waugh, Evelyn, 89, 94; *Officers and Gentlemen* (1955), 133; *The Ordeal of Gilbert Pinfold* (1957), 213
Weaver, J. R. H., 248
Webster, Maj. W. B., 142–3
Wehrmacht, 127
Weiss, Julian, 304, 310, 373
Wellington, 19, 33, 44, 45, 64
Wenninger, Oblt.z.S. Ralph, 46

Wessel, Horst, 101
West, Nigel, 148
West Indies, University of the, 342
Westminster Bank, 130
Wheeler, Ernest (uncle), 37, 53, 56–7
Wheeler, Hildreth (uncle), 37, 53, 57
Wheeler, Capt. Hugh Bernard (father), 35–7, **170**; appearance, 39, 314; character; 53–4, 57; military career, 37–8, 44, 47–8, 49, 50, 66; marriage, 36, **38**; married life, 39, 44, 46–7, 48–9, 52–5, 171; divorce, 53, 55–6, 67, 171, 340–1; mental illness, 54–5, 171, 190; abuse of his children, 57, 171, 214, 341; prematurely declared dead, 58, 66; death, 56; PER relationship with, 53–4, 55–7, 171, 214, 341
Wheeler, Col. John Langford (grandfather), 36–7, **36**, 53, 56–7, 58
Wheeler, Lionel (uncle), 37, 43
Wheeler, Lydia (*née* Porter) (grandmother), 36, **36**
Wheeler, Margery (aunt), 37
Wheeler, Max, 371
Whinnom, Keith, 234, 249, 354, 368
Whirlwind (clipper), 16
Who's Who, 339, 340
Wight, Colin, 200, 267, 269–70
Wilde, Oscar, 92
Wilhelm II, 186
Williams, Miss (governess), 18
Williams, John, 267
Williamson, Henry, *The Labouring Life* (1932), 99
Wilson, Prof. Edward, 233, 249, 250, 251, 265
Wilson, Edward Adrian, 26
Wilson, Mary Agnes, 32
Wilson, Terence, 373
Wind, Edgar, 253, 335–6
Wind, Margaret, 253, 335–6
Windsor, Duke and Duchess of, 129–30
Winneba, Gold Coast, **153**
Winnicott, Donald, 210
Wisconsin, University of, 41
Wolfe, Gen. James, 79
wolfram, 142
Wolof, 322
Women's Royal Naval Service (WRNS), 198, 204
Woods, Michael, 370
Woolf, Virginia, *To the Lighthouse* (1927), 193
Woolley, F/O Harold (Rollo), 164–5
Worcester, HMS, 26
Worcester College, Oxford, 246, 277
Workman, Col. Riley, 194–5
Wright, T. E., 225, **226**
Wyatt, James, 252
Xalapa, 212
Yale University Press, 316
Yarnton Manor, 89–90, 155, 225, 332
Young, Maj. C. T., 159
Yundum, Gambia, 145
Zamora, 260
Zola, Émile, 103
Zurara, Gomes Eanes de, 314, 317
Zürich, 123

www.ingramcontent.com/pod-product-compliance
Lightning Source LLC
Chambersburg PA
CBHW030433190426
43202CB00035B/39